A MAGNA CARTA FOR CHILDREN?

The UN Convention on the Rights of the Child is the most widely ratified human rights treaty, yet children still face poverty, violence, war, disease and disaster. Are the rights we currently afford to children enough? Combining historical analysis with international human rights law, Michael Freeman considers early legal and philosophical theories on children's rights before exploring the impact and limitations of the Convention itself. He also suggests the ways we may rethink children's rights in the future, as well as identifying key areas for reform. This book will appeal to an interdisciplinary audience who are interested in children's rights, childhood studies, the history of childhood, international human rights and comparative family law. It is a *crucial* restatement of the importance of law, policy and rights in improving children's lives.

MICHAEL FREEMAN is Professor Emeritus of English Law at University College London. He is the Founding Editor of the *International Journal of Children's Rights*; Former Editor of the *International Journal of Law in Context*; General Editor of the *International Library of Medicine, Ethics and Law* and of the *International Library of Family, Society and Law*; and former Editor of the *Annual Survey of Family Law* and of *Current Legal Problems*. He has published in the areas of Family Law, Child Law and Policy, Children's Rights, Medicine, Ethics and the Law and Medical Law, Jurisprudence and Legal Theory, and other areas of law and social policy.

A MAGNA CARTA FOR CHILDREN?

Rethinking Children's Rights

MICHAEL FREEMAN

CAMBRIDGE
UNIVERSITY PRESS

CAMBRIDGE
UNIVERSITY PRESS

University Printing House, Cambridge CB2 8BS, United Kingdom

One Liberty Plaza, 20th Floor, New York, NY 10006, USA

477 Williamstown Road, Port Melbourne, VIC 3207, Australia

314–321, 3rd Floor, Plot 3, Splendor Forum, Jasola District Centre,
New Delhi – 110025, India

79 Anson Road, #06–04/06, Singapore 079906

Cambridge University Press is part of the University of Cambridge.

It furthers the University's mission by disseminating knowledge in the pursuit of
education, learning and research at the highest international levels of excellence.

www.cambridge.org
Information on this title: www.cambridge.org/9781107152823
DOI: 10.1017/9781316591468

First published 2020

Printed in the United Kingdom by TJ International Ltd. Padstow Cornwall

A catalogue record for this publication is available from the British Library

Library of Congress Cataloging-in-Publication Data
NAMES: Freeman, Michael D. A., author.
TITLE: A Magna Carta for children? : rethinking children's rights / Michael Freeman.
DESCRIPTION: Cambridge, United Kingdom ; New York : Cambridge University
Press, 2020. | Series: The hamlyn lectures | Includes bibliographical references and index.
IDENTIFIERS: LCCN 2020031362 (print) | LCCN 2020031363 (ebook) | ISBN
9781107152823 (hardback) | ISBN 9781316606674 (paperback) | ISBN 9781316591468
(ebook)
SUBJECTS: LCSH: Children (International law) | Children's rights. | Children – Legal
status, laws, etc. | Convention on the Rights of the Child (1989 November 20) | Magna
Carta. | Children's rights – Government policy. | International law and human rights.
CLASSIFICATION: LCC K639 .F74 2020 (print) | LCC K639 (ebook) | DDC 341.4/
8572–dc23
LC record available at https://lccn.loc.gov/2020031362
LC ebook record available at https://lccn.loc.gov/2020031363

ISBN 978-1-107-15282-3 Hardback
ISBN 978-1-316-60667-4 Paperback

To the memory of Janusz Korczak, *z' l*
(*May he be remembered for a blessing*)

CONTENTS

vii

CONTENTS

viii

The Hamlyn Trust owes its existence to the will of Miss Emma Warburton Hamlyn of Torquay, who died in 1941 at the age of eighty. She came of an old and well-known Devon family. Her father, William Bussell Hamlyn, practised in Torquay as a solicitor and JP for many years, and it seems likely that Miss Hamlyn founded the trust in his memory. Emma Hamlyn was a woman of strong character, intelligent and cultured, well-versed in literature, music and art, and a lover of her country. She travelled extensively in Europe and Egypt, and apparently took considerable interest in the law and ethnology of the countries and cultures that she visited. An account of Miss Hamlyn by Professor Chantal Stebbings of the University of Exeter may be found, under the title 'The Hamlyn Legacy', in volume 42 of the published lectures.

Miss Hamlyn bequeathed the residue of her estate on trust in terms which it seems were her own. The wording was thought to be vague, and the will was taken to the Chancery Division of the High Court, which in November 1948 approved a Scheme for the administration of the trust. Paragraph 3 of the Scheme, which follows Miss Hamlyn's own wording, is as follows:

> The object of the charity is the furtherance by lectures or otherwise among the Common People of the United Kingdom of Great Britain and Northern Ireland of the

knowledge of the Comparative Jurisprudence and Ethnology of the Chief European countries including the United Kingdom, and the circumstances of the growth of such jurisprudence to the Intent that the Common People of the United Kingdom may realise the privileges which in law and custom they enjoy in comparison with other European Peoples and realising and appreciating such privileges may recognise the responsibilities and obligations attaching to them.

The Trustees are to include the Vice-Chancellor of the University of Exeter, representatives of the universities of London, Leeds, Glasgow, Belfast and Wales and persons co-opted. At present there are eight Trustees:

Professor Rosa Greaves, University of Glasgow
Professor I. R. Davies, Swansea University
Ms Clare Dyer
Professor Chantal Stebbings (representing the Vice-Chancellor of the University of Exeter)
Professor R. Halson, University of Leeds
Professor J. Morison, Queen's University, Belfast
The Rt Hon. Lord Justice Sedley
Professor A. Sherr, University of London (Chairman)

From the outset it was decided that the objects of the Trust could be best achieved by means of an annual course of public lectures of outstanding interest and quality by eminent lecturers, and by their subsequent publication and distribution to a wider audience. The first of the Lectures were delivered by the Rt Hon. Lord Justice Denning (as he then was) in 1949. Since then there has been an unbroken series of annual

Lectures published until 2005 by Sweet & Maxwell and from 2006 by Cambridge University Press. A complete list of the Lectures may be found on pp. xii–xvi. In 2005, the Trustees decided to supplement the Lectures with an annual Hamlyn Seminar, normally held at the Institute of Advanced Legal Studies in the University of London, to mark the publication of the Lectures in printed book form. The Trustees have also, from time to time, provided financial support for a variety of projects which, in various ways, have disseminated knowledge or have promoted to a wider public understanding of the law.

This, the sixty-seventh series of lectures, was delivered by Professor Michael Freeman at the University of Leeds, the University of Nottingham, and University College London. The Board of Trustees would like to record its appreciation to Michael Freeman and also to the three institutions which generously hosted these Lectures.

AVROM SHERR
Institute of Advanced Legal Studies, London
Chair of the Trustees

This book contains an expanded version of the Hamlyn Lectures delivered by me in November 2015 at the University of Leeds, where my academic career began in 1966, the University of Nottingham, where it might have begun had they not rejected me, and UCL, where I have been since 1969. In fact, the lectures were a cut-down version of the book. I first attended a Hamlyn Lecture in the early 1960s: it was one of Barbara Wootton's on crime, the first Hamlyns given by a woman. It is extraordinary to be reminded that it was 1990 before a woman gave another series of Hamlyns! But we only had to wait five years more for Brenda Hale to be the third. Her lectures, the 47th of the series, were the first to explore family issues and therefore the first to have any focus on children. My lectures twenty years later were the first to concentrate entirely on children, in particular on children's rights. This is not a subject with which Miss Hamlyn would have had any acquaintance, but one which, interestingly enough, the first Hamlyn lecturer, Lord Denning, was an early advocate, perhaps *malgré lui* (see his judgment in *Hewer* v. *Bryant* (1969)). What, I wonder, would he make of my lectures? Or the Convention? I did once describe him in an appraisal I wrote of his family law jurisprudence as a 'bastion of reaction'! To his credit he responded in a handwritten letter, which I treasure. And he did advocate that corporal punishment should be abolished in schools, before 'Europe', as he put it 'makes us do it'.

I am grateful to the Hamlyn Trust for giving me the opportunity to give the Hamlyn Lectures 2015. Particular thanks are due to Professor Avrom Sherr, who accompanied me to all three lectures and who negotiated reimbursement of expenditure for the secretarial assistance. I was delighted that eminent judges were prepared to take time to chair the lectures: I am most grateful to Sir James Holman, Lord Justice MacFarlane and Lord Woolf, who each chaired a lecture.

The text does not purport to be a comprehensive treatment of children's rights. It is selective in its choice of subjects and in states covered. It is sad that standard books on human rights pay so little attention to children's rights. Were human rights to fall with the European project, at least they would not necessarily take children's rights with them. It is important that children's rights should survive and prosper. We have to see the Convention of 1989 as a beginning, no more. We can build on it, and we must. You can judge a society by the way it treats its weakest members. We could do a lot better. The tone would disappoint Miss Hamlyn, who was rather complacent about the virtues of English law. It is important that she gets a rude awakening. If just a few common people of England are made aware of the state of childhood in England today, this book will have succeeded.

This text was written in 2016 but, unfortunately, publication has been delayed due to my serious illness.

Michael Freeman

ACKNOWLEDGEMENTS

In thanking those who have assisted it is difficult to know how far back to go. My initial debt may be to my parents who first stimulated my thinking about children's rights. Since then, a large number of thinkers have encouraged the development of this project: countless conferences, many conversations, and academic literature have nourished my thinking about children's rights. A special debt is owed to Philip Veerman, who introduced me to the work of Korczak many years ago, and to Elizabeth Szwed, who involved me in her 'Justice For Children' pressure group and nourished my interest in Korczak. Amongst others who have assisted me, I must mention Priscilla Alderson, Laura Lundy, Aoife Nolan, my former PhD student Noam Peleg, Carrie Menkel-Meadow, Coby de Graaf, Bernadette Saunders, Alice Margaria, John Eekelaar, John Tobin, Lucinda Ferguson, Ann Quennerstedt, Anne McGillivray, Karl Hanson, Jane Williams, the late Malfrid Flekkøy; and many good friends in the children's rights community – Julia Sloth-Nielsen, Helen Stalford, Tara Collins, Gertrud Lenzer, Mark Henaghan, Jane Stoll, Alice Hearst, Olga Khazova, Velina Todorova, Kathryn Hollingsworth, Rhona Schuz, Ya'ir Ronen. I am also grateful to colleagues who answered my questions and to Deborah Burns who assisted the production of this book and to Esther Gershing without whose help the bibliography would not exist.

xix

PRELUDE

It is impossible to enter the tangled terrain of children's rights without a concept of a child as a guide. It is easy, deceptively so, to take our understanding of 'child' from the Convention on the Rights of the Child (CRC). Article 1 of this proclaims that a child is

> every human being below the age of eighteen years unless under the law applicable to the child, majority is attained earlier.

When I first studied children's rights in the 1970s, this was about as far as we went. We took it as a given that the concept 'child' embraced all those under eighteen years of age, at least two of Shakespeare's 'ages of man' (*As You Like It*, II, vii, 143). We ignored the obvious differences between babies, children proper (whatever that means) and adolescents or youth. Concepts like 'evolving capacities', maturity and vulnerability were passed over with little contemplation. Maturity (Buss, 2009; Todres, 2012), vulnerability (Herring, 2014), development (Grugel and Piper, 2011) are now vigorously debated and contested within and across disciplines. The first book on the human rights of adolescents appeared only recently (Bhabha, 2014; and see now UN Committee on the Rights of the Child, 2016) – note, 'human' rights. And Priscilla Alderson has written of 'young children's rights' (2008), and with fellow researchers has explored the participation rights of premature babies (Alderson, Hawthorne and Killen, 2005).

During the CRC's gestation period (it took ten years), there was no consensus as to when childhood began. Pragmatism prevailed, there being no philosophers present. That the drafters got as far as they did may be explained as an example of what Cass Sunstein has called, though not in relation to the CRC, incompletely theorised agreements (Sunstein, 1995/6, and see Tobin, 2013). The gulf between Catholic and liberal states was left gaping. A compromise was affected by designing a paragraph in the Preamble which recognised life before birth, and permitted states parties to choose their own start date for the beginning of life. But the rights, if any, of the unborn child (Alston, 1990; Cornock and Montgomery, 2011; Joseph, 2009) are no nearer being resolved than they were at the onset of negotiations in 1979. Reconciling the pregnant woman's rights with those of the unborn baby – and much hinges upon language, since I could have labelled it [sic] as 'foetus' – may prove impossible. Two dignities remain on a collision course (Siegel, 2013). The definition of 'child' in Article 1 of the CRC is expressed to be 'for the purposes of the present Convention', but not surprisingly it has taken over as the definition of a child. It was congruent with standard practice anyway. An inevitable consequence is that all persons under eighteen are lumped together under one category. It is not uncommon to refer to all persons under the age of eighteen as 'kids', which, apart from being derogatory, as kids are baby goats, it infantilises adolescents (Abramson, 1996a).

It is becoming almost as difficult to determine when childhood ends. It is often said it is getting longer (Future

Foundation, 2000, see *The Independent*, 29 May 2000). To impose closure at the age of eighteen is arbitrary, though it reflects what is generally felt appropriate (but see Grover, 2004). But the CRC permits recruitment into the armed forces at fifteen (an Optional Protocol raises this to eighteen), steers clear of interfering with domestic policies on the age of criminal responsibility (Cipriani, 2009), and on the age at which marriage is permitted, thus leaving both dismally low in many countries (in England, it is ten and sixteen, respectively). Veerman (2010) and Desmet (2012) have both pointed to the 'ageing' of the Convention (see also Freeman, 2000b). The twenty-eight years since the Convention was finalised have seen developments in neuroscience which make us question our understanding of adolescence (Steinberg, 2014). The evidence is now clear that adolescence is a period when significant changes in brain structure and function occur. Important changes in brain anatomy and activity take place far longer into development than was previously thought (Casey, Jones and Somerville, 2011). Such evidence was put to the US Supreme Court in *Roper* v. *Simmons* in 2005, and must have influenced its decision to declare the death penalty unlawful where the crime is committed by a juvenile. Subsequently, it led the court to come to the same conclusion where the sentence was life imprisonment without parole (see *Graham* v. *Florida*, 2010). In *Graham*, there is explicit reference to neuroscientific evidence. Justice Anthony Kennedy stated that:

> Developments in psychology and brain science continue to show fundamental differences between juvenile and adult minds. For example, parts of the brain involved in

3

> behavior control continue to mature through late
> adolescence. (2010: 17)

This use of evidence has continued. In *Miller* v. *Alabama* and in *Jackson* v. *Hobbs* (2012) it was invoked to rule out life without parole for homicide committed by juveniles.

The implications of neuroscientific evidence are profound. They suggest the brain is not fully developed until about the age of twenty-five, and that it declines from about forty-five years. Should we reconsider our whole criminal justice system to take account of this evidence? And, what are the implications of this evidence from neuroscience for civil and political rights? It seems likely that sixteen-year-olds may soon be given the right to vote. Opponents will inevitably point to neuroscience. Justice Scalia did just this in his dissenting opinion in *Roper* v. *Simmons*. He criticised the American Psychological Association: in *Hodgson* v. *Minnesota* in 1990 it had submitted an *amicus curiae* brief arguing that adolescents should be permitted to make decisions about abortion without involving their parents.

What looks like inconsistency – both having one's cake and eating it – can easily be explained. It is more likely that criminal activity is impulsive, whereas the decision to terminate a pregnancy is considered. Similarly, the exercise of voting in an election. This certainly seemed to be the case with sixteen-year-olds in Scotland, who in 2014 were given the vote in the independence referendum. It can thus be argued that neuroscience should not affect the trend, exemplified by Article 12 of the CRC, to pay more and more attention to children's input into decision-making in areas such as divorce, care and medical questions. Neuroscience may yet come to assist us understand concepts in the CRC like the 'evolving capacities' of children (in Article 5), and better inform us as to when a child is capable of forming his or her own views so that account can be taken of them in accordance with the relevant child's 'age and maturity' (see Article 12). It may enable some content to be poured into the *Gillick* competence test (1986). It may offer us some guidance on whether the judicial retreat from *Gillick* when a child refuses medical treatment can be justified. Why is it easier to accept a child's decision when it is an acceptance of treatment (see *Re R* (1992); *Re W* (1993); Freeman, 2007b)?

This conflict between autonomy and protection, we will see, has dogged the modern study of children. In the nineteenth century, the need for protection led to the child-saving movement. In the latter third of the twentieth century, there was a shift to emphasising the autonomous child, capable of agency, though this image co-existed with that of the vulnerable child. The image of the autonomous child features prominently in childhood studies literature which has blossomed since the 1980s (Alanen, 2011; Alderson, Hawthorne and Killen, 2005; Corsaro, 1997; James, Jenks and Prout, [1998] 2002; Mayall, 2003; Prout, 2005). But the emphasis on protection (and prevention) remains, though this is now looked at more critically than was once the case. This is not surprising as more forms of abuse emerge and new ways of exploiting children are uncovered (Davies, 2014; Furedi, 2015; Wild, 2013). But, as Richard Farson noted more than forty years ago, we must protect not only children, but also their rights (1974). To take one simple example, make it unlawful to punish children physically and you will take a major step towards the elimination of child abuse (Freeman and Saunders, 2014). English law retains the 'compromise' position that reasonable chastisement is a defence if the parent commits only a common assault (see Children Act 2004, s. 58, and below, p. 136).

The Convention on the Rights of the Child of 1989 is the clearest and fullest statement of children's rights. It is one of the nine core human rights treaties, all of which are of relevance to children, who are, of course, human beings. It is tempting to regard it as a definitive code of children's rights but this would be to ignore a number of considerations.

It was drafted without the input of children and reflects a top-down understanding of children's interests. In the twenty-eight years since, there has developed an awareness of a different picture that would emerge from a bottom-up construction of children's rights. There are now advocates who wish to approach children's rights in this way (Liebel, 2012a; Vandenhole, 2012); see, however, the highly critical riposte of Gertrud Lenzer (2015). In relation to human rights more generally, see De Feyter (2007) and De Gaay Fortman (2011). There is nothing new in this. As long ago as 1928, Janusz Korczak wrote of children that 'They [children] ought to be trusted and allowed to "organise" as "the expert is the child"' (Korczak, 1928, English translation, 2009: 33). Korczak was critical of the Declaration of Geneva of 1924 (the 'Geneva lawmakers'). Writes Korczak, 'The child is neither given nor trusted to be able to act on his/her own "The Child-nothing. We-everything"' (2009: 25). How different would the Convention look if there had been input by children? (Liebel, 2013). Would it have reflected more the interests of children of the Global

South? For example, what would the education/work equation have looked like? Would there have been greater emphasis on socio-economic rights than civil and political ones? Would there be new rights, perhaps the right to vote? Or the right to work? Would children have pursued a rights strategy at all, perhaps preferring an ethics of care approach? Or a greater emphasis on well-being? (Ben-Arieh et al., 2014). There are children starving in Britain today for many of whom the right of association – to take but one rather obvious example – is meaningless (Chakrabortty, 2015).

A second reason why the 1989 text cannot be regarded as definitive is that the world changes ever more rapidly. The CRC was finally constructed as the Berlin Wall was pulled down, and with it the beginning of the end of Communism. The CRC reflects a world emerging from the Cold War. It is rooted in the historical context of the last days of the Cold War. Poland proposed a Convention as a riposte to the United States which, with Jimmy Carter as President, was pushing rather for a Convention against Torture. The United States dropped its opposition to a Children's Convention when it was able to insert a basket of civil and political rights. But it pushed for this more because it wanted to make what became the CRC a less attractive package for the Communist bloc. The Convention was thus negotiated against the backdrop of power politics which changed contemporaneously with the finalising of the document. A few years later we might have had a different Convention.

The end of Communism is not the only cataclysmic rupture. The rise of a capitalist China, an epidemic of civil wars in Africa, wars of religion in the Middle East and elsewhere, 9/11 and its aftermath – the 'war on terror', Guantánamo (which warehoused more than a few children), Islamophobia and antisemitism, the collapse of economies, the refugee crisis. We are more aware of the impact of globalisation, of the results, real and potential, of climate change, of the challenges of the IT revolution (it is difficult to believe that the World Wide Web was only invented in 1989), of the ways the reproduction revolution can question the meaning of life itself (reproduction without sex, a plurality of parents, human enhancement, sex selection, saviour siblings). We have also awakened to new forms of abuse polluting the lives of our children, like cyber bullying and grooming. Childhood has become 'toxic' (Palmer, 2006), children are exploited (Wild, 2013) in ways barely imaginable to those who formulated the CRC in the 1980s (the global sex trade is but one example, O'Connell Davidson, 2005).

This is a book about children's rights. Children's rights are a sub-set of human rights. Had children not been marginalised, seen as 'becomings' rather than as 'human beings', separate treatment of children might not have been necessary. The same might be said about the Convention on the Elimination of All Forms of Discrimination Against Women (CEDAW) and the Disabilities Convention. There is a view that we should be working to a future when a children's Convention is superfluous. This vision was seen by Richard Farson (1974) and John Holt (1974), the child liberationists of the 1970s. But children do need protection, justifying a degree of paternalism – I long ago called this 'liberal paternalism' (Freeman, 1983). I now prefer 'limited' paternalism. It is important, therefore, that we retain children's rights, whilst not regarding the CRC as the definitive statement of these rights, or even thinking that children's rights can be reduced to a set of rules. We need to go beyond rules to change structures, embrace new forms of governance (Falk, 2013), rethink justice and citizenship, change our values (Minow, 1986: 297). These are major ventures and I can only sketch the beginnings of such an agenda. This I attempt to do in the coda of this book in its final chapter.

Is it Wrong to Think of Children as Human Beings?

PART 1

Is it Wrong to Think of Children
as Human Beings?

1

Are Children Human?

Is it 'very strange' to think of children as having rights? Is a child's 'main remedy' to grow up? These are the views of two leading philosophers, Harry Brighouse (2002) and Onora O'Neill (1988), and doubtless many others. This is not as I see it, as I intend to show in this book. My focus will be on the importance of recognising children's rights, not just for children, but for society as a whole. I first explain why it has taken so long to recognise that children have rights.

The second part of the book focuses on a landmark in the history of childhood, the Convention on the Rights of the Child (CRC, 1989). Attention will be drawn to critiques of it. These will be answered. Limitations will be exposed.

The final part of the book looks to the future of childhood, on alternatives to rights, on well-being, 'happiness', on whether it is right to 'ghettoise' children. Do they need a separate convention, or should we just consider them as human beings with human rights?

Hitherto, those who have written on human rights have tended to ignore children. Mahoney's 'challenge' of human rights (2007) may speak 'directly to contemporary audiences' (Gearty, 2011), but it says nothing about children's rights. Charles Beitz's *The Idea of Human Rights* (2011) has a section on women's rights (Beitz, 2011) but nothing on the rights of children. Donnelly devotes just ten lines to children (2003), Nickel (2007) little more in his *Making Sense of Human*

13

Rights. Griffin at least concedes children should acquire rights 'in stages – the stages in which they acquire agency' (Griffin, 2008: 94), and he devotes a whole chapter (Griffin, 2008: 94) to children to illustrate what is considered to be the 'scope' of human rights. The most recent accounts of human rights (Buchanan, 2015; Klug, 2015; Posner, 2014) are similarly remiss. Standard books on child welfare also tend to overlook the contribution that children's rights can make on this: as an example, see Esping-Andersen (1990).

Taking Children's Rights Seriously

The most celebrated account of rights by a legal and political philosopher in recent years implores us to 'take rights seriously' (Dworkin, 1977), but it certainly does not take children's rights seriously (Freeman, 2014). Similarly, Rawls' failure to address justice within the family necessarily meant a failure to address children's issues and so also their rights (Rawls, 1971; cf. Okin, 1979).

Historians of human rights are similarly remiss. Lynn Hunt writes in *Inventing Human Rights* (2007) of developments in the seventeenth and eighteenth centuries of the education of 'boys' so that they could achieve rational autonomy (Hunt, 2007), but confines herself otherwise to the ways European history has seen children as objects of concern, not future adults. Micheline Ishay's otherwise excellent *The History of Human Rights* (Ishay, 2008), discusses only children's rights to protection. Neither Hunt nor Ishay so much as mentions Ellen Key (1909); Eglantyne Jebb (1929); Janusz Korczak (1920, [1928] 2009) or the child liberation movement of the 1970s. It is inconceivable

14

that a thinker (and activist) as significant as Korczak would have been ignored had his/her brief been women's rights or gay rights.

Yet a book purportedly to chart 'the rise and rise of human rights' (published in 2002) can totally ignore children's rights (Sellars, 2002). Meanwhile, the very different 'The End of Human Rights' (Douzinas, 2000) – a powerful indictment of the discourse and practice of human rights – mentions the CRC only *en passant*, and then only to tell us that the United States hasn't ratified it (Douzinas, 2000: 139). (At the time of writing, we now have a President, Donald Trump, who certainly will not ratify the CRC.) This is the only reference to children and their rights in a 400-page book. And Samuel Moyn's engagement with some of 'the leading interpreters of human rights' (Moyn, 2012) gives no space to any child's rights advocate (or, for that matter, any feminist).

Even historians of childhood tend to overlook children's rights. For obvious reasons I exonerate Philippe Ariès (1962) and others whose focus is on the pre-modern world. So too can Melvin Konner be forgiven: his *Evolution of Childhood* (2010) is truly awe-inspiring, a vast panorama of what we know about children and childhood. There is a brief reference to children's 'responsibility', but none to the absence of any rights. Sommerville (1990) has a chapter on the 'Liberation of Childhood', and A. S. Neill's 'Summerhill' is discussed but, this apart, there is no reference to children's rights or to any of the classic twentieth-century advocates. Cunningham's history (2005) devotes a few pages to developments relating to children's rights. Jebb, Neill and Holt are discussed, and there is a brief reference to the Convention. Peter Stearns, a leading historian of childhood, in his *Human Rights in World History* focuses only on children's rights to protection, so that his cursory reference to the Convention discusses only child labour and the non-applicability of capital punishment for crimes committed by children (Stearns, 2012). In Roger Cox's *Shaping Childhood* (1996) there is more on an early opponent of children's rights, Hannah More (see Stott, 2003), than on any advocate of them.

It is 'not a defence to invoke the argument that children's lives have passed relatively unnoticed' (Linda Pollock observes that what we know about children comes from 'moral and medical tracts, religious sermons, and the views of contemporary "experts"' (1983: 22; see also Hiner and Hawes, 1985: 167). Whilst this is clearly so as regards earlier times, there is ample recorded data about the rise of the children's rights movements. There is no excuse for a book published in 2001 to ignore the CRC, the 1970s liberation thrust, Key, Korczak, but proudly conclude with the 1959 Declaration, as Colón and Colón do in a book of nearly 600 pages on the history of children (2001). But Colin Heywood (2001), who offers us a fascinating account of children's lives from the Middle Ages to the beginning of the twentieth century, omits all reference to children's rights, though the opportunity arose any number of times.

Do Children's Rights Matter?

It would be reassuring to think that this question did not need to be posed, that the answer is so obvious. But there has been a backlash against human rights generally (see, for example, Posner, 2014), and children's rights are unlikely to escape censure or worse. Accordingly, we must be prepared to respond to critics with arguments to justify why children's rights are important.

John Tobin (2015) divides possible justifications into four separate arguments, and here I follow his schema.

The commonest answer heads straight for the CRC (or incorporating legislation if this technique has been applied). But this does not tell us why we have the Convention. In this particular case it does assist a little because the CRC contains a more copious Preamble than is usually the case. This gives us the moral case (or at least a moral case).

It refers to 'the inherent dignity' and 'inalienable rights of all members of the human family' as being 'the foundation of freedom, justice and peace in the world'. There should be no distinction such as race, sex, language, religion, etc. (but note the omission of age). Paternalism is accepted ('Childhood is entitled to special care and assistance'). The child is to grow up in a family environment 'in an atmosphere of happiness, love and understanding'. Protection extends 'before' birth, but we are not told how far back this protection stretches. To conception? To viability? Are gametes protected? Are zygotes? (Burgess, 2010; Curtis, 2014). It could conceivably give children the right to be loved – it doesn't. But it is found elsewhere, for example, in Japan and Israel (see Veerman, 1992; see further, Liao, 2006).

Another way to justify children's rights is to ground them in *law*, specifically the Convention. Many rights are embedded in the Convention. In some states the Convention has been incorporated into the domestic law (Lundy et al., 2013). Where this has been done, there should be remedies where there is a breach. But, otherwise, the Convention appears relatively toothless. In time, the Third Protocol may provide an avenue of redress, but at present it offers few grounds for optimism (R. Smith, 2013; Spronk, 2014).

There is also a *political* case. Children's rights have become part of the vocabulary of policy-makers. This may be in part the result of a greater awareness of human rights generally, albeit coupled with hostility to their implications. Tobin comments, specifically in relation to Australia, 'children's rights can no longer be dismissed as a marginal consideration, reflecting the utopian aspirations of international law' (Tobin, 2015: 2).

There is also an *instrumental* justification, that is the adoption of a rights-based approach has the 'capacity to lead to more effective and sustainable policies in matters relating to children' (Tobin, 2015). And it has done so, albeit patchily. Thus, it has had an impact in reforms such as the recruitment of child soldiers, on child labour, and on cultural practices such as female genital mutilation (FGM).

Early Legal Statements about Children

Early legal statements are conspicuously silent on children's rights. Thus, the Ten Commandments (*Exodus*, repeated in *Deuteronomy*), arguably the most influential of all legal codes, contains a clear normative pronouncement on parent-child relations, but it is in terms of respect for parents, and is silent on what obligations, if any, parents owe to children (Giordano, 2015; Silverman, 1978). It is not, therefore, surprising that in early modern times children were being prosecuted before ecclesiastical courts for abusing parents, but that prosecutions of parents for beating children appear not to have taken place (Helmholz, 1993).

One of the earliest recognitions of children's rights is found in the Massachusetts Body of Liberties of 1641. Parents are instructed not to choose their children's marriage partners, and not to inflict unnatural severity against their children. It also gives children the 'free liberty' to complain to the Authorities for redress: we don't know whether any did sue. This was also the law that prescribed the death penalty for children over seventeen who disobeyed parents, though there is no evidence that executions ever took place (Hawes, 1991). It is significant that this only applies to relatively mature children.

Locke and Modernity

In John Locke (1632–1704), we see the earliest attempt to constrain parental dominance. It is, he tells us, a 'temporary Government which terminates with the minority of the child' (1690: para. 67). The bonds of this subjection are like swaddling clothes. Unlike Thomas Hobbes, he did not believe that parents (and he included mothers in this) had 'an authority to make laws and dispose as they please of their lives and liberties' (1690: para. 66). Children like adults had natural rights which needed to be protected. Parents needed to prepare children for their freedom because this was God's will. Parents had an obligation to 'preserve, nourish and educate' their children. Children were not their parents' property, but God's property. (Martin Luther 150 years earlier was the first to assert that children did not belong to their parents, but to God.) Children 'are

19

not born in a full state of Equality, though they are born to it'
(1690: para. 55). Parents must bring their children to a state
where they are capable of independence.

Locke's paternalism is attenuated: it begins to look like
what I have called 'liberal paternalism'. I now prefer to call this
'limited paternalism' (below, pp. 202, 380). Of course, Locke got
there first! Locke cannot accept that there could possibly be any
conflict between parents and children. The child's good was
identified with the parents' wishes. As Worsfold explained
(1974: 146), 'parental benevolence is sufficient to ensure the
fulfilment of children's rights'. Locke did not question the age
of majority, then twenty-one, nor distinguish babies and twenty-
year-olds – parental power is to be exercised over both. But in
later writing (Locke, 1690), Locke introduced a developmental
understanding of a child's nature. His psychology of childhood
envisaged a clear distinction between a child lacking reason and
an educated adult. The goal of education was to produce
a rational man. I see Locke as sowing the seeds of a modern
approach to childhood. We are to that extent all 'Locke's children' (Archard, 2015).

Early Advocates of Children's Rights
and Their Critics

Jean-Jacques Rousseau (1712–1778)

Jean-Jacques Rousseau cannot be ignored but, as Heather
Montgomery pithily remarks (2009: 158), he 'championed
the view that children should be treasured for what they
were, left alone to play, and be protected as far as

possible from the adult world'. These may be seen as conflicting views, as Montgomery does, or a recognition of two sides of children's rights – autonomy and protection. For Chris Jenks (1996: 74) these different images of childhood are 'informative of the shifting strategies that Western society has exercised in its increasing need to control, socialise people in the transition to modernity'. Rousseau elevates childhood to a special place of innocence.

Rousseau is essentially peripheral to debates about children's rights, but his idiosyncratic book *Emile* (1762) cannot be ignored. (Nor can the discussion of Sophie's education). It is a manifesto on how to 'preserve the integrity of the growing child as it (*sic*) passes from innocence to virtue' (Cox, 1996: 65). The most significant argument, and the clearest break with Locke, hinges on his different approach to dependence and authority. For Locke, a child had to defer to adult authority until capable of rational thought. For Rousseau, by contrast, the child was to be dependent on things, rather than people, because things belong to nature and cannot corrupt, and people belong to society and are, as a result, corrupted.

Francis Hutcheson (1694–1746)

One of the clearest early pro-children's rights arguments is to be found in the writings of Francis Hutcheson (1755), Adam Smith's teacher, and the thinker to whom we owe the iconic 'the greatest happiness of the greatest number', forever associated with Jeremy Bentham. In his view, children had rights that needed to be respected. He maintained a child was not simply parents' property, but:

21

> a rational agent with rights valid against the parents – tho'
> they are the natural tutors or curators, and have the right to
> direct the actions, and manage the goods of the child, for its
> benefit during its want of proper knowledge. (1755: 192)

Hutcheson's contemporary, Sir William Blackstone (1723–1780), the leading eighteenth-century English jurist, wrote in the 1750s that parents had 'obligations' to their children to maintain, protect and educate them (Blackstone, 1765–1769). This broke new ground only in that he included education. Of course, it was not framed in rights language.

Thomas Spence (1750–1814)

The first book/pamphlet specifically on children's rights was written at the end of the eighteenth century by Thomas Spence (1796). Entitled *The Rights of Infants*, it followed Spence's radical agenda. It was published in 1797 and is perhaps the first publication with such a title (Bonnett and Armstrong, 2014; Rudkin, 1927). It is a brief tract which emphasises the importance of protecting children from poverty and abuse, and was ahead of its time in this, but its main targets were aristocratic privilege, inequalities of wealth and the ill-treatment of women. Peter Stearns argues in a recent paper that the tract cannot be considered as a 'first' for children's rights, though it certainly pointed in that direction (Stearns, 2016). Spence argued that children's rights extended to a full participation of the 'fruits of the earth' (quoted in Bonnett and Armstrong, 2014: 4) (see Appendix 1).

Spence is barely remembered today. This was an era when revolutionary ideas flourished (Israel, 2011), but were also attacked. Hannah More (on whom see Stott, 2003) used what she saw as a *reductio ad absurdum* argument to attack those who advocated rights for women.

> It follows that the next influx of irradiation which our enlighteners are pouring on us, will illuminate the world with the grave descants on the rights of youth, the rights of children, the rights of babies. (1799: 172–3)

French Revolution and its Aftermath

The French Revolution did not address children's rights, though it showed some interest in expanding education. However, it offered one intriguing reform. During the Revolution's radical phase, legislation sought to remove the distinction between legitimate and illegitimate children (a reform also advocated by Spence). But this reform did not survive, and it is not in the Napoleonic Code of 1804 (Brinton, 1936).

Neither Spence nor More made much of an impact, and we hear little further of children's rights for a half century. An article with the title 'The Rights of Children' appeared in 1852 (Siogvolk, 1852). But it is J. S. Mill's refusal in *On Liberty* (1859) to extend his 'liberty' principle to children – he coupled them with 'backward nations' – which better reflects the orthodox opinion of the mid-nineteenth century. Mill does not even think it necessary to give a reason to exclude children. Mill's contemporary in France by contrast, Jules Vallès, attempted to establish a league for the protection of the rights of children in the aftermath of the Paris Commune. He dedicated a novel, *L'Enfant*, to all oppressed children (1879, English translation, 2007).

Child-Saving Movement

This was the era of the child-saving movement (Katz, 1986; Tiffin, 1982). It gave us juvenile justice (Platt, 1969), limits on child labour, and compulsory education (Bowles and Gintis, 1976). Children are objects of intervention rather than legal subjects (Fitz, 1981, and see Hanson, 2015). Society's concern for the child is seen very much in terms of the child's usefulness to society (Cregan and Cuthbert, 2014: 129; Meyer, 1973). Distinguishing children from adults becomes a conceptual means of rationalising, controlling, even exploiting children (Sartorius, 1975). Children become a convenient focus for public ills. By personalising causes the social reality of trouble can be astutely ignored, and was (Schur, 1965; Wright Mills, 1967).

Karl Marx (1818–1883)

That Karl Marx (Roth, 2008) saw value in children's rights will come as a surprise to many – it certainly shocked me (and his most recent biographer: Sperber, 2013). After all, in *On The Jewish Question* he berated those who spoke of 'so-called rights of children' (Marx, 1843). But in 1840, Marx and Engels called for recognising the right of children to a free public education (Marx, 1840). He reiterated this in 1868. 'The *rights* of children and juveniles must be vindicated'. He added that provision for education and other legislation protecting the rights of children had to be 'enforced by the power of the state' (Marx, 1868). Marx saw the right of education as a 'genuine social right of citizenship, because the aim of education during childhood is to shape the future of adulthood' (quoted in Marshall, 1965). Marx adds that no parent and no employer ought to be allowed to use juvenile labour, except when combined with education. This echoed Robert Owen's utopian vision in 1824 (Owen, 1817). Marx was clearly less interested in children than with what, with education, they might become – the 'investment motive' is prominent yet again.

Kate Douglas Wiggin (1856–1923)

By the end of the nineteenth century there had been much legislative activity to protect children. Legislation in the United Kingdom even – latterly in 1889 – made cruelty to children a criminal offence, though it was another nineteen years before incest was criminalised in 1908. But there was still little discussion or advocacy of children's rights before the First World War. In the United States, there was Florence Kelley (1859–1932), who as early as 1905 asserted a 'right to childhood'. And Kate Douglas Wiggin, the author of the best-selling novel *Rebecca of Sunnybrook Farm*, the story of a rambunctious rule-breaking ten-year-old orphan, who wrote an article for Scribner's magazine entitled 'Children's Rights' (1892). In it she drew a distinction between child protection – the child's right to special protection from extreme forms of abuse and neglect – and children's rights, which included an independent legal identity, a degree of autonomy from parents, and the right to a 'free, secure, healthy, bread and butter childhood', unburdened by heavy labour. In answer to the question 'Who owns the child?' Wiggin answered pointedly: no one. 'The parent is simply a divinely appointed guardian.' Wiggin's idea that children have a right to a proper childhood, and that adults have a duty to serve as their stewards, remains a challenge even today.

Ellen Key (1849–1926)

There was also Ellen Key in Sweden, who looked to the twentieth century as 'the century of the child', much as, she claimed, the nineteenth century had been the 'century of the woman' (Key, 1900, 1909)! It became rather the century of the 'child professional' (King, 1981; Koops and Zuckerman, 2003; Rose, 1990). Like many social reformers of the period, she was a eugenicist. Nevertheless, she argued for important reforms. She looked, for example, to child-centred education and the end of corporal punishment, which is, she argued, both ineffective and not only humiliating to the victim but is so also to the person who administers it. She commented (Key, 1909: 155):

> When a mother is ashamed of the bad behaviour of her son she is apt to strike him – instead of striking her own breast! When an adventurous feat fails he is beaten, but he is praised when successful. These practices produce demoralization.

She also argued that children should have the right to choose their own parents.

Schools, she writes commit 'soul murder' (Key, 1909: 203). The desire for knowledge, 'the capacity for acting by oneself, the gift of observation, all qualities children bring with them to school, have, as a rule, at the end of the school period disappeared'. Her vision for the future sees an end to child labour, state intervention to tackle child abuse, and compulsory training of women in the 'care of children, hygiene, and sick nursing' (Key, 1909: 317). It is (she uses the analogy) the equivalent of military service for men.

Janusz Korczak (1878–1942)

More significantly, there was, of course, that icon of children's rights, Janusz Korczak in Poland (1920, 2007), who emphasised the need to love and respect children, and significantly also drafted what is arguably the first modern charter for children, although it is not set out as such (see Appendix 2). He died as he lived, putting children first. It is poignant that he is best remembered for the manner of his death, voluntarily accompanying 192 children transported by the Nazis from the Warsaw Ghetto to the extermination camp of Treblinka (Lifton, 1988).

His work has only recently become known about in this country. In part this is because he wrote in Polish, but is also because he challenged the accepted paradigm (Kuhn, 1962). He was a polymath, an innovative educator, a doctor/paediatrician, a novelist (he wrote several children's novels including *King Matt I*), and much else. He was the first to set up a children's parliament. He developed the concept of children's courts. He was the first to establish a children's newspaper. This ran for thirteen years (1926–1939) and had a circulation of 50,000 copies. He has been rightly dubbed 'the king of children' (Lifton, 1988).

Korczak believed that children were 'complete' human beings, not merely persons engaged in the process of becoming adults.

> Children are not people of tomorrow, but are people of today. They have a right to be taken seriously, and to be treated with tenderness and respect. They should be allowed to grow into whoever they were meant to be – the unknown person inside each of them is our hope for the future.

He thus rejected, what remained orthodoxy until the 1980s, the idea:

> that the child is not now but will become later, does not know anything but will do so, is not capable of doing anything but will learn, makes us live in a perpetual state of expectation...For the sake of tomorrow we fail to respect what amuses, saddens, amazes, angers, and interests him today. For the sake of tomorrow, we steal many years of his life.

For Korczak, two rights were particularly important: the right to receive love and the right to respect. He developed these in two longer texts for parents and teachers. *How to Love a Child* was prepared on the battlefields of the First World War and published in 1920, and *The Child's Right to Respect* written in the 1920s and published in 1928. He wrote:

> People speak of the old with weighty respect. They speak of the child patronizingly and condescendingly. This is wrong, for the child too deserves respect. He is still small, weak. He does not know much, he cannot do much as yet. But his future – what he will be when he grows up – commands us to respect him as we respect the old.
>
> The child is not dumb; there are as many fools among children as there are among adults. Dressed in the clothing

of age, how often do we impose thoughtless, uncritical, and impractical regulations. Sometimes a wise child is shocked by a malicious, senile, and abusive ignorance. (Ibid.: 33)

Korczak worked in the worst of circumstances and experienced how immensely important it was that adults treated children with respect and love. Abuse, he believed, caused deep scars:

> There are many terrible things in the world, but the worst is when a child is afraid of his father, mother or teacher.

But Korczak does not ignore the rule of gentle paternalism (liberal paternalism). He believed:

> We have to instruct, guide, train, restrain, temper, correct, caution, prevent, impose, and combat. (Ibid.: 27)

> Since he has no vote why go to the trouble to gain his good opinion of you? He doesn't threaten, demand, say anything. (Ibid.: 20)

> But, we do not like it when children criticise us. They are not permitted to notice our mistakes, our absurdities. We appear before them in the garb of perfection. We play with children using marked cards. We win against the low cards of childhood with the aces of adulthood. Cheaters that we are, we shuffle the cards in such a way that we deal ourselves everything.

And there are many more words of wisdom! He didn't construct a 'children's code' as such, but one can be pieced together from his writing (see my reconstruction, below pp. 437–9). It includes rights that still make us think.

Russian Revolution

One of the least known attempts to propagate children's rights occurred in Moscow in the immediate aftermath of the 'October Revolution' (see Liebel, 2016; Veerman, 1992: 281, 435). The Declaration of the Rights of the Child (1918) emerged out of the Communist rejection of the educational system of Tsarist Russia. The Declaration contained seventeen principles. These include an affirmation that the child is a person in his/her right, and not the property of their parents, the state or the society. Under Stalin less than twenty years later, the child became state property and was expected to spy on their parents (Figes, 2007). Also enunciated is the principle that children should participate in the making of the rules that govern their lives, almost a prototype for CRC, Article 12. Religious education was for the child to choose, and no child was to be oppressed because of his/her convictions. Like the liberationists of the 1970s, the Declaration gave children the freedom to express their thoughts 'just like adults'. None of this was ever operationalised but as an ideological commitment it is a fascinating insight into what might have been. Walter Benjamin, after a visit to Moscow in 1927, remarked 'Bolshevism has abolished private life' (1996–2003, vol. 2: 30).

Declaration of Geneva and UN Declaration of 1959

In the aftermath of the First World War, we had the Declaration of Geneva in 1924 (Marshall, 1999), spearheaded by Eglantyne Jebb (1929), who also founded Save The Children (and see

Kerber-Ganse, 2015; Milne, 2008; Mulley, 2009). The Declaration captured the mood of the time, it stressed society's obligations to children, rather than their rights. Its Preamble explains where it is coming from: 'Mankind owes to the Child the best it has to give'. It was another thirty-five years before children's rights received international attention again, although this is to overlook the Conference on the African Child in Geneva in 1931 (Marshall, 2004). But how many have noticed this conference? Two hundred attended, only seven of them black! The Declaration of 1959 was broader in coverage. The emphasis was still on protection and welfare. There is no recognition of a child's agency, the importance of a child's views, nor any appreciation of the concept of empowerment.

The 1960s might have been expected to see a flowering of children's rights. It didn't. But at the very end of the decade Poland persuaded the United Nations to proclaim 1979 as the International Year of the Child (IYC) (Freeman, 1980, 1983: 24–6). Memories of IYC in the United Kingdom include a Children's Parliament, which voted to keep the cane in schools (one wonders if any of the delegates had been caned at school!), a party in Hyde Park on a wet July weekend – more a mud bath!; and the prominent role in the year played by Jimmy Savile (Davies, 2014; Furedi, 2015), now exposed as a major child sex abuser (J. Smith, 2016).

Child Liberation Movement

The 1970s were very different, or supposedly so. This was the decade of the short-lived child liberation movement. It is associated with the Summerhill school experiment (Cooper, 2013;

Neill, 1968), calls for society to be free of schools (Illich, 1973), but more particularly with a number of American radicals (Gross and Gross, 1977). The most significant were John Holt (1974) (see Byrne, 2016) and Richard Farson (1974). The flavour of their (rather similar) manifestos can be sensed by examining the rights each of them would bestow on children. There were some English advocates of child liberation too, for example A. S. Neill (1973) and Paul Adams (1971).

Holt argues for the right to equal treatment at the hands of the law; the right to vote (and no minimum age) and take a full part in political affairs; the right to be legally responsible for one's life and acts; the right to work for money; the right to privacy; the right to financial independence and responsibility (for example, the right to own property, establish credit, and sign contracts); the right to direct and manage education; the right to travel, to live away from home, to choose or make one's own home; the right to receive from the state whatever minimum income it may guarantee to adult citizens; the right to enter into quasi-familial relationships, on the basis of mutual consent; and the right to do, in general, what any adult may legally do.

Farson's 'Bill of Rights' (he calls them 'Birthrights') contains many of the same entitlements. He is clear that the foundational right is the right to self-determination. He argues that children should be given the right to alternative home environments; the right to responsive design ('society must accommodate itself to children's size and their need for safe space'); the right to information ordinarily available to adults; the right to design their own education; the right to freedom from physical punishment; the right to sexual freedom ('the right to all sexual activities that are legal among consenting adults'); the right to economic power; the right to political power (or at least the right to vote).

Two radical blueprints – a reflection of the 'permissive' 1970s. It is easy to ridicule this thinking. Even easier when the manifestos are augmented, as they are by Holt, to include the right to use drugs, and by Farson to include the right to sexual freedom. Holt at least appreciates the dangers in seeing children as 'love objects' (Holt, 1974: ch. 11). He observes:

> Children don't like being used as love objects, even by people they like. They want the right to refuse, to set the terms, the ground rules, on which at any moment the relationship will proceed. (1974: 82)

This, we must remind ourselves, was written ten or more years before we 'discovered' and recognised sexual abuse of children, and a generation before paedophile grooming, etc. assumed the profile that it has today. It was the era of Jimmy Savile, Rolf Harris, Gary Glitter and many lesser known individuals who treated children as sexual objects (I deliberately omit the word 'love') (Davies, 2014).

But Farson dismissed such scepticism:

> asking what is good for children is beside the point. We will grant children rights for the same reason that we grant rights to adults, not because we are sure that children will then become better people but more for ideological reasons, because we believe that expanding freedom as a way of life is worthwhile in itself. And freedom, we have found, is a difficult burden for adults as for children. (Farson, 1974: 31)

Holt was similarly cynical about those who would deny children access to drugs. He wrote, 'adults use them excessively and unwisely' so how can we justify denying this 'pleasure' to children? (Holt, 1974: 194, 201). This is most unpersuasive: is it not important to break the cycle?

Farson and Holt were not alone. Best remembered of others at this time, perhaps because he offered some constructive machinery, is Howard Cohen (1980). Noting that we all rely on the capacities of others – we use doctors, lawyers, financial advisors – why shouldn't children? He argued that any rights currently enjoyed by adults which children could exercise with the aid of agents are rights which children should have, and, he added, this should apply to 'all children' (H. Cohen, 1980: 60). The task of the agent would be to 'supply information' in terms which the child could understand, to make the consequences of the various courses of action a child might take clear to the child, and do what is necessary to see that the right in question is actually exercised (H. Cohen, 1980: 60). Cohen calls this person an 'agent', but she/he looks more like a counsellor. Why, we may ask, if the child is capable of appointing an agent, is he/she not capable of acting without one?

Did the child liberation movement influence what happened next? Is there any link between the liberation movement and the proclamation of 1979 as the International Year of the Child? And what influence did this 'year' have, if any, on the initiative to formulate a Convention? Perhaps it was one of the catalysts for change. It would be nice to think that the child liberationist 'movement' of the 1970s had some influence on the decision to proclaim the IYC, but this is doubtful. The movement was short-lived and at the time very much marginalised.

The writing of Neill (1968), Farson (1974), Holt (1974), Coigney (1975), H. Cohen (1980), and other lesser-known authors (e.g., Gerzon, 1973; Gottlieb, 1973; Gross and Gross, 1977) are significant, and they deserve a reassessment (and see Byrne, 2016).

The liberation movement was not entirely adult-led, as Young-Bruehl thinks (2012: 9). It is also worth remembering that at the same time there were youth movements proclaiming the need for liberation. A well-known one was Youth Liberation of Ann Arbor in Michigan (see Gross and Gross, 1977: 329). This is an onslaught on 'adult chauvinism' – age *in itself* deserves no recognition. It goes beyond youth liberation to target sexism, bureaucracy, racism, colonisation. It talks of youth of the world unity 'in our common struggle for freedom and peace'. It attacks compulsory education, the trial of children by adults – it advocates a jury of *their* peers. It asserts the right to be economically independent of adults. It was a true example of the 'counter-culture' at work (Roszak, 1968: 95) (and see Appendix 3).

It was in the 1980s that what we call the childhood studies movement emerged. We began to accept that children were 'beings' not just 'becomings' (Qvortrup, 2009) (see below, p. 41).

Feminism and Children's Rights

Thus far, the discussion has focused on 'children', as if all children were the same. The development of children's rights tended to accept this essentialist coding. But, of course, children cannot be neatly packaged in this way; there are gender, age, race and sexual orientation differences, only to mention four of the most 'obvious'. I will here concentrate on gender. Feminism/gender studies has avoided collapsing gender differences. Discourses on children's rights often started from the premise of the universality of childhood (Taefi, 2009). They commonly took a gender neutral approach. Girl children are subjected to additional burdens and have fewer rights, whatever the CRC says (see Article 2). Sex selection is taken advantage of (in India, for example) with the result that in parts of that country less than 800 girls are born to every 1,000 boys. China's one-child policy (Greenhalgh, 2008; Naftali, 2016) aborted in 2015, led to the disappearance of 8.9 million girls in the period 1980–2000 (Ebenitern, 2011). In much of the world girls are subjected to cultural practices like genital cutting (FGM) (E. H. Boyle, 2002); forced into marriage when still comparatively young children (Fruilli, 2008); deprived of education, so poignantly described by Malala Yousafzai (2013) (Morrow, 2013). Their mobility is restricted (Porter, 2011). In parts of the world 'son preference' is endemic (Ratpan, 2012).

Childhood studies should have appreciated this. Initially, it didn't. Much of the work of children's rights scholars take the universality of childhood as unproblematic (see Berman, 2003: 103). Today, there is a burgeoning of literature which explores gender as integral to the study of childhood.

But it is really striking how little interest the 'second wave of feminism' took in propagating children's rights. Shulamith Firestone, the author of *The Dialectic of Sex* (1970), was the egregious exception. Perhaps her oppressive yeshiva education made her aware of the child's need for autonomy. Whatever the explanation, she was clear that if women were to be taken seriously they had to adopt the child's cause too.

But feminists today have more than made up for this. Barrie Thorne (1987) saw the parallels between the situations of women and children: 'the fates and definitions of children have been closely tied with those of women' (Thorne, 1987: 95). Feminist studies were instrumental in deconstructing naturalised images of motherhood and childrearing (Hays, 1996). Such representations were shown to be socially constructed and therefore not universal givens. Feminist theory also has 're-visioned women as active speaking subjects' (Thorne, 1987: 88), and with this has come support for the agency of children (Oswell, 2013). But, paradoxically, emphasising the gendering of children has also undermined children's agency, seeing them as 'becomings', as adults in the making (Thorne, 1987: 92–3). This is now challenged not only within childhood studies, but also by feminists. The 'exaggerated view of children as unagentic, blank slates' (Martin, 2005: 457) was shown to be largely an ideological position promoted by the powerful, that is predominantly men in the Global North (Burman and Stacey, 2010). Different views have been expressed as to the impact of the CRC on women (C. P. Cohen, 1997; Minow, 1990; Olsen, 1992).

What is Guggenheim Getting At?

One of the most interesting critics of children's rights today is Martin Guggenheim. He entitles his book *What's Wrong with Children's Rights*, to which he doesn't append a question mark. There are some wild assertions in the book, for example, all US decisions are consistent with the CRC. He appears to have scant knowledge of the Convention. These are not my concerns here (but see Freeman, 2007).

We need to examine the root of his argument – often glossed over because it is found in the Preface. He believes that children's rights have 'staying power' because they serve adults as well. They are a 'useful subterfuge for the adults' actual motives'. They are useful also to mask 'selfishness' by invoking a language of altruism. He sees a constant stream of cases in which children's rights are invoked by adults to gain some advantage over other adults. I see very little evidence of this in England.

Guggenheim would recast children's rights claims to 'what is fair and just for children'. But this is much the same as a best interests test (Federle, 2009; 2017).

The Convention: A Preliminary Note

And so to the Convention. There is a danger in forefronting this, that it is taken as the last word on children's rights. To do this is to adopt the status quo as unproblematic. I certainly do not intend to do this.

But one cannot get away from the preliminary conclusion that the CRC is a magnificent achievement. It is, and will remain, a landmark in the history of childhood. Together with the World Summit for Children in 1990 (and the Millennium Development Goals of 2000, see below, p. 267, and now see also the Sustainable Development Goals of 2015, below, p. 298) it constitutes recognition by the world that children have that most precious of rights – the right to have rights (Arendt, 1964; Menke, 2014). True, not all children have even this basic right. One-third do not even have their births registered or, for that matter, their deaths. They come and go, and it is as if they never existed. Many asylum-seeking and refugee children fit this description (Bhabha, 2014). Even so, world leaders waxed lyrical about children at the World Summit. One, Margaret Thatcher, referred to children as 'our sacred trust' (perhaps a 'secret trust'!)

The CRC then is a milestone in the history of childhood – the danger is that it may become a 'millstone' (Drabble, 1965). It includes a recognition that children are 'beings', and not merely pre-adult 'becomings'. Korczak saw this in the 1920s, Jens Qvortrup in 1970. With the emergence of childhood studies in the 1980s this became the new orthodoxy. But it had to shift the consensus of leading social scientists from a range of disciplines: Emile Durkheim (1890) and Talcott Parsons (1951) from sociology; Margaret Mead (1969) from anthropology; Jean Piaget (1955) from psychology. Having conceded that children were 'beings', the next question was 'were they full beings'. Those who championed the Convention were prepared to acknowledge that children could be agents. They did this in Article 12, in many ways the pivotal provision in the CRC, though as we will see Articles 13, 14 and 15 are at least as significant (see below, p. 100). The English and US legal systems had already said as much, in *Gillick* (1986) and *Tinker* (1970), respectively. But the Convention did not confer 'citizen-ship' on children, for example, and most obviously, there is no mention of the right to vote. Worldwide this would have been difficult to lay down as a universal structure since the CRC was drafted when half the world was in a Communist stranglehold (it was finalised in the same month as the Berlin Wall fell). So, it has left children as little more than 'semi-citizens' (E. Cohen, 2009).

There were controversies: for example, over adoption (not a concept within Islamic jurisprudence), over religion, and a meta-norm in some countries, over the question of children's duties, firmly entrenched within African legal systems (Sloth-Nielsen and Mezmur, 2008; Twum-Danso, 2003) (and also in Israel, see Bainham, 2006). These had to be negotiated before a Convention could emerge (Johnson, 1992), indeed, including the very definition of 'child'. When did childhood begin and when end? Catholic countries believe life begins at conception, but others (the majority), that it begins at birth. The birth view prevailed (see Article 1), but the battle scars remain, as may be apparent from the ninth paragraph of the Preamble. This speaks of a child's needs 'before as well as after birth'. One premise of the Convention is the 'dignity' of the child (Preamble, paragraph 1). But, of course, the right to abortion is increasingly linked to a woman's dignity (Dixon and Nussbaum, 2012; Siegel, 2010, 2012, 2014). How this conflict of dignities is to be resolved is a task for another day!

Cass Sunstein (1995–6) explains (though not in the context of the CRC) why consensus was achieved despite profound fractures of ideology. He talks of 'incompletely theorized' agreements: agreements reached by consensus in circumstances where there is disagreement as to the principle underpinning the agreement. In other words, the lack of a coherent philosophy (for which the drafters are often criticised) actually facilitated the construction of the Convention.

There are vague and inchoate concepts in the Convention: best interests in Article 3, about which so much has already been written (Freeman, 2007a; Zermatten, 2006). There are concepts about which there is little or no agreement.

'Family' and 'culture' are two examples. There is language used, though not deliberately so, to enable the Convention to become a 'living instrument', like 'violence' in Article 19. (See below, p. 135.) Spanking a child is clearly embraced by this word, but the Convention's drafters were not brave enough to outlaw the smacking of children specifically.

The reporting mechanism, though very weak, also enables a continuing jurisprudence to evolve, so that more and more content can be poured into the Convention. This gives the Convention some dynamism. It can move with the times and take into account new developments like cyber bullying (Cheung, 2012; Hinduja and Patchin, 2011); international surrogacy (Tobin, 2015); grooming and slavery, human enhancement (Fukuyama, 2002; Kahane and Savulescu, 2015); and cloning, neuroscience and global warming and climate change. New problems and new sensitivities can be responded to also through Optional Protocols, and there have been three so far. The General Comment (there are twenty of these thus far) is another way of keeping abreast of the novel, and filling in gaps in the Convention. But new issues continually confront us: sexting (Crofts et al., 2015), radicalisation (Guru, 2013; Stanley and Guru, 2015) and breast ironing, are three of the latest. These raise issues of the limits society should impose on a child's autonomy.

One concept in the CRC, given a prominent place – it is one of the governing principles – is development. This is another of the concepts which is not defined in the Convention, and on which there is a developing jurisprudence. There is a full investigation of this by Noam Peleg (2017, 2019). He shows how the Committee on the Rights of the Child 'implicitly employs mainstream developmental psychology', and was silent when it came to explaining the child's 'legal right to development'. Thus far, he notes, it has not provided 'a coherent, distinct and meaningful interpretation of the child's right to development' (Peleg, 2017, 2019).

This is significant because one of the failings of the CRC is the 'disjunction between the expressions in rights-based advocacy for children and their visibility in development discourses, on the one hand, and their continuing vulnerability, on the other' (Grugel, 2013: 19).

We will return to this later. But, for now, it is worth emphasising one of the reasons why there may be dissatisfaction with the CRC in the Global South is that, whilst children may be gaining more rights 'in theory', this is not being translated into meaningful improvement in their well-being, particularly in the Global South.

Could it be that the Convention reflects the lives of children in the more prosperous North more than it does those living in the much poorer South? The Convention is not strong on socio-economic rights. Nor are legislatures in translating what rights there are into practice (Nolan, 2011). Poverty, preventable diseases, malnutrition and war still plague much of the Global South, and more than twenty-eight years of the Convention have done little to eradicate these evils.

But Why are Rights So Important?

The language of rights can make visible what for long has been suppressed. As Carrie Menkel-Meadow explains (1987: 52):

> Each time we let in an oppressed group, each time we listen
> to a new way of knowing, we learn more about the limits of
> our current way of seeing.

As an example, look at the *Williamson* case (2003). It was an attempt by Christian fundamentalist parents and teachers at fundamentalist schools to challenge the state's abolition of corporal punishment in schools. This, remarkably, had only finally happened in 1998. The case was fought as a battle between parents and teachers and the state: children were not parties to the litigation nor were they represented. They (or rather their backsides) became contested territory. This injustice caused Baroness Hale of Richmond bravely to say in her judgment:

> This is, and always has been a case about children, their
> rights, and the rights of their parents and teachers. Yet
> there has been no one here or in the courts below to speak
> on behalf of the children. The battle has been fought on
> ground selected by the adults. (*Williamson*, para. 128)

Her judgment, she exclaimed, 'is for the sake of the children'. From a children's rights perspective the case was about whether children's rights to be free from corporal chastisement at school could be trumped by their parents' religious convictions. But the case was fought as if the issue were whether the state had the legitimate right to undermine parents' beliefs.

Rights are important, 'uniquely valuable' (Buchanan, 2015), because they are inclusive: they belong to all members of humanity. They are universal. Once they depended on gender and race and on sexual orientation. Women were non-persons, black persons were kept in subservience by institutions such as slavery and apartheid. It is not insignificant that the word 'boy' was applied to black adult men, and girls remain 'girls' even during adulthood!

But, just as concepts of gender inequality have been a key to our understanding of womanhood, so the 'concept of generation is key to understanding childhood' (Mayall, 2002: 120). It has always been to the advantage of the powerful to keep others out. It is therefore not surprising that adults should wish to do this to children. Of course, the flipside of inclusion is exclusion. The powerful regulate space – social, political (E. Cohen, 2009), geographical (Valentine, 2004). They define the realm of participation, as they have done in the CRC (see Article 12 and the following Articles 13, 14 and 15). They marginalise significance. They impede development.

Rights are indivisible and interdependent. Denying certain rights undermines other rights. If we deny children the right to be free from corporal chastisement, we so undermine their status and integrity that other rights may fall as well. A child denied the right to education (see CRC, Article 28) will lack the ability to exercise many other rights. This applies with force across categories of persons. So, for example, freedom from child abuse (Article 19) is more likely to create a society where there is no domestic violence, than one where abuse of children is prevalent. Thus, it is all the more surprising that feminists have until recently shown such little interest in advocating rights for children.

Rights are important because they recognise the respect their bearers are entitled to. To accord rights is to respect dignity (Kateb, 2014; Milbank, 2013; cf. Rosen, 2012). There is much more discussion of dignity today than there has been at any time since Kant ([1797] 1996) (see McCrudden, 2013), but little or none in relation to children. Michael Rosen thinks children do not possess dignity. This surprises Milbank (2013) and Dellavalle (2013: 446), and so it should. As Dellavalle points out, although young children may have difficulties in articulating arguments, they can nevertheless communicate in ways 'more respectful of the truth, truthfulness, and rightness than the communication which takes place between fully rational...adult humans' (Dellavalle, 2013: 446). Rights are thus an affirmation of the Kantian principle that human beings are ends in themselves and not means to others' ends (Kant, [1797] 1996).

For the powerful, and as far as children are concerned adults are always powerful, rights are an inconvenience. The powerful would find it easier to rule if those below them lacked rights. Decision-making would be swifter, cheaper, more efficient, more certain. It is hardly surprising that none of the civil and political rights we have today were freely bestowed. They all had to be fought for. Oddly, there is one exception to this. Children were presented with the gift of the CRC. They didn't fight for it or bargain for it. The gift did not include the vote. It is therefore important that we see rights as 'trumps' (Dworkin, 1977: ix). This is to emphasise that they cannot be knocked off their pedestal or chipped away at because it would be better for others, parents, teachers, social workers, the medical profession, or even society as a whole were these rights not to exist.

Rights are important because those who have them can exercise agency (Oswell, 2013). Agents can be decision-makers. They can be citizens. As we will see (see below, p. 91), the CRC does not confer full citizenship rights. Even the much-lauded Article 12 stops short of conferring full participation rights (e.g., in relation to education, see King, 2004; Lundy, 2007; A. B. Smith, 2007). Agents can negotiate with others. They are capable of altering relationships, of effecting changes in decisions. Agents can shift social assumptions and constraints. There is now clear evidence that even the youngest child can do this (Alderson, Hawthorne and Killen, 2005). As agents, rights-bearers can participate. They can make their own lives rather than having their lives made for them. And participation is a fundamental human right: it enables us to demand rights. We are, of course, better able to do so where there is freedom of expression (Mill, 1859: ch. 2), of assembly and association. All of these freedoms are set out in the CRC (see Articles 13, 14 and 15), but they are commonly denied children. Freedom of information is also fundamental, but it too is rarely forthcoming to children.

Rights are also an important advocacy tool, a valuable weapon in the battle to secure recognition. They provide moral argument for advocacy. Giving people rights without access to those who can present those rights, and do so expertly, is of little value. In 2014, the Third Protocol to the CRC came into operation. This introduced a new 'complaints procedure' for children (see, further, below, p. 222), but how effective can it be in an age of austerity with massive reductions in spending on public services? Not many children will be able to finance their own challenges to governmental failure before the Committee on the Rights of the Child in Geneva (Lee, 2013; R. Smith, 2013; Spronk, 2014).

Rights offer legitimacy to pressure groups, lobbies, campaigns, to both direct and indirect action, in particular to those who are disadvantaged or excluded. They offer a way in; they open doors. It is thus hardly surprising that some of the best statements of the case for rights have come from minority scholars like Mari Matsuda (1987), Kimberlé Crenshaw (1988), and Patricia Williams (1998), or from those arguing the case for the excluded such as Martha Minow (1990). For Alan Hunt, rights have the capacity 'to be elements of emancipation' (A. Hunt, 1990). But, he adds, they must become part of an 'emergent common sense' to be part of a strategy for social transformation. As Kate Federle explains (1994: 343), 'rights flow downhill'. (See below, p. 55.)

Thus, the task of the children's rights advocate becomes clear. It is to demonstrate that the case for children's rights is so morally right that people will wonder how they can ever have thought otherwise. And we can help to negotiate this common sense through our social practices. Certainly, the social practices of those who work with children can help to construct a new culture of childhood.

Rights then are also a resource: they offer reasoned argument. They support a strong moral case. Too often those who oppose rights can offer little or nothing in response. Opponents of anti-smacking laws go on the attack and tell us it never did them any harm, or like the claimants in the *Williamson* case, reel off epigrams from the *Book of Proverbs* as if the 'wisdom' of an earlier millennium provided closure to a contemporary debate (and see Greven, 1992). They help us define injustice.

Rights are a militant concept (H. Cohen, 1980). Without rights the excluded can make requests, they can beg or implore, they can be troublesome; they can rely on, what has been called, *noblesse oblige*, or on others being generous, kind, cooperative or just intelligently foresighted. But they cannot demand because there is no entitlement (Bandman, 1973).

Rights are valuable commodities (Wasserstrom, 1964). They are necessities, not luxuries (Alderson, 2003: 14). It is instructive to reflect upon what a society without rights would look like. It would be morally impoverished. It might be ruled by a benevolent dictator, but if his standards dropped there would be no cause for complaint. A world with claim-rights by contrast is one in which 'all persons...are dignified objects of respect' (Feinberg, 1966). Throughout history children have not been accorded either respect or dignity. Only, finally, with the passing of the Convention have children acquired at long last that most significant of rights...the right to have rights (Arendt, 1964; Bhabha, 2014).

Why Have Children Been Denied Rights?

Many reasons, many rationalisations, have been proffered for denying rights to children. There are four main justifications, or alleged justifications, none of them convincing and largely jettisoned today by their proponents.

First, there was the view that children were merely the property of their parents. Expressed as overtly as this, it didn't survive the nineteenth century (Mason, 1994), but it limped on, cloaked in the pseudo-science of the 'blood tie'. Mia Kellmer-Pringle's response that we must eradicate the attitude that:

> a baby completes a family, rather like a TV set or
> fridge...That a child belongs to his parents like their other
> possessions over which they may exercise exclusive rights.
> (Kellmer-Pringle, 1980: 156)

is dated only because of the consumer items it cites, but not in the salutary warning it offers. In the same year, Andrews (1980) was asking in the leading social work journal whether blood was thicker than local authorities. Both were writing in the aftermath of horrific cases of child abuse, most notably that of Maria Colwell (Field-Fisher, 1974; Howells, 1974). But, forty years on, these crimes persist (see the case of 'Baby Peter' in R. Jones, 2014), and, indeed, have seemingly got worse, with abuse on an industrial scale, as male predators in Rotherham, Rochdale, Oxford, and doubtless many other places prey on girls (and boys) they regard as their property.

Secondly, rights are regarded as public coinage. It is thought they are not as important in the private domain. For children this is seen as a walled garden of 'Happy, Safe, Protected, Innocent Childhood' (Holt, 1974: 22–3). Of course, this is a myth. The curtain of privacy cloaks all manner of evils: sexual abuse, FGM, forced marriage, religious indoctrination (Dwyer, 1994), even slavery (bonded labour, sexual slavery). It also stifles the opportunities children might have to participate in the public arena, to communicate their views to decision-makers. And, when they succeed in communicating their opinions in public, they are deemed 'out of place', and met with patronisation or, more commonly, ignored

(Hine, 2004). Not a great deal of thought has been given to what the 'standpoint' of children might be on the public/private divide (Alenen, 1994). For example, where does the school fit? Is it the focal point of childhood, a space where they naturally belong? Is it an extension of the family? It performs many of the same functions. But school is also a place where children learn about the world, about the place they will occupy in it, about power and inequality (Bowles and Gintis, 1976). Schooling is an imperative for economic development, and as such, it is a key investment, though not all education takes place at school. As far as children are concerned, the school may well be experienced as private, rather than public. Certainly, in so far as the language of rights has any meaning in the school setting, they inhere in parents, not their children. This is clear not only from domestic legislation, but also from the CRC, European jurisprudence, and from the UK courts' interpretation of the European Convention on Human Rights (ECHR).

Not all children are at school. Many, perhaps 10 per cent of the world's children, are in work and many of them are in hazardous forms of labour. Many more – no one knows how many – are engaged in low status work in the home environment. For such children the 'heartless world' has been installed in the 'haven' (Lasch, 1977). Also hidden are the many 'young carers', perhaps as many as a quarter of a million in Britain alone.

The most interesting group of children to test the public/private binary are street children. They are not a category of children recognised as such by the CRC (Ennew, 2000: 169). The street is 'a metaphor' (Wells, 2009: 29). Street children are out of place (Ennew, 2000): they don't belong on the street, which is adult territory. They are an anomaly, not really children, and not quite 'human'. We see children on the streets as nuisances, truants, members of gangs, a 'blot on the landscape', but not as 'street children'; they are in Rio, Nairobi and Bangkok (Ennew, 2003). The number in the Global North will increase substantially with the refugee crisis. But Charles Dickens recognised the phenomenon (in *Oliver Twist* and elsewhere). Of course, the public/private dichotomy is illusory – this I have discussed elsewhere (Freeman, 1975).

The third reason why childhood was thought to be a rights-free zone was that children were not truly persons yet but only on their way to achieving this status. A child was seen as an adult in the making. . .the child is 'work in progress'; the adult is the finished product. Nick Lee put it well when he stated we were expected to make 'sense of childhood through adulthood. . .Children's lives and activities in the present are- . . .envisaged. . .as preparation for the future' (Lee, 2001: 8). Of course, the implicit assumption is that adults are the finished product, that they can act in society, can participate 'independently in serious activities like work and politics', 'whilst children's instability and incompleteness mean that they are often understood only as dependent and passive recipients of adults' actions' (Lee, 2001). Children were seen as 'becomings', and not yet 'beings'.

This view of childhood was nourished by a number of disciplines, in particular by developmental psychology (Burman, 2008) (the work of Piaget, 1955 especially prominent); social anthropology (Lancy, 2015), for example, the work of Margaret Mead (1969); sociology (Durkheim, 1890; Parsons, 1951). In a nutshell, this saw children as 'inadequate, incomplete and dependent' (Allison James, 2009: 37). Of course, this conception of the child left no space for the agentic child. And this radically different model of the 'child' was to become a key feature of the emergent paradigm within the new childhood studies.

The fourth reason why rights were denied to children is that it was supposed that they lacked the competence to exercise them. This can be answered in a number of ways. In brief, there are two answers. First, there is evidence that children are much more competent than critics would have us believe. Secondly, rights protect interests and children certainly have these; indeed, the CRC clearly protects interests rather than the exercise of will (see, for agreement, Tobin, 2013).

Kate Federle, in a series of important articles (1993, 1994, 2017), has pointed to the problems which 'capacity' has caused those who wish to construct a case for children's rights (Federle, 1993). Noting that 'having a right means having the power to command respect' she argues:

> But if having a right is contingent upon some
> characteristic, like capacity, then holding the right
> becomes exclusive and exclusionary. . .claims made by
> those without the requisite characteristics of a rights holder
> *need not be recognised.* (Federle, 1994: 344)

Whereas many powerless groups in the past (ethnic minorities, women) have been able to redefine themselves as competent beings, this route is not as open to children, so that 'powerful elites decide which, if any, of the claims made by children they will recognise' (Federle, 1994).

Federle offers a searing indictment of rights theories (classical and modern) which, she shows, link having and exercising rights to capacity. She appears, initially at least, to find greater promise in feminist theory, which de-emphasises 'the significance of competency in rights talk by focusing on individual relationships between children and adults' (Federle, 1994: 354). But it is to the writings of Martha Minow (1987) that she turns, and she is right to find shortcomings in these. As Federle observes, 'the emphasis on relationships presupposes a connection between adults and children that merely under-scores children's dependencies rather than rendering them irrelevant' (Federle, 1994: 356). And, more significantly, she notes that 'when our rights talk speaks of children's rights in relationships, it forecloses an honest assessment of the power we have over our children' (Federle, 1994). Thus, 'tying rights to relationships' is nothing more than a 'sophisticated' version of the argument that 'children should have rights because of their incompetencies' (Federle, 1994). It is Federle's conclusion that there is a need to re-conceptualise the meaning of having and exercising rights. The kind of rights she envisions are 'not premised upon capacity but upon power or more precisely, powerlessness' (1994: 365). Rights are seen from this perspective more as inhibitions on the ability of those with power. And this creates 'zones of mutual respect for power that limits the kinds of things we may do to one another' (1994: 366). Her argument is that this has 'a transformative aspect as well, for the empow-ering effects of rights would reduce the victimization of children because we would no longer see them as powerless beings' (Federle, 1994).

This is an intriguing argument, and the message that 'rights flow downhill' (Federle, 1994: 365), if true, would be of great comfort to the disadvantaged everywhere. But, even aside from the problem Federle acknowledges – how children actually claim rights' violations within this conceptual structure – there are difficulties with this thesis. How, for example, does this carefully-constructed case transcend the common objection to rights that what is on offer is formal acknowledgement rather than anything of substantive value? Additionally, Federle's thesis would seemingly lead to the conclusion that certain children, children with special needs, poor children, refugee children, should be given more rights than other children if there is to be any equalisation. I doubt if this is intended or would be morally justifiable. There is also the problem that the same formal right accorded to two different children, one of whom was already endowed with some 'power' (by reason of genetic inheritance, social status or education) would not be of the same value to each. Just as there are different childhoods, so there are differently situated subjects. Different children might 'need' different rights, might wish to claim different rights, or ought to have different rights claimed on their behalf. But this comes close to a recognition that the having or the exercising of rights is tied to competence. That rights and power are linked. Federle's thesis may also oversimplify power: that children lack rights is not necessarily an indication that others have power, or power over them. And power itself can often be fragmented and diffuse.

But Why Rights for Children?

Some who accept the moral importance of rights are nevertheless sceptical, or even dismissive, when the question is raised as to whether children should have rights.

One argument put is that the importance of rights and rights-language can be exaggerated. This is not the same argument that I shall be putting in Chapter 14 that rights by themselves are not enough. Rather, this argument points to other morally significant values, such as love, friendship, compassion, altruism, which raise relationships to a higher plane. This argument may be thought particularly apposite to children's rights, especially in the context of family relationships. Perhaps in an ideal moral world this might be true. But this is not an ideal world – certainly not for children.

A second argument is in one sense related to the first. It makes the assumption that adults already relate to children in terms of love, care and altruism, so that the case for children's rights becomes otiose. This idealises adult-child relations; it emphasises that adults and parents in particular have the best interests of children at heart. That most do does not undermine the point. There is a tendency for those who proffer this argument to adopt a *laissez-faire* attitude towards the family. An obvious example runs through the writings of Goldstein, Freud and Solnit (1979, 1986). A policy of minimum coercive intervention by the state fits neatly with their 'firm belief as citizens in individual freedom and human dignity' (1979: 12). But it hardly needs to be asked *whose* freedom and *what* dignity this is thought to uphold. It is difficult to see how the creation of a private space can be said to protect the humanity of the child.

The third argument is also embedded in a myth. This sees childhood as a golden age, as the best years of our life. Childhood is seen as synonymous with innocence, as the time when, spared the hardships of adult life, they enjoy freedom, and experience joy. Whilst adults work, they play. The corollary of avoiding the responsibilities and adversities of adult life in childhood, so the argument runs, is that there is no necessity to think about rights, a concept which we must assume is reserved for adults. Whether or not the premise underlying this were correct or not, it would represent an ideal state of affairs, and one which ill-reflects the lives of many of today's children. But for many this idyllic image of childhood is illusory, even utopian (Holt, 1974). Indeed, it is just plain wrong, with poverty, disease, malnutrition, exploitation and abuse rife in all parts of the world (Mapp, 2011; Wells, 2009; Wild, 2013). Childhood today is said to be 'toxic' (Palmer, 2006), 'under siege' (Bakan, 2011). Children have even been said to be 'an endangered species' (Max, 1990).

Onora O'Neill and Obligations

A more oblique challenge to children's rights (or rather on the way morally to justify them) is mounted by Onora O'Neill in a much-quoted article (1992, originally 1988). She does not question the view that children's lives are a public concern, rather than a private matter. Nor does she query the aim of securing positive rights for children. What she does question is whether children's positive rights are best grounded by appeals to fundamental rights. She claims rather that they are best grounded by embedding them in 'a wider account of fundamental obligations' (1992: 25). The strategy of her argument, as she puts it, is:

> That theories that take rights as fundamental and those that take obligations as fundamental are not equivalent. The scope of the two sorts of theory differs and does so in ways that matter particularly for children. A constructivist account of obligations has theoretical advantages which constructivist accounts of rights lack, though rights-based approaches sometimes have political advantages which obligation-based approaches do not. . .[T]hat in the specific case of children, taking rights as fundamental has political costs rather than advantages. (O'Neill, 1992)

I do not deny that children's dependency is very different from that of other groups, but I do not think it is as different as O'Neill would have us believe. To some extent it is artificially produced. The lessons of history tell us this, and our own experiences and intuitions enable us to realise that many adolescents have the capacity to be less dependent than many adults. For example, if competence were the test, rather than age, we could with confidence give the vote to some fourteen-year-olds, and disenfranchise many adults (Lindley, 1986: 125–33). Some (clearly not all) of it can be ended by political if not by social change. They may not be changes of which we necessarily approve – an example might be encouraging children to be gainfully employed. But there are changes which would decrease dependency. The reciprocal dependency argument can also be over-played. There are parents who need to be loved and shown affection by their child. Some child abuse, it is thought, can be explained in this way – children who cannot, or more likely are not old enough to show affection being abused by inadequate parents. Certainly, some older children perceive a parent's dependency in this way.

A third difference I have with O'Neill follows on from the second. She perceives children as a special case. Whilst she concedes that the fact that children cannot claim rights is no reason for denying them rights, the claiming/ waiving dilemma seems to be at the root of her thinking. Although she does not say as much, this commits her to the will theory of rights. A series of inconclusive test matches may, as Neil MacCormick ([1982] 1984) memorably suggested, have been played out between the will and interest theories of rights. But I think he showed convincingly that, in the case of children's rights at least, the interest theory is more coherent and has greater explanatory power. Children have interests to protect before they develop wills to assert, and others can complain on behalf of younger children when those interests are trampled upon. The theoretical underpinning of the CRC adopts the interest theory as its inarticulate premise (Tobin, 2013).

It cannot be right, as O'Neill asserts, that the 'child's main remedy is to grow up' (1992: 39). This underestimates the capacities and maturity of many children (Alderson, 2008). We expect children to be criminally responsible at the age of ten. Our policy-makers are clearly oblivious to neuroscientific evidence (T. Mahoney, 2009, 2011). This is discussed below, p. 332.

O'Neill also ignores the impact on adult life that parenting and socialisation have. A child deprived of basic children's/human rights will grow up differently from one raised in a rights environment. To take one simple example: there is evidence to suggest that a child disciplined by spanking may develop a lower IQ than a child reared in a non-violent home (Straus et al., 2014). Of course, a child deprived of rights may not grow up at all (R. Jones, 2014).

My differences with O'Neill are numerous. Summarised briefly her views are:

(1) She cannot envisage a children's movement. I can. Indeed, there are both historical and contemporary examples of this phenomenon.

(2) She thinks the dependency of children is very different from the dependency of other oppressed groups. She concedes that appeals to children's rights might be important if children's dependence on others were like that of other oppressed groups. But, she argues, there are four ways in which the dependence of children is different from that of other oppressed groups:

   (a) It is not artificially produced, though she concedes it can be artificially prolonged.

   (b) It cannot be ended by social or political changes by themselves.

   (c) Others are not reciprocally dependent on children, whereas slave-owners, for example, need their slaves.

   (d) The 'oppressors' usually want children's dependency to end.

Rights versus Interests

A commonly-expressed criticism of children's rights is that the exercise of such rights may conflict with the best interests of that child or the best interests of others.

The first of these criticisms pits the two sides of children's rights against each other. It raises the question of how to resolve the conflict which occurs when the exercise of autonomy by a child is thought (by adults) not to be in the child's best interests. Two points may be made. First, the Convention explicitly provides (in Article 12) that the 'child has a right to express views' on all matters affecting him/her. This includes the child's perception of best interests (Article 3). However, participation rights are accorded on the basis of age and maturity. Secondly, and linked to this, there are limits to the exercise of autonomy. This was grasped by John Stuart Mill in his *On Liberty* (1859), though not in relation to children. Liberty, in his view, does not extend to selling oneself into slavery. And there is his famous dangerous bridge example (Mill, 1989: 96; originally 1859). He poses the dilemma of what to do when you see someone crossing an unsafe bridge. Mill himself was in no doubt: you pulled him back. But suppose our hypothetical bridge-crosser is intent on committing suicide? Do we have the right to frustrate his exercise of autonomy – his last such exercise? For the bridge-crosser substitute a thirteen-year-old Jehovah's Witness who needs a blood transfusion and is refusing it on religious grounds, or a sixteen-year-old anorexic who is refusing consent to treatment. Let us assume that both are competent.

A recent English case may serve as an illustration (as, indeed, may Ian McEwan's recent novel *The Children Act* (2014)). The case's central character is Angela Roddy. She was nearly seventeen, and a mother. She wanted to sell her story to a tabloid newspaper. There were injunctions to stop this, designed to protect her and her family from undue publicity by prohibiting their identification. The judge allowed Angela to proceed, following the *Gillick* ruling. He defended the right of a child who has sufficient understanding to make an informed decision to make her own choice. There was need, he said, to recognise 'Angela's dignity and integrity as a human being' (McEwan, 2014: 968). She was, of course, almost an adult, but she had given birth to the baby when only thirteen, and in a glare of considerable publicity, although her identity had not been revealed, because the Roman Catholic Church had paid for her not to have an abortion. Had she tried to sell her story at the earlier time, the court would have applied wardship principles – the best interests test – and prevented her from telling her story to the press. But now, any decision would need to be grounded in the ECHR (and the CRC as well, if this were incorporated into English law, as I argue below, it clearly should be). And she would have rights under the ECHR and the CRC to publish her story. The judge, however, found she also had rights, as her parents or the court might wish to assert them on her behalf, '(a) to keep her private life private and (b) to preserve and protect the family life she enjoys with her parents and other members of her family' (2014: 963). The court, in other words, would not allow her to make a mistake.

Paternalism

This injection of paternalism is explained by John Eekelaar (not in relation to the *Roddy* case) as the situating of children's rights within dynamic self-determinism. The goal of this is 'to bring the child to the threshold of adulthood with the maximum opportunities to form and pursue life-goals which reflect as closely as possible an autonomous choice' (Eekelaar, 1992: 53). It is also explained by Jane Fortin (in a comment on *Roddy* and on this dictum) 'as gentle paternalism which bears the hallmarks of commonsense' (Fortin, 2009: 259). There are, she adds, 'respectable jurisprudential arguments for maintaining that a commitment to the concept of children's rights does not prevent interventions to stop children making dangerous short-term choices, thereby protecting their potential for long-term autonomy' (Fortin, 2009).

My own view is similar, though it is closer to Eekelaar's than to Fortin's. It was explained over thirty years ago in *The Rights and Wrongs of Children* to be rooted in liberal paternalism (Freeman, 1983: 54–60). Since then I have had opportunities to fine-tune this theory, in particular in cases where judges have removed rights from adolescents when they have refused to consent to medical treatment (Freeman, 2007b). I am critical of these decisions (see *Re R*, 1992; *Re W*, 1993). Others have argued that where such a dangerous, potentially life-threatening choice is made 'liberal paternalism demands intervention by adults' (Lowe and Juss, 1993).

There is not a simple answer to this, or a simple solution. But there must be less emphasis on what these young persons know – less talk in other words of knowledge and understanding (Alderson and Goodwin, 1993) and more on how the decision they have reached furthers their goals and coheres with their system of values. We need to understand their experiences and their culture. We must engage with them. Just imposing treatment upon them, as has happened all too frequently (see Hagger, 2003), achieves nothing in the long term. We must situate these disputes and their court resolutions not just in terms of the psychological impact they have on the young person in question – it was described by one as like rape – but with an appreciation of what they say about our concept of childhood. This is dramatically illustrated by the case of *Re E* (1993), fictionalised by Ian McEwan (2014), in which a competent young man was forced to undergo treatment until his eighteenth birthday when he was allowed to say 'no'. He died a few days after. The striking contrast is with the paranoid schizophrenic in a secure psychiatric hospital permitted to refuse a leg amputation: he was sixty-eight, and had killed his wife (*Re C*, 1994).

Why Children's Rights Come First

The promotion of children's rights – placing them on a pedestal – may also undermine the rights of others, sometimes as in the case of the conjoined twins (*Re A*, 2001) or in a situation where the parent is a child (for example, see *Birmingham CC* v. *H*, 1994), the rights of other children. This is a common criticism. One who has expressed it is Martin Guggenheim in his *What's Wrong with Children's Rights* (2005). But there are good reasons why the interests of children should rule. These have been rehearsed often (Dwyer, 2010), so a brief account is all that is necessary here.

Children are, of course, especially vulnerable. They have fewer resources – material, psychological, relational – upon which they can call in situations of adversity. They are usually blameless. They didn't ask to come into this world. For too long they have been regarded as objects of concern (sometimes, even worse, as objects – one is reminded of Mia Kellmer-Pringle's already quoted stinging criticism (above, p. 51) of those who think children complete a home rather like typical consumer durables), not as persons (1980). They have been regarded as 'becomings', not 'beings'. Even today, more than twenty-eight years after the CRC, they remain voiceless, even invisible, and it matters not that the dispute is about them.

There is also a concern amongst some who are committed to rights for children that reducing them to a specifically-named children's Convention may have the opposite effect from that intended. It may weaken them rather than, as it is intended to do, strengthen them. The danger, as they perceive it, is that a code for children can have the effect of removing children from the general human rights framework, leaving them in a ghetto, and making human rights generally the exclusive province of adult society (see, e.g., Hanson, 2015; Pupavac, 2011; Reynaert, Bouverne-De Bie and Vandevelde, 2009). There are developments which support these concerns, as well as those which should allay fears.

As examples where concern is justified, look at workplace practices, at the increase in bonded labour, and in child trafficking (Rao, 2013), and in the global sex industry (O'Connell Davidson, 2005); or at the way criminal law has developed for children. More promisingly, concerns may be deflated by examining laws which have strengthened children's status in civil proceedings and provisions like Article 19 of the CRC, which enhance the protection accorded children in abusive environments (but see Gal, 2011). The promotion of children's rights may undermine the interests of others, particularly of parents. But emphasising children does not necessarily imply the interests of others must be neglected. As Barbara Bennett Woodhouse reminds us:

> A truly child-centred perspective would. . .expose the fallacy that children can thrive while their care-givers struggle, or that the care-givers' needs can be severed from the child, which can lead to the attitude that violence, hostility and neglect toward the care-giver are somehow irrelevant in the best interests calculus. (Woodhouse, 1993: 1825)

The Relational Model: A Note

This leads neatly into a brief discussion of the relational model of child rights (Nedelsky, 1993). This attaches to the liberal model of children's rights, which I have not questioned in this chapter, the ethics of care, first developed in the writings of Carol Gilligan (1982). The ethics of care is foundational for the relational model. 'The relational model focuses on the concrete person and emphasises the fabric of relationships between (the rights-holder and others)' (Zafran, 2010: 192). There is a close connection between the relational model and the development of alternative dispute resolution (ADR) techniques, such as mediation. The liberal model, by contrast, is structured around the binary solution. It is often said that adversarial procedures are harmful to children, and this may be so. But ADR has a propensity to silence the child, who may feel even more marginalised than in a traditional trial.

The relational model fuses the ethics of rights with the ethics of care. As a result, rights are protected within a system which upholds relationships (Minow and Shanley, 1996). Its advocates claim that rights do not go under, but I am sceptical. They also claim that it is possible to continue to use the concept 'right' without prejudicing other values, in particular care and responsibility.

Certainly, it may lead to the formulation of rights not found in the Convention. One suggestion is 'love' (Liao, 2015). Zafran (2010: 195) suggests three: the right to meaningful family relationships, the right to parental care, and the right to development (on which see Grugel, 2013). But how would it play out in intractable conflicts? For example, in disputes about medical treatment, religion (male circumcision is an example), education? How would relational rights help a court confronted with the issues in *Wisconsin* v. *Yoder* (1972) or the *Gillick* litigation or the *Williamson* case? At least it may be supposed that the children would have been involved in *Williamson*, and not just the objects of it.

Children's Rights and the Capability Approach: A Note

The capability approach (CA) can be traced to Amartya Sen (1999) and Martha Nussbaum (2000). Scholarship is now emerging which attempts to show it offers insights into children's rights (Biggeri, Ballet and Conim, 2011; Dixon and Nussbaum, 2012; Stoecklin and Bonvin, 2014). The approach is not without its critics; Dean (2009) describes it as a 'beguiling concept'. Of course, as Stoecklin and Bonvin concede (2014: 1) 'children's rights and the capability approach are not of the same nature: children's rights are a social reality and the capability approach is a perspective to reflect on it'. The capability approach draws our attention to the gap between formal rights and real freedoms. But this only draws attention to the failures of the rights approach which the CRC exemplifies. We are all aware of the dangers of seeing words on a document as embodying deeds.

The question posed is thus how to turn rights into capabilities. What are capabilities? They are not, we are told, resources or commodities. And Nussbaum and Sen cannot agree what they are. So Nussbaum has drawn up a list of essential capabilities, but Sen believes that they should be left to the initiative of local actors. Further capabilities do not coincide with 'functionings', that is what people are and what they actually do. Two people displaying the same kind of functioning might enjoy different level of capabilities. The goal is to encourage autonomous choice of a life that is valuable to the individual. This leaves little or no space for paternalism.

Hence, CA 'insists...people should be provided with real opportunities which extend beyond resources and formal rights; they should be left autonomous in deciding about the way they want to use these opportunities and not be constrained toward compliance with specific norms or official directives' (Stoecklin and Bonvin, 2014: 3). A liberal's paradise!! And what of children? CA appears to recognise evolving capabilities, though it seeks in support not Article 5 of the CRC, but rather Article 12, 'the masterpiece for child participation' (Stoecklin and Bonvin, 2014: 4).

A full account of CA in relation to children is given in Reynaert and Roose (2014). It is their view that 'both the framework of children's rights and the capability approach are characterised by a strong egalitarian individualism, which supports an understanding of agency and the individual responsibility of people' (Reynaert and Roose, 2014: 176). In their view, the framework of CA is important because it is better able 'to accommodate the diversity of human beings and the complexity of their circumstances' (Dean, 2009: 263). It is also comprehensive, covering as it does all dimensions of human development (Robeyns, 2005: 96).

A capability is about more than just what people effectively do and be; it is about their freedom to live the kind of life they have reason to value. Does it matter that they value pinball rather than poetry (to recall a Benthamite example)? Or join ISIS rather than the Koran study group? CA conceptualises the individual from an egalitarian individualism point of view, so that agency and autonomy are emphasised. Does this apply to children as well? Macleod (2015) recognises that, to quote Shakespeare, there are seven ages of man – or more. At each of these stages, capabilities are shaped in different and distinctive ways.

2

Interlude: Taking A Deep Breath

Where We Are At – Reflections on Current Thinking –
Towards A Critique

Universalist and Particularist Ethics

Children's rights are situated within the culture of modernity, in which the emphasis is on the universal and upon objective knowledge (Hartas, 2008). The ethical foundation is that individuals are atomistic units and require an authority to establish objective rules to govern their lives. When children's rights are seen, as the dominant tendency is to do, as a universal code, most obviously as in the CRC, it has attracted criticism for relying on a deterministic understanding of who the child is (Gould, 2004). Determinism has played a formative role in the constructions of childhood.

Carol C. Gould (2004) argues instead for a human rights framework that is less universal and abstract and more concrete. She distinguishes between abstract and concrete universalism. She recognises that we have appealed latterly to universalist norms to confront cultural practices that violate human rights. I have tried to do this in previously published articles (Freeman, 1995, 2002). Gould puts forward her conception of concrete universality as a way of making room for 'universal norms such as equal freedom and human rights' (Gould, 2004: 5).

It is conventional for human rights advocates to seek their support in Western concepts of liberal autonomy. A clear statement of this is formulated by Ronald Dworkin in *Taking Rights Seriously*. He argues:

> Government must treat those whom it governs with concern, that is, as human beings who are capable of suffering and frustration, and with respect, that is, as human beings who are capable of forming and acting on intelligent conceptions of how their lives should be lived. Government must not only treat people with concern and respect, but with equal concern and respect. It must not distribute goods or opportunities unequally on the ground that some citizens are entitled to more because they are worthy of more concern. It must not constrain liberty on the ground that one citizen's conception of the good life. . .is nobler or superior to another's. (Dworkin, 1977: 272–3)

This may fit (or may have fitted in 1989) the agenda set by the Global North, which privileged its way of looking at the world (and at childhood), and embodied this image in the norms of the Convention. The Convention has been criticised as culturally biased (Harris-Short, 2003). It has also been critiqued as 'neo-liberal'. This is supported by Kate Swanson's *Begging as a Path to Progress* (2010), based on research in Ecuador (a state seemingly in the vanguard of propagating children's rights). It enacted in 2003 the Código de la Ninez y Adolescencia with the input of children and adolescents. But at the same time, used militarised policing of the streets to drive the indigenous poor from the area of Quito where they congregate to beg. There was a conflict between poor children's rights to survive (see Article 6 of the CRC) and neo-liberal economic policies which involved attracting tourists to Ecuador.

Development

'Development' is the 'primary metaphor' through which childhood is made intelligible, both in the everyday world and 'also within the specialist vocabularies of the sciences and agencies which lay claim to an understanding and servicing of that state of being' (Jenks, 1996: 36).

'Development' means different things to different scholars and to different disciplines. Contrast the interpretation given to the concept by economists or by Amartya Sen, for example, with that we find in developmental psychology, the work of Erica Burman as an example. The Convention refers to the child's right to development in this second sense (see Article 6). And, so significant is it that it is coupled with 'life' and 'survival', and set out as the first norm in the Convention to proclaim a right for children. It is, however, not defined.

Could it be that the two concepts of 'development' are not all that different, but rather different conceptions of the same concept? More still, that economic/cultural understandings of development and psychology's interpretation of the development of children can be traced to the same historical roots? If this is right, it may shed light on a number of questions relating to children.

What are these historical roots? The clue may lie (this should please Miss Hamlyn) in an inter-discipline less popular now than a generation ago, namely 'law and development studies'. I introduced it into Lloyd's jurisprudence text, but space considerations have meant that it is not in the latest editions.

A parallel can be drawn between the way countries develop – an example would be South Korea – going from underdeveloped to developed in a generation, and the way children advance from being 'becomings' to fully fledged 'beings': both the Global South, much of it victims of Global North imperialism and colonialism, and children, the victims of 'childism' (Young-Bruehl, 2012) and so of prejudice and disempowerment. This is to suggest that children and poor countries both go through stages of development. Adults, like the Global North, have aspirations that children, as also the Global South, will come in time to reach the standards set by their superiors. The difference is that for most of the Global South, this is unattainable. It is fantasy to imagine that Africa, as the victim of the environment and of exploitation, as well as of self-inflicted corruption, can ever haul itself up to North American or European goals, though this is to ignore what China, South Korea, Singapore have achieved (Fukuyama, 2011, 2014).

If we pursue this argument, we can see children as a bit like colonies. Is this what John Stuart Mill intended to convey when he compared children to 'barbaric nations' (Mill, 1859)? One clear similarity is the way space is regulated for both colonial peoples and children. Is it incongruous to think that the dispersal technique employed against children in the United Kingdom takes its name (the mosquito) from the pest which restricts the lives of children in the Global South? Colonies were treated like children. A top-down strategy was employed, with language, educational structures, governmental institutions and legal concepts and systems imposed by the colonial parent and any 'disobedience' ruthlessly punished.

Children Today: Impact of Globalisation

Globalisation – the 'macro flows of population information and economics' (Ongay, 2010: 373) has had and will continue to have a major impact on children's lives, as well as upon our understandings of childhood. There is a global interpretation of childhood, which takes its cue from the Global North, which tends to be based on the comfortable world of children and to impose this environment as a norm on children in less favourable circumstances. A good illustration is the accepted norm in the Global North that children should attend schooling, and not be engaged in work activities (Liebel, 2007).

Are we living in a 'borderless world' (Ohmae, 1990) or a global economy? Are our children 'growing up global' (Katz, 2004)? There is certainly more movement of economic activity across national borders than there was a few years ago. In some countries children's living standards have improved, with better access to health care, education and maternity services. Globally, according to the WHO (2013) infant mortality rates have come down; in 1990 they were 61 per 1,000 live births, by 2013 34 per 1,000. But there have not been significant improvements in the global distribution of income. The top 20 per cent of the global population owns 83 per cent of resources, leaving the bottom 20 per cent to enjoy just 1 per cent of the world's income. Even in a prosperous country like the United Kingdom, poverty blights the lives of a substantial number of children (27 per cent). Child poverty reduced dramatically between 1998/99 – 1.1 million children were lifted out of poverty. But under current government policies it is projected to rise, with an expected 600,000 more children living in poverty by 2020, the year we were told by Tony Blair it would be finally conquered.

But poverty in the United Kingdom pales into insignificance when compared to the plight of children in the Global South. According to UNICEF, 22,000 children die each day due to poverty, and they die quietly in some of the poorest villages on earth, even more invisible in death than they were in life. About 28 per cent of children in developing countries are underweight or stunted. If this trend continues, the Millennium Development Goal (MDG) target of halving the proportion of underweight children will be missed by 30 million children. (On MDG, see below, p. 267.) About 72 million children of primary school age in the Global South were not in school in 2005: 57 per cent of them were girls. In much of the Global North, malnutrition is not the problem, rather it is obesity. If the world were to spend 1 per cent less each year on weapons, the money saved could put every child into school.

Where Do Children's Rights Come From?

(i) Dignity

'All human beings are born free and equal in dignity and rights', proclaimed the Universal Declaration of Human

Rights (UDHR) in 1948. The two International Covenants on Civil and Political and Economic, Social and Cultural Rights in 1966 emphasised that these rights were rooted in the inherent dignity of the human person. Jürgen Habermas (2010) sees dignity as the source from which all human rights are spelled out. Kevin Hasson (2003) sees it as 'the ultimate value' that gives coherence to human rights. For Yehoshua Arieli (2002), it is 'the cornerstone and the foundation on which the United Nations sought to reconstruct the future international order of mankind and of public life in general'. All these noble aspirations obviously applied to children as well, but this was never acknowledged at the time. Children were not in the minds of those who drafted the UDHR or the 1966 Covenants, even though the catalyst was the Holocaust and a million and a half children were exterminated by the Nazis (Dwork, 1991).

No international law document defines 'dignity', and it slipped effortlessly into the CRC's Preamble in paragraph 7 and into several provisions (see Articles 28 and 37(c)). Its roots are deep (Rosen, 2013; Sensen, 2011) in Judaeo-Christianity and in Roman thought, particularly in Cicero's *De Officiis* (*On Duties*, 1991, originally 44 BCE). For Cicero, dignity (*dignam hominis*) is what separates man from animals. In a passage, which has been very influential, he argues:

> It is essential to every inquiry about duty that we keep before our eyes how far superior man is by nature to cattle and other beasts: they have no thought except for sensual pleasure and this they are impelled by every instinct to seek; but man's mind is nurtured by study and meditation...From this we see that sensual

pleasure is quite unworthy of the dignity of man
(*dignam hominis*)...And if we will only bear in mind
the superiority and dignity of our nature. (I. 105–6) (See
further Lane, 2014: 277–84.)

Another important source is the Bible. The word is not
found in either Testament, but the concept is. In *Genesis*,
we are told that man is created in the image of God (*imago
dei*) and in the likeness of God. In *Psalms*, we are told that
God made man a little lower than the angels and crowned
him with glory and honour (*Psalms*, 8.5). Dignity is understood as flowing from a relationship with God and is inherent. It does not derive from a legal mandate, a human quality
or individual merit.

Modern thinking about dignity begins with Pico
della Mirandola (1463–94) (1998, originally 1486). In what
is seen as a core text of the Renaissance, he argued that
dignity of men is based initially on their capacity to choose
their own place in the chain of being. In his view, what
elevated human beings above the rest of nature is that they
can choose their own fate. 'Thou (man) art the moulder
and maker of thyself' (Mirandola, [1486] 1998: 5) (see
further Nauert, 1995).

Immanuel Kant is generally regarded as the founder of
modern thinking on dignity (see his *Metaphysics of Morals*,
[1797] 1996). For Kant, 'dignity' is an absolute value, enjoyed
by all human beings. Of human nature he says:

> Man regarded as a person, that is, as the subject of
> a morally practical reason...he is not to be valued merely
> as a means...he possesses a dignity (*Würde*, absolute inner

77

worth) by which he exacts respect for himself from all
other rational beings in the world.

Kant explained that there were things which could not be
understood in terms of their value. These things could be said
to have dignity. Value is necessarily relative because it depends
upon a particular observer's judgement of that thing. These
things 'which are not relative are "ends" in themselves'. A thing
is only an end in itself if it has a moral dimension. For Kant, the
human being is the end, and is entitled to unequivocal ethical
respect. No person should be depersonalised or dehumanised
by the state or by any other individual. The dignity of humanity
in each (*Würde*) demands respect. And it is independent of
a Supreme Being or any other external source. Kant explicitly
links the moral duty of the individual to rights, which he saw as
sacred and inviolable.

The Kantian understanding is an important source
for the idea that human rights are based on the inherent
dignity of the human person. It was undoubtedly influential
in the drafting of the UDHR (Donnelly, 2003). Most significant is Kant's argument that 'humanity itself is a dignity'
(Kant, 1996: 193). Although Kant does not specifically address
the applicability of this to children, there is no reason, I would
argue, for not doing so. This follows from the way Kant takes
the traditional concept of dignity, which saw dignity as
a special status or rank, and made it universally applicable
(but see Rosen, 2012, 2013). Dignity commands respect by
other individuals, by civil society and by the State. What is
entailed by 'respect', especially in its political elements, is
realised through human rights.

(ii) Respect

Ronald Dworkin (1977) emphasises the importance of respect. The most important right is the right to have rights (Arendt, 1964; Benhabib, 2012; Bhabha, 2011). Slaves – and there are more slaves in the world today than when slavery was 'abolished' nearly 200 years ago – have no rights because as non-persons they do not even get to the starting gate. Jews were tattooed with a number by the Nazis: they forfeited their identity as persons before their lives were extinguished. Women were not persons – the US Supreme Court actually said this in *Bradwell* v. *Illinois* (1873) – until relatively recently. The UK Parliament can pass an Equality Act as recently as 2010 and exclude children (see my discussion in Freeman, 2010: 2–4).

Dworkin's explanation of 'respect' has already been quoted earlier in this chapter. It is rather a pity that he never tested it out with reference to children. But then he never expressly addressed children's rights, though he trod dangerously around them. Thus, in *Law's Empire* (Dworkin, 1986), he writes of the dilemma facing a judge who thinks the best interpretation of the US constitutional equal protection clause would outlaw distinctions between the rights of adults and those of children, but realises that these distinctions have never been questioned in the community. His view is that it would be 'politically unfair' for the law to impose that view on a 'community whose family and social practices accept such distinctions as proper and fundamental' (Dworkin, 1986: 402). Substitute 'African-Americans' for 'children' in this argument, and Dworkin's reasoning collapses, as it does if the subject is women. The inherent inconsistencies unravel

when we realise that Dworkin succumbs to childism
(Young-Bruehl, 2013), that his inarticulate premise is that
children are not quite human, still 'becomings', not yet
'beings'. It is sad to think that, on this question, one of the
giants of the last generation of legal and political thinkers
was so out of touch.

(iii) Vulnerability

The third consideration, the vulnerability of children, was
rarely fully articulated until recently (Herring, 2014). Thus,
for example, it was only 'thinly analysed' (Buss, 2009: 28) in
US Supreme Court decisions. In the United States, the turning
point was the death penalty charge in *Roper* v. *Simmons*. The
Court gave three reasons for distinguishing adults and adolescents when culpability for criminal offences was the issue.
First, adolescents have less impulse control, bad judgement,
and were less responsible. Secondly, they were more exposed
to peer pressure and other negative influences. Thirdly, their
characters were less fixed. The evidence cited came exclusively
from developmental psychology. The decision was hailed as
progress in the inter-disciplinary integration of developmental psychology and the law (Scott, 2006). Buss points to
hazards in this triumphalism:

> First, any rights built upon developmental research are
> vulnerable to attack if the match between research findings
> and legal age lines is not complete. Second, a reliance on
> this research to formulate rights for children raises serious
> questions about our approach to various adult rights.

Third, the analysis calls into question our approach to other rights for children particularly autonomy rights. And fourth, declaring that adolescents are less responsible for their own actions sends a message that is both politically and developmentally counterproductive. (Buss, 2009: 30–1)

Even Lawyers Were Children Once

3

The Convention on the Rights of the Child and Its Principles

The Convention on the Rights of the Child (CRC) is the most ratified, and most swiftly ratified, international treaty in history. Only the United States, which played a dominant role in its formulation (C. P. Cohen, 2006), has not as yet ratified (Gunn, 2006). Somalia ratified in 2014, South Sudan in May 2015.

United States' Opposition

US steadfast opposition to becoming a party can be explained in a number of ways (Browning, 2006). I was once told, after I gave a lecture at the University of Illinois in Urbana in 1994, that it was a Communist conspiracy. In fact, Communism was in its death throes. More seriously, the CRC is thought by American critics to be anti-family, in particular there was concern that it might undermine home schooling (Farris, 2012; Glanzer, 2012). The religious 'Right' saw it as anti-religion. A further obstacle was that the United States executed offenders who committed capital offences when still children. This is no longer so (see *Roper* v. *Simmons* (2005), in which the Supreme Court is thought to have been influenced in part by the CRC to end the death penalty for juveniles) (T. Mahoney, 2011). There is also the mechanics of getting a treaty accepted by the two Houses.

There is a belief in the United States that American law already gives children the rights conferred by the CRC, so that acceding to it is a meaningless exercise (Guggenheim, 2005). This is clearly not the case (Freeman, 2007c; Fortin, 2009), but even if it were, ratification by the United States would be of symbolic importance and set an example to poorer and less rights-conscious countries.

Why Ratify?

But what should surprise us more are the states that have ratified.

We need an explanation of why states which were clearly in breach of the CRC committed themselves to undertake obligations which they had no intention of implementing. There is the get-out of reservations. There is liberal recourse to this. There is also flagrant breach of Articles. It may be that states believe that commitment to the CRC enhances their legitimacy. Or, it may be, as Hafner-Burton and Tsutsui (2005) argue, because even mere symbolic commitment has the effect of encouraging compliance, even if this takes time. They refer to this as the 'paradox of empty promises'. It may be the result of non-governmental organisations (NGOs) and other human rights advocates now having an additional tool to use to exert pressure (Keck and Sikkink, 1998). Hafner-Burton and Tsutsui (2005) argue that what is important is whether a support system emerges after ratification, alerting those prepared to listen to abuses. Globally, UNICEF plays its part. There are many such organisations in the United Kingdom; examples are CRAE and the Global Initiative on Eliminating Violence

Against Children. In relation to the latter, it is of note the way that a particular provision in the CRC (Article 19) has acted as a magnet for reform, as yet unsuccessfully. But what of countries that have no such structure in place (see Hathaway, 2007)?

The Achievement

The Convention has a number of positives. Given the history of childhood, that we have a Convention at all is an achievement. It is without question a landmark in the history of childhood. ILO Conventions apart, and their scope is very limited, there are no precedents. There were attempts to draw up Bills of Rights for Children (American Bar Association, 1979; Farson, 1974; Korczak, 1928), but none is as comprehensive, or as significant, as the CRC.

It enables us to talk for the first time of the human rights of children (Freeman, 2010). It recognises children as rights-holders, at least as semi-citizens (E. Cohen, 2009). It gives children that most important of rights, 'the right to possess rights' (Arendt, 1964). No longer is it 'very strange to think of children as having rights' (Brighouse, 2002). The child's 'main remedy is not to grow up', as Onora O'Neill asserts (O'Neill, 1988). The CRC recognises that children are 'beings', and not merely 'becomings' (Korczak, 1928). They are, of course, both (and see Uprichard, 2008). The Convention recognises children as decision-makers (see Article 12, and Alderson, 2008; Bluebond-Langner, 1978). (It recognises that rights bite in the private arena as well as in the public sphere, so that we can talk of rights within the family.) It accepts that children must not only be protected,

87

but that their rights must be protected too (see Farson, 1974). It offers children a package of rights. These are invariably referred to as the three 'P's (protection, provision and participation, as to which see below, p. 131). A number of critics have noted the absence of a fourth 'P', namely power (John, 2003: ch. 2).

It has had an impact on courts worldwide, even in the United States (see *Roper* v. *Simmons*, 2005). It has influenced legislatures, and therefore has had an impact on legislation. When the CRC was finalised in 1989, only seven states had outlawed the practice of corporal punishment by parents. By the end of March 2017, fifty-two states had anti-smacking laws, Montenegro being the most recent. A number of states have incorporated the Convention into their domestic law (see Lundy et al., 2013).

It has had an impact too on policy-makers. Neither the Millennium Development Goals nor the Sustainable Development Goals would have been possible without the Convention.

It has had an impact as well on research, the growth in which has been exponential. It has nourished at least two journals, *Childhood*, which commenced publication in 1994, and the *International Journal of Children's Rights*, which I have edited since it started in 1993. It has stimulated the growth of a library of monographs, perhaps as many as 100, and also many edited collections. In short, there is more scholarship on children's rights now than there has been in the whole of history leading up to 1989. But the relationship between the Convention and research is not all positive. The Convention has acted as a stranglehold on researchers: there is a tendency for the CRC to be taken as the final word, as unproblematic. As a result, it was some years before researchers began to point to gaps in the Convention (Freeman, 2000a), to its ageing (Veerman, 2010). For example, by lumping together all those between birth and eighteen under the category 'child', the interests of adolescents are neglected (Bhabha, 2014). The interests of girl children, gay children, children in the Global South, refugee and asylum-seeking children (Bhabha, 2011), children with disabilities (Sabatello, 2013), Roma children, children of imprisoned parents (Scharff-Smith, 2014), are all either marginalised or ignored.

It has encouraged the development of institutional structures such as ombudspersons for children. The first ombudsperson, in Norway, was established before the CRC (as to which see the account by the first holder of the position, Malfrid Flekkøy, 1991, and see Melton, 1991). The relationship between the ombudsperson and the new complaints procedure (Optional Protocol No. 3, 2013, operative 2014) will depend on a number of factors, in particular what assistance is available to the child to pursue a grievance.

The Convention has opened our eyes to aspects of children's lives not always thought justiciable, such as standard of living, poverty and play. It has also made us think critically about childhood, including its history.

It has stimulated the development of regional charters and other codes: only the African Charter on the Rights and Welfare of the Child 1990 has as yet emerged. The CRC is focused on the 'child', not it should be noted 'children'. Its premise is the 'universal' child (R. Smith, 2013). In 1989, there was little discussion of 'global childhood' (Katz, 2004) or of the gulf between the 'Global North' and the 'Global South' (Cregan and Cuthbert, 2014). What is it to be a child and what constitutes childhood, as we understand it, is historically, socially and politically contingent, and emanates from the Global North. And it is against Northern standards that Southern societies are judged (Wells, 2009). It has influenced interpretation of the ECHR (Fortin, 2009). New codes have also emerged, following the CRC's precedent: for example, there is now a draft one on the rights of the dying child (see Appendix 6). It has left its mark on global politics (Grugel and Piper, 2011: 73).

The Convention: Its Pre-History

Prior to the Convention there had been two Declarations, in 1924 and 1959, respectively, and it was Poland that proposed enacting the second of these, as it stood, into a Convention. Poland also proposed that the 1959 Declaration should contain an appeal to governments, 'requesting them to adjust their respective legislation to the Principles expressed in the Declaration' (UN Doc. E/CN.4/780). But the Netherlands spoke for the majority of states in arguing that it was not time to conclude a Convention since 'the great economic, social and cultural differences and the greatly divergent views on morality and religion...in the Member States (would) give rise to many problems'.

They were not insoluble, but it was thirty years before a Convention finally emerged. The CRC was ten years in the making, and many differences and problems had to be surmounted. Some of these have already been referred to, and will not be further discussed here. The relatively swift collective change of mind – it did after all take a generation – has to be explained.

Why Did We Get the CRC?

Geraldine van Bueren (1995: 13) suggests a number of explanations. There were already positive moves in the direction of children's rights in a number of jurisdictions. Court decisions such as *Gault* (1967) and *Tinker* (1970) in the United States and *Gillick* (1986) in England anticipate the CRC. So does the creation of institutions like the ombudsman in Norway in 1981 (Flekkøy, 1991). These developments demonstrated that the 1959 Declaration had outlived its usefulness, that its vision was too narrow. Children needed more than protection: their 'citizenship' rights needed to be recognised too. (Of course, they still are not – at best today children remain 'semi-citizens' (E. Cohen, 2009).)

Secondly, it was coming to be appreciated that to be effective more was required than a declaration which prohibited the 'denial' of rights to children, rather, a code of specific rights tailored to the demands of a specific group. Children were not alone in this: the same applied to women, the disabled (Sabatello, 2013), refugees, etc.

Thirdly, it came to be acknowledged, though it had been understood for a century (see, for example Jules Vallès' response to the Paris Commune), that children required a higher standard of protection in some areas of their lives than was found in international law then, and often still is now;

for example, against the imposition of the death penalty (see *Roper* v. *Simmons*, 2005), and life imprisonment without parole (*Graham* v. *Florida*, 2010).

Fourthly, to be 'effective', some of these require principles of interpretation which are innovative in the context of international law. Van Bueren cites the best interests of the child principle (now in Article 3 of the CRC), and the evolving capacities of the child, which is emphasised in Article 5.

Fifthly, twenty years had passed since the second Declaration, since which time there had been 'a spawning of international, regional and bilateral agreements which dealt with specific issues of children's rights. This...created a need for uniformity in international standards' (Van Bueren, 1995: 14).

Sixthly, it was acknowledged that two goals had to be met, which the Declaration had failed to do: a Convention needed to be both comprehensive and accessible to children.

Seventhly, the proclamation of 1979 as the International Year of the Child acted as an 'emotional magnet drawing states towards the idea of a convention' (Van Bueren, 1995).

In addition, world conscience was awakened to the plight of children in the Global South in particular, the lives of whom were blighted by disease, wars, malnutrition and extreme poverty. Images of child soldiers, of mutilated limbs, of starving babies and, from the early 1980s, the ravages of HIV/AIDS, made us ask questions about the legitimacy, the limits, and the appropriate uses of humanitarian intervention. Could the law achieve more than the charitable appeal? What are/were the limits of effective legal action?

The lives of children in the Global North did not penetrate public consciousness or concern in the same way, nor should it have done so, but child abuse in all its forms, particularly sexual abuse, and child poverty attracted more public attention in the period of gestation of the Convention than it had in previous years.

One thing which seems to have had little or no impact on those who formulated the Convention was the 1970s child liberation ferment. It was far too radical a blueprint.

The Principles

The Convention is informed by a number of principles:

(1) the non-discrimination principle (Article 2);
(2) the best interests principle (Article 3(1));
(3) the inherent right to life, survival and development (Article 6);
(4) participation rights (Article 12).

Non-discrimination

Little needs to be said here about non-discrimination. In a global world, particularly one characterised by gross imbalances in the 'basic goods of human flourishing' (Finnis, [1980] 2011). This has resonance for refugees and asylum seekers and for children displaced by civil wars and other conflicts (Bhabha, 2014). There are non-discrimination principles in earlier human rights treaties, but none is as broad as that in the CRC. It offers protection against discrimination on grounds of status, expressed opinions, activities, as well as those of a child's parents, legal guardians and family members. But this principle applies only to condemn discrimination against a class of children: black children as under apartheid, girl children where there is a lower age of marriage for girls, gay children, children with disabilities, children of a particular religion, etc. It does not apply to the most obvious form of discrimination from which children suffer, namely lacking rights which persons over eighteen have. Thus, it is not a recognised form of discrimination to give voting rights to eighteen-year-olds but not to those who are seventeen. Despite Article 2, adultism remains firmly entrenched.

This is fundamental. It tells us in the clearest of terms about the ideology of the Convention. Just compare the CRC with CEDAW. The goal of CEDAW (1969) is unequivocal: it is to extirpate sexism wherever it is to be found. It too has its critics, for example Catherine Mackinnon (2006) – it is beyond my brief to debate this. CEDAW may fail to achieve this, but its aspiration is manifest, that women should enjoy equality with men. The Convention on the Elimination of All Forms of Racial Discrimination is similar, perhaps even stronger and more comprehensive (Donner, 1994). On Article 2, see further Abramson, 1996b; Besson, 2005.

Case Study: Children with Disabilities

There may be between 150 and 200 million children with disabilities in the world today. That we can be no more accurate than this is but one indication of their invisibility. The CRC does not ignore them – Article 2 is the first provision in a human rights treaty to include disability within its prohibited grounds of discrimination. It is also the first to include an article on disability (Sabatello, 2013). Article 23 requires states to 'recognise that a mentally or physically disabled child should enjoy a full and decent life, in conditions which ensure dignity, promote self-reliance and facilitate the child's active participation in the community'. It also requires states to recognise the right of a child with a disability to have effective access to special care and assistance, emphasising in particular education, training, health care services, rehabilitation services, preparation for employment and recreation opportunities 'in a manner conducive to the child's achieving the fullest possible social integration and individual development, including his or her cultural and spiritual development'.

However, children with disabilities are, despite these noble sentiments, worse off than their non-disabled peers. They are more vulnerable to infanticide and premature death (UNICEF, 2012); are commonly removed from families; subjected to inhuman and degrading treatments (sterilisation was once almost routine, A. Cohen, 2016); and are more likely to be denied health services and education (more than one-third of the 67 million children who are out of school have disabilities). The literacy rate amongst persons with disabilities is 3 per cent – it is 1 per cent for women. This undermines employment prospects, aggravates poverty and adds to the welfare budget. One in five of the world's poorest people has disabilities.

The CRC has failed to make an impression on the lives of children with disabilities. What is most troubling, says Maya Sabatello (2013: 468) is that violations of the Convention have passed 'unnoticed'. Children with disabilities have tended to be invisible. They have been seen as objects of charity and not as rights-bearers. Jones and Basser Marks (1997: 184) support this, seeing the Convention's focus as on the disabled child's welfare needs rather than his rights. This is reflected also in Article 23 itself.

This emphasis on welfare needs has two particular problems. Meeting the welfare needs is costly and therefore a burden on states, even if they are only expected to comply as far as 'available resources' permit. Further, because of the stigma associated with disability, it is not uncommon for parents to assume a position of denial, which frustrates the child's access to services to which she/he might be entitled under Article 23. In the Global South, the birth of a child with disabilities may not be registered, the child might be abandoned or locked indoors to save face.

The CRC adopted the traditional model of disability, which saw the answer in non-discrimination. But the principle of non-discrimination permits different treatment if the distinction is based on reasonable and objective criteria. If children with disabilities appear or behave differently, 'the criterion is commonly used, thus in practice, permitting and legitimising discrimination and segregation' (Sabatello, 2013: 470). Examples are separate education for children with disabilities (this is not viewed as discrimination), and the sterilisation of intellectually disabled adolescent girls, initially for eugenic reasons ('Three generations of imbeciles are enough' *per* Holmes J in *Buck* v. *Bell*, 1927) (A. Cohen, 2016), and more recently, allegedly, to protect the girl from sexual abuse.

The Convention on the Rights of Persons with Disabilities (CRPD) followed lengthy pressure from disability activists and three years of intensive negotiations at the United Nations. It wasn't formulated top-down, as the CRC had been; persons with disabilities were heavily involved, as were their representative organisations. One session was opened to enable a group of young persons with disabilities to 'make the case for themselves'.

The CRPD is said to take a 'social, inter-relational approach to disability, calling attention to the interaction between...impairment, society, and context, rather than focusing, as traditionally was the case, merely on the medical deficit' (Sabatello, 2013: 470). Its purpose is 'to promote, protect and ensure the full and equal enjoyment of all human rights and fundamental freedoms by all persons with disabilities, and to promote respect for their inherent dignity' (Article 1).

Case Study: Transgender Children

Little attention has been paid to the lives and rights of transgender children (but see now CRAE, 2016, and in the United States, Felders, 2006 and Gilliam, 2004). The UN Committee on the Rights of the Child (2016) in its examination of the United Kingdom raised a number of concerns about the discrimination experienced by these children, including the bullying and violence they encounter at school. There are research indications that 91 per cent of boys and 66 per cent of girls experience harassment and isolation, and this encourages them to leave school as early as possible. The Equality Act 2010 mandates schools to respect gender reassignment as a protected characteristic, whether there have been medical procedures or not. But protection is undermined because the Equality and Human Rights Commission is not permitted to take up a complaint without parental consent (Women and Equalities Committee, 2010).

Some countries, for example, Spain, permit underage children to undergo gender reassignment. English law does not. As our tolerance of LGBTQ youth increases, so their visibility will manifest itself. References to England's only gender identity clinic rose from 97 in 2009–10 to 1,419 in 2015–16. Children as young as three have been referred. They are a highly marginalised group, barely acknowledged to exist. There was no discussion of their problems during the drafting of the Convention. However, whilst obviously all the provisions in the CRC apply to these children, some have particular resonance:

Article 2, protecting against discrimination;
Article 19, protecting against all forms of violence;
Article 24, the right to the best possible health care;
Article 29, education rights, to include a broad-based curriculum responsive to their particular needs.

More needs to be done to help this small marginalised group. Access to specialised services and treatment needs to be increased, and assessment periods for prescription of puberty blockers and cross-sex hormones need to be speeded up. There are far too many suicides, often the result of the system failing these children.

Best Interests of the Child

The best interests principle may puzzle the unwary (Archard, 2015). What, they may ask, is a paternalist mandate doing in a Convention which purports to confer rights on children, and which emphasises their agency? (see Alderson, 2016; Alderson and Goodwin, 1993; Alderson, Hawthorne and Killen, 2005; Oswell, 2013). Others may be critical of a principle which prioritises the interests of children (Reece, 1996).

There are several reasons why in all actions concerning a child, the child's best interests should be a primary consideration. The CRC does not go as far as the laws of Finland and of Scotland, which require the child to be consulted by parents before the parents take any major decision impacting on the child's interests. The Convention only applies this best interests standard to decision-making by public bodies like courts. It means, in effect, decisions like building a new road, going to war and restructuring a school syllabus could be governed by the best interests principle in Article 3 (and see the direct/ indirect distinction discussed below, pp. 102–9).

Margaret Thatcher grasped the essential point when she said: 'children come first because children are our sacred trust'. This high-minded sentiment was belied by her policies. For example they saw child poverty increase dramatically during her premiership.

A number of arguments have been put forward to justify prioritising children's interests. First, children are more vulnerable. In a world run by adults, there is a danger that children's interests would otherwise be overlooked.

Secondly, children must be given the opportunity to become successful adults. Penelope Leach (1994: 265) argues that children are important because they are 'our future'.

Thirdly, as Libby Purves (1993) put it, 'we invited [children] to life's party'. This argument only has force in relation to parents: 'it ignores the interests of someone who had no control over whether the child was born' (Reece, 1996: 280).

Fourthly, and again this argument only has purchase in the parent-child context, sacrificing oneself for one's child is the very essence of what being a good parent is. The biblical story of King Solomon and the two 'harlots' (I *Kings* 16–28) is commonly invoked as an example.

Fifthly, there are arguments which appeal broadly to utilitarianism. Thus, it has been said, care of children is a 'prime priority' if we want to build a 'strong, good and powerful nation for the future' (Baroness Strange, during a House of Lords debate on what became the Children Act 1989, *Hansard*, HL vol. 502, col. 519, 6 December 1988). For Stephen Parker too, it maximizes the welfare of society (1994: 38).

The reconciliation of the best interests principle with the emphasis on the child as an agent in Article 12 (and the following Articles) has led to some doubting whether the CRC is coherent. In my opinion, it is possible to interpret the two provisions so as to rule out any dissonance between them. Article 12, in stressing that there is to be assured to the child the right to express views freely in all matters affecting the child, must be interpreted as including within 'all matters' what is in his/her best interests. A Convention which purports to uphold children's rights should be interpreted expansively so as to give effect to as many rights as possible.

The best interests principle is intuitively right but will always be beset with the criticism that it is vague, indeterminate, contingent on the values of the decision-maker and on culture (Piper, 2000). One danger of invoking a best interests standard is that other policies can creep in behind the 'smokescreen' of what is at first glance an innocuous principle. It can cloak prejudices: not long ago it was used as a rationalisation to penalise lesbians in custody disputes (Reece, 1996). Critics like Irène Théry have argued that it is 'an alibi for dominant ideology, an alibi for individual arbitrariness, an alibi for family and more general social policies for which the law serves as an instrument' (Théry, 1989: 81–2). Guggenheim (2005: 65) believes it is 'deeply antithetical to the rule of law'.

Of course, as Robert Mnookin pointed out forty years ago, 'deciding what is best for a child poses a question no less ultimate than the purposes and values of life itself' (Mnookin, 1975: 260). What is encompassed by 'best interests' depends on how the concept is understood. It was Michael King and Christine Piper who drew our attention to the fact that:

> The broad range of factors – genetic, financial, educational, environmental and relational – which science would recognise as capable of affecting the welfare of the child are narrowed by law to a small range of issues which fall directly under the influence of the judge, the social workers or the adult parties. Among social problem construction theorists the issue is usually presented in terms of political ideology. By reconstructing the social dimension of any issue concerning the welfare of the child on such matters as housing, education, healthcare and financial security in ways which emphasise individual responsibility and the failure to accept that responsibility or perform those duties expected of a child carer, law in capitalist societies effectively depoliticises social problems and reinforces liberal, individualistic ideology to the detriment of socialist notions of collective or governmental responsibility. (King and Piper, 1995: 30)

Different societies also operate with different conceptions of what is in a child's best interests. As a simple example, take an issue with which English courts have had to grapple recently. A Muslim father wants his son to be circumcised, the Christian mother objects. Both parents genuinely believe that they are putting their son's best interests first. They differ on what this requires. The Court of Appeal (*Re J*, 2000 and also see *Re S*, 2005) thought it was not in the five-year-old's best interests to be circumcised against the wishes of his primary carer (the nominally Christian mother). But note the way the case was conceived as a dispute between parents, and note there is no attention paid to the child's views. And was the court taking a short-term view of best interests? On a longer-term view, perhaps circumcision was in the boy's best interests. Courts can only make, and must make a decision now on the facts known to them. They (and we) cannot follow up cases, fascinating though that would be.

It has become increasingly clear that some actions and some decisions affect children directly, others less directly. The CRC says the best interests principle applies 'in all actions concerning children'. The Committee on the Rights of the Child in its General Comment No. 14 (2013) explained (para. 19):

> The term 'concerning' refers, first of all, to measures and decisions directly concerning a child, children as a group or children in general, and secondly, to other measures that have an effect on an individual child, children as a group or children in general, even if they are not the direct targets of the measure.

Later in the Comment we are told that all cases have to be considered 'individually'. So, which is it? If one thing is clear, it is that the Committee is not clear!

In *ZH (Tanzania) (FC) v. Secretary of State for the Home Department* (2011), a case concerning the deportation of a failed asylum seeker, Lady Hale compared decisions which directly affect the child's upbringing (with whom the child is to live) and decisions which affect her only indirectly (where one or both parents are to live). In the former case, best interests are the 'determining' consideration: in the latter, only 'a primary' consideration, that is they must be considered first, but can be outweighed (see further Fortin, 2011).

So many actions concern children that a very large case law has grown up, and not just in UK jurisprudence and ECHR case law (Eekelaar, 2015). In fact, there is no best interests principle in the ECHR, but for many years the European Court of Justice (ECJ) has operated as if there were one in Article 8 of the ECHR. In *Yousef v. Netherlands* (2002), the Court ruled that, where the rights of parents and a child were at stake in a case directly about children, the child's rights must be the 'paramount' consideration.

Decisions which Directly Affect the Child

First, let us look at decisions which are directly about the child. Such cases may be either private law disputes (e.g., a contact dispute between parents) or a public law dispute (e.g., whether a care order should be made). In *Re G (Children) (Residence; Same-Sex Partner)* (2006), the House of Lords said that it was 'only as a contributor to the child's welfare that parenthood assumes any significance. In common with all other factors bearing on what is in the best interests of the child, it must be examined for its potential to fulfil that aim'.

As an example of a public law case, see *Flintshire County Council* v. *Mrs L D and Mr G* (2014). The children had special needs and were at risk of suffering significant harm. The question was whether long-term fostering was sufficient or was it necessary to move straight to adoption. The judge emphasised the need to make a 'holistic' assessment of the children's welfare.

Decisions which Affect the Child only Indirectly

Secondly, there are decisions which only indirectly affect children. A good illustration is the decision of the South African Constitutional Court in *S* v. *M* (2008). The South African Constitution provides that 'a child's best interests are of paramount importance in every matter concerning the child' (Section 2) (Bill of Rights) Article 2, section 28(2). The court had to consider what part the best interests principle should play when the child's primary carer was given a custodial sentence. Sachs J stated:

> The purpose of emphasising the duty of the sentencing court to acknowledge the interests of the children is not to permit errant parents unreasonably to avoid appropriate punishment. It is to protect the innocent children as much as is reasonably possible. . .from avoidable harm.

As a consequence:

> The children will weigh as an independent factor to be placed on the sentencing scale only if there could be a more

> appropriate sentence. . .one which is a non-custodial
> sentence. For the rest, the approach merely requires
> a sentencing court to consider the situation of children when
> a custodial sentence is imposed and not to ignore them.

English courts adopt a similar approach (see *HH* v. *Deputy Prosecutor of the Italian Republic*, 2012). As Lord Judge had to concede in that case:

> Sadly the application of this principle cannot eradicate
> distressing cases where the interests of even very young
> children cannot prevail. (See further, Scharff-Smith, 2014.)

As already pointed out, the ECHR does not refer as such to the best interests of the child. This is not surprising given that in 1950 this principle was not in the forefront of policy-making. But courts are now reading Article 8 of this Convention to incorporate the best interests principle. As an example, look at the case of *Neulinger and Shuruk* v. *Switzerland* (2010). A mother and a child argued that their Article 8 rights had been breached by a Swiss court which had held that the child could be returned to Israel pursuant to an application under the Hague Child Abduction Convention. The European Court of Human Rights (ECtHR) held that the order was an interference with the mother's and child's rights under Article 8, but it had been in accordance with law. The issue was therefore whether 'a fair balance between the competing interests at stake, namely those of the parents, those of the child, and those of public order had been struck, within the margin of appreciation afforded to States in such matters. . .bearing in mind that the child's best interests must be the primary consideration' (para. 134). The court added, rather confusingly, children's 'best interests must be paramount' (para. 135). What was needed, it said, was a full examination of the child's circumstances. So:

> The Court must ascertain whether the domestic courts conducted an in-depth examination of the entire family situation and of a whole series of factors, in particular of a factual, emotional, psychological, material and medical nature and made a balanced and reasonable assessment of the respective interests of each person, with a constant concern for determining what the best solution would be for the abducted child in the context of an application for his return to his country of origin. (para. 139)

The ECtHR concluded that it was not satisfied that returning the child to Israel would be in his best interests.

I have always believed that applications in child abduction cases should be governed by the best interests principle, but that is not what the Abduction Convention provides. The court in *Neulinger* acted as if the Convention was in line with my preferred solution. It treated the decision as if it were one about a child, whereas the Hague Abduction Convention is about the appropriate forum in which the decision should be taken (Schuz, 2013, 2015). In other words, such decisions are to be characterised as only affecting the child indirectly, which is manifestly absurd. (Child abduction is discussed further below, p. 109).

Another area of law where courts have attempted to distinguish direct and indirect impact on children revolves around border control. *ZH* (see above, p. 103) was about a decision to deport a mother. Her two children (aged twelve and nine) were UK nationals. The parents had separated. The father was HIV positive. If the mother were removed, the children would either have to go with her or stay with the father. The UK Borders, Citizenship and Immigration Act 2009, section 55 provides that, in relation to immigration, asylum and nationality, arrangements must be made to ensure that these functions are discharged having regard to the need to safeguard the welfare of children who are in the United Kingdom.

The Supreme Court assumed that if the mother were deported, the children would go as well, and considered that the harm they would suffer would be greater than the competing considerations of upholding the state interest in border control. Lady Hale indicated that the children were only affected indirectly but nevertheless, and rather puzzlingly, added their interests had to be considered 'first', but could be outweighed. And Lord Kerr made this even clearer:

> Where the best interests of the child clearly favour a certain course, that course should be followed unless countervailing reasons of considerable force displace them. It is not necessary to express this in terms of a presumption but the primacy of this consideration needs to be made clear in emphatic terms. What is determined to be in a child's best interests should customarily dictate the outcome of cases such as the present, therefore, and it will require considerations of substantial moment to permit a different result. (para. 46)

Both judges sought support in decisions of the Australian Federal Court (*Teoh* 1995; *Wan* 2001). The Court of Appeal used the same reasoning in *EV (Philippines)* v. *SSHD* (2014). But, having concluded that the children's education would be best served by their remaining in the United Kingdom, decided this was outweighed by the need to uphold immigration control.

Cases where the child's health will be harmed if a parent is deported also raise acute conflicts. Clearly, the United Kingdom is not the 'hospital of the world' (*per* Maurice Kay LJ in *Re SQ (Pakistan)* v. *Upper Tribunal* (2013) – ironic given that our hospitals only survive because we employ foreign-trained medical professionals!). How then is a court to react when a parent is to be deported and this will result in a child having to go or return to a country where his/her health will be badly affected? The question arose in *AE (Algeria)* v. *Secretary of State for the Home Department* (2014). Leave to remain in the United Kingdom was refused to parents of a child with spina bifida. The case was returned to the Upper Tribunal for it to reconsider its application of the best interests principle. The Court of Appeal said a 'structured' approach was called for, with the best interests of the child as 'a primary consideration'. His mother and the children were overstayers and the father was an illegal immigrant. The court conceded that the child was faced with being returned to a country where the 'differentials in relation to medical, social and educational support as (compared to the UK) are very substantial indeed'. On a best interests test the conclusion should have been obvious, but the court ruled that it would not be inappropriate for 'the future cost and duration of (the child's) treatment and care in this country to play a part in the balancing exercise as matters relating to the economic wellbeing of this country, given the strains on the public finances' (para. 9).

There is a distinction between what Mnookin (1975) calls 'current interests' and 'future-oriented interests'. And, as we have just seen, there may be a conflict between them. Current interests focus on experiential considerations. This was understood by Mnookin when he observed that what makes a person 'happy' at seven may have 'adverse consequences' at thirty, or at seventy. Mnookin asks:

> Should the judge decide by thinking about what decision the child as an adult looking back would have wanted made? In this case, the preference problem is formidable, for how is the judge to compare 'happiness' at one age with 'happiness' at another age? (Mnookin, 1975: 260)

Investing in a child's future is risky, leading Piper (2010) to advocate 'more child-centred' decision-making for children. There are areas of law involving children where there is less focus on the child's welfare. Two of these are outlined below.

Child Abduction

The problems of, and issues raised by, international child abduction, apart from their intrinsic interest, are significant for two reasons: first, they demonstrate that the '3 Ps' classification (see below, p. 131) does not always fit. Secondly, and this is also one of the reasons why it doesn't, is that the Hague Convention on International Child Abduction of 1980 pays scant attention to children's welfare, let alone their rights (Schuz, 2013, 2015). I turned down an offer to be a UK representative at the drafting conference, insisting that the Convention would turn the clock back to a time when children were treated as items of property. I also thought it undermined women, whom I perceived, rightly as it has turned out, were likely to be the principal abductors. My image was of a young English woman fleeing from a violent husband in some nasty country and bringing their children to safety in the United Kingdom. (In the late 1970s one was not expected to be politically correct (Siberman, 2003).)

The structure of the Hague Convention is to return the child to the jurisdiction where she/he was habitually resident before the act of wrongful removal. The Convention defines jurisdiction. Only where one of a limited number of defences is raised do considerations of a child's welfare come into play.

The contrast between this Hague Convention and the CRC is remarkable. Had the Abduction Convention been negotiated a few years later, the dissonance would have been unacceptable. As it is, we have children returned like packages to uncertain futures, perhaps to an abusive parent (Freeman, 2007a). In the worst case with which I am familiar, a nine-year-old boy who was to be returned from Israel to Belgium took to his heels and was never seen again. The mother went to prison for five years for kidnapping him, though it is not clear how complicit she was in her son's escape (*RB* v. *State of Israel*, 2014).

The Hague Convention lacks a provision comparable to Article 12 of the CRC. But, ironically, Hague Convention, Article 13(2), which permits the court to decline to return a child where the child objects and the court considers that the child has reached an age and degree of maturity at which it is appropriate to take account of his/her views, was in 1980 ahead of its time in recognising the child's right to participate. But, as Beaumont and McEleavy (1999: 177–8) point out, this provision does not reflect an endorsement of children's rights, rather a pragmatic concern that it would be difficult to return a recalcitrant adolescent and forcibly doing so would get a bad press.

The child's views only emerge when an Article 13(2) objection is raised, and not otherwise. In *Re M* (1994), the child's objections became patently obvious when he kicked up such a fuss that he had to be taken off the plane taking him back to the jurisdiction where he had been ordinarily resident. The reasons for not routinely seeking the child's views are most unconvincing: that it causes delay, and will not achieve anything anyway. It is true that the return of the child is intended to be a summary process, but rather sad that we can have thought only thirty-seven years ago that a child's whole future could be disposed of in summary fashion.

These cases cry out for the child to be separately represented. In the absence of this, the child is represented by the abducting parent. This may easily cast a shadow over the child's case. Predictably, in reported cases, children seem more likely to be successful where they are independently represented.

The Convention's failures are beginning to be acknowledged. There was to have been a Protocol, but this has disappeared from the agenda of the Hague Conference. Some judges have recognised the problems. Baroness Hale in *Re D* (2006) will have spoken for many when she said:

> No one intended that an instrument designed to secure the protection of children from the harmful effects of

> international child abduction should itself be turned into
> an instrument of harm. (para. 52)

Thus, there is more understanding that if a child is to be returned, it may be necessary to put in place protective measures to ensure the child's safety (see *Re E*, 2011). Even more significant, as was discussed above, p. 105, are developments in ECtHR jurisprudence which lay down an underlying norm to the effect that a child's return cannot be ordered without first considering his/her best interests (see *Neulinger and Shuruk* v. *Switzerland*, 2010). This development has been criticised by the UK Supreme Court in *Re S* (2012), and by Stephens and Lowe (2012). It is said that it undermines the whole design of the Hague Convention, but similar criticisms can be made of other European case law (an example is *A* v. *United Kingdom*, 1998). This criticism fails to appreciate the rationale of supranational law.

Adoption and the Child's Best Interests

Adoption was only established in England in 1926. It became a very popular institution: in 1968 there were 24,831 orders. There has been a steep decline since. 1968 saw the introduction of 'legal' abortion, the mid- to late 1960s the increased availability of contraception (particularly the 'pill'). In addition, it became easier for single mothers to keep their children. The development of medically assisted reproduction offered an alternative for the infertile, though its success rates were low and, where not subsidised by the NHS, it was prohibitively expensive. Today, there are only a little over 5,000 adoptions a year and that is more than there were a few years ago, the recent growth in adoption having been stimulated by a governmental push to give children permanency.

Adoption orders are 'final and for life' (*Re B*, 1995). There is no right to adopt (*Fretté* v. *France*, 2003). It is possible to construct models of adoption which would not satisfy the ECHR. English law certainly complies with it (*YC* v. *United Kingdom*, 2012). The ECtHR said:

> family ties may only be severed in very exceptional circumstances. . .everything must be done to preserve personal relations but where the maintenance of family ties would harm the child's health and development, a parent is not entitled under Article 8 to insist that such ties be maintained. (para. 134)

In 2012, the Adoption and Children Act 2002 underwent pre-legislative scrutiny to consider reforms (these are now in the Children and their Families Act 2014). No judicial concern was expressed. What happened next could not have been anticipated.

The Supreme Court had to consider a closed adoption against the wishes of the parents where there was no evidence that they had harmed the child or any other child (*Re B*, 2013; Doughty, 2013). The Court endorsed Hedley J's analysis in *Re L* (2007, quoted above, p. 152), and therefore had to explain why it was upholding the care order based on risk of future emotional harm in the context of adoption being 'the last resort' (para. 74), 'where nothing else will do'. In the Court of Appeal, Rix LJ wondered whether the case was an example of the state exercising its 'precautionary responsibilities'. This explains why Lady Hale asked the Supreme Court about the proportionality of a care order with a care plan for adoption. The result has been a torrent of appeals (Masson, 2014).

Re B was an appeal against a care order, where the plan presented to the court was adoption. *Re B-S* (2013), by way of contrast, was an appeal against a High Court order refusing leave to oppose adoption orders under Adoption and Children Act 2002, section 47(5).

The result of these decisions has been to make it more difficult to obtain an adoption order. Since adoption can offer the best chance of giving a child love, security and stability, and breaking the cycle of neglect and abuse, this is a regrettable trend. Children have the right to a permanent placement. Many will not now get this elementary right. The number of adoption orders has declined for the first time in five years: 4,690 looked-after children were the subject of adoption orders in 2016. This is 12 per cent down on the previous year, despite the fact that the number of looked-after children increased by 1 per cent. This may be attributable to the number of unaccompanied asylum-seeking children increasing. It is an unfortunate consequence of *Re B* and *Re B-S* that children who might have been adopted find themselves deprived of this second chance. Did the judges who saw adoption as a last resort appreciate the implications of using language like 'where only adoption will do'?

Best Interests and Culture

Different societies have different perceptions of childhood. Ariès, however discredited his thesis, drew attention to this half a century ago. Today, there remain divisions of opinion on such questions as to whether children should work, when they be permitted to marry and whom, and when they can be held criminally responsible, as Ncube recognises:

> the normative universality achieved in the definition and formulation of children's rights have to contend with diverse and varied cultural conceptions of childhood, its role, its rights and obligations. (1998: 5)

He describes some aspects of the traditional African conception of childhood that are very different from the model found in the developed world of the Global North.

The reconciliation of best interests and cultural norms can pose problems. To accept cultural relativism is to give up on best interests, as we would understand them. Millions of girls have been subjected to FGM, and whole populations of girls remain at risk. But, although it is identity-conferring, its consequences are so harmful that we are right to reject it as an abhorrent practice, and as not being in girls' best interests. The contrast with ritualistic male circumcision (the Jewish practice of *brit milah*, for example), which is not harmful in that it does not have long-term harmful consequences and on balance has beneficial results, for example, may make it less easy to acquire HIV, is so great that one wonders how any association can have been made between them. But male circumcision is under attack in much of Europe (Schuz, 2015).

Life, Survival and Development

The third of the General Principles in the CRC is in Article 6, the inherent right to life, and to the maximum extent possible survival and development. The right to life is the only right in the Convention described as 'inherent'. This has several implications. It is non-derogable, even in times of war and public emergencies when the life of the nation is threatened. The death penalty is not allowed. The prohibition antedates the CRC (it is in the International Covenant on Civil and Political Rights 1966, Article 6(5)), and is stated explicitly in Article 37(a) of the CRC. The United States, not a state party to the CRC (indeed, one of the reasons why it has not ratified), only abolished the death penalty for under eighteens in 2005. A number of states still use it in breach of the Convention, including China, Pakistan, Iran and Saudi Arabia.

The CRC is unique in emphasising survival and development. Other core human rights treaties protect the right to life, but stop short of stipulating survival and development.

The reference to survival targets the positive obligations on states parties to prolong children's lives. It must be understood together with the obligation in Article 24 to 'strive to ensure that no child is deprived of his or her right of access to such healthcare services'. The UN Committee on the Rights of the Child has sensitively linked Articles 6 and 24 to the evidence on the social determinants of health (WHO, 2008). In particular, the Committee drew attention to the 'many risks and protective factors that underlie the life, survival, growth and development of the child', which it said 'need to be systematically identified in order to design and implement evidence-informed interventions that address a wide range of determinants during the life course' (CRC Committee, 2013: 6). The Convention attaches these positive obligations to states, but it is clearer now than may have been the case in the 1980s lead up to the Convention that these obligations need to be seen as global responsibilities (Orbinski, 2008). What percentage of Africans with HIV/AIDS have access to retroviral drugs? In 2003, it was 0.1 per cent (Cullet, 2003: 143). It will have increased since, but not substantially. Another example is famine, the relief of which is a global responsibility, even where a state deliberately starves its population, as in North Korea. But we give more attention today to child obesity (Voigt, Nicholls and Williams, 2014) in the Global North than to starving children in Africa (Armstrong, 2013; Pogge, 2008).

Right of Participation

The fourth of the General Principles is the most significant. It certainly broke new ground. It acknowledges that children are beings and, accordingly, agents (Alderson, 2015; Oswell, 2013). The conceptualisation of children is shifted, as I wrote in 1992, from 'protection to autonomy, from nurturance to self-determination, from welfare to justice' (Freeman and Veerman, 1992: 3). CRC, Article 12 states in paragraph (1):

> States parties shall assure to the child who is capable of forming his or her own views the right to express those views freely in all matters affecting the child, the views of the child being given due weight in accordance with the age and maturity of the child.

The rights set out here apply to the situations envisaged in other Articles in the Convention. Examples are the best interests principle in Article 3, so that children should have input into what is in their best interests, and the provision in Article 9, which deals with the problem which arises when a child is separated from a parent and for whom proceedings may be needed to determine where and with whom that child shall live, 'all interested parties (must) be given an opportunity to participate in the proceedings and make their views known'. Children are most obviously 'interested parties'. It is not so very long ago that Butler-Sloss LJ had to remind us that children were not like packages to be carted about (see *Re W*, 1992). No longer items of property or ways of completing a family (Kellmer-Pringle, 1980), children are now 'principals' (Pais, 1991: 76), persons, and not objects of concern (Butler-Sloss, 1988).

In England, the right of participation can be traced to the *Gillick* case in 1986. The House of Lords held that 'parental right yields to the child's right to make his own decisions when he reaches a sufficient understanding and intelligence to be capable of making up his own mind on the matter requiring decision' (*per* Lord Scarman, *Gillick*, para. 189). The initial impression is that English law complies with Article 12. But what level of understanding and intelligence counts as 'sufficient'? (Reder and Fitzpatrick, 1998). Thus, a child, admittedly after leave from a court, can apply for a child arrangement order. Courts making decisions about a child's upbringing, albeit in a limited range of circumstances, are required to have regard to the 'ascertainable wishes and feelings of the child concerned', in the light of that child's age and understanding (Children Act 1989, section 1(3)(a)). Local authorities, before making any decision concerning a child whom they are looking after or proposing to look after, are required to ascertain the wishes and feelings of that child, so far as that is reasonably practicable (Children Act 1989, section 22(4)). There is a range of provisions in the Children Act 1989 permitting a child of sufficient understanding to be able to make an informed decision on the right to refuse to submit to a medical or psychiatric examination or other assessment where one of a number of protection orders is being sought.

Despite this, the courts are less happy with children who refuse medical treatment. They have ruled that the *Gillick* principle does not confer upon a competent child a power of veto over treatment, but merely allows him/her to give valid consent to such treatment. This has the strange consequence that a girl of fifteen who is *Gillick*-competent can consent to her pregnancy being terminated, but should she refuse to consent, an abortion can nevertheless take place.

Article 12 embodies an important principle. It must, of course, be put into practice if it is to have any value. This is acknowledged by the Committee on the Rights of the Child, which in General Comment No. 5 (2009) was critical of those who appeared 'to "listen" to children', this being 'relatively unchallenging'. But 'giving due weight to their views requires real change' (para. 12). It therefore adds that listening to children should not be seen as an end in itself, but rather as a means for states to make their actions on behalf of children increasingly more sensitive to the implementation of children's rights.

Children as Beings

This required a paradigm shift in thinking about children. The disciplines which had nurtured the 'becoming' model had begun to question received 'truths'. Janusz Korczak had, of course, done so some sixty years earlier. He had written in 'How to Love a Child':

> Children are not the people of tomorrow, but are people of today. They have a right to be taken seriously, and to be treated with tenderness and respect. They should be allowed to grow into whoever they were meant to be – the unknown person inside each of them is our hope for the future. A hundred children – a hundred individuals who are people – not people-to-be, not people of tomorrow, but people now – right now – today. (Korczak, 1920)

And Gertrud Lenzer had asked, as early as 1961, whether there was 'sufficient interest' to establish a sociology of children (Lenzer, 1991).

The work of Piaget was shown to be of limited value. The thought and reasoning of young children were demonstrated to be much more sophisticated than Piaget had claimed. As Woodhead and Faulkner (2000: 25) explained: 'What appears to be "faulty" reasoning actually indicates children's ingenious attempts to create sensible meanings for, what are, to them nonsensical situations and contexts'.

The structural functionalist agenda of Talcott Parsons was also critiqued. It placed too much emphasis on the role of social structures and institutions in shaping society, and so left little space for the part that individuals, including children, could and did play in society. Wrong (1991) famously accused Parsons of having an over-socialised conception of man. The structure/agency debate began to awaken an interest in children, in particular in the part they played in the growing-up process, and in socialisation.

There were important investigations too. Good examples are Myra Bluebond-Langner's study of the private worlds of dying children (Bluebond-Langner, 1978), and Priscilla Alderson's research on children's consent to surgery, which showed a capacity so to do much earlier than we had been led to believe (1990). Berry Mayall (2000: 21) was able to conclude:

> Children are social actors. . .they take part in family relationships from the word go; they express their wishes, demonstrate strong attachment, jealousy and delight, seek justice.

There has since been a huge growth in child-focused research, which demonstrates the agency of children; they are very much 'beings'. Examples are work on how children negotiate their parents' divorce (Smart, Neale and Wade, 2001), and how they cope with an abusive environment (Saunders and Goddard, 2008). That children are beings does not mean that they are not also becomings. The Convention recognises this with its references to age and maturity (Article 12) and to 'evolving capacities' in Article 5. As far as adults are concerned, the law recognises the concept of the 'has been', but adults are beings, never (save in cases of learning disability) becomings or less.

If children were only becomings, the CRC would have emphasised the importance of their best interests, as it does, and concentrated on provision and protection rights exclusively. But because it accepts children are also beings, it gives them 'a voice'. It recognises the dangers of wrapping them in silence. Hence, the roster of participation rights in Articles 12–17. It should be added that the provision on education in

Article 29 states one of the aims of education to be the development of a child's personality, talents, and abilities to their fullest potential.

Participation in Education

A most obvious subject to test out Article 12 is education. If, as seems likely, schools are to become academies and with this the end of parent governors (see *The Guardian*, 17 March 2016), then the status of children in relation to education decision-making won't look as bad as it does now. But, at present, children play no role to speak of. So, as far as they are concerned it will get no worse.

Children have no consultation rights, and teachers are not under any obligation to take cognisance of their views. Children are not allowed to become school governors. English law gives them no rights to be notified that they are to be excluded from school. They have no rights to appeal exclusion, and no rights to attend a review panel, which may be convened at their parents' request. Only pupils over eighteen have these privileges, and they are not children. Ironically, Department of Education Guidance (2012: 4) says that children should be 'enabled and encouraged' to participate in the exclusion process. There is evidence anyway that children's contributions to hearings have been ignored (Children's Commissioner's Inquiry, 2012: 52–3).

It is clear that we are in breach of Article 6 of the ECHR, and this was held in relation to Croatia in *Orsus* v. *Croatia* (2010). It follows from the *Croatia* ruling that children should be given access to a court or a tribunal to challenge exclusions, but this is not as the UK state reads it. However, the Children and Their Families Act 2014 provides for pilot schemes to test appeal procedures. It is envisaged that all disabled children will be covered. Included in the Act are General Principles, one of which stresses the importance of participation in decision-making when working with children with special educational needs.

There are a few positives we can take from this quagmire of rules. We now have 'pupil participation guidance' (Education Act 2002). This applies to nursery schools as well. But blink and you miss it! In 2014, the pupil participation guidance was cut down to size; it is now two pages long, gives the text of Article 12, which schools are told they do not have to take any notice of, with a list of web addresses and little else! This could have come straight from *Yes Minister*!

There is a new duty on governing bodies to invite and consider the views of school students, which was laid down by the Education and Skills Act 2008, but has not yet been brought into force. Only two in every five children surveyed for the Children's Commissioner said that their school was good at listening to new ideas. Only 10 per cent of children surveyed thought that their ideas were listened to 'a lot'. Only one-third believed that their ideas had been listened to at all.

It is a firmly-entrenched principle that education bodies educate children in accordance with parental wishes (Education Act 1996). Parents may exclude their children from sex education classes – it is surely no coincidence that the United Kingdom has one of the highest teen pregnancy rates in Europe. Children have no rights in this area. And only those over sixteen may opt out of acts of collective worship. Parents' rights are again stronger – they may exclude their children of any age from religious education, in effect making a visit to the National Gallery a frustrating experience.

The *Williamson* case, referred to above, p. 49, is instructive. The Supreme Court refused to allow parents' beliefs in corporal punishment to trump children's rights to physical integrity. Fundamentalist Christian parents were not allowed to challenge legislation which outlawed such punishments. The interest in the case is two-fold: first, the marginalisation of the children, only spoken for by Baroness Hale; and secondly, the pathetic defence on the ban on corporal punishment by the government, which must be seen to be believed:

> the parents could attend school on request and themselves administer the desired corporal punishment when the child comes home after school, or if the need for immediate punishment is part of the claimants' beliefs, they could educate their children at home. (2005, para. 405)

Participation in Legal Proceedings

Until relatively recently, the courts of England and Wales were not open to children. If they wanted to litigate, to sue for negligence, for example, they could only do so through a 'litigation friend'. This will normally be a parent. The court can remove the parent and substitute another adult where the parent is acting improperly or against the best interests of the child (*Re Taylor's Application*, 1972).

The Children Act 1989 introduced major reforms. A child may now bring a case to court without a litigation friend or guardian ad litem with the court's permission or where a solicitor considers that the child is able, having regard to his/her understanding, to give instructions, and has accepted instructions from the child. The 1989 Act conferred capacity upon children to apply for section 8 orders. These were then called residence, contact, prohibited steps and specific issue orders, and now less clumsily child arrangement orders. Children thus have the ability to restructure their living arrangements, in effect to 'divorce' their parents. One can imagine situations where this might occur: a row leading to an adolescent walking out; a girl wanting to live with her boyfriend and his more liberal and/or tolerant parents; an abused child seeking refuge; a child wishing to escape from an environment of domestic violence; a Polish child wanting to remain in the United Kingdom when his parents return to Krakow. The last of these scenarios mirrors the notorious *Polovchak* v. *Mese* case in 1985 in the United States, and more recently the politicised fight over the destiny of Elian Gonzalez (De la Cava, 2015). The English cases have had a far lower profile (Freeman, 1996a).

In brief, these cases establish that even if it is accepted that the child applicant has sufficient understanding, the court retains a discretion when deciding whether or not to grant leave. The legislation is silent as to the considerations that should guide the exercise of judicial discretion. This is very different from where leave is being sought by an adult. The contrast reflects the welfare orientation of the judicial role where children are concerned.

Some of the reported English cases appear, to adult eyes, to be about trivial matters. An example is the fourteen-year-old girl who wanted to live with her boyfriend's family, and go on holiday with them to Bulgaria. The judge took the view that Parliament intended the jurisdiction to be exercised only as regards matters of importance. A Bulgarian vacation hardly met this criterion.

There is a difference of opinion as to whether the question of leave is governed by the welfare principle. In *Re C*, it was held that it did. This has the effect of acting as a filter, thus taking away the court's jurisdiction on what it considers to be in the best interests of the child. This would seem to conflict with both the ideology of the Children Act 1989 (Fox Harding, 1991a, 1991b) and to be in breach of the CRC, Article 12. Subsequent cases have taken the view that the paramountcy principle did not govern the leave issue, though have stressed that applications should be examined cautiously (*Re SC*, 1994). Of greater importance is the case of *Mabon* v. *Mabon*, 2005.

The case was about three boys (aged seventeen, fifteen and thirteen) whose parents were divorcing. Their mother was seeking a residence order. There had been a welfare report and the boys were represented by a guardian. However, the boys wanted to instruct their own solicitor. This was rejected by the first instance judge, but allowed on appeal. The Court of Appeal ranked freedom of speech by articulate adolescents as more important than judicial invocation of welfare to protect them.

Thorpe LJ conceded there were very limited circumstances in which it would not be appropriate to permit a competent child the opportunity to participate. Where there was obvious risk of harm to the child and the child was incapable of appreciating the risk, the judge could find that 'sufficient understanding' had not been demonstrated. Of course, listening to children is one thing, taking their views seriously is something else. Research by May and Smart (2004) found that in only one-quarter of their sample of cases was there any record of children's views. They also found that where children's wishes did not coincide with those of the welfare officer, it was rare for the children's views to prevail.

There is substantial evidence as to what 'competence' means. One of the earliest pieces of research, by Weithorn and Campbell (1982) remains of interest. They compared the responses of nine-, fourteen-, eighteen- and twenty-one-year-olds to hypothetical problems of decision-making about medical and psychological treatment. The fourteen-year-olds did not differ from the adult groups on any of the major standards of competency. Even the nine-year-olds were as competent as the average adult, according to standards of evidence of a choice, and reasonableness of that choice. This is consistent with Lewis's finding (1983) that when elementary school children were given unlimited access to the school nurse for routine medical care, their health care behaviour was very similar to adults with similar demographics. Gary Melton (1984) thinks these findings offer us 'a conservative estimate of children's capacities', it seems the more autonomy you give children, the better they are at exercising autonomy. Research by Peterson-Badali and Abramovitch (1992, 1993) throws light on children's understanding of the role of lawyers. They found that even the youngest (aged nine to eleven) had an adequate appreciation of the concept of defence counsel in the criminal process.

There is also evidence of children's competence to participate in divorce custody decision-making (Garrison, 1991; Parkinson and Cashmore, 2009). Garrison found that fourteen-year-olds performed as well as eighteen-year-olds in stating with which parent they wanted to live. But, she warns, her findings 'assessed competence rather than actual performance' (Garrison, 1991: 85), and real-life factors, such as stress, may adversely affect decision-making abilities.

Rights at Home

The right to participate in decisions taken in the home environment must be placed in a particular context: parents hold the whip hand. In most European countries it is unlawful to smack children. In England it is still permitted, so long as it is no more serious than a common assault. If children are to be given rights within the family, they must be protected from legitimate assaults. It was banned:

in prisons in 1967;
in state schools in 1986;
in children's homes in 1991 (a child adopted from a home forfeits this protection);
in private schools in 1998;
in foster care in 2002;
in day care and childminding in 2003.

Since then there have been numerous attempts but obstacles have always been placed in front of reform. A Consultation Paper in 2000 (Department of Health, 2000) was a disingenuous attempt to mould public opinion. The 'Swedish model' was ruled out before a number of options were put. All of these permitted smacking, what was described as a 'loving smack'. This is a form of discipline which offers no space for discussion.

The striking contrast is to be found in the law of Finland (Savolainen, 1986–7). Its Child Custody and Right of Access Act 1983 states that before a parent who has custody:

> makes a decision, on a matter relating to the person of the child, he or she shall, where possible, discuss the matter with the child, taking into account the child's age and maturity and the nature of the matter. In making the decision, the custodian shall give due consideration to the child's feelings, opinions and wishes.

This has provided the model for a similar provision in Scotland (Children (Scotland) Act 1995, section 6). The Scottish Law Commission was attracted to the Finnish precedent because it had value, in that it could influence behaviour. This is despite its obvious failing, that it was 'vague and unenforceable'. There is considerable force in this argument. This is as it should be, and in England children have these rights in just about every environment save the family. This is all the more odd given that statutory guidance tells parents that not giving children opportunities to express their views, deliberately silencing them, or 'making fun' of what they say or of how they say it are regarded as indicators of emotional abuse (HM Government, 2013: 85). They can change a child's name without his/her consent until the child attains his/her sixteenth birthday. The child may be adopted, and this may be accomplished in the absence of consent by the child. The court only has to have regard to the child's wishes and feelings.

When parents separate, they do not usually resort to court to determine child arrangements (Blackwell and Dawe, 2003). If they do, they will be met by a new presumption inserted by the Children and their Families Act 2014 that parental involvement in a child's life will further their welfare. But does it necessarily do so? And can this be squared with the deeply-rooted presumption that the child's welfare is paramount where such a dispute arises? The original proposal was to the effect that that involvement meant an equal sharing of time. This was dropped. Courts therefore now work within a structure which requires them to have regard to the child's ascertainable wishes and feelings, as also any harm suffered and educational needs. The new legislation in no way strengthens the child's status. The presumption of parental involvement assumes a greater profile than any cognisance taken of children's views. OFSTED's children's rights director found that a very clear majority of children questioned (72 per cent) thought the future of a child's relationship with a parent should depend on what the child wanted (Morgan, 2011: 15). Although a small sample, the findings are in line with larger samples in better known research (Smart and Neale, 1999).

4

The Convention: Norms and Themes

The last chapter discussed the general principles, as identified by the Committee on the Rights of the Child. This chapter considers some of the main rights in the Convention, using the standard taxonomy of protection (including prevention), provision and participation.

Classification of Rights: The Three 'P's

It has become so common to break the rights in the CRC into these three categories that the classification is rarely proble-matised (Alderson, 2000: 440; Hammarberg, 1990; Lansdown, 1994; Qvortrup, 1996: 36). To add 'power', as Mary John does (John, 2003), injects some sociology but barely disturbs the normative framework. Ann Quennerstedt (2010), by contrast, offers some probing insights, critical reflections, on what she calls the hampering effect of the three 'P's.

We owe the classification to Thomas Hammarberg (1990), who broke the CRC down in this way for pedagogical reasons. He was trying to educate an ignorant and hostile audience. But he set a trend and, twenty-seven years on, we still follow it.

It is first worth noting that we do not break adults' rights up in this way. This cannot be because adults do not need protection, provision and participation rights (citizen-ship). They are more taken for granted where adults are concerned, it is true. But the demands are similar, though protection/paternalism is less easy to justify (G. Dworkin, 1972), and the provision needs are different (employment rather than schooling, for example). The tripartite division assumes there are discrete entities; that there are clear boundaries, no interpretational questions; that the categories can be objectively differentiated. In other words, they exist, are value-free and there are no overlaps. Also, there is no controversy as to where a particular right is to be fitted in. This is all very legalistic (Shklar, 1964).

Does anything hinge on this conventional categorisation? It may be that arguing the case for a new right to be recognised may be more difficult (but it might be easier) if it does not readily fit into one of the ready-made categories. There is no evidence that this is happening, or any that Quennerstedt's preferred solution (2010: 625–9), to use conventional human rights categories, would surmount any of these problems, or that research would be carried out better without the stranglehold of the conventional model. Where it falls short is in explaining rights which do not fit neatly into any of the categories, for example, a right to a safe environment (provision, protection and, arguably, participation) or a right to housing (Van Bueren, 2016) or a right to work. But none of these is guaranteed by the Convention.

The best answer is that the rights in the Convention are interdependent, and nothing much hinges on what classification is adopted, or whether there is a classification at all. I retain the conventional division for convenience only.

The Convention encompasses a broad range of rights. There are over forty substantive provisions. Indicative are the obligations of states parties to ensure the survival and development of children (Article 6(2)), seen as one of the General Principles; to tackle infant and child mortality (Article 24); and to ensure that all children have access to health care (Article 24). It mandates states to make primary education compulsory and free, and to make secondary and higher education accessible to all, and also to encourage school attendance and reduce numbers of children who drop out from school (Article 28). Pursuant to the ILO Minimum Age Convention of 1973, it confers upon children 'the right to be protected from economic exploitation and from performing any work that is likely to be hazardous or to interfere with education' (Article 32(1)). (And see below, p. 169.)

The Convention also gives children the right to a name from birth (Article 7(1)); the right to free expression (Article 13(1)); freedom of conscience, thought and religion (Article 14); freedom of association and of peaceful assembly (Article 15); and privacy rights (Article 16). This extends to the child's correspondence. The right to rest and leisure are also recognised, and within this are included play and participation in cultural life and the arts (Article 31).

Children's Protective Rights

The claims to protection made on behalf of children are very different from the assertion that children should have greater independence or more autonomy. As Michael Wald argued:

> They do not change the status of children. The
> intervention advocated entails substituting one adult

> decision-maker for another, rather than giving children
> the choice of deciding whether they like the conditions in
> which they find themselves. (Wald, 1979: 263)

The intervention is usually invoked by adults, rarely by children themselves. Of course, protection as rights is a highly paternalistic notion. We do not ask children if they want to be protected. If we did, it is conceivable that some would opt for the abusive environment they know over the uncertainties of the alternative. This is clearer when we look at less obvious targets of protection, like that against taking indecent photographs (see Protection of Children Act 1978, as amended by Sexual Offences Act 2003, section 45). This applies to sixteen- and seventeen-year-olds who oddly can consent to marriage, but not to having a pornographic photograph taken of them (see Gillespie, 2004).

The *Munro Review of Child Protection* (Department of Education, 2012: 25) made the point that:

> Children and young people are a key source of information
> about their lives and the impact any problems are having on
> them. . .it is therefore puzzling that the evidence shows that
> children are not being adequately involved in child
> protection work.

The Committee on the Rights of the Child recognises the right of every person to others' respect for his/her dignity and physical integrity, and equal protection under the law (CRC Committee, 2007: para. 16): 'The dignity of each and every individual is the fundamental guiding principle of international human rights law'. This right, found in the original

International Bill of Human Rights, is, the Committee notes, expanded upon in the Convention:

> There is no ambiguity: 'all forms of physical and mental violence' does not leave room for any level of legalized violence against children. Corporal punishment and other cruel or degrading forms of punishment are forms of violence and the state must take all appropriate legislative, administrative, social and educational measures to eliminate them. (CRC Committee, 2007: para. 18)

Parties to the Convention are bound also to take all appropriate measures to protect children from all forms of violence, injury or abuse, neglect or negligent treatment, maltreatment or exploitation, including sexual abuse (Article 19(1)). Corporal punishment may not be specifically targeted, but taken together with the 'best interests' principle in Article 3, is clearly within 'violence', and arguably may amount to torture in some situations (Article 37(a)). Looked at from the victim's perspective, this may well be how it is experienced. It recognises also that some forms of traditional cultural practices, such as FGM, are abusive (Article 24(3)).

The Committee's response to those who point to the omission of corporal punishment from Article 19 (and also from Article 28 on school discipline) is that the Convention is 'a living instrument'. Its interpretation develops over time. It nevertheless remains the case that states have 'an immediate and unqualified obligation' to eliminate corporal punishment (CRC Committee, 2007: para. 22). Less than one in four states have seized the initiative: at this rate it will take a century to rid the world's statute books of this example of legalized violence.

It is no answer to distinguish and defend reasonable or moderate chastisement, though there are attempts to do so (Coleman, Dodge and Campbell, 2010). It is most unfair to parents, given no guidance as to what is reasonable. It fails to protect children or uphold their dignity: it is designed as much to humiliate as to deter. It is no answer to adopt the English compromise (in Children Act 2004, section 58) which, put into lay language, permits hitting a child so long as it does not leave a mark. How is this interpreted by the ordinary 'parent with a buggy', who rarely dips into the Children Act 2004?

There is a concern that making it unlawful to hit children will lead to greater intervention into the family, more prosecutions, more care proceedings (Thompson, 1992). But this is not the experience of countries which have passed such legislation (Durrant, 1999 on Sweden). It is more likely that outlawing corporal punishment will result in less abuse and so fewer prosecutions, a decline in the number of care proceedings, and also to less delinquency and violent crime, and thus to a reduction in the prison population.

Article 19 is not the only provision in the CRC which protects against abuse and neglect. Article 6, discussed briefly above, p. 133, as one of the General Principles, is intended to ensure that every child has the right to survival and development. The Committee on the Rights of the Child has requested states parties to interpret this holistically to cover physical, mental, spiritual, psychological and social development (and see Scherer and Hart, 1999). And Noam Peleg points to other aspects of development: personal, moral and talents (2013: 103), which can be seen if other Articles are examined, in particular Articles 18, 23, 24, 27, 29 and 32. Of course, survival and development must apply to all children, and so the non-discrimination principle looms large as well in a world where, two generations after the Holocaust, we witness the resurgence of racial hatred and discriminatory practices against First Peoples, Roma and many other minorities.

Protecting Girls

Girl children suffer discrimination in many parts of the world. They are aborted or destroyed at birth as a consequence of policies like China's 'one child' interdict (Greenhalgh, 2008) (jettisoned only in 2015); deprived of education in Pakistan, Afghanistan and elsewhere, an evil brought to the world's attention by the shooting of Malala in October 2012 (Yousafzai, 2013); forced or coaxed into marriage when much too young (Kitson, 2016) (the Committee has many times chided states which have different marriage ages for girls and boys, drawing attention to the negative impact this has on girls' health, education and social development). Girls are also more likely to fall victim to sexual exploitation: that 272 schoolgirls can be abducted from a school dormitory, and 'disappear', as happened in Nigeria in 2014, strains credulity (Orr, 2014). Many of the girls have not been rescued; many are now mothers. One particularly invidious example of gender discrimination affecting girls is the political weapon of mass rape against subjugated populations. The United Nations estimated that between 20,000 and 50,000 women and girls were raped during the Bosnian conflict in the early 1990s (see, further, MacKinnon, 2006).

Victimised Children

There is discrimination also against children with disabilities (and see above, p. 94). There have been improvements in their status in the recent past, but there is no room for complacency (Sabatello, 2013). There are many further examples of the 'marginalised other' amongst child populations (Simmons, 2011): refugee children (Liden and Rusten, 2007); street children (Rizzini and Butler, 2003); stateless children (Bhabha, 2014); trafficked children (Rafferty, 2007); asylum-seeking children, particularly those who are unaccompanied (Connolly, 2015); undocumented children (Vandenhole et al., 2011); traveller children (Kiddle, 1999); indigenous children (Blanchet-Cohen, 2015); children belonging to cultural and ethnic minority groups (Douglas and Walsh, 2013; Woolley, 2009) subjected to serial attempts at genocide, ethnic or cultural cleansing or ethnocide (examples of which are found in Darfur, in Rwanda in 1994, in Cambodia by the Khmer Rouge, in Burma/Myanmar, Bosnia, and earlier in Australia and North America). All these have suffered discrimination and, worse, cleansing. There are also 'abandoned' children (Panter-Brick and Smith, 2000).

'Disappeared' Children

Another group of children were targeted in Argentina between 1976 and 1983 (Cregan and Cuthbert, 2014). They were either children of 'left wing' parents or themselves had identified with radical causes. A reign of terror (the 'dirty war') was pursued by a junta through the systematic kidnapping of those opposed to it. Over 30,000 victims of this terror disappeared, some for nothing more serious than being suspected of holding different views. On one occasion, sixty high school students 'disappeared' for having joined a school council (Goldman, 2012). The term 'ideocide' has been coined to categorise this form of oppression (Appadurai, 2006). The Argentinian experience has led to a new international Convention, and to the recognition of a new human right, the right not to endure forced disappearance (McCory, 2007). But this still occurs: an example (mentioned above, p. 137) is the abduction by Boko Haram of nearly 300 girls from a school dormitory in 2004.

Protecting Children from Disciplinary Violence

The Convention's protective barrier stretches beyond physical abuse to include emotional abuse (in the CRC called mental violence), sexual abuse and neglect, as well as maltreatment and exploitation. It will be observed that corporal punishment is not singled out. This omission was criticised by Cynthia Price Cohen (1984), who argued that 'in order for children's rights to be adequately protected, children must be regarded as entitled to human dignity' (C. P. Cohen, 1984: 129). Much abuse started as punishment (Zigler, 1980: 27). Today's abuse, in particularly tragic cases of the death of a child, is frequently yesterday's punishment. Indeed, corporal punishment is a form of abuse. This will be recognised in years to come (Straus, 2000). Fifty-two states have made it unlawful to hit children. England has not done so. A Consultation Paper in 2000 ruled out removing from those with parental responsibility the freedom to punish a child with what it called 'a loving smack' (*Protecting Children*, 2000: 1).

The twentieth century saw a move away from using violent disciplinary measures against children. It ceased to be a judicial punishment in 1948, though the birch continued to be used in the Isle of Man until 1993 (and see *Tyler* v. *United Kingdom*, 1979–80). It was finally abolished in schools in England and Wales in 1998, though it survives in madrasas, yeshivas and, presumably in theory at least, in Sunday schools. Reform was anticipated here in 2017, but did not materialise.

Parents may still smack their children, but they may not mark their bodies (Children Act 2004, section 58). The oxymoron 'a loving smack' still rules. It is 'simply a fact of childhood' (McGillivray, 1997: 211). It is deeply embedded within culture, and resistant to change. For too long, Saunders comments (2015: 246), 'children have been punished for being children'.

In more than forty countries it remains lawful for children to be sentenced to caning, whipping and flogging. Over seventy countries still permit corporal punishment in schools. The paddle continues to be used to beat children in nineteen US states, a practice upheld by the Supreme Court (*Ingraham* v. *Wright*, 1977). It is endemic in African schools (Gwirayi and Shumba, 2011, on Zimbabwe; Burton, 2008, on South Africa; Mweru, 2010, on Kenya; Twum-Danso, 2003, on Ghana). It is common in India (Raj, 2011); in China and Korea (Kim et al., 2000); in Arab schools in Israel (Khoury-Kasabri, 2012); in Thailand (Nelson et al., 2009). In most of the world parents retain the freedom to inflict corporal punishment on their children. There has been some progress, with fifty-one countries having followed Sweden's lead, and removed this right (more accurately privilege, see Hohfeld, 1923). Sweden made it unlawful for parents to hit children as long ago as 1979, and Scotland is about to do so.

Of all the reforms needed, it is perhaps the easiest to accomplish. And it is one of the most important. The expressive function of law cannot be underestimated (Sunstein, 1995). The law is a symbol of what is right and what is wrong, and has the capacity to effect change in behaviour and in attitudes (Freeman, 1974: 45–69). True, social engineering's weakest spot is the family. But, nevertheless, we should not discount the impression it can make. It is likely to be most effective when it is not used in isolation. It should therefore be integrated into the zero tolerance onslaught on domestic violence, currently being pursued, and into the attempt to eliminate FGM, a problem which we awakened to only in the very recent past.

The cane in school instilled fear into the student population even when you were not the one receiving it. It was enough that you were a witness. It was even enough that you knew the teacher had access to a cane. Corporal punishment is used by those in power on those who have inferior status. Exposure to physical punishment is a badge of inferiority; slaves were flogged, prisoners birched, members of the armed forces whipped, wives subjected to the power of the hand, as well as the power of the purse (Bell and Newby, 1976: 164). Violent punishment was the commonest technique employed to reinforce subjugation. Today, children remain the sole category left. No one today suggests reintroducing corporal punishment in prisons or in the navy, but you don't have to dig very deep to find support for bringing back the cane in schools.

The most recent attempt to outlaw the physical punishment of children in England and Wales was by means of a Private Member's Bill in the House of Lords in 2015. There seems to be little prospect of reform succeeding in the immediate future, yet it is inevitable that it will be effected eventually. It is as if King Canute had returned to hold back the waves.

One of the obstacles to reform are the compromise measures already put into operation. These limit, rather than banning, corporal punishment. Anne McGillivray (1997: 211) has written of 'a shifting geojurisprudence of licit and illicit body contacts (which) explicitly define rather than reject the legitimacy and inhumanity of violent parental responses to children'. The attention given to which instruments and which parts of the body would be laughable were the subject not so serious. In New South Wales, for example, a child may be hit so long as it is below his/her shoulders, and the pain caused is transient, though this is left undefined. In Canada, you may not hit a child until she/he reaches the age of two. (I have this sick image of two-year-olds birthday cards, but let's not go there!) Children may not be physically punished once they reach the age of twelve. Why twelve? Could it have something to do with puberty? Between two and twelve they may be hit, but not on the head, or with an instrument. I am reminded of the regulations which governed the use of the cane in English schools which prescribed the length of the cane that was permitted according to the age and gender of the child (Newell, 1972). And in England and Wales, reasonable chastisement, as defined in the middle of the Victorian era (see *R* v. *Hopley*, 1870), is permitted as long as it does not meet the test for occasioning actual bodily harm in the Offences Against the Person Act 1861. The average parent is, of course, intimately familiar with the statute and the case law!

There is increasing empirical evidence that hitting children does not achieve positive outcomes (Gershoff, 2016). The latest research even suggests it may affect a child's intelligence (Straus, et al. 2014). This seems intuitively right since reasoning with a child is likely to encourage thinking and language skills, and thumping a child teaches only that violence is an answer, which she/he soon learns it isn't. Evidence also suggests that behavioural development and relationships with significant others may be adversely affected (Benjet and Kazdin, 2003; Gershoff, 2013; MacKenzie et al., 2013). Of course, it may also lead to serious injury or even death (Nielssen et al., 2009). Many of the most notorious child abuse cases started as attempts to discipline a child.

It is debatable whether it is possible to separate corporal punishment and child abuse (Newell, 1989a). Much depends on how child abuse is defined – see the discussion above. If broadly, as with David Gil (1970: 6) and the National Commission of Inquiry into the Prevention of Child Abuse (1996), it is a form of abuse. If narrowly, as David Archard (1993: 149) conceives it, only severe physical punishment would meet the threshold. The line between them is very fuzzy. English law hinges on the concept of significant harm. Most smacking clearly does not cause significant harm, though judges are developing this concept to incorporate practices not envisaged by the legislature, for example ritualistic, non-therapeutic male circumcision (*Re G*, 2015).

Sexual Abuse

The protective barrier extends to a wide range of abuse. Attention today is so concentrated on sexual abuse that it is difficult to grasp how recently it was recognised as a social problem. It could have been responded to so much earlier, but other interests, male and professional, blocked its being brought out into the open (Smart, 1999). Instead, a discreet veil was drawn over it. In 1884, it was described by the London Society for the Prevention of Cruelty to Children as 'an evil which is altogether too unmentionable' (1884: 5–6). The public was, however, sensitised to the problem of child prostitution by William Stead in 1885, and the age of consent to lawful sexual intercourse was raised from thirteen to sixteen. Sexual abuse within the family was not discussed publicly: it was thought to be exclusively a vice of the poor, linked to low intelligence and a product of overcrowded sleeping conditions. Incest only became a crime in 1908 (Bailey and McCabe, 1979). As regards children, the offence was replaced and widened in 2003 (see below, p. 147).

A Royal Commission on Venereal Diseases in 1916 did not question the provenance of childhood infections. And the *Lancet* in 1923 was similarly obtuse. The best advice it could give was that girls in institutions should not share 'towels, baths or bedrooms'. There was not even the hint of a suspicion that these girls might have been sexually abused. But since it was commonly believed that you could cure yourself of a venereal disease by having sex with a virgin, this was hardly surprising – this folk myth was resurrected in South Africa recently to target HIV/AIDS. In both contexts we might say that it was not rape or abuse, but rather 'misdirected medical effort' (Smart, 1999: 398).

There were calls for legal reforms as early as the 1920s but it was the 1990s before these reforms were implemented (see Pigot, 1989; Criminal Justice Act 1991). The response at the time was to blame the victim (Ryan, 1976). Radical reforms had been recommended in a Departmental Committee report in 1925 (*Sexual Offences Against Young Persons*, 1925), but these met legal resistance. It was a remarkable document which would have put England in the vanguard of the battle to confront sexual abuse. Legal opposition was based on 'a specific understanding of childhood as a phase of both resilience and insignificance. Children did not matter in this scheme of things, at least working class girls. . .did not matter. On the other hand, men. . .did matter; they were recognised as legal subjects' (Smart, 1999: 403). When, more than sixty years later, the Butler-Sloss Cleveland report looked forward to a time when children would be persons in their own right, not merely objects of concern (Butler-Sloss, 1988: 245), what may have been overlooked was that in relation to sexual abuse, they had hardly become even objects of concern. Has all that much changed? One of the lessons of the Jimmy Savile revelations is not so. Certainly, there is a sense of *déja vu* as we hear of men of importance taking advantage of weak young women (Davies, 2014; Furedi, 2015).

It took a strange saga in Teesside in the mid-1980s to awaken our consciousness and our conscience to the sexual abuse of children. I had written about it in the 1970s, but had been advised to take it out of my book, *Violence in the Home* (Freeman, 1979) since, I was assured, it didn't happen! It was published as an article in *Current Legal Problems* (Freeman, 1980). I doubt if it caused a ripple then – it is certainly not read now.

What should cause surprise is not that 'Cleveland' happened, but that a 'Cleveland' was so long in coming. The exposure was clouded by revelations of ineptitude, of inter-professional rivalry, of the way and the battleground upon which initiatives for reform were fought. We will never know how many of the children removed from parents in Cleveland were sexually abused. We are therefore unlikely ever to discover whether the paediatricians, Marietta Higgs and Geoffrey Wyatt, were Midases who turned everything they touched into sexual abuse or, like many pioneers, were more sinned against than sinning. They certainly made mistakes and at the time this became the focus of attention. But in the perspective of history, Cleveland will be remembered as the place where we first faced up to the iniquity of the sexual abuse of children (Freeman, 1998).

It has been estimated that as many as 20 per cent of girls in England have been sexually abused. Fewer boys are victimised in this way, but a substantial number (perhaps 5 per cent) are. One-third of sexually abused children are the victims of other children or adolescents. Of course, the question of 'how many' depends upon how sexual abuse is defined. There is no universally accepted definition of what constitutes child sexual abuse. How far does 'sexual' extend? A much-quoted definition (Schechter and Roberge, 1976) defines it as:

> the involvement of dependent, developmentally immature children and adolescents in sexual activities that they do not fully comprehend and to which they are unable to give

informed consent or that violate the social taboos of family roles.

Working Together (2015) expands upon this – the first edition in 1980 did not even draw attention to its existence. We are now told it includes 'non-penetrative acts such as masturbation, kissing, rubbing and touching outside of clothing', and 'non-contact activities, such as involving children in looking at, or in the production of, sexual images, watching sexual activities, encouraging children to behave in sexually inappropriate ways, or grooming a child in preparation for abuse'. The width of this definition offered principally in guidance to social workers and other professionals may be too great. As I wrote in March 2015, there are hordes of school parties visiting an excellent exhibition at the Wellcome Museum in London on sexology. Technically, the teachers appear to be sexual abusers. The opportunity for a moral crusader to step in and challenge these visits should send alarm bells ringing, not least because the Tory government, elected in 2015, wants social workers who turn a blind eye to child abuse sent to prison.

The net has also been cast wide by the latest Sexual Offences Act in 2003 (Hoyano and Keenan, 2010; Spencer, 2004). Activities, including some which are harmless and certainly should not be the business of the state, now attract the criminal sanction (H. L. A. Hart, 1963; cf. Devlin, 1965; Syrota, 1996). The 2003 Act goes for 'overkill' (Spencer, 2004: 352). The legislation sends out the message that all sexual activity with children is wrong. The target is the paedophile, but children themselves can be criminalised for what has long been regarded as innocuous, a stage in the growing-up process. For example, if two fifteen-year-olds kiss or pet, one or both has committed sexual exploitation. That a prosecution is unlikely (CPS, 2003) is beside the point. Worse still, there can be a situation where both parties are victims of abuse, but the law deems one of them to be the perpetrator. Look at the startling case in 2011 of *R (E)* v. *DPP* (2012).

A twelve-year-old girl, who had herself been groomed over the Internet by an adult male, filmed herself engaging in sexual activities with her two sisters, aged two and three. It was the view of the multi-agency strategy group, the police dissenting, that it was not in the best interests of any of the children to bring a prosecution. She was nevertheless brought to trial, now aged fourteen, in the Crown Court. The case was adjourned pending the outcome of a judicial review. It was argued, unsuccessfully, that CPS guidance was unlawful in that it failed to give sufficient attention to cases where the child was both victim and perpetrator. The court rejected the argument, holding that prosecution policy was to be decided by the CPS, not by the courts. The decision to prosecute was quashed on a different ground, namely that the CPS had failed to take into account the best interests of the children, contrary to its own guidance (and, of course, CRC, Article 3). She was treated as a paedophile, when she was rather a victim. Hollingsworth (2013: 794) describes the decision to prosecute as 'bizarre', given that the 2003 Act deems children under thirteen incapable of consenting to sexual activity and as being victims in all cases involving sexual activity regardless of actual content.

Sexual Exploitation

The protective umbrella encompasses also sexual exploitation. Probably, the first to write on this was Judith Ennew, and that as recently as 1986 (Ennew, 1986). That it was a novel phenomenon – much more likely a newly discovered one – is brought out strikingly when she compares two articles from *The Observer*, one published in 1984, the other in 1985. The conventional 'Margate' in (iconic) 1984 is followed by lists of exotic/erotic places to visit and indulge a year later. We are offered 'sexy' Vienna, and Athens, where, we are told, hotel and tour guides will do the 'procuring' for you. Sex tourism is as old as tourism.

Article 34 of the CRC expects states parties to commit to protecting children against sexual exploitation and sexual abuse. Neither sexual exploitation nor sexual abuse is defined. A lot less was known about sexual exploitation in the 1980s than now. But attempts to tackle it go back a long way: the first international treaty was in 1921.

The victims are the poor and many of them are children. Children are exploited in many ways, and not all of them are sexual.

Commercial Exploitation

There is also commercial exploitation. Wild (2013) has edited a collection of essays on the theme of exploiting children which focus on a variety of examples of commercial exploitation, many of which are not sexual; junk food manufacturers and child obesity (Lobstein, 2013; see also Handsley et al., 2014; Mills, 2013); violent entertainment (Warburton, 2016; see also Bakan, 2011). And none of his essays discuss two of the latest examples of child exploitation, namely radicalisation (Stanley and Guru, 2015) to fight for the cause of ISIS (the girls may well be recruited for sexual reasons, as kidnap victims of Boko Haram are); and the merchants of death who ferry refugees across the Mediterranean in unseaworthy boats (many, including a disproportionate number of children, perish).

Intervention Questions

The very concept of intervention itself is problematic. Whom does it protect and against what? Non-intervention is a form of intervention (Olsen, 1985). Article 19 of the CRC looks to eliminate child abuse, but what constitutes it is not self-evident. It is a social construction (Hacking, 2000). To take a simple example, physically punishing a child is regarded as abuse by some (unfortunately, a minority), and by others as acceptable behaviour. Archard (1993: 149) confines abuse to 'something serious enough to warrant (state) intervention' (a rather circular definition). Gil (1970), by contrast, defines it as anything which interferes with the optimal development of a child (is this over-extensive?). Arguments surrounding definitions of child abuse reflect different understandings of childhood and of appropriate child development (Ashenden, 2003; Smart and Neale, 1999). It has been argued that these conflicts may be intractable (Stoll, 1968).

Much depends on who is doing the defining and for what purpose. Lawyers may define child abuse differently from doctors or social workers. 'Abuse' may be distinguished from 'an accident'. But it is not always easy to do so. They are not distinct categories. Rather, they are labels created by doctors, police, social workers, coroners, judges – people who have the authority to decide whether a particular act or omission is to be designated as deviant.

Protective intervention can also backfire. The history books are littered with examples of well-intended interventions which far from advancing children's welfare have positively harmed them. The US decision in *Re Gault* (1967) illustrates this dramatically. Gault, aged fifteen, made an obscene telephone call. Had an adult done this, the penalty would likely have been a fine. But 'for his own good' Gerald Gault was sent to a reformatory until he came of age – in effect a six-year sentence. This was overturned on appeal, but we must assume many juveniles before *Gault* did not challenge such 'benevolent' sentences. Another illustration is the way post-apartheid labour legislation has had the unintended consequence of exacerbating poverty, and so hunger among children who, prior to this legislation, had worked seasonally or as part-time workers (Levine, 2003).

The State, Parents and Children

We don't choose our parents: some of us get lucky, some not so. We don't licence parents (LaFollette, 1989). Most children probably result from acts of sexual congress where the last thing on the minds of the participants is the creation of a new, helpless and vulnerable human being. Most muddle through, and produce adequately socialised individuals who continue the generation game. But some fail. A child dies each week at parents' hands, and many more are physically, sexually and emotionally abused by parents, their partners and relatives, and older siblings. Every few years we are confronted by a scandal, a Maria Colwell (Howells, 1974), a Jasmine Beckford (Parton, 1986), a Victoria Climbié, a Peter Connolly (R. Jones, 2014). Invariably, the state (its social workers) is blamed; the state (those who are responsible for its macro policies) escapes with little opprobrium attached. The parents go to prison, and emerge a few years later to continue the saga, no better equipped than they were (Parton, 1986).

The cases we hear about are but the tip of the iceberg. The state could not cope with intervention every time a child was abused, and so it defines abuse narrowly (rather as Archard, 2015, see above, p. 150), and steers clear of the expansive interpretation associated with David Gil (1970), and prescribes the threshold for intervention as 'significant harm' (Children Act 1989, section 31(2)). 'Significant' is defined no further, but will be interpreted differently by different decision-makers; for example, judges and police with their different experiences may see conduct through different lenses and mediated by different ideologies.

The judicial response is to tolerate 'very diverse standards of parenting, including the eccentric, the barely adequate and the inconsistent' (Hedley J in *Re L*, 2007, para. 50). The judge pointed out that it was not 'the provenance of the state to spare children all the consequences of defective parenting' (ibid.). In *Re B* (2013, para. 143) Baroness Hale made much the same point: 'the State does not and cannot take away the children of all the people who commit crimes, who abuse alcohol or drugs...or who espouse antisocial political or religious beliefs'.

And in the same case, Lord Wilson of Culworth agreed with the submission of counsel that:

> Many parents are hypochondriacs, many parents are criminals or benefit cheats, many parents discriminate against ethnic or sexual minorities, many parents support vile political parties or belong to unusual or militant religions. All of these follies are visited upon their children, who may well adopt or 'model' them in their own lives but those children could not be removed for those reasons. (*Re B*, para. 28)

It has also been affirmed that:

> the courts are not in the business of social engineering. The courts are not in the business of providing children with perfect homes. If we took into care and placed for adoption every child whose parents had a domestic spat and every child whose parents on occasion had drunk too much then the care system would be overwhelmed and there would not be enough adoptive parents. So we have to have a degree of realism about prospective carers who come before the courts. (*North East Lincolnshire Council* v. *G & L*, 2014)

That parents have responsibilities was clearly formulated by Blackstone in his *Commentaries* (1765) in the mid-eighteenth century, and the child-saving movement in the nineteenth century saw the beginnings of the implementation of a 'rescue' ideology. But there was a reluctance to criminalise child cruelty. It was two-thirds of a century before legislation began to catch up with laws on cruelty to animals. Even then they gave children less protection than domestic animals were afforded.

There were discussions about rights, but most certainly not about the rights of children. Indeed, a major stumbling block to getting the legislation passed in 1889 was the belief that we should not interfere with the sacred rights of fathers (Behlmer, 1982).

Today's child cruelty legislation dates from 1933. It was amended in 2004 to protect children from excessive corporal punishment, and again in 2015, when a reform was tagged on to the Serious Crime Act 2015. Is its survival a sign that it has stood the test of time or, more likely, that the children's lobby remains relatively weak, and children themselves the only major disenfranchised section of society? Since its language is antiquated and since our knowledge and understanding of child abuse and neglect are so much greater, it is difficult to think beyond the indifference interpretation.

The 2015 reform targeted child neglect. This is significant because, though sexual abuse and exploitation grab the headlines, neglect is where the action is. Nearly 50 per cent of protection plans relate to cases of child neglect. The reform (see section 66) was instigated by lobbying by Action For Children, a children's charity. The government was satisfied that the existing law was satisfactory. It is now clear that injury and harm caused by wilful neglect include psychological injury and harm.

The importance of this should not be underestimated. It removes an inconsistency between the criminal law and family law, the latter long regarding emotional/psychological harm as triggering intervention to protect a child. If we add to this the lesser standard of proof in the family court – a balance of probabilities as against beyond reasonable doubt – we can appreciate the dissonance in approach between social care professionals and the police and the criminal courts, though parents may have found it difficult to understand why their children were removed when all they received in the family court was a slap on the wrist (a caution).

The 2015 reform will better enable us to protect children. But it also raises once again the question as to how appropriate it is to use the criminal law to tackle child abuse and neglect. English law does not spell out what responsibilities parents have (Scots law by contrast does), so, it may be claimed, not giving them the doctrine of fair opportunity (H. L. A. Hart, 1968). It does, however, give them a defence if they are of low intelligence, the House of Lords having held in 1981 that 'wilfully' meant either intentionally or subjectively reckless. Lord Keith explained: 'a parent who has genuinely failed to appreciate that his child needs medical care, through personal inadequacy or stupidity or both, is not guilty' (*R v. Sheppard*, 1981: 418). I wonder if there is any other crime to which stupidity is a defence!

There are arguments against using the criminal law. Offences are difficult to prove: there may be no witnesses or no reliable witnesses. Not guilty verdicts may reflect these difficulties, rather than innocence. The parent may see acquittal as a vindication of her/his behaviour. This may well encourage repetition and the distinct possibility that this time the result will be worse – for the parent, and of greater concern for the child. It may also make therapeutic intervention more difficult, if not impossible.

There is no reason to believe that successful prosecutions deter the offender or others. Rather, they tend to confirm the parent in his/her negative self-image. There is also the very real danger that a parent who fears criminalisation may neglect or delay seeking medical treatment for an injured child because of concern about this consequence.

Children who do not get the love and care they need may find it difficult to establish healthy relationships later in life, thus neglecting their own children. They may also suffer the effects of post-traumatic stress disorder, abuse drugs and/ or alcohol. They are also more likely to engage in delinquent behaviour.

Children have the right to expect at least the basic necessities of life: food, shelter, clothing, education, basic health care (see above, p. 334). Many, even in prosperous countries such as the United Kingdom, do not get these basic goods of human flourishing. There are 13 million people living in poverty in the United Kingdom today, of whom 2.3 million are children; 1.5 million children in poverty live in families with a working parent. The Commission stresses poverty is not a 'transient' experience.

The right to be loved is altogether more difficult to grasp. It is recognised in Israeli law, and is found in the Preamble to the CRC ('a child should grow up in an atmosphere of happiness, love and understanding'). A moral right to be loved is arguable (Cowden, 2012; Liao, 2015). A legal claim to be loved seems a step too far. Can we really impose a duty on others to love? Liao thinks we can. He uses scientific and neuroscientific literature to substantiate the claim he makes. He is not concerned that he is deriving an 'ought' from an 'is'. Even were he not doing this (and see Hume, 1740), he does not make a convincing case. Cowden hypothesises that the right to be loved may be an example of what Joel Feinberg has called a 'manifesto right' (1970: 252). Manifesto rights are the natural seeds from which rights grow (ibid.), laws that ought to be made. But is it a law that ought to be made? Can loving ever become a duty? How would a child or the state or some representative of the child enforce such a duty? Can love be taught? It is possible that state policies may frustrate the development of a loving relationship, for example, by imprisoning a parent or recruiting him into the armed forces to fight abroad or by removing children from their parents (it was reported in December 2015 that there has been an increase in the number of babies removed at birth (*The Guardian*, 15 December 2015, and see also Freeman, 1980). The CRC already copes with these problems in so far as it can. Of course, it does so without any reference to 'love'. Examples are:

Article 7 (child has right to know and be cared for by parents);
Articles 9 and 10 (child's right not to be separated from parents against their will);
Article 18 (assistance to parents to perform child-rearing responsibilities);
Article 20 (children deprived of family environment are entitled to special assistance from the state).

Liao also argues for 'institutional arrangements that would adequately provide for children's various essential needs'. An example is the compulsory parenting class. But it is difficult to see how this could be enforced. It encounters the same obstacle as do proposals to license parenthood. Sanctions are likely to hurt the very children for whom the right to be loved is designed. And, anyway, how do you teach 'love', which should be spontaneous? Would prospective parents be compelled to undergo a love test? Would this be a written examination or would there be a 'practical' as well? We are into the Brave New World of Aldous Huxley and Margaret Atwood! But these are worlds noted for their absence of rights. The right to be loved does not stand up to critical examination. That ideally children should be loved by their parents does not mean that this is a right children have.

Protection: A Case Study – Sexting

Sexting is a good example of a practice which adult authority and young persons interpret differently. Adults/the 'Law' sees the practice as child pornography, and criminalises it. Young people see it as 'a vital part of their social life and the building of their identity' (McGrath, 2009: 2). Sexting refers to the 'digital taking and distribution of images of nude/semi-nude persons through mobile phone or social networking sites' (Crofts et al., 2015: 1).

Sexting is becoming 'normal' amongst teenagers (UK Government Child Exploitation Online Protection Centre, 2015; *The Guardian*, 11 November 2015). How much of it there is, is not known, but the Protection Centre is notified of a serious incident on average once a day.

Teenagers do not use the word 'sexting'. They prefer 'nudes', 'nude selfies' and 'dodgy pix'. In some cases girls fall victim to, what they call, 'snaking' – a boy befriends them, leads them on, asks for a photo, which he then distributes. In one case it reached soldiers in Afghanistan. In September 2015, a fourteen-year-old boy was told his details would be held on a police database for ten years for making a naked image of himself and sending it to a classmate.

A most notorious case was decided in Florida in *AH v. State of Florida* (2007): a seventeen-year-old boy took digital images of himself having consensual sexual intercourse with his girlfriend aged sixteen. They emailed the images to another computer. They did not show anyone else, but the police got wind of the existence of the images, obtained a search warrant for the computer and found the images. The couple were both charged and convicted of producing, directing or promoting a photograph or representation that they knew to include the sexual conduct of a child. The boy was also charged with possession of child pornography. The girl appealed her conviction, but it was upheld, the court finding a compelling state interest in protecting children from sexual exploitation. This compelling state interest exists irrespective of the age of the exploiter, and is undoubtedly 'triggered by the production of 117 photographs of minors engaging in graphic sexual acts'. A criminal prosecution was said to be the least intrusive way of upholding the state's compelling interest.

In England, legislation followed a moral crusade (Gusfield, 1963) by a well-known moral entrepreneur, Mary

Whitehouse. The Protection of Children Act 1978 made it a criminal offence to take an indecent photograph of a child. There is no definition of 'indecent'. It is left to the courts to determine what is indecent by looking to ordinary standards of decency (*R* v. *Stanford*, 1972). Community standards are applied, and neither the context nor the intention of the maker of the image is relevant. The definition of indecency is accordingly wide (Gillespie, 2010: 211).

The law is being used for purposes for which it was never intended. It was designed to tackle paedophilia and preparatory acts surrounding it, but it is being used to suppress adolescent sexuality. It is an excessive use of the law, and it is unlikely to succeed. Where next? Masturbation as a crime?

Radicalisation

The categories of abuse are never closed. The latest to emerge is complex. There is nothing wrong with radicalisation when we approve of the ends sought by the 'radicals'. Without radicals there would have not been children's rights, or indeed any rights. But when the objective is the violent overthrow of Western values, and the recruitment of disaffected youth as foot soldiers, there is legitimate concern.

There has been little research on radicalisation as yet (Guru, 2013). It is defined as the process by which people come to support terrorism or violent extremism and in some cases to join terrorist groups. It has to be approached carefully. It is in many cases an exercise of autonomy. But, given the danger to self and the harm to others, intervention to intercept recruitment is easy to justify. Even were there only danger to the recruit himself, we would have prima facie a simple case for paternalistic intervention. To adapt Mill's famous example, there are many unsafe bridges on the road to Damascus (Mill, 1859). Radicalisation operates as a kind of sociological trap: its recruits have no way out but on, often to their deaths. To keep this in perspective, remind yourself of the Kitchener World War One poster – 'Your Country Needs You!'. Radicalisation does not have to be violent, but it usually is.

A family where a convicted terrorist lives will constitute a significant risk to any child who resides there. Keeping children out of school – home schooling or using unregulated schools or taking them on rallies designed to stimulate radicalism may set alarm bells ringing. There are no simple solutions: intensified surveillance may lead to families going elsewhere, for example, to a conflict zone, increasing the risk of the children suffering harm. Intervention is the orthodox answer but the labelling process may create terrorists (Becker, 1963), and it may lead to nursery staff for example having to divert their attention to 'spotting tomorrow's terrorists' (Crown, 2014).

There is now a counter-terrorism strategy embedded in Prevent and Channel programmes. These focus on vulnerable individuals suspected of being a terrorist threat. There has been a frenzied attempt to tackle radicalisation with little signs of success.

Wrongs and Rights: Dilemma of Child Criminality

The rights of children who do wrong, as I expressed it many years ago (Freeman, 1980, 1983), continues to perplex. Every so often, it causes a moral panic (S. Cohen, 1972; Pearson, 1983), as happened when two ten-year-olds brutally murdered a toddler in Liverpool in 1993. This case (the *Bulger* case) has become a backdrop to our thinking about juvenile crime for a generation, and itself raised many human rights questions.

Such questions evoked international responses pre-CRC. There were the Beijing Rules, the Riyadh Guidelines, the Havana Rules and the Vienna Guidelines (Schabas and Sax, 2006). Some basic principles were codified in the CRC, and subsequently elaborated upon in a General Comment (2010). Of importance are Articles 37 and 40; Article 37 because it sees detention as a last resort; Article 40 because it sets out principles to ensure a fair trial. Geraldine van Bueren (2006) notes the tensions involved in upholding these standards. How to create a child-centred criminal justice system focusing on the child's welfare, which is not necessarily safeguarded by lawyers, which also recognises that traditional juvenile justice is dependent upon lawyers?

We get some assistance from the jurisprudence of the ECtHR. It has ruled on the legality of pre-trial detention in *Giuveç v. Turkey* (2009). It has expressed its 'misgivings' about the practice of detaining children in pre-trial detention (ibid.: para. 109). In this case, the Court concluded there had been inhuman and degrading treatment. This conclusion was reached by assessing a chain of factors: the child's age, the length of the detention, in prison with adults, failure to provide adequate medical care for his psychological problems, and failure to prevent his repeated attempts to commit suicide (ibid.: para. 98).

Minimum Age of Criminal Responsibility

On the question of the minimum age of criminal responsibility (MACR), the ECtHR has been less helpful. Is this a question best left to states to decide? Should 'a margin of appreciation' play a role here? How low can it get before there is international intervention? England and Wales has one of the lowest ages in Europe. In almost every other European country the boys who killed James Bulger would not have been subjected to criminal sanctions. Not surprisingly, therefore, the Committee on the Rights of the Child has repeatedly castigated the United Kingdom for the 'internationally unacceptable MACR in England and Wales'. The abolition of the *doli incapax* presumption – one of the consequences of the *Bulger* case, where if it was ever going to work, this was the case – in effect reduced the MACR in England and Wales from fourteen to ten (Asquith, 1996; Freeman, 1997b; King, 1995).

Governments have repeatedly refused to accept the UN Committee's recommendation to increase the MACR. The absurdly low age exposes children to the harms of criminal justice system before they are out of primary school. In Scotland, by contrast, a child cannot be prosecuted under the age of twelve. We seem to take no account of the alternative non-criminal processes available to address childhood offending, such as family group conferences.

The Committee has said that twelve should be the absolute minimum, but offers no further guidance on what the appropriate age is. The Council of Europe Guidelines on Child-Friendly Justice in 2010 merely indicates that it shouldn't be too low (Committee of Ministers of the Council of Europe,

2010). The ECtHR held in *T* v. *United Kingdom* (1999) that imposing criminal responsibility on a ten-year-old (one of the boys who killed James Bulger) as not in itself a violation of Article 3 of the European Convention. It might not decide the same way today. The Court in *T* v. *United Kingdom* was concerned that a ten-year-old like Thompson received a fair trial, that he was properly represented. More recent cases point to the need for the child to be able to participate effectively in his trial (see *Salduz* v. *Turkey*, 2008), where the Court stressed 'the fundamental importance of providing access to a lawyer where the person in custody is a minor' (ibid.: para. 60).

Protection: A Case Study – The Migrant Child

One group of children in special need of protection are migrant children, whether they are refugees, asylum seekers or economic migrants. According to UNICEF (2016) we are witnessing the largest movement of children since the Second World War: nearly 50 million children have migrated across borders or have been forcibly displaced. More than half of that number (28 million) have fled violence and insecurity. They are amongst the most vulnerable people in the world today. In 2015, nearly half the child refugees came from just two countries, Afghanistan and Syria. A disproportionate number is admitted to Germany and far too few to the United Kingdom. The United States has 3.7 million child migrants, more than anywhere else. Many are unaccompanied, all of them are vulnerable to exploitation and abuse. Many are victims of trafficking. As we have seen, international law was slow to recognise children: it has been even slower in acknowledging the migrant child. It should not have been so. CRC, Article 2 imposes an obligation on states parties to treat all children as rights-bearers, irrespective of their status. Article 22 gives asylum-seeker children the same rights as refugees (their status under the Refugees Convention and its Protocol notwithstanding).

The CRC offers a variety of protections to the migrant child. Most obviously, because they are children, the best interests principle in Article 3 applies. The UN Committee on the Rights of the Child accepts that the child's best interests are only a primary consideration, not the paramount consideration, a conclusion readily seized upon by Australian courts (*Teoh*, 1995). Nevertheless, it does mean that children's interests are prioritised (*Marion*'s case, 1992). This is morally compelling given the experiences children on the move have; being trafficked, sold into slavery, forced into marriage, coerced into prostitution, and often losing educational opportunities and therefore frustrating future life chances. That the drafters were aware of this is reflected in the fact that the only provisions in the CRC which make the child's best interests paramount both have resonance for migrant children, namely adoption (Article 21), and separation from parents (Article 9).

There are several other provisions in the CRC which should protect the migrant child. Article 6 articulates an 'inherent right to life', which may come as a shock to those involved in the drama on the Mediterranean. This article emphasises the importance of survival and development, but in all the discussion about closing our doors and of letting them drown, etc.,

I have heard nothing of Article 6. Also significant is Article 11(1), which targets the 'illicit transfer and non-return of children abroad'. As are Articles 19 and 20, the latter of which deals with the protection of children who are deprived of family environment, temporarily or permanently. There are special protections for refugee children: see Article 22(c). The right to be protected from economic exploitation (trafficking and the sale of children, Article 32), and from the harms caused by illicit drugs (Article 33) are potentially valuable to children with disabilities. Sexual exploitation is targeted by Article 34. Anything omitted is swept up in 'all other forms of exploitation prejudicial to any aspects of a child's welfare' (Article 36). The first two Optional Protocols, the first dealing with the sale of children, child pornography and child prostitution, the second with the involvement of children in armed conflict, are also valuable protective instruments.

The structure is thus there for migrant children to be treated comparably with children from the home state. Why then are there so many gaps and shortfalls in practice?

The first problem is the identification of children who are at risk. Many of the children will come without documentation. It is common for there to be a dispute as to the child's age. The critical boundary is eighteen. Above eighteen, the CRC does not apply. Below eighteen, it does. In the United Kingdom, an asylum seeker identified as a child is diverted into the care of child protection authorities, and if assessed as at risk will in normal circumstances be placed in care until they attain majority. Sadly, most are then returned to their 'home' country, although they have by then integrated into British society; in 2014, 6,000 were returned to Afghanistan to await uncertain futures, a blot on our humanity, but a policy unlikely to be reversed.

With so much hinging on whether the young person is under eighteen or not, the methods used for age assessment have come under scrutiny, and wisely so. Estimates are made on the basis of appearance, or by using bone scans in some countries, for example, the United States and Australia (Bhabha and Crock, 2007; Crock, 2006). Rather more sophisticated procedures using 'holistic methodologies' (Crock, 2006) operate in the United Kingdom, involving age assessments by a range of professionals, whose task is to evaluate physical, cognitive and psycho-social development indicators. European countries also favour the use of experts, and a holistic approach to a child's state of development (Office of High Commissioner for Human Rights and UNICEF, 2012). The UNHCR Guidelines (1997) require the benefit of doubt to be given to the child if the exact age is uncertain.

A further concern is that immigration officials do not always spot that a child is the victim of trafficking or smuggling. In theory, they should be able to do so. With the use of profiling and statistical data from law enforcement, in the United Kingdom they are trained to identify child migrants at risk. The CRC, and the UN Convention Against Transnational Organised Crime, establish important safeguards to protect children who are victims of trafficking or other forms of transnational organised crime. Such children are to be cared for through the 'lens of child protection, not the criminal law'.

States often do not observe this obligation. They commonly detain children whom they designate as 'irregular' or find to be undocumented.

The conditions in which these young persons are detained are unacceptably low. There have been suicides. It is clear that detaining children in prison-like facilities is a flagrant breach of international standards, including those in the CRC. The policies pursued are in striking contrast to those to protect 'Kindertransport' children escaping Nazi Europe in 1939.

Whether the age of criminal responsibility could be tinkered with without considering evidence from neuroscience is also contentious. As neuroscience hints at raising the minimum age of criminal responsibility, English law in effect lowered it when in 1998 it disposed of 600 years of history and abolished the *doli incapax* presumption. It was motivated to do this by a moral panic caused by the *Bulger* case in 1993.

Work/Education Conundrum

It seems so obvious to us in the Global North that education to as high a level as possible should be pursued as a goal and that work should not get in the way of this. We have raised the school-leaving age in Britain to eighteen: it was sixteen not very long ago.

One of the main impetuses behind the establishment of the International Labour Organisation (ILO) (Alcock, 1971) was to improve the working conditions of children, but it was only in 1973 that it decided to take the initiative in combating child labour. ILO Convention No. 138 tried to lay down a minimum age for admission to employment as a universal standard, though it added several flexibility clauses to accommodate the needs of less-developed economies. But it was perceived by many that it reflected the culture, needs and traditions of the wealthier Global North, and there were few ratifications.

Interest in child labour was rekindled by the CRC, Article 32 of which emphasised that children were to be protected from 'economic exploitation' and 'any work. . .likely to be hazardous or to interfere with the child's education, or to be harmful to the child's health or physical, mental, spiritual, moral or social development'.

It is significant that a shift was made in the CRC from seeing children's work as a matter of labour regulation to situating it within human rights (Cullen, 2007). The CRC, implicitly at least, distinguished permissible and unacceptable child labour. The distinction was subsequently articulated by the International Programme for the Elimination of Child Labour when, a few years later, it differentiated 'child labour' from 'child work', the one benign, the other deleterious, and thus to be rooted out (White, 1999).

This distinction has now found its way into ILO Convention No. 182, adopted in 1999. This is one of the most swiftly ratified of all ILO Conventions. Ratifying states are required to target the worst forms of child labour as a matter of urgency. 'Child' is defined as a person under the age of eighteen, as would have been expected. This reflects, however, the thinking of the more prosperous parts of the world.

The key provision is Article 3; this lists the types of work which are prohibited. Some are obvious, such as slavery and trafficking as well as compulsory labour, including compulsory recruitment into the armed forces; others, perhaps a little less so, for example prostitution, the production of pornography. 'Hazardous work' is not defined, but Recommendation 190 attempts one. It is defined there as:

> work which exposes children to physical, psychological or sexual abuse, work underground, under water, at dangerous heights or in confined spaces; work with, dangerous machinery, equipment or tools, or which involves the manual handling or transport of heavy loads, work in an unhealthy environment. . .work under particularly difficult conditions, such as work for long hours or during the night.

The Convention also emphasises the 'importance of education in eliminating child labour' (Article 7(2)). It speaks of the rehabilitation and social integration of working children, and, where appropriate, vocational training for those removed from the worst forms of labour. It also envisages account to be taken of 'the special situation of girls' (ibid.).

What has been the impact of ILO Convention No. 182 (Fodella, 2008)? There have been some positive results. Was the ILO simplistic or merely being over-optimistic, when it announced in 2006 that 'it is within our capacity to make this "a world without child labour?"' (ILO, 2006: ix). And is the answer an end to child labour? Is this perhaps just another example of Global North speak? And of those on 'top' imposing a solution on those at 'the bottom' that they believe to be good for them?

A large majority of countries have adopted legislation, or amended existing legislation, either just before or soon after ratifying the Convention, to prohibit trafficking in persons or children under eighteen. The ILO CEACR records that such legislative measures were nearly always accompanied by the introduction of stiffer penalties. And similar measures have been taken by many countries to target prostitution and pornography. It is worthy of note that the CEACR has requested countries to extend the prohibition on the commercial exploitation of children to boys, where it had only applied to girls. The CEACR has asked some countries to introduce legislation to target the client of a child prostitute.

As far as 'hazardous work' is concerned, since the concept is itself open-textured, what constitutes that which can be regarded as the worst form of child labour is left to the discretion of Member States. But it is significant that many countries have legislated what activities or occupations can be so regarded. Of course, the legislation is far from uniform. The CEACR has on occasions requested countries to adopt measures to prohibit children under eighteen from engaging in types of work it considers to be hazardous. It did this in relation to children employed as camel jockeys in Qatar and the United Arab Emirates, and as horse jockeys in Mongolia. Also encouraging is the large number of countries which have adopted Programmes or Plans of Action to tackle one or more of the worst forms of child labour, for example, sub-regional projects in Cambodia and China dealing with the trafficking of children for sexual exploitation.

There are also sub-regional programmes aimed at withdrawing children from commercial sexual exploitation and integrating them into school, whilst importantly providing economic alternatives to the families who, as a result, are deprived of a wage-earner. Such a project exists among the main Anglophone countries of West and East Africa. There are also National Plans of Action, including ones to protect and rehabilitate young victims and punish those who have victimised them. Some countries have also adopted measures to combat child pornography on the Internet (Livingstone and O'Neill, 2014). There are Action Plans to criminalise the sale, production and possession of child pornography. There are also seminars organised to train teachers, school psychiatrists, police and magistrates about the Internet-related risks of sexual exploitation. Measures have also been taken by countries to combat the worrying increase in the virulent malaise of child sex tourism.

Some progress has also been made in relation to hazardous work. The CEACR reports many countries, and many measures, including time-bound programmes (TBPs), to prevent the employment of children under eighteen in hazardous work, as well as to provide for the rehabilitation of such children, where they have been so engaged. In some areas TBPs prioritise certain forms of hazardous work, such as hazardous agricultural activities and hazardous work in the urban informal economy. In others, specific sectors are targeted, for example, the construction industry, the manufacture of fireworks, sugar cane plantations. Indeed, a whole plethora of other examples can be found, such as deep-sea fishing in Indonesia, carpet-weaving in Nepal, seafood processing in Pakistan. In terms of numbers of children involved, the CEACR reports places where substantial withdrawals have taken place. For example, the report on El Salvador notes that nearly 30,000 children were prevented from engaging in hazardous work as a result of TBPs.

The quoted statistics, and thus mainstream opinion which heavily relies on these, and the data thus far given, offers reasons for optimism. Thus, in 2000, just after the promulgation of ILO Convention No. 182, the number of economically active children aged five to fourteen years was estimated to be 211 million. By 2004 there had been a decrease of 11 per cent.

Most of the identified progress occurred in South America, where the number of working children dropped from 17.4 million in 2000 to 5.7 million in 2004, a decline in the activity rate from 16.1 to only 5.1 per cent. The decreases in Asia and the Pacific and in sub-Saharan Africa fell in the same period only marginally: from 19.4 to 18.8 million in the former; from 28.8 to 26.4 million in the latter.

Have children been consulted? All the initiatives discussed thus far have been adult-led. Where does Article 12 of the CRC fit in? Does it give children a role in unpacking the work/education dilemma? The evidence from sociology and anthropology is that children create their own worlds rather than accept a world imposed upon them (Mayall, 1994).

Should we therefore pay more attention to how children perceive their own experiences? There are a number of studies on children's meanings of work. We have evidence from a number of European countries, including Britain, Germany, Italy and Scandinavia, from South America and from Africa. There is, for example, important research about Germany (Hungerland et al., 2007). This found that work was not perceived first and foremost as a social problem that had to be tackled, rather as an example of where children needed to be taken seriously 'as reflective, active subjects in all imaginable aspects of their lives' (2007: 258).

Mainstream thinking can easily gloss over this. Judith Ennew (2002) noted that in the developing world 'children have economic and other responsibilities to fulfil within families and communities'. Work can be seen as a learning experience, where knowledge and skills to enable them to live and interact in the societies of which they are a part are cultivated. There is a vast difference between working in the fields with parents and extended family, and 'arduous labour in sweatshops to service the needs of the developed world' – needs which will increase as the demand for more and more £1 shops increases with austerity.

Work can be part of a child's identity. So, 'listening to children's feelings, perceptions and views is an essential source of evidence on the way work affects their development, especially psychosocial aspects of development' (Ennew, 2002). We tend to use the language of 'hazard' and 'harm', but we must not ignore children's perceptions of this.

In the light of this, two related developments must be noted: the growth of working children's social movements and organisations; and legislative attempts, notably one in Bolivia in 2003 (Liebel, 2015), to take the exploitation out of children's work by paying a living wage.

All the initiatives thus far discussed have been adult-led. But we must not overlook Article 12 of the CRC. Has it had any impact on this work/education relationship? Can children act as change-makers? There is evidence of their doing so. The growth of working children's social movements and organisations is significant (Liebel, Overwien and Recknagel, 2001). These leave us in no doubt that working children can speak out for themselves. The organisations that have developed consist mainly of children between the ages of twelve and sixteen. Most of these children work under conditions which violate their human dignity and hinder their development. They claim rights modelled, it would seem, on the CRC, but tailored to their situations. Manfred Liebel (2004) quotes the 'twelve rights' formulated by the West African Children's organisations in 1994 as an example. A number of demands are set out:

the right to vocational training in order to learn a job;
the right to stay in the village and not move away;
the right to carry out our activities safely;
the right to access to fair justice in case of problems;
the right to sick leave;
the right to be respected;
the right to be listened to;
the right to a light and limited type of work, adapted to our
    ages and abilities;
the right to have health care;
the right to learn to read and write;
the right to express ourselves and organise ourselves. (Liebel,
    2004, 2007)

Liebel (2004) notes that 'In Latin America and in Africa, a right is demanded which is not included in the CRC, namely the right to work'. These children see themselves as individuals who can design their lives and who can contribute something to society. There have been a number of Mini World Summits of Working Children. One held in Dakar in 1998 proposed that all the world's children should one day be able to decide whether they worked or not. There is the danger of 'double marginalisation' (Liebel, 2004): the child/adolescent denied citizenship rights and unable to participate in the organisation of society, and the worker as devalued, and more so because regarded as a lesser being. The organisations respond to this by insisting not only on questions affecting them, but on being able 'actively to co-decide'. As an example, they have demanded a seat and a voice on ILO Committees. This is a challenge to dominant views of children and childhood, even to those held by norm-setting bodies like the United Nations and the ILO.

As is the recent Bolivian legislation (Ley 548 Codigo Nino, Nina y Adolescentes, 2014; Liebel, 2015). It is described by Liebel as 'the first law in the world to have come into existence with a decisive input from children' (Liebel, 2014: 491). Others regard it as a backward step. It is estimated that 800,000 children, 491,000 of whom are under fourteen, work in Bolivia, that is about one in four of the child population.

The Code is designed to ensure that children who work are not exploited. All children and adolescents (from the age of twelve) working for an employer have the right to social security. Adolescents must not be treated less favourably than adults. An example of this, outside labour law, is the provision in the 2008 Constitution (Article 16(a)) prohibiting any kind of violence against children, in the family or in society.

With the establishment of a union of working children and adolescents in Bolivia in 2003, the claim for a right to work was articulated, not an easy claim to formulate in the face of opposition from international bodies and orthodox thinking. Liebel explains (2015: 594) that 'the Code tries to reconcile the

ILO Conventions on Child Labour, which aim at putting a comprehensive prohibition into practice, with the fact that the work of hundreds of thousands of children is a reality in a wide variety of forms and contexts in Bolivia'.

If children are going to work anyway, then the Bolivian model is attractive. But as a solution it looks to be rather short-term, even short-sighted. Can we really be sure that whatever the protections, children will not be exploited, treated harshly, even abused? And does this expedient not offer them a closed future, with little or no opportunity to seek a better life?

(ii) Agency and Children's Right to Participate

The welfare paradigm, which sees children as lacking the capacity and maturity to understand and assert their own needs, has been challenged by new paradigms, including children's rights and children as social actors and citizens. Within these new paradigms, children are no longer seen as dependent, vulnerable, at-risk victims of divorce and passive objects of law, but are seen as subjects with agency (Hunter, 2007: 237).

Agency

Agency is often referred to as the capacity to choose, act and influence. Ruth Lister (2004: 39) sees agency as a 'conscious capacity influenced by self-identity'. It is linked to citizenship. It is much more than just acting and influencing. It is a concept involving complex awareness of spatial and temporal responsibilities, multiple belongings, and the negotiation of capacity through other eyes (Mentha, Church and Page, 2015). An important factor is the ascription of capacity: how others perceive us to be. This is particularly significant in the context of children, especially young children.

Agency is at the core of identity. 'Identity' has been defined as 'an agentic core of personality' (Nsamenang, 2006: 6). It is through this that individuals situate themselves as among and against (ibid.). Only relatively recently have we come to recognise the agency of children. Children were 'becomings', not 'beings'. In the opinion of the leading sociologist of children, Berry Mayall (2002: 3), children were defined: they did not define (Hunter, 2007: 283).

Participation

Without agency there can be no participation, and participation is key to the enforcement of rights.

The right to participate is one of the four General Principles in the Convention on the Rights of the Child (United Nations, 1989). The key provision is Article 12(1) which states:

> States Parties shall assure to the child who is capable of forming his or her views the right to express those views freely in all matters affecting the child, the views of the child being given due weight in accordance with the age and maturity of the child. (See above, p. 117.)

There was little discussion of the agency of children until relatively recently, as we have seen. That children have rights is still contested by philosophers like Onora O'Neill and Harry Brighouse, and lawyers such as Michael King and Martin Guggenheim. Sociologists/anthropologists, such as Olga Nieuwenhuys and Karl Hanson have been critical of the decontextualized way in which state responsibilities and also legal procedures are discussed in the literature. Despite this, the recognition of the agency of children has deep roots. Plato understood it, as did the authors of *Genesis*, the New Testament and the *Qur'an* (see Wall, 2010).

Wyness (2013) stresses that there are five emerging narratives in the literature about children and young people's participation:

(1) participation can be seen as embedded in children's 'everyday lives', routine and ongoing rather than exceptional and event-based;

(2) participation is relational, enacted and created with others, rather than reifying the individual person with agency;

(3) participation is recognised as emotional and embodied, rather than solely rational and intellectual;

(4) participation is material as well as political, including the economic; and

(5) the distribution of participation should be considered, in how it follows or creates (in)equalities, identities and differences.

General Comment No. 12 (CRC Committee, 2009) stresses that children have the right to be heard as individuals and as a group of children. In its analysis of Article 12, the General Comment emphasises some of its implications:

- Children's rights under Article 12 are not discretionary.
- A child should be presumed to have the capacity to form a view. It is not for the child to prove this capacity. The right to express a view has no age threshold and a child need not have comprehensive knowledge to be considered capable.
- Non-verbal communication should be recognised as expressing a view just as verbal communication.
- Children should be supported to enable them to participate – and they may well need information to clarify their views and assistance to express them. They should be able to express their views 'freely', without being unduly influenced or pressured.
- The ambit of Article 12 is wide, relating to 'all matters affecting' the child and not just those where a right is specified in the Convention. The child's views must be given 'due weight', that is, to be considered seriously when the child is capable of forming a view.
- Children should have feedback on how their views have been taken into consideration. (CRC Committee, 2009: 3)

In providing this literal analysis of Article 12, the UN Committee on the Rights of the Child implicitly addresses many of the challenges faced in trying to implement children's and young people's participation (see Lansdown, 2010; Tisdall, 2014). The Committee emphasises that *all* children have the right to participate (and not just older children or articulate children); that they should be supported to do so; that their views should be weighed seriously in decision-making; and that they should know what has happened to their input.

The term participation has evolved and is now widely used to describe ongoing processes, which include information-sharing and dialogue between children and adults based on mutual respect, and in which children can learn how their views and those of adults are taken into account and shape the outcome of such processes.

The CRC Committee has also recognised the right to participate effectively in trials and that the child needs to comprehend the charges, and possible consequences and penalties, in order to direct the legal representative to challenge witnesses, to provide an account of events, and to make appropriate decisions about evidence, testimony and the measure(s) to be imposed (CRC Committee, 2007: para. 46). The Committee adds that '(t)aking into account the child's age and maturity may also require modified courtroom procedures and practices' (2007: para. 46). The Committee has also provided further guidance on the significance of Article 12 for criminal justice proceedings in its General Comment No. 12 on the child's right to be heard. It observed that 'a child cannot be heard effectively where the environment is intimidating, hostile, insensitive or inappropriate for her or his age' and that '[p]roceedings must both be accessible and child-appropriate', which means that '(p)articular attention needs to be paid to the provision and delivery of child-friendly information, adequate support for self-advocacy, appropriately trained staff, design of court rooms, clothing of judges and lawyers' (CRC Committee, 2009: para. 34). It held with regard to the juvenile justice context that '(i)n order to effectively participate in the proceedings, every child must be informed promptly and directly about the charges against her or him in a language she or he understands, and also about the juvenile justice process and possible measures taken by the court' (CRC Committee, 2009: para. 60). 'The proceedings should be conducted in an atmosphere enabling the child to participate and to express her/ himself freely' and '(t)he court and other hearings of a child in conflict with the law should be conducted behind closed doors' (2009: paras 60–1).

The broad remit of the principle was affirmed by the Committee on the Rights of the Child in its General Day of Discussion in 2006. Article 12 was described as a 'new social contract', which recognises the right of children to speak, to participate and to have their views taken into account (CRC Committee, 2006). The Committee has also highlighted the relevance of Article 12 to health care decision-making. For older children, the General Comment on Adolescent Health and Development recognised that the right to express views freely and have them taken into account is fundamental to achieving adolescents' right to health and development. The Committee has also noted that the Convention requires states to ensure that young people have opportunities to participate in decisions affecting their health and to obtain adequate and age-appropriate information (CRC Committee, 2003). In its General Comment on Implementing Child Rights in Early Childhood (CRC Committee, 2005) it stressed the right to express views and feelings and that these should be 'anchored in the child's daily life at home and in his/her community; within the full range of early childhood health, care and education facilities'. This requires adults to adopt a child-centred attitude, listening to young children and respecting their individual points of view. Adults must show 'patience and creativity by adapting their expectations to a young child's interests, level of understanding and preferred ways of communicating'. The germ of a child-friendly approval can be detected here. It stressed here that younger children have the right.

Gillick *Case*

In England the right of participation can be traced to the *Gillick* case in 1986. The House of Lords held that 'parental right yields to the child's right to make his own decisions when he reaches a sufficient understanding and intelligence to be capable of making up his own mind on the matter requiring decision' (*per* Lord Scarman, ibid.: 189). The initial impression is that English law thus complies with Article 12. So, a child, admittedly after leave from a court, can apply for a child arrangement order; courts making decisions about a child's upbringing, albeit in a limited range of circumstances, are required to have regard to the 'ascertainable wishes and feelings of the child concerned', in the light of that child's age and understanding (Children Act 1989, section 1(3)(a)); before making any decision with respect to a child whom they are looking after or proposing to look after, a local authority is required to ascertain the wishes and feelings of that child, so far as that is reasonably practicable (Children Act 1989, section 22(4)). There is a range of provisions in the Children Act 1989 permitting a child of sufficient understanding to make an informed decision, and giving a child the right to refuse to submit to a medical or psychiatric examination or other assessment where one of a number of protection orders is being sought (see Children Act 1989, section 22).

Conceptual Autonomy

The importance of 'conceptual autonomy' was recognised first by Barrie Thorne (1987). It was explained by Jens Qvortrup (1991) thus:

> In a world dominated by adult interests and with adults having the power of definition, children are supposed to become autonomous. . .it is a precondition for knowing about children's own life situation, that they become liberated from adult-centred categorizations and be given conceptual autonomy. (Qvortrup, 1991: 17)

The importance of appreciating this is all too easy to overlook. We may take an interest in whether children regard a particular activity as harmful to them, but assume our concept of harm is the same as theirs. Our slapstick may be defined by them as 'violence', and thus within the Article 19. Our postponement of punishment for the weekend may be defined by us as sensible cooling-off time, but to a child it may be torture, and thus also encompassed by Article 19. Hanson (2015: 431) sees the Third Protocol (above, p. 48) as 'a symbolically significant marker of children's conceptual autonomy'. But it was adult initiative which saw a complaints procedure eventuate, not demands from children or children's groups. Litigious competence comes with confidence that the legal system is on our side and works for us. Carlin, Howard and Messinger explain that a competent subject will take initiative and will see the law (here the CRC) 'as a resource for developing, furthering and protecting his interests' (1966: 70; see also Friedman, 1971).

The main instrumental value of the Third Protocol may be as a further string to the bow of NGOs keen to develop children's rights, rather than specifically for children themselves.

Civil and Political Rights

The Convention also recognises that the child has some basic civil and political rights. In much of the world, no one has rights of free expression, freedom of assembly, freedom of association, etc., and therefore extending these rights to children will achieve very little.

Freedom of Expression

As far as freedom of expression is concerned, neither the 1924 nor the 1959 Declaration refers at all to this right. The US Supreme Court did in *Tinker* v. *Des Moines*, but this decision was soon being distinguished. Thus, we can see the provision in CRC, Article 13 as a radical innovation. It does not recognise total freedom of expression. Article 17(e) places a duty on states parties to encourage the development of guidelines to protect children from material that may harm them. The sort of injurious material they may have had in mind is illustrated by *The Little Red Schoolbook* case in 1978 (*Handyside* v. *United Kingdom*). The publisher claimed that his right to freedom of expression had been breached by the United Kingdom seizing and destroying copies of the book. The book was intended for children aged twelve upwards. It contained information on sex and contraception. The UK government argued that the infringement was necessary in a democracy to protect morals. The ECtHR concluded that there was a margin of appreciation to permit the banning of a book. This is top to bottom jurisprudence at its most discriminatory. It eats into freedom of expression with a vengeance. It prioritises welfare, or one view of this, over rights. What if the applicant had been a sixteen-year-old adolescent? Would the court have approached the case differently? But should it take a paternalist view when the challenger is an adolescent?

Freedom of Thought, Conscience and Religion

There is no right which illustrates better the inherent dignity of man than freedom of thought, conscience and religion. Article 14 of the CRC provides that states parties shall respect the right of a child to these freedoms. There has only been limited discussion of them, because traditionally they were seen more as parental rights relating to a child's upbringing (Langlaude, 2007). More states parties have expressed reservations to Article 14 than to any other article in the CRC (Scolnicov, 2011: 150). There is some irony in this, because as Mill (1859) pointed out, religious freedoms were the first to take root. Why reservations are allowed despite being incompatible with the object and purpose of the CRC is not puzzling. It is largely a concession to Islamic nations which do not accept freedom of religion.

Freedom of Religion

The Convention does not give the child a right to choose his/her religion (Detrick, 1992: 26). This might be a convenient lacuna, or a question deliberately left open for interpretation in the light of Article 18 of the International Covenant on Civil and Political Rights (ICCPR).

Religious Identity

This is determined at birth, and reinforced in the educational process. Thus, it is significant that the ECHR recognises in its First Protocol the importance of states respecting the rights of parents to ensure education and teaching in conformity with their educational and philosophic conviction. It is clear that it is parents' rights that are the concern. Children's rights (not surprisingly) were passed over in early 1950s' documents. Parents relied on philosophic convictions, unsuccessfully, in the well-known *Williamson* case (discussed above, p. 45). But why a belief in hitting children should be thought a 'philosophic' conviction escapes me! It should be stressed that we are talking of parents' convictions, and not children's. Where adolescents are concerned, this may be of significance. Some will wish to forge a new religious identity. Many more will reject religion altogether. Many will be brainwashed by their education, others by proselytising organisations such as Jews for Jesus. This makes Justice Douglas' concern in *Wisconsin* v. *Yoder* (1972) (below, p. 192) unrealistic – once an Amish, always an Amish!

Once, the right to exercise religious freedom was invoked only in curriculum disputes and similar conflicts. Now it is felt most acutely when Muslim adolescent girls invoke the right, as they see it, to dress as their religion requires. So, a pupil in Luton wanted to wear a jilbab to school. This full covering was not acceptable to the head teacher, who decided that the girl should wear an alternative which was acceptable to mainstream Islam (and apparently had been to this pupil, when she joined the school at the age of eleven). Only Lady Hale of the judges in the House of Lords seemed to appreciate that a little girl had become a young woman (she was now fourteen), and was more conscious of her body. She was not to be estopped from changing her view of the correct attire. But the House of Lords decided that it was within the legitimate discretion of the head teacher to decide, as she had done, on a school uniform, which met the requirements of mainstream Islam and which did not threaten or pressurise other girls as the jilbab may do (see *Begum*, 2006).

Freedom of Association and Assembly

Freedom of association and of assembly are set out in separate articles in the CRC, but they are closely related. Together, they enable children and especially adolescents to participate in group activity. Freedom of association enables child workers to form trade unions. But it is not limited in this way; street children have successfully used Article 14. Does it extend beyond the political to include social and cultural associations? Similar words in the ICCPR were given the widest interpretation by the Privy Council in *Collymore* (1967): they may be 'religious or social, political or philosophical, economic or professional, educational or cultural, sporting or charitable'. Polonius could not do better! (see *Hamlet*, II, ii, 392–6).

Freedom of peaceful assembly can only be restricted in the interests of national security or public safety, public order and the protection of public health or morals, or in order to protect the rights and interests of others.

(iii) Children's Provision Rights

Education

Education, it has been said, should be available, accessible, acceptable and adaptable (Tomaševski, 2004).

The Convention devotes two Articles to education, the only right given more than a single article. The first of these, Article 28, distinguishes three levels of education, primary, secondary, and higher and vocational (a unique example of extension of childhood beyond eighteen). The states parties' obligations are different as regards each level: they get progressively less. The Article mainly addresses access. The second article, Article 29, prescribes standards relating to the content of education. It focuses on the goals of education.

We need to distinguish a right to education and rights in education (Lundy, 2012). A right to education, though clearly one of the most important child rights, is a right which has huge implications for adults, particularly parents, who are relieved of their children for 200 days a year and who know, or expect, that their children will be 'socialised' by teachers, even if theirs is the primary obligation; and also for society as a whole, the prosperity and stability of which depends on an educated population (Lansdown, 2001).

Education can also be seen as a 'conduit' for other human rights (McCowan, 2012). But school is also a site where children may experience violence and humiliation at the hands of teachers and fellow pupils. The cane has passed into history in England, finally being removed from English schools in 1998, but bullying remains endemic. In the United States, corporal punishment remains lawful (*Ingraham* v. *Wright*, 1977). An attempt to outlaw it in 2011 failed (Lenzer, 2015: 286). Corporal punishment is still commonplace in Asia. It remains a method of punishment in seventy-one countries. A poll conducted for the *Times Educational Supplement* in 2015 discovered that 40 per cent of parents and 14 per cent of pupils thought the cane or the slipper should be reintroduced in English schools. The Convention (Articles 19 and 37, as well as the 'best interests' principle in Article 3) makes it clear that this is unacceptable, and the Committee on the Rights of the Child is routinely critical of the practice wherever it exists. Of course, it is denied an opportunity to condemn the United States, which is not a state party (Freeman, 2014; Freeman and Saunders, 2014; Saunders and Goddard, 2010).

Education rights can be seen as relating to access, content and relations within education (Quennerstedt, 2011). What is understood by the right to education should be straightforward. But it raises many questions. Is it about access to educational institutions, schools, academies, etc.? To a particular form of educational experience? Does learning the Koran by rote satisfy this criterion? Is a Yeshiva diet of the Talmud in Yiddish enough? Do they foreclose a child's right to an 'open future'? (Feinberg, 1980). Or is this just an illusory ideal anyway? Should all forms of enhancement be disallowed? Does this include education itself? Does it depend upon how we define education?

A number of authorities have stressed how important it is to distinguish quantitative and qualitative questions when discussing the right to education (Beeckman, 2004; McCowan, 2010). Examples of the former include whether there are enough places and whether they are accessible to all children.

In 2012, 58 million primary school-aged children were not in school (UNESCO, 2015). It is important that schools are free; the best schools may be prohibitively expensive. Not surprisingly, children most likely not to be in school are poor, live in less developed countries, or are girls. Many meet two or even three of these criteria. Worldwide, 92 per cent of boys of primary age and 90 per cent of girls are enrolled in school. In the least developed countries, the numbers fall to 83 per cent and 79 per cent, respectively (UNESCO, 2014).

The latter relates to standards; do the local schools provide a good learning environment? Quantitative and qualitative issues cannot always be separated. As an example, consider the way English schools did, and some still do, decide at eleven whether a child should get an academic education, or one which is more vocational. The school place allocated depended upon an examination only partly, because another consideration was availability of places. Geography could count for as much as performance in an examination. (I failed the 11-plus!)

Katrien Beeckman (2004) notes that measurement of the extent to which the right to education has been implemented has usually concentrated on the quantitative, mainly on access questions, so that where qualitative questions are addressed they are translated into quantitative answers. She maintains that 'measuring the human right to education calls for the development of rights-based indicators, capable of reflecting the norms, principles and values underpinning human rights in general, and the right to education particularly', for example, whether teaching and learning processes are open, interactive and participatory.

The right to education raises many questions. To what education? The CRC emphasises 'primary' education, UNESCO (2000) 'basic' education. Is there a distinction? Is 'basic' pre-primary (Herczog, 2012)? Or just included within it?

How does one weigh parents' rights against those of their children? How relevant is Article 12? Look at the celebrated US Supreme Court case of *Wisconsin* v. *Yoder* in 1972. Amish parents saw no need for their children to attend school after the age of fourteen. Thereafter, they would imbibe the Amish way of life on the farm – a version of home schooling. Mr Justice Douglas spoke to the children and concluded that this view was shared by them. But what if a child had disagreed with the parents? To what extent should notice have been taken of his/her view? The Supreme Court upheld the parents' claim. Chief Justice Burger explained: 'the primary role of the parents in the upbringing of their children is now established beyond debate as an enduring American tradition' (ibid.: 232). But it is Mr Justice Douglas' partial dissent which holds the greatest interest. He wrote:

> It is the future of the student, not the state or the parents, that is imperilled by today's decision. If a parent keeps his child out of school. . .then the child will be forever barred from entry into the new and amazing world of diversity that we have today. The child may decide that this is the preferred course, or he may rebel. It is the student's judgment, not his parents', that is essential. . .if he is harnessed to the Amish way of life his entire life may be stunted and deformed. The child, therefore, should be given an opportunity to be heard before the State gives the exemption which we honor today. (Ibid.: 244–5)

There is a potentiality for conflict also where parents allow their religious convictions to take precedence over their child's best interests. There are faith schools and faith schools. Some are open to a plurality of viewpoints, others have closed minds and, to take one example, refuse to acknowledge evolution. There are schools in London today which teach children that the world was created by 'g-d' (children aren't even allowed to spell his/her name fully) in six days about 6,000 years ago. These include state schools, many with excellent secular education, and they have charitable status with the tax advantages which accompany this. A child's right to education should be valued because it opens their minds, not because it fills them with nonsense. A school which taught that the Holocaust hadn't happened would be closed down, its teachers sacked, never allowed to teach again.

The right of children with disabilities to education raises important issues. The CRC neglected them, and many of the issues which it should have addressed were taken up in the Disabilities Convention in 2006 (Sabatello, 2013). Before this, there was the Jonntien Declaration (UNESCO, 1990) which signalled the beginning of a turnaround in international attitudes to vulnerable groups of children, recognizing that they too had human rights. The implications of this for children with special educational needs were developed in the Salamanca Declaration in 1994 (UNESCO, 1994). In place of segregation, the thrust was towards inclusive education and this became the dominant model in many countries. Nevertheless, children with disabilities remain a group apart, deviant and discriminated against (Allan, 2010). The goal may be inclusion within mainstream schooling, but many still remain in special schools. There are presumably cases where there is some conflict between parents and their children, one opting for mainstream, the other for special schooling, but I have not seen any research on this.

Health

Article 24 of the Convention recognises that children have the right to the highest attainable standard of health, to facilities for the treatment of disease, and to access to health care services. But these services may be inaccessible, expensive or the quality may be poor. Standards in the Global South may be badly affected by the loss of doctors and nurses to the Global North. The CRC is curiously silent about what the right to health in Article 24 involves. It also evades addressing many of the truly difficult questions, such as the child as a research subject, the child and consent to medical treatment and, more controversially, whether the child can refuse medical treatment. Mortality rates in the developing world are improving, but they are still grossly disproportionate in comparison to those in the developed world. Health care in the developing world is constrained by poverty, famine and drought. Children's rights to health are not only rights in themselves, but without them many other rights would falter.

Although the focus is naturally on Article 24, a number of other Articles are relevant to the issue of health. Pre-eminent amongst them is Article 6, which recognises the child's right to life, and to survival and development to the maximum extent possible. In 2013, the Committee on the Rights of the Child stressed that the 'many risks and protective factors that underlie the life, survival, growth and development of the child need to be systematically identified in order to design and implement evidence-informed interventions that address a wide range of determinants during the life course' (General Comment No. 15: 6). Also highly significant are Articles 2 and 3, referring to non-discrimination and best interests respectively (and see above, pp. 93 and 137). Nor should the importance of Article 12 on child's participatory rights be overlooked: it has importance on two levels. First, it requires that children have input into the development of health care policy (CRC Committee, 2009: 20), and on the planning and implementation of health care services. Secondly, it makes us come to terms with including children in decision-making about their own health. The work of Priscilla Alderson (1990, 2008, 2014) is most reassuring and enlightening. The CRC Committee (2009: 20) is also supportive, stressing that children should be included in decision-making processes as their capacities evolve. The research of Myra Bluebond-Langner on dying children is also eye-opening (1978) (see also above, p. 121). The ideal of Article 12 can only work if children are given information about proposed treatments and their effects and outcomes (Kilkelly and Donnelly, 2011).

Since the CRC, the Council of Europe (2001) has got to grips with health care and children. Its Guidelines prescribe 'health care policy and practice' centred on children's rights, needs, characteristics, assets and evolving capacities, taking into account their own opinion. Children who come into contact with the health care system retain their Convention rights to education, privacy, play, rest and leisure, contact with parents, etc. They have the right to be protected from abuse, sadly a right breached quite commonly, it would appear from a number of recent revelations. A particularly bad example is the case of Myles Bradbury, a cancer specialist at Addenbrooke's hospital in Cambridge, who abused young cancer patients (*The Times*, 2 December 2014). The judge described his conduct as a 'gross and grotesque breach of trust'. They have the right to be protected from exploitation. They have the right to religious freedom: this becomes contentious when its exercise is harmful to what we consider the child's best interests (the Jehovah's Witness child who is refusing a blood transfusion, for example, and see above, p. 62).

Issues on Traditional Practices

The Convention addresses one aspect of this in a separate paragraph. Article 24(3) requires states to take 'all effective measures' to abolish traditional practices prejudicial to the health of the children. The CRC gives no examples; it was easier to achieve consensus by leaving it open. But it was FGM that was the main concern of the drafters of Article 24(3). This is endemic in the Horn of Africa and is common among Muslims, many of whom believe it is a Koranic injunction – it is not (Slack, 1988). The practice is commonly perpetrated on young girls between the ages of three and eight. It is found primarily in areas where there is considerable poverty, where hunger, insanitary conditions and illiteracy are rife, and where there is little in the way of health care facilities. It is also pertinent to note that the economic and social status of women tends to be very low where FGM is prevalent. Legislation in England and Wales prohibited FGM in 1995. It became an offence to take a girl abroad for any form of genital mutilation in 2005. It has been criminalised in many other countries.

More than 125 million women and girls live with FGM, and 30 million girls are at risk of being cut in the next decade. The European Parliament estimates that half a million women and girls in Europe have been subjected to FGM, and that 180,000 are at risk of having to undergo it each year (European Parliament, 2009). The Report *Violating Children's Rights: Harmful Practices Based on Tradition, Culture, Religion or Superstition* (International Council on Violence against Children, 2012) indicts the devastating failure of international and regional human rights mechanisms to provide the necessary challenge. But FGM is now under attack. It will survive going underground, affirming what Herbert Packer (1968) referred to as 'the limits of the criminal sanction'. A 'crime tariff' will be created to protect the shady entrepreneur, the price will go up, and the quality down. Is FGM beyond the tentacles of the law? Is education the answer? The law, it would appear, is a blunt instrument. The answer may lie in education (Ford, 2005).

As already observed, FGM is not the only traditional practice prejudicial to the health of children. Other cultural practices include uhuthuala (seduction amongst the Xhosa), trokosi (sexual slavery in Ghana), the targeting of children as witches in Burundi, and the killing of Albino children in Tanzania. The Committee on the Rights of the Child (2003) had the opportunity to discuss this further when it produced its General Comment on the Right to Adolescent Health, but it held back from offering more than a passing reference to FGM. Nothing is therefore said about early marriage (Kitson, 2016) or son preference (Ratpan, 2012), or about traditional practices in the Global North, such as corporal punishment and male circumcision.

Male Circumcision

Male circumcision was banned by the Roman Emperor Hadrian in 130 CE, but has not been outlawed since, not even by the Nazis. But ritualistic male circumcision (the Jewish practice of *brit milah*, for example) has increasingly been attacked (Adler, 2016). To date, English law can offer no more than two somewhat contradictory *obiter dicta*, one that it is lawful (Lord Templeman in *R* v. *Brown*, 1993); the other that it constitutes 'significant harm' and thus potentially acts as a trigger for a care order and the removal of the child from his parents (Sir James Munby, President of the Family Division in *Re B and G*, 2015).

It has come under attack in Scandinavia, where a leading Norwegian newspaper published a virulently antisemitic cartoon in 2013 reminiscent of *Der Sturmer* (a Nazi publication in the 1930s); in the Netherlands, where a medical committee wanted it to be limited to those aged eighteen and over; and in Germany, where a court in Cologne ruled against it, and outraged Chancellor Merkel, who promptly promoted legislation to reverse the Cologne decision (Auroque and Wiesing, 2005).

The Dutch case is particularly striking. It is 'for adults only'. Somewhat odd in a country, one of three, the others being Belgium and Luxembourg, where children can consent to euthanasia! Clearly, consent is what worried the Dutch doctors. We are not told what they think of infant baptism. Neither circumcision nor baptism is reversible. The consent defence looks weak, especially if it can be shown that circumcision is in the boy's best interests. It will confer on him a religious and cultural identity. It is also a prophylactic and since its benefits outweigh its harms, it can be said to be therapeutic. However, whilst this is also its ostensible rationale, the real reason for FGM is to control female sexuality (Cutner, 1985). A boy is only 'harmed' by circumcision if a few transient moments of pain constitute harm. By contrast, the results of FGM are grave and permanent (and see Feinberg, 1992; Morris et al., 2016).

It is unfortunate that the two procedures should have become associated. FGM is abhorrent and indefensible. It is a hostile act, often performed in insanitary conditions, sometimes to satisfy an outlandish belief (such as that the clitoris is a masculine feature and will grow to the size of a penis if not excised). Male circumcision is not a traditional practice, but a religious institution, a core belief of the Jewish people, which can be traced back to biblical injunction in the book of Genesis. It is a benevolent act, doing for a child what he would give his consent to were he able to do so. Far from its being abusive, it is arguably abuse to deny a Jewish or Muslim boy a circumcision. Whether an act is abusive depends in part on context (Freeman, 1992a: 102–3). In relation to significant harm I have argued that 'significant' has to be situated within relationships, that abuse in one context is not necessarily abuse in another. Context must include culture and religion. There are limits to this: we cannot exculpate practices we believe to be objectively harmful merely because they are prevalent amongst a particular group. Here lies a clue to the difference between FGM and male circumcision. FGM can only be defended by invoking a cultural relativist value system. Relativists regard all values as the product of the customs, practices and beliefs which have developed within a particular tradition. They deny that any value has any authority, epistemological or moral, outside of this cultural context.

Identity and Cure

A question upon which controversy rages centres on the conflict between identity and cure. The best example concerns the deaf community and its prerogative, as it sees it, to protect those with hearing loss from merchants of hearing who come bearing cochlear implants. I must declare an interest, having watched my grandson develop from a two-year-old in a totally silent world to an articulate twelve-year-old at the top of his class; yes, I go for cure and do not mourn his loss of identity. Nor does he! The decision was taken by his parents in his best interests. Should we have waited until he was capable of participating in the decision-making process, when he was *Gillick* competent? This would have been foolhardy to the point of being criminally negligent. It cost the state £60,000 – he will repay that back many, many times over.

Consent Issues

On many of the most contentious issues in health care the Convention is silent. A number of these questions relate to consent.

At what age may a child consent to medical treatment? Does the same age apply to all medical treatments and procedures? When, if at all, may a child refuse medical treatment? When may a child enrol/be enrolled in a medical trial? When may a child donate an organ? So far were these questions from the minds of those who drafted the CRC, that it totally ignores health professionals.

English law has answers to these questions but they are far from definitive. It distinguishes a number of categories of children. There are children of sixteen and seventeen, who are usually deemed competent; Family Law Reform Act 1969, section 8 reduced the age at which a child can consent to sixteen. But this only applies to diagnosis and treatment, so that bone marrow and organ donation and non-therapeutic research are excluded and are governed by common law principles. The most controversial question is whether section 8 applies to refusals to consent to treatment also, or only to consent. The Court of Appeal held in *Re W* (1993) that it did not.

A child under the age of sixteen may consent to medical treatment if *Gillick* competent, but a refusal to consent may be overridden. As pointed out above, adults determine whether a child satisfies this test. In reality, the view taken by adults of what is in a child's best interest undermines the input into health care decision-making that children are permitted (Kilkelly and Donnelly, 2011). The child's space is also invaded by Article 3 of the CRC, which appears to transfer power to adults to determine what is in a child's best interests, although, as pointed out above Article 12 must apply to Article 3 as well.

The autonomy conferred on mature children by *Gillick*, and reinforced by Article 12, will often have to cede to the child's best interests, even possibly to the public interest. There may be a space here for what I have previously called 'liberal paternalism', and now prefer to call 'limited paternalism'. This would permit interference with a child's autonomy where the child's decision would result in death and thus deny him/her any future (Freeman, 1992b). To use an example drawn from Mill (1859), we deny you the autonomy to sell yourself into slavery because this would be the last exercise of autonomy. It would mean that a child does not have the right to choose death? Clearly, we should allow a *Gillick* competent child to choose between different types of life-sustaining treatment (Gilmore and Herring, 2011). But euthanasia? Does the dying child have the right to die?

Sexual Health

The Convention is weak on the issue of sexual health. There are provisions on ante-natal care and on post-natal care. This is a failing, and it is surprising. Surprising because the Committee on the Rights of the Child (2013: 13) is concerned about high rates of pregnancy amongst adolescents. It has now recommended health systems and services to meet their need, including family planning and safe abortion services, so that girls can make 'autonomous and informed decisions' regarding their reproductive health. The Catholic Church has continued to be obstructive, with a 'liberal' Pope who has more problems with contraception than with hitting children (*The Guardian*, 11 February 2015), of which he apparently approves.

An important consideration is the preservation of the girl's confidences. This is not an issue faced by the Convention's drafters, and the Committee also has not really got to grips with it.

Of course, it is a highly sensitive question, more so in the developing world. As far as English law is concerned, the answer is clear. The then President of the Family Division stated in 2001 that 'Children, like adults, are entitled to confidentiality in respect of certain areas of information. Medical records are the obvious example' (*Venables* v. *News Group Newspapers*, 2001). But where very young children are concerned, and parents are making decisions, hiding information from parents would make no sense, and 'the doctor's duty of confidentiality is owed to the family unit of parent(s) and child' (Jackson, 2013). *Gillick*, followed in *Axon* (2006), has put it beyond doubt that a child who meets *Gillick* criteria has a right to have her views respected. As a result, it is likely that any other conclusion would mean fewer girls would seek contraceptive advice and more would resort to back street abortions. (See Appendix 6 with the Trieste Draft Convention recognising this.)

Mental Health

The Convention clearly includes a child's mental health within 'health' (Article 24). But this has passed relatively unnoticed (Eide and Eide, 2006; Woolf, 2012). There is a tendency instead to concentrate on childhood obesity (Voigt, Nicholls and Williams, 2014). The two conditions may be related, but this is not necessarily the case. A child's mental health can be affected by a variety of factors, many of which are the subject of other provisions in the CRC, for example by bullying and now by cyber-bullying, by displacement from home or country. Refugee children cannot be expected to have the resilience to withstand pressures on their mental health. Holocaust survivors – those still alive today will have been children – retain the mental scars of their experiences. The mental health of Syrian children fleeing violence only to see others drown may similarly be irrevocably damaged.

Childhood obesity was cited for a good reason. The physiological effects, for example type 2 diabetes, are well known. The psychological ones less so. There is clear evidence that it can lead to loss of self-esteem, feelings of loneliness and depressive symptoms, particularly in girls (Erickson et al., 2000; Strauss, 2000).

Mental health services for children are the Cinderella of the health system, inadequately resourced and falling well short of child-friendly standards.

The Committee on the Rights of the Child (2016) is concerned that there is no comprehensive strategy to ensure that the needs of children suffering mental health problems are not overlooked, and their access to vital services is facilitated.

Environmental Health

It is estimated that three million children under the age of five in the developing world will die from illnesses related to dangerous environmental conditions. 300 million of the world's children live in areas with extreme air pollution, with toxic fumes six times the accepted international guidelines (UNICEF, *Clear the Air for Children*, 2016). Global air pollution contributes to 600,000 child deaths a year, more than are caused by HIV/AIDS and malaria combined.

Poor children in developing countries suffer much worse environmental health than do children living in richer, developed nations. The CRC does not explicitly recognise the right to a healthy environment. Only the San Salvador Protocol and the African Charter do this. The San Salvador Protocol recognises both a right to health, as well as the 'right to live in a healthy environment and to have access to basic public services'. The African Charter adds to the right to health a right of all peoples to 'a general satisfactory environment favourable to their development'.

Amongst the threats to environmental health are chemicals in the environment. Children are most vulnerable to these chemicals, which can impair immune systems and damage organs. Another cause of death and disease is water pollution. Over 1 billion people each year are exposed to the risk of illness and death as a result of lack of access to clean water and exposure to waterborne diseases as a result of inadequate sanitary water disposal. Diarrhoea is the cause of 4 million illnesses a year, the overwhelming majority of which result in death. Children are the main victims. Another threat is posed by marine pollution: bathing in polluted seas, eating contaminated fish, exposes the consumer to mercury poisoning and to whatever detritus has been dumped at sea. There is also air pollution to which children whose lungs are not properly developed are particularly sensitive.

Some progress is being made to tackle these issues. Twenty years ago, David Ezra could shock us with an article title like 'Sticks and Stones May Break My Bones, But Tobacco Smoke Can Kill Me' (1994). Much of the world was then in denial. We now have a Tobacco Convention (Gostin, 2014). Its objective is to prevent present and future generations from the devastating health, social, environmental and economic consequences of tobacco consumption, and exposure to tobacco smoke, by providing a framework for tobacco control measures to be implemented by the states parties at national, regional and international levels to reduce the prevalence of tobacco use and exposure to tobacco smoke.

Environmental tobacco smoke ('passive smoking') is a significant health risk to young children. Children who are exposed to environmental tobacco smoke are more likely to suffer from reduced lung function, respiratory tract infections and respiratory irritations. Children who smoke are even more likely to suffer in these ways. The Tobacco Convention establishes general principles and rules to guide the development of protocols that will formulate specific obligations. These obligations include regulations to control smoking by pricing, taxing, labelling and packaging (Gostin, 2014). Some progress is being made but powerful corporate merchants of death remain adept at finding their way round the law. Smoking is in decline: now less than 17 per cent of the population smoke (*The Guardian*, 19 September 2016).

Children and Medical Research

Medical research will not necessarily be in the best interests of the child who is the subject of the research, it is in the interests of children as a class. The world was rightly horrified when it learnt of Mengele's 'twin experiments'. Medical research with children can be especially valuable in trying to tackle medical problems which affect children. How does the English legal system respond? The Nuremberg code is clear: the voluntary consent of the human subject is absolutely essential. But research may need to be conducted on children who lack capacity or competence.

The common law in general accepts consent for the treatment of a child from a person with parental responsibility, or from a child aged sixteen or who is *Gillick* competent.

The courts can overrule the child and holders of parental responsibility if it is in the best interests of the child to do so (*Re W*, 1993). Legislation does not deal with consent to research. Family Law Reform Act 1969, section 8(1) is confined to therapeutic and diagnostic procedures, and the court in *Gillick* did not discuss the issue of research; it follows that we do not know whether a researcher can rely on consent given by a *Gillick*-competent child. The Court of Appeal in *Re W* could have considered this but seemed to be more concerned with protecting the medical profession from litigation than with the child's autonomy interests.

The court contented itself with saying that it was 'highly improbable that a child could be considered sufficiently mature in *Gillick* terms to consent to research'. The court also speculated that it was highly unlikely that a court would permit research to be conducted on a *Gillick* mature child against his/her will.

The law, more than forty years after *Gillick*, is in poor shape. From a children's rights perspective it is most unsatisfactory. The Royal College of Paediatrics and Child Health (2000) takes a more sweeping brush to these questions. It is in no doubt that the implication of *Gillick* is that a *Gillick*-competent child may consent to enrolment in a research project. This is in line with research findings (Alderson, 1990), and certainly with the thrust towards the empowerment of children.

One difficult case arises where research is not in the best medical interests of the child, but is in the best interests of the child as more broadly interpreted, to take into account emotional, social and other welfare interests (*Re Y*, 1997).

Global Climate Change: A Case Study

Global climate change constitutes a challenge to us all. There is consensus that its impact will be felt by children more than today's adults, and not only because they will outlive most of them.

UNICEF's *Unless We Act Now* (2015) is the fullest account of the impact of climate change on children (see also Hayward, 2013). It is clear, in so far as anything is in a world plunging from crisis into crisis, that there is no greater threat facing the world's children than climate change, and it is increasing.

UNICEF offers a number of key messages:

- children will bear the brunt of climate change;
- it will make existing inequities even worse; the poorest and most vulnerable will be harmed 'first, hardest and longest' (2015: 8);
- the trajectory of climate change can and must be interrupted;
- now is the time for action; and
- children deserve to live in a world free from the threatening effects of climate change.

Over half a billion children live in areas with very high levels of flood occurrence, the majority of them in Asia, and nearly 150 million in areas of high drought density. Children also suffer from heat-induced stress; babies under one are particularly vulnerable.

The CRC does not mention climate change – it did not have the profile then that it does now, but it is clearly covered by Articles 6 and 24 ('the dangers and risks of environmental pollution'). Household air pollution causes 4.3 million deaths annually; 13 per cent of these are deaths of children under the age of five.

Lethal and debilitating diseases, including malaria and dengue fever, are highly susceptible to changes in the climate. WHO estimates that 88 per cent of the burden of disease attributable to climate change occurs in children under five. Two-thirds of deaths from malaria are of children under five – 800 per day. Dengue fever affects about 50 million people and kills 15,000 persons a day. It is the most rapidly spreading mosquito-borne viral disease in the world, facilitated by climate change increasing globalisation, as well as migration.

Climate change forces us to confront the question of intergenerational justice. Our behaviour affects the lives of our children, and their children, and so on. What attitude should we take towards their interests? What obligations do we have towards citizens of the future (and non-citizens)? Rawls concerned himself, and then only briefly, with obligations towards future members of our own community. Even this question 'subjects any ethical theory to severe if not impossible tests' (Rawls, 1971: 284). Rawls adopted a similar view to that which he had to our obligations to non-nationals. The practical implication of this is that we ought to observe a 'just savings' principle. But can this principle offer us any guidance on how to distribute the costs of climate change? How much should the current generation save? Does this depend on whether it is a wealthy or a poor one? A problem for Rawls and others like him is that he is not 'globally focused' (Armstrong, 2013: 196). We need a normative theory which recognises that, as John Donne acknowledged, no man is an island (Donne, 1650).

One worth exploring is suggested by David Miller (2009). He proposes that richer countries should bear the costs of mitigating climate change, and that in so doing they should make equal sacrifices to their standards of living. He acquits the poorest societies of any of the responsibility for mitigating climate change. He maintains that we ought to allow the poorest societies to increase their emissions if doing so is necessary to tackle their poverty (2009: 146). For the rest, he argues that the costs of mitigating climate change should be the same for each society: he calls this 'a principle of equal sacrifice'.

Armstrong (2013: 198) asks two questions. First, is it just? It would endorse inequality. It would mean that a country making a disproportionately large contribution to the problem would continue to do so. The second question looks odd. It seems to suggest that, although Miller's is not an egalitarian principle, in that it does not require equal emissions, in another sense it apparently is 'because it argues for equal sacrifices to deal with the problem' (Armstrong, 2013). Does this mean Miller accepts global egalitarianism?

Socio-Economic Rights

Aoife Nolan apart (2011, 2013), very little attention has been paid to children's socio-economic rights. Article 4 is one of the least commented-upon provisions in the CRC. It provides:

> States Parties shall undertake all appropriate legislative,
> administrative and other measures for the implementation
> of the rights recognised in the present Convention. With
> regard to economic, social and cultural rights, States
> Parties shall undertake such measures to the maximum
> extent of their available resources and, where needed,
> within the framework of international co-operation.

The wording of this Article is significantly different from its predecessor and model in International Covenant on Economic, Social and Cultural Rights (ICESCR), Article 2, in that the words 'progressive realisation' are omitted. The Committee on the Rights of the Child in General Comment No. 5 (at para. 7) states that these words are to be implied. This reflects political reality, but detracts from the goal of improving children's lives by legitimating procrastination. It justified the UK government in 2000 proclaiming the end of child poverty by 2020, even subsequently giving this commitment legislative force. But it has not prevented the Conservative Government elected in 2015 threatening to repeal the Act. Child poverty remains a blot on the landscape of our polity.

'Progressive realisation' was initially working. Child poverty reduced dramatically between 1998 and 2011/12: 1.1 million children were lifted out of poverty. Since 2010, the number of children in absolute poverty has increased by half a million. There were 4.1 million children living in poverty in the United Kingdom in 2016–17 (30 per cent).

We are now progressively reinstating poverty. The Institute for Fiscal Studies projects that, as a direct result of tax and benefit decisions made since 2010, the number of children in relative poverty will rise to 4.3 million by 2020, the year when child poverty was supposedly going to end.

It has been assumed that this was the fault of their parents (or parent). However, the evidence now shows that nearly two-thirds of British children living in poverty are in working families. For many, work is not a route out of poverty. Further, it is predicted that the Conservative Budget will lead to an increase in child poverty and inequality. As the planned tax and benefit cuts take hold, recent declines in income inequality will reverse, and child poverty rates will begin to increase again.

The United Kingdom is not the only wealthy nation in which child poverty remains deeply embedded. The United States is similarly blighted. The US Children's Defense Fund's *State of America's Children* (2014) reports that: 'children are the poorest group in the nation'. One in five children are poor, of whom 40 per cent live in extreme poverty. The youngest children are the poorest; more than one in four children under the age of five are poor, that is 5 million children. Almost half of them (2.4 million) are extremely poor (Children's Defense Fund, 2014).

Child poverty has been discussed as an example of provision, but, as a blatant example of child maltreatment it fits equally into the protection category. Would moving it to child abuse concerns have an impact on our responses to it? Would we be more likely to respond positively after re-categorisation? The image of the abused child (these linger for many years) is more graphic and challenging than that of the poor one – unless the child is in Africa – the malnourished Ethiopian child preys on our consciences in ways that hungry children in Edgware do not. How much impact did the news that children in Britain today went hungry in school holidays have?

A Decent Standard of Living

The Convention (Article 27) states that children have the right to an adequate standard of living. Parents have the primary responsibility to ensure this, but the state is expected to support them.

It is apparent that many children do not enjoy an adequate standard of living. Many live in extreme poverty. For far too long we knew too little about this. Children's experiences used to be invisible, hidden from the view even of social scientists. We now are possessed of data and the picture of deprivation which emerges is dismal and distressing.

What we now know is that children who live in low-income families are exposed to risk factors to a much greater extent than their peers in better-off families. Their development can be stunted by care arrangements (child abuse and domestic violence), racism, etc. (Garbarino, 1998). Evans' research review (2004) concluded that poor children in the richest nation, the United States, were exposed to more family disturbances and violence, had less social support, and also had parents who were less responsive and were more authoritarian. Seccombe (2002) supplemented Evans' list, adding poor health, stress, difficulties at school (even dropping out) and becoming parents when still a teen. Both Evans and Seccombe believe that the environment should also be explored to understand the lives of poor children: low-income neighbourhoods are more dangerous and offer poorer services.

This data is replicated in research in Britain, and elsewhere in Europe. Bradshaw (2001, 2002) found that poverty in Britain and in other European countries is associated with child mortality and illness, child abuse, teen pregnancy, low-standard housing, poor school achievement and youth delinquency.

These research findings are important: they tell us that poor children perform badly in comparison to their better-off peers. We knew this already. What this does not tell us is how individual children experience their everyday lives (Lister and Beresford, 2000; Ruxton and Bennett, 2002). In response, there have been studies which address children's own experience of growing up in poor families (Ridge, 2002; Roker and Coleman, 2000). These studies show that many children in low-income families are materially and socially deprived: they cannot access things and activities that are commonplace to their better-off peers. Significantly, they also found that children show insight into what the experiences are like growing up in a poor environment. Also, that they worry about their future.

Who loses out in poor families? Many studies show that it is women and children (Pahl, 1989), but some suggest children's needs are prioritised (Middleton, Ashworth and Braithwaite, 1997). There is evidence that parents can shield their children from the worst effects of poverty, but this ability declines as the poverty gets more severe.

Elder's work (1994) remains of interest today. He showed that there is no simple effect of socio-economic environment. Over a life course, a child's adjustment, he found, depended upon a number of factors; the child's age and gender, the original class of the family. It was changes in family life, rather than deprivation of material resources, which appeared to be most damaging to the welfare of children. Of major importance is marital compatibility. The problem with this approach is it diverts attention away from social policy towards the families' internal lives. For bad policies, read 'bad parents'.

There is agreement now that the first three years of a child's life are the most important in their development (Shonkoff and Phillips, 2000). Children whose early care is inadequate never make up the deficit. As adults they are less successful. 'Growing up and living with persistent poverty is detrimental to one's psychological, physical and educational health' (Wadsworth et al., 2008). There is a 'pervasive tendency for children born to socially disadvantaged families to have poorer health, education and general welfare' (Fergusson, Horwood and Boden, 2008).

This is recognised by the Convention (as well as in earlier international norms). The UDHR (Article 25) lays down that 'everyone has the right to a standard of living adequate for the health and well-being of himself and his family'. ICESCR, Article 11(1) also recognises the right of everyone to an adequate standard of living. ICESCR, Article 20, affirms 'the widest possible protection and assistance be accorded to the family, as the national and fundamental group unit of society'.

There was thus nothing novel in Article 27 of the CRC, other than its specifying it was focused on children.

None of these international legal instruments throws much light on what is meant by an 'adequate standard of living'. There are lists: food, clothing, housing and medical care, necessary social services, social security. But there is no further definition of what the term 'adequate standard of living' should mean.

The ICESCR Committee has, however, issued a General Comment (No. 4) and this further elaborates on the concept in relation to housing. Adequate housing requires sustainable access to natural and common resources, safe drinking water, energy for cooking, heating and lighting, sanitation and washing facilities, means of food storage, refuse disposal, site drainage and emerging services. See further, Van Bueren, 2016.

Article 27 has not been successfully implemented. Even a cursory glance at the statistics reveals this.

Global Poverty

Global poverty is illustrated by the following data:

- 2,600,000,000 people live on less than US$2 a day;
- 1,4000,000,000 people live on less than US$1.25 a day;
- 27 per cent of children in developing countries are estimated to be underweight or have stunted growth (United Nations, 2007a);
- 67 million children of primary school age were not in school in 2009, 57 per cent of them were girls (United Nations, 2007b);
- 760,000 children under five die each year from diarrhoea;
- Almost half the population of developing countries are, at any given point of time, suffering from health problems related to poor water and sanitation (United Nations, 2000);
- 2 million children under thirteen live with HIV;
- 21,000 children died today.

Extreme poverty is declining. Most of the decline has occurred in China and to a lesser extent in India. It has declined much less in sub-Saharan Africa. The very wealthy remain. Many do not even pay taxes or what might be considered the appropriate taxes (Dorling, 2013).

Through tax havens, transfer pricing and many other similar policies, both legal and illegal, billions of dollars of tax are not paid. The much-needed money would help developing (and for that matter developed) countries provide important social welfare and social services for their populations.

Some tax avoidance, regardless of how morally objectionable it is, is legal and the global super-elite are able to hide away trillions of dollars, resulting in massive losses of tax revenues for cash-strapped governments, which then burden ordinary citizens further with austerity measures, for example, during an economic crisis. Yet this super-elite is often very influential in politics and business. In effect, they are able to undermine democracy and subvert capitalism at the same time.

As the global financial crisis has affected many countries, tackling tax avoidance would help target those more likely to have contributed to the problem, while avoid many.

The onslaught on poverty was recognised in the Millennium Development Goals, which were to be accomplished by the end of 2015. This was never likely to happen, and has not done so.

Right to Benefit from Scientific Progress

One overlooked right which one would hope would get more attention is the right to benefit from scientific progress and the application of science (Gran et al., 2013). There is far from true recognition even for adults (Chapman, 2009). Article 15 of the ICESCR states that states parties recognise the right of everyone:

217

(b) To enjoy the benefits of scientific progress and its applications.

Subsequently, the Venice Statement in 2009 emphasised three duties that states parties should undertake to put Article 15 into practice: to respect, to protect, to fulfil.

Very little has been written on Article 15 (but see Gran et al., 2013). Audrey Chapman (2009) finds three rights embedded in the right to benefit from scientific progress. The first is to access the benefits of scientific progress and technology without being discriminated against, so there must be free participation in the cultural life of the community. Secondly, there must be adequate protection against the harmful effects of science and technology. The third right is to protection of intellectual property. And without academic freedom, none of these rights is likely to be achieved. Nor will they be without resources. William Schabas (2007) takes this further, arguing that science has tended to focus on problems which affect the wealthy, rather than the poor. Money was poured into research to find a cure for erectile dysfunction which could have been used in the fight to eliminate malaria from which one child in the world somewhere, but mainly in Africa, dies every 30 seconds (2007: 297).

The right to benefit from scientific progress is closely connected to a number of rights in the CRC, most obviously health (Article 24), survival and development (Article 6). The interdependence of the CRC and Article 15 of the ICESCR can be seen by appreciating that children will be better able to benefit from scientific progress if the right to education in CRC, Article 28 has been put into effect.

The Internet is clearly an invaluable tool to expand the knowledge base of children. But it is not universally available, and can easily increase the gap between children in the Global North and the Global South. The advancements in technology are, however, a double-edged sword. They assist us to exercise our rights, but they can also be deployed against us. Young peoples' space is constrained by the use of the 'mosquito', a device which emits a frightening sound which can only be heard by young ears. Internet technology is also used to facilitate the trafficking of young people, clearly in breach of the Optional Protocol to CRC on the sale of children, child prostitution and child pornography (2000).

The right to enjoy the benefits of scientific progress and its applications (REBSPA) may improve children's lives. It may also make them more vulnerable and aggravate inequality. It may lead to improvements in wellbeing, in particular to health, but it may also lead to greater controls upon them. To get the benefits of scientific progress requires good education, for girls as well as boys.

More research on the implementation of Article 15 is called for. There is a gap in children's rights scholarship waiting to be filled.

5

Enforcing Children's Rights

Rights are valuable commodities but without remedies they have only expressive value. The CRC paid little attention to this rather obvious point, and, as a result, barely addressed the question of how children were supposed to enforce the rights in the Convention. This should not surprise us. Were we really taking Article 12 seriously (Daly, 2018: 43)? How many of the leading cases on children's rights were brought by children? Most, I suspect, were initiated by those wishing to gainsay children's rights! Mrs Gillick? Nothing could have been further from her mind. Williamson? Fortunately, Baroness Hale was on hand to speak for the children.

Article 4 of the CRC requires states parties to 'undertake all appropriate legislative, administrative, and other measures for the implementation of the rights' in the Convention.

Children should be at the centre of government decision-making – children come first. But children's rights can easily be ignored, and are. Hence the need for a senior Cabinet Minister with responsibility for children's rights.

With regard to social, economic and cultural rights, they are to undertake such measures to the maximum extent of their available resources. It is up to states parties to determine how best to implement their treaty obligations. The UN Committee is 'seriously concerned' about the effects that 'recent fiscal policies have had on children: they are disproportionately affecting disadvantaged children'. The Committee urges the United Kingdom to introduce a statutory obligation to consider children's needs 'when developing laws and policies affecting children'. They should adopt 'comprehensive action plans', designed to ensure children in the United Kingdom have the best start in life. Lundy et al. (2012: 19) say in their study of the legal implementation of Convention rights that there is a trend towards 'consolidated children's statutes'.

There is no international court. Enforcement mechanisms include a reporting process (see CRC, Articles 43–44). States parties report every five years to the Committee. NGOs and other interested bodies may submit alternative or shadow reports. The reports are examined by the Committee, which produces 'concluding observations' and recommendations, identifying shortcomings in the states parties' performance. The Committee does not have the powers of a court. It cannot impose sanctions if recommendations are not implemented. It cannot even compel an errant state party to submit a periodic report. Reports are late or missing and some are economical with the truth. The Committee adopts an 'advisory and non-adversarial' approach, relying on diplomacy, not the force of sanctions (Kilkelly, 2001). Despite all its limitations, the reporting process can carry moral weight.

The enforceability of children's rights at domestic level depends in part on whether or not the CRC enjoys the status of national law. Where it is automatically incorporated into domestic law, it can form the basis of court action in a domestic court. Where this is not so, redress may be more difficult to obtain, all the more so where the litigated right was not accepted in the legal system (Kilkelly and Donnelly give the example of child participation, 2011: 146).

The United Kingdom has not incorporated the Convention, and it is unlikely to do so. Many other states have done so. The case for incorporation is argued later in this book (below, p. 407).

Complaints Procedures: Communications

The spectre of children hauling their governments before an international court fills me with glee! This is unlikely to happen in the foreseeable future, if ever. But, as a result of Optional Protocol No. 3, operative since 2014, children are able to take complaints about breaches of their rights to the Committee on the Rights of the Child (Y. Lee, 2010). This is not the first example of such a procedure – the African Charter on the Rights and Welfare of the Child of 1990 explicitly permits 'communication' from 'any person, group or (recognised) non governmental organisation' (Article 44). There is 'little evidence of widespread usage' (R. Smith, 2013: 307). Under Protocol No. 3, the Committee can receive and consider both individual and inter-state complaints concerning the application of the CRC.

It is doubtful whether the CRC complaints procedure will be used any more than its African predecessor. And it will divert attention away from the establishment of a court, if this were ever a possibility. There are a number of reasons why we cannot expect too much from Protocol No. 3. It presupposes that children know their rights. On the whole they do not. There is far too little human rights education in schools, a great pity because they could learn about their responsibilities as citizens at the same time (Guru, 2013), rather like a document produced in South Africa by the National Children's Rights Committee which emphasises the moral correlativity of rights and responsibilities (see Appendix 5).

Even where children know their rights, they may well find it difficult to access the system. In addition to competence, they will need 'legal competence', the ability to use the system. They will require to have the confidence that the system will work for them. Few adults have legal socialisation, and even fewer children are likely to feel confident enough to negotiate the complexities of an alien process. And they cannot go straight to the Committee. They must first exhaust all domestic remedies. By the time they have done this, it is probable that they will no longer be children. A lot may depend on how easy they find it to get adult representation, on finding pro bono lawyers, on eliciting the support of children's organisations. Rhona Smith (2013: 315) points to the failure of the Protocol to provide for 'a neutral curator, guardian or litigation friend to be appointed to help the child'. But why 'neutral'?

Smith (2013: 317) is also concerned about how people will react to a further 'piercing the veil of the family', that it will be a step too far, that parents will be deprived of their 'natural law right to bring up their own children'. But surely the new powers will in most cases strengthen parental authority, not weaken it. This will not always be so. I can imagine the issue in the *Williamson* case (above, p. 45) taken to the Committee. But it is more likely that it will be challenges on issues of socio-economic rights that find their way to the Committee, questions like housing and poverty, where there is consensus between parents and children, not conflict. Courts have shown that socio-economic rights are enforceable (Langford, 2009; Nolan, 2011). Where legislatures and courts fear to tread, the Committee may in time step in, but many barriers must first be surmounted.

Children's Rights Institutions

When the CRC was under discussion, the possibility of requiring states to set up domestic human rights institutions to protect children's rights was mooted, but it is not to be found in the final text. Article 4 imposes implementation obligations on states parties. The Committee on the Rights of the Child has interpreted this Article to include an obligation that states parties should establish independent children's rights institutions (ICRI).

UNICEF's Office of Research and the European Network of Ombudspersons for children define an ICRI (2013: xi) as a

> public body with independent status whose mandate is to monitor, defend, and promote human rights and which has a focus on children's rights, either as specialized or because it carries out activities specifically focusing on children, with an identifiable department.

Norway was the first to establish a children's ombudsman. It did this in 1981. The first ombudsperson, Malfrid Flekkøy, wrote up her experiences in what remains the fullest account of one ombudsperson's understanding of her role (Flekkøy, 1991). Initially, the trend was to separate the work of children's rights and human rights institutions.

The functions of ICRI institutions for children are:

(1) to influence policy-makers and practitioners to take greater account of children's rights;
(2) to promote respect for the views of children;
(3) to raise awareness of child rights amongst both adults and children;
(4) to ensure children have effective means of redress when their rights are violated.

Representing Children

We do not expect adults to participate meaningfully in legal proceedings without representation. What then should be the role of the lawyer in enhancing child participation in legal proceedings?

A number of scholars, particularly in the United States, have remarked that law schools do not 'adequately prepare' law students to handle cases involving children (Kelly, 1998; Kelly and Ramsey, 1983; Weinstein, 1997). I suspect that law schools in Europe – less exposed to the influence of legal ethics and lawyering skills courses – are more open to this indictment. Not surprisingly, those representing children (I include the non-lawyer *guardian ad litem* (GAL) in this) are often confused about the nature of their role. One would anticipate a clear correlation between such confusion and the quality of the representation which results (Shepherd and England, 1996). The result is that lawyers are largely left on their own to determine how to represent children. It is therefore not surprising that this failing is seized upon by those who would wish to cut down on legal representation for children. Emily Buss

(1999) is one such critic, pointing out that, as a result, lawyers bring their own 'predilections to bear' on the determination of what role to assume.

Legislation is of little assistance. Nor do international conventions assist: CRC, Article 12(2) refers only briefly to representation, and Articles 4 and 9 of the European Convention on the Exercise of Children's Rights, which allude more fully, say nothing as to the special representative's role. The legal profession's ethical regulations hardly assist. They are primarily directed at the representation of adult clients (Lyon, 1987).

Within academic literature there has been vigorous, even heated, debate over the role of the representative. Should she represent the child's best interests or advocate for the child's wishes as a lawyer does when representing an adult? (Buss, 1999: 1700–2). Should the representative preserve confidences, as she would with an adult client? What if not revealing confidences may expose the child to danger? Perhaps the two positions are not watertight. Perhaps an absolutist position is a wrong one to adopt. Perhaps different approaches are called for with children of different ages. It is difficult to represent a child's wishes when she cannot express them (Peters, 2007: 40). It is difficult not to advocate where the child is *Gillick*-competent. But, even here, difficult questions arise when what the adolescent demands (and I use this term advisedly, rather than 'wants') will harm her. For example, she refuses a medical examination because she knows that this will demonstrate she is being sexually abused. Or she suffers from anorexia nervosa and will not be force-fed (*Re W*, 1993). Or she is a Jehovah's Witness and objects to a medically directed blood transfusion, or a heart transplant (*Re E*, 2003).

There is a widespread assumption (which is not shared by Katherine Hunt Federle (1996) whose views are considered later below, p. 236) that the advocate's role, whether she is a lawyer or a GAL, is to present the child's best interests. That this gives the representative vast discretion has to be acknowledged. Thus, Green and Dohrn (1996), introducing the Fordham Conference proceedings, can talk of it, in relation to a pre-verbal child, as 'unparalleled in scope'. And they comment on the 'inevitability of bias and personal value-determined judgments...including the class, race, ethnic and religious assumptions that underlie notions of child rearing and family life' (1996: 1290).

There are two principal concerns. Randi Mandelbaum expresses them thus:

> First, there is unease caused by the fact that these determinations [i.e. of best interests] are beyond the scope of a legal representative's expertise and therefore may require attorneys to make decisions that they are not well-suited to make. Second, there is concern that the determinations that legal representatives are making may not be what is best for children. (2000: 35)

Lawyers, as has already been said, are not trained to represent child clients. They know little about child development, child psychology; have little insight into interviewing children or counselling them. In many cases their clients (children or adults, but the problem may be accentuated when children) will be from a different class or race. What the lawyer deems to be best may well be based on the only value system she knows, her own (Lopez, 1989).

We should not be surprised that the very idea of the independent representation of children has come to be challenged. Two opponents are Martin Guggenheim (1999) and Emily Buss (1996, 1999). Guggenheim, in a number of articles, has argued that lawyers for young children are not needed. Buss finds them necessary but carves an alternative role for them as 'educators' and enforcers of statutory guidelines.

Guggenheim's views are significant: he is the co-author of the AAML standards for custody and visitation proceedings. But they are also flawed. He explains how the role of counsel for adults is based on the central principle of 'individual autonomy' (Guggenheim, 1999). Unimpaired adults have the inherent power to make *all* the important decisions concerning their lives. As far as children are concerned, Guggenheim distinguishes inherent autonomy rights and autonomy rights based upon the law of a particular subject area. So, the first question is: is the child:

> of sufficient age, intelligence, and maturity to be
> 'unimpaired' as defined by the Model Rules. If the answer is
> 'yes', the inquiry should cease. In these circumstances,
> children are empowered by established principles to set the
> objectives of the litigation. If the answer is 'no', then it is
> necessary to continue the inquiry by examining whether
> and to what degree children are supposed to have
> autonomy rights in the particular subject under
> consideration. (Guggenheim, 1999)

His view seems to deem children under twelve 'impaired'. With those under twelve, the lawyer must examine the relevant legislation and case law in the particular area. Thus, he takes the hypothetical case of the eleven-year-old pregnant girl who seeks permission to terminate her pregnancy. He assumes that the law requires written consent of a parent or a judicial waiver to have an abortion, and the case law dictates the waiver must be granted if she is found to be 'mature and well-informed enough to make the abortion decision on her own' (Guggenheim, 1999) or if the judge finds that the abortion is in her best interests.

He contrasts the abortion scenario, where the lawyer should argue the girl's case 'because she possesses a substantive constitutional right' with children's rights in the adjudicating phase of a child protection proceeding, which has 'virtually nothing to do with empowering children' (Guggenheim, 1999). He says (and this is reminiscent of the Goldstein, Freud and Solnit thesis (1979)) that children 'have no more right to insist that the state intervenes to protect them from inadequate parents than to insist that the state stay out of their lives' (Guggenheim, 1999). As with Goldstein, Freud and Solnit (1979), the posited law is unquestioned and unproblematic. Do we really want to avert our eyes from complaints of abuse until these are substantiated, when, as we well know, many of the 'impaired' children will be irreparably impaired or indeed dead? In England, no abused child will not be separately represented in care proceedings. It is strange to encounter a defence of the opposite position. It is much more the point that 'lawyering for children' should be brought in at much earlier stages. This would, however, take the debate into 'ombudswork' and other crisis intervention strategies, which there is not the space to consider here.

Buss is unhappy about lawyers taking any positions in litigation until children are developmentally capable of understanding the nature of the proceedings and the significance of their role as decision-maker (Buss, 1999), before such time she sees lawyers as educators and protectors of statutory fidelities. It is her view that until children are capable of understanding their sense of themselves and their sense of themselves in relation to others they will not be able to be empowered. She defines empowerment with regard to child clients as:

> the transformation of the child client's perception of his influence in the litigation process and the creation of an appetite for the exercise of that influence. The influence in question has two targets: (1) the process and outcomes of litigation and (2) the perceptions of the client held by the client and others. (Buss, 1999)

And how many adult clients have this, one wonders!

Her focus then is not on whether or how young children should be represented, but on the questions of whether and when children are able to be empowered. She acknowledges that empowerment is not the only goal of lawyer-child client relationships, but she explains that her abilities to be empowered extend to all of the other reasons why lawyers should seek to engage in traditional lawyer-client relationships with their child clients. Not until what she calls 'late childhood' (apparently about ten to twelve) do children, she argues using developmental literature (Buss, 1999), attain developmental capacity so as to form a relationship with a lawyer-representative.

If these proposals are directed at reducing bias and discretion, they will not achieve their purpose. In making the determination of when a child is sufficiently mature, there is bound to be discretion. Buss as much admits this:

> Each lawyer will bring her own predilections to bear – predilections about the children's needs and abilities, about the legal process, and about the lawyer's place in the process. And it is these predilections. . .that will determine what model of representation the lawyer will assume. (Buss, 1999)

It is also significant that both Guggenheim and Buss, in advocating the aggressive enforcement of the law 'as it was written by the legislature and interpreted by the courts', in arguing that representatives for young children should 'limit their advocacy to ensuring statutory fidelities' (I assume a consensus of opinion here) believe that this eliminates bias and discretion. It clearly does not do so.

Children need representation. Why? First, because the judge cannot adequately protect children's interests. Nor can the parents. The first of these statements may contain a less obvious truth than the second, but it is difficult to gainsay either. Guggenheim says that young children's interests in child protection proceedings can be adequately represented by either the parents, the child welfare agency or the presiding judge. Even if the court could do this in theory (exercising its *parens patriae* role), in practice it is not possible. The goal – to allow the child's best interests to prevail – is a mirage without knowledge of the child's perspective. And the judge is not likely to get this from talking to a child in the artificial (non-natural) atmosphere of a court, even if he does try to interview the child in as child-friendly a manner as is possible in his ante-chamber. Likewise, a judge cannot conduct out-of-court interviews with persons who may be able to provide important information about the child's life experience and the circumstances that brought the case to the court's attention. The input and participation of the child, without a representative, will be limited and the court will miss critical information.

Nor are the parents adequate representatives of a child's interests. There will often be a conflict of interests between parents and children. In child protection cases this will be obvious: in other cases perhaps less overtly so, but it will be there nonetheless. We cannot pin our faith in child welfare bodies to represent the child's interests. They are overwhelmed, underfunded and highly bureaucratic, and their interests may not necessarily coincide with those of the child. The ideological frameworks within which they work may also conflict with what is best for this child. Nor may they allow the child's wishes and feelings to prevail, even to be introduced as an alternative perspective.

That children need to be represented has come to be accepted. The views of Guggenheim and Buss – and they are not alone – had to be examined, if only to understand their concerns. Those of us who argue for greater participation by children, argue also for better representation. Those who are to represent children need to be better trained. Of course, the reality is that lawyers need to be better trained! The point I am making here has been made forcefully in the context of race, ethnicity and culture and impressively in the context of domestic violence (Alfieri, 1990). Too rarely do lawyers understand their clients' lives. A test like the 'best interests' one could be opened up, its subjectivity reduced, if this understanding were broadened. There is a need, for example, for cross-cultural training (Duquette and Ramsey, 1987): social work and family therapy both recognise this, but law is only now coming to do so.

Children need to be represented for many reasons. The US Fordham Conference summarised these (Fordham Conference, 1996). Without representation the 'best result' (1996: 1327) cannot be obtained. Representation redresses the 'imbalance of power' and addresses the need to minimise the risk of harm to the child that 'flows from contact with the legal system' (Fordham Conference, 1996). One might stress also notions of fairness and efficacy. The mediating effect of a representative might also be pointed to, though this is not a point I would want to overplay.

The question remains as to how best representation is to be achieved so as to maximise child participation. I have myself (if obliquely) argued for substituted judgement (Freeman, 1983). It is child-focused but it does not give much guidance as to how to determine the child's perspective and, as a result, can end up involving a type of reasonable child test. The uniqueness of this child thus gets glossed over. Is there a better approach?

One I find appealing is Jean Koh Peters' 'child-in-context' approach. She set this out in *Representing Children in Child Protective Proceedings: Ethical and Practical Dimensions* which was originally published in 2007. (See also Peters, 2018.) In essence, she says, this is:

> the concept of the child-in-context, the child understood on her own terms in ways that she would be able to understand and endorse. (Peters, 2007)

Peters' book is insightful throughout. It contains far too much to address here. I have selected a few points, mainly related to a child's participation. She is for maximising this wherever possible. Even a newborn child she believes can contribute some amount to her lawyer's representation and 'the lawyer must strive to incorporate every percentage of the client's contribution into the representation' (2007: 419–54). She suggests three default practices. First, what she calls 'relationship default': a lawyer should begin her representation as she would any other lawyer-client relationship, by meeting the client and trying to ascertain the client's goals. Secondly, 'competency default': presume the child 'can understand the legal issues' in the case and 'express a subjective perspective or offer critical information about them'. Thirdly, 'advocacy default': all lawyers whose child clients can express a view relevant to the legal representation should proceed in the first instance as if the stated view *is* the goal of the representation. The book offers guidance on how to proceed if the child's ability to participate is limited. Where children are too young to participate fully, she is concerned that all aspects of representation remain true to the child's realities and perspectives. She discusses ten principles of good communication with clients (2007: 84–9). There are seven questions to keep the lawyer honest with herself (2007: 65–9). I like the suggestion that the lawyer write a letter to the client explaining why she is making a particularly significant decision.

Lawyers, to represent children well and enhance their participation in proceedings, must open themselves up, listen, question when they do not understand, and recognise difference. They must understand their child clients' lives and the communities within which they live. Because there is such an obvious difference in a lawyer–child-client relationship, namely age, I have glossed over so many other, and often equally significant, differences: class, ethnicity, race, culture, gender (Hing, 1983). Perhaps these differences are greater when we move outside the more traditional divorce–custody battle, though it is clearly there too. That is one of the reasons I have focused rather more on child protection issues, where the race and culture questions are often greater.

I have often warned in the past of the perils of marginalising children. The side-lining or ignoring of these wider cultural issues will prove as troublesome. And, of course, at most its source is hardly different.

Representation has a further dimension. It can advocate for social justice. This representative will transcend the narrow contours of legal justice. S/he will see her/his role as an advocate for change, pushing out the boundaries of traditional lawyering. If the legislature will not act to give children better lives, then we must look elsewhere. There are precedents in Latin America, post-apartheid South Africa, India and elsewhere, impressively documented by Aoife Nolan (2011). Political lawyering (Bellow, 1996; Lopez, 2005) is not what my generation were taught at law school. We read cases and more cases.

Yet history tells us that lawyers have often been in the vanguard for social change. Leaving aside the obvious examples, Gandhi and such like, we should not forget that one of the first articles on children's rights in the modern era was written by Hillary Rodham, now Clinton (many years before she failed in her bid to become president of the United States) (Rodham, 1973).

Representation and Justice

Lawyers who represent children do so for several different reasons. It is common to say they give children a voice (Ross, 1996). Equally common it is said they empower (Federle, 1996; Woodhouse, 2003). Another view is that they are there to protect children against themselves, parents, the state. Most lawyers would say they want to assist the child to get justice. At the very least, procedural justice. Some will also be concerned to create or extend substantive rights for children, and some will even see their role as the pursuit of social justice (Brooks, 2006).

The lawyer who adopts the procedural justice approach is concerned with access, and does not challenge the system (Pitts, 2005). She/he works within the system. This constrains him/her. She/he is confined to arguing about legal rights, and cannot challenge the status quo. Where the problem cannot be solved within the existing paradigm but requires structural change, this lawyer cannot move and is stuck in a stranglehold and cannot find a solution.

The lawyer who adopts the legal justice approach seeks to enlarge the rights of children. She/he pushes boundaries: *Brown* v. *Board of Education*, *Re Gault* and *Tinker* are three well-known American examples where lawyers achieved important freedoms for children. But this strategy does little to address 'systemic problems that create risks for children, such as racism, poverty, poor schools, lack of economic opportunity, and lack of access to healthcare' (Appell, 2006: 701). She adds:

> The individuating aspect of legal justice approaches disregards children's developmental, economic and psychological dependencies by viewing the child as separate and discrete. (2006: 701)

Children as Enforcers

Geraldine van Bueren (1995: 1) alerted us more than twenty years ago to the fact that if children were going to enjoy their rights, 'they must be acknowledged to possess the necessary procedural capacity to exercise and claim their rights and freedoms'. It is only in the last ten years or so that we have begun to see this in practice. Children can play a 'key role' in making their rights count (Vuckovic Sahovic, 2012: 10; see also Liebel, 2012a: 28). The Committee on the Rights of the Child has encouraged children to get involved in its activities, to be proactive. In General Comment No. 12 (2009) it urged states parties to facilitate the formation of groups and organisations so that children's views will be heard on matters which affect them. It stresses the importance of participation in the decision-making process, and the value of organisations such as school councils. The mediating role of NGOs is also valuable.

The response has been positive, though there is no room for complacency. Children's organisations have begun to see the value of putting in independent shadow reports to the Committee. An example is the work of Funky Dragon

(2011) in Wales. In states as diverse as Australia, China, Denmark, India, Lesotho, Peru, Serbia, Thailand and the United Kingdom, organisations have emerged committed to offering an alternative view of children's lives. This is encouraging, but all is not positive. The impact that children have made thus far on the implementation of the CRC is not great.

Nevena Vuckovic Sahovic, once a member of the CRC Committee, notes that the impact made by children on questions of legal implementation is very limited. In her view, progress is unlikely to be made 'in the absence of an independent, professional and child-sensitized judiciary', which few countries have (Vuckovic Sahovic, 2012: 9). We in the United Kingdom certainly have an independent and a professionalised one, but too few of our judiciary understand the dynamics of childhood. There are egregious exceptions, of course. We should not forget that it was judges who kick-started children's rights (in *Gillick*).

6

Criticisms of the Convention

A number of criticisms have been made of the Convention on the Rights of the Child (CRC).

Understandably, there are critics (Archard and Macleod, 2002; Reynaert et al., 2009, 2010a, b, 2012). There are those who think it does not go far enough. Those who are opposed to children's rights generally. Those who dislike encoding children's rights within an international normative code. And those who think there are better routes to take to improve the lives of children (King, 1997). The main criticisms of the Convention can be stated briefly and responded to with little difficulty.

(1) It is said that children lack the capacity to have or exercise rights. There are two answers to this. First, it is not true that children lack capacity (Alderson, 2012). Secondly, this criticism presumes that the basis of children's rights is 'the exercise of will', but it is clear that the Convention is protecting children's interests (Thomas and O'Kane, 1998), and even the youngest baby has legitimate interests (Alderson, 2012). Indeed, so do foetuses. This, of course, raises the question of abortion and women's rights. This is too big a subject for this book. However, you can have interests without having rights: a dead person has an interest in respectful disposal of his/her body.

(2) Is it anti-family? A criticism commonly made of the CRC is that it is anti-family, by which is meant it is anti-parents.

It is seen by some, including many in the United States, as operating to the detriment of the interests of the family. Thus, Goldstein, Freud and Solnit (1979), writing before the Convention, argued that the only right children could have was the right to autonomous parents (for a critique see Freeman, 2007b). A generation on, Martin Guggenheim (2005) could argue in much the same way. He writes of parents' rights as 'sacred', but children's rights are summarily dismissed (see Freeman, 2007b). That it is thought to be anti-family is supposedly one of the reasons why the United States has not ratified the Convention. Many of these critics are believers in a 'nightwatchman state' (Nozick, 1973), and in policies like home schooling (e.g., see Farris, 2012; Glanzer, 2012). A careful reading of the text, far from supporting this interpretation, points to a very different conclusion. First, the Preamble identifies the family as 'the fundamental group of society and the natural environment for the growth and well-being of...particularly children'. It adds, 'children should grow up in a family environment, in an atmosphere of happiness, love and understanding', in John Holt's 'walled garden' (Holt, 1974, and above, p. 51). Secondly, and most significantly, Article 5 emphasises that states parties are to 'respect the responsibilities, rights and obligations of parents' to provide appropriate direction and guidance in the exercise by the child of his rights (and see Freeman, 2017). Thirdly, Articles 18 and 27 state that parents have primary responsibility for the care of their children. States are deputed to assist parents to carry out their responsibility. Fourthly, Article 29(c) states that one of the goals of education is to be the development of respect for the child's parents.

Fifthly, children must not be removed from their parents unless it is necessary in the best interests of the child (see Article 9). Taken together, these provisions convincingly support the conclusion that the criticism is well wide of the mark. There is no textual evidence that the CRC is anti-family. It is significant also that parents' rights are set out before any of the rights conferred upon children, the first ones of which are in Article 6.

(3) Is the status of parents recognised sufficiently? There are two answers to this. The first confronts the criticism face on. The history of childhood makes it obvious that there is a need to curb parental rights. It is salutary that we now talk of parental responsibilities rather than parental rights (for example, in the English Children Act 1989). It is not so long ago that children were seen as the property of their parents. Legacies of this remain. To take examples just from England, look at the *Williamson* case (and Baroness Hale's brave intervention), *Re T* (1998) (the liver transplant decision), and *Re A* (2001) (the conjoined twins case). But we shouldn't ignore the effect that this may have on children's rights: a shift towards parent responsibility can easily undermine child rights, and may already be doing so (Bainham and Gilmore, 2013; Erlings, 2016).

Secondly, the critics have clearly leapt to the conclusion they wanted to find without thoroughly examining the Convention. Guggenheim for example, seems to have a weak grasp of the Convention (Freeman, 2007b). A careful examination of the Convention reveals, that, if anything, it is over-protective of parents. There are at least eight articles of the Convention, starting with Article 5, which put parents first.

I will not give the full list: it can be found elsewhere (Tobin, 2013). The conclusion is that the Convention is not guilty of this alleged offence. The Convention, incidentally, nowhere defines 'family', perhaps a sensible precaution given the rapid developments in the concept.

Some of those who are critical of the Convention argue that the Convention does not go far enough in recognising the status of parents. They will say that Article 5 is a case in point: deference to parental rights and responsibilities is subject to the child's evolving capacities. And, further, it must be exercised so as to guide and assist the child to exercise his/her rights. A good example is the provision in Article 19, which limits the disciplinary measures that parents may use. 'Violence' is not permitted, and this limits the ways parents can physically chastise their child, in effect ruling out all falling short of occasioning actual body harm.

(4) It is Eurocentric. Another commonly-voiced criticism is that the CRC is Eurocentric, that it favours the interests and concerns of the Global North. It is said to reflect a Western conception of childhood (Harris-Short, 2003; Pupavac, 2011; Todres, 2012). This is the brunt of the attack by cultural pluralists/relativists (the difference is not always sustained in the literature). It is true that the CRC was largely constructed by delegates from the Global North, and also true that it would have greater legitimacy had the Global South been more involved in the drafting process. But there was determined and constructive participation in that process from a number of countries in the Global South.

Further, the Convention is open to different cultural norms. This can be seen as early as Article 1, with the recognition of different interpretations of 'child', though the conflicts are based on religious differences concerning when life begins, rather than economic development.

(5) The drafting process is too top-down. Closely linked to this criticism is one I myself have made as long ago as 1998. It is today encapsulated as the shortcomings of the 'top-down' approach. That language was not used in 1998. I wrote: 'The Convention encodes a set of rights and takes an image of childhood from the perspective of the adult world, looking in almost as an external observer on the world(s) of children' (Freeman, 1998: 439). It is a criticism that children had no input into the deliberative process that bore fruit as the CRC. In these terms, the CRC adopts a top-bottom trajectory. Of course, all of those who wrote the Convention had experienced childhood. Even lawyers were children once! (Lamb, 1823). It wasn't a strange land of which they knew nothing. It is a pity that we know so little about those who constructed the Convention (Holzscheiter, 2010). What kind of childhoods did they have? Were they brought up in a 'walled garden' with the proverbial silver spoon (Holt, 1974)? Or did they experience poverty? Violence? How are they regarded in their own countries? Highly or just as window dressing? True experts or 'jobs for the boys'? Or persons unlikely to rock the boat?

(6) Is there too much emphasis on civil and political rights? Another criticism is that the CRC pays much more attention to civil and political rights than it does to social, economic and cultural rights. This reflects the dominant role in the drafting process played by the democratic Global North. This distortion is aggravated by the fact that the

implementation of social, economic and cultural rights is subject to the availability of resources (see Article 4): not so civil and political rights. Dean (2002: xv) notes that 'the status of welfare rights as an element of human rights remains curiously ambiguous which invariably subordinates it to the civil and political rights of citizenship'. He sees these rights as 'fragile and difficult to enforce' (see also Jonsson, 1996; Khadka, 2013). Since welfare rights are more important for children than civil and political rights – especially so in the poorer Global South – it may be argued that the CRC allows states to get away with purporting to improve the political status of children without doing much to support better material conditions and environments for them. But the more civil rights children have, the more likely it is that their economic conditions will improve. Children with voting rights are likely to be feared by elites which hitherto have run roughshod over their interests. This criticism has substance, but it is difficult to imagine the Convention stripped of a 'progressive realisation' clause.

(7) A criticism, increasingly voiced, is the purportedly 'neutral' way in which the Convention is supposed to operate. Khadka (2013: 620) refers to the 'apolitical' nature of the CRC. It is sad to think such naivety existed, that we could believe that rights without a modicum of social justice would work. The criticism goes not so much to what the CRC does, as what it does not do, and perhaps cannot do.

One reason why this failing was not picked up initially was/is the tendency to examine the Convention for what it says, and not for what is missing from the text. Since the CRC says nothing about the redistribution of resources, much critical comment stops short of commenting upon the inequalities it leaves untouched. Dean (2002: 202) explains:

> rights may constitute the welfare subject as a heroic
> consumer, entitled to equality of opportunity within a neo-
> liberal regime, as a juridical subject, entitled to substantive
> equality, as a passive client, entitled to the benefits of state
> controls, as a participating citizen, entitled to social
> inclusion within a conservative regime.

Thus it becomes necessary to link children's rights to a particular political model.

(8) The most serious criticism of all is that the Convention has failed to achieve its goals. To make this criticism convincing we must first seek out the reasons why the world community in the late 1970s and in the 1980s was so committed to a rights agenda for children. We have already seen that it couldn't even agree a definition of a child. The initiative came initially from Poland, then a Communist country purporting to live by a Marxist ideology which saw rights as a fraud on the proletariat. That Marx himself saw value in giving children the right to education (see above, p. 26) can be discounted: hardly anyone appears to know this, even now. Poland was of course the homeland of Janusz Korczak, an icon of children's rights. But how influential was his vision, utopian almost, of a future in which the key concepts surrounding children were respect and love? The Poles remembered him – did anyone else? In 1979, when Poland first mooted a Convention – actually adopting the UN Declaration of 1959 as a Convention – his name was hardly known outside Poland and Israel (where a sculpture of him and the children graces the

entrance to Yad Vashem). His writings only began to appear in English after the CRC was finalised.

(9) There are other criticisms of the Convention. I made some of these as long ago as 2000 (Freeman, 2000c) and Philip Veerman, in an excellent recent article did so too, and referred to the 'ageing' of the Convention (Veerman, 2010). In brief, there are gaps in the Convention. Certain groups of children were marginalised. Insufficient attention was given to girl children, to gay children, to children with disabilities, to child refugees and asylum-seeking children, to abandoned children, to indigenous children, to children of prisoners. Issues were not always addressed properly: the age of criminal responsibility, early and forced marriage, child soldiers. Citizenship questions (the right to vote?) were largely ignored. Socio-economic rights were not given sufficient attention (Nolan, 2011, 2013). Do children have the right to food? Or housing? (Van Bueren, 2016). The enforcement machinery was weak. Thus, for example, there was initially no complaints procedure. The Committee itself is weak and not professional enough. It has some members with scant knowledge of the issues, and some with little interest in or concern for children. It is imperative that it is professionalised if confidence is to be restored in it.

Protocols have addressed two of these criticisms. There is now a complaints procedure, operative from 2014 (see Egan, 2014; Y. Lee, 2010). The provision on child soldiers is now more realistic. Another Convention (the UN Convention on the Rights of Persons with Disabilities) has effected improvements as far as children with disabilities are concerned (Sabatello, 2013). But other failings remain. The policing process remains weak. Reports are late or missing, criticisms are ignored. There are too many reservations (Hathaway, 2007). Should we be grateful for small mercies, or should we look to something better?

7

Beyond the Convention

The CRC provides us with a normative framework, nothing more. And it is *a* framework, not the only one. There has been a tendency to assume it offered a definitive programme, and required only attention to implementation, putting the Convention into practice, examining obstacles, establishing institutions (for example, ombudswork), debating incorporation (Lundy et al., 2012). This is despite the fact that we know the Convention is largely about the perceived needs of children in the Global North (Harris-Short, 2003) and might look very different if children themselves had had input into its provisions (Lundy et al., 2015). Despite Article 12, the motivating force behind the Convention was the 'image of the child as victim', with the street child then the representative icon (Ennew, 2002). That it became the victim of abuse, mainly sexual abuse, is of little consequence (Poretti et al., 2014), other than broadening concern to a wider range of children, including those from middle-class backgrounds. Now (in 2018) it is the asylum seeker and the refugee, as millions flee to Europe from war-torn Syria, Afghanistan and elsewhere in the Global South.

Concern for, and advocacy about, children's rights was limited until the passing of the Convention in 1989. My own experience as editor of the *International Journal of Children's Rights*, the first issue of which appeared in 1993, bears this out: to publish I had to be proactive. Few unsolicited articles were submitted. Was there a university course on children's rights anywhere in 1993? Most of the early work post-Convention was philosophical and explored the moral foundation of children's rights (Archard, 1993; Freeman, 1992b); some was highly critical (Purdy, 1992, 1994, and see Campbell, 1994; McGillivray, 1994; and, of course, O'Neill, 1988). There was little empirical work and hardly any of an interdisciplinary nature.

The early post-Convention years saw the growth of childhood studies, and the recognition that children were beings, and not merely becomings. One result of this was research which investigated children's own perspectives on welfare issues such as child labour (Liebel, 2004; Nieuwenhuys, 1994); recruitment into the armed forces (Honwana, 2005); street children (Ennew, 2002; Hecht, 1998); prostitution (Montgomery, 2001; O'Connell Davidson, 2005); abandoned children (Panter-Brick and Smith, 2000).

One concern with the Convention project, expressed even before we had the CRC, is that a Convention for children can easily create the impression that these are the only rights children have, so that human rights generally come marked 'for adults only'. Raes (1997: 13) expressed this concern when arguing that 'the implementation of children's rights will not ameliorate their fate but could very well result into an even greater control on children's lives'. Whether it does that or not, there is the danger that children may be ghettoised.

In 2007, Karl Hanson asked whether children's rights research was theoretical enough. He added:

> Doing scientific research on a subject. . .pushed
> forward. . .from an activist's perspective is not an easy

> understanding as it catches...a researcher between their role
> of a distant scientific observer, and the role of a human rights
> advocate wishing to contribute via research findings to make
> the realisation of children's rights come closer to reality.
> (2007: 635–6)

But this has not been the result. There is a mixed picture, but on the whole we have not made much progress in realising the programme set out in the CRC. There have, however, been advances in theory but these are commonly, and perhaps unsurprisingly, the work of theorists, not activists. There are exceptions, of course: the work, particularly the latest work, of Priscilla Alderson (2012, 2016); the research of Manfred Liebel (2008); Karl Hanson's many essays (2007, 2011, 2012; Hanson and Lundy, 2017). And childhood studies academics have begun to bridge the gap between their work and that of children's rights activists and scholars. Leena Alanen (2010) has argued the need 'to take children's rights seriously'. Berry Mayall (2000) has published several papers on the relationship between the sociology of childhood and children's rights, and Virginia Morrow (2012) has explored the value that childhood studies can find in the work of children's rights thinkers and practitioners.

I argued some years ago that advocates of children's rights had much to learn from the childhood studies movement (Freeman, 1998, 2007b), and returned to this subject again recently (Freeman, 2015). In the 2015 article I called for a 'dialogue between scholarships' (2015: 647). Most significantly, they need to take cognisance of the following pertinent question asked in an Editorial in *Childhood* in 1998, and even more pertinent now:

> Given our proliferating insights into the very different
> sorts of childhood worlds, how can we conceptualize
> universal conditions of children's welfare that would
> constitute legitimate foundations for international
> children's rights activism? (Editorial, 1998: 131)

The implications of this go to the roots of the whole project. It
raises the question whether monism is totally flawed. Were we
right to seek a universal set of norms? Or would we have been
better advised to adopt a pluralist vision? Pluralists believe
that there are many reasonable conceptions of the good life,
and many reasonable values upon which the realisation of
a good life depends. This must be distinguished from cultural
relativism, which holds that all values are conventional. It is
difficult to ignore the attractions of relativism. It is rooted in
egalitarianism, in liberalism, in modernism; it is anti-
assimilationalist, anti-imperialist, it is hostile to ethnocentr-
ism. It is sympathetic to the traditions and rights of indigenous peoples. It asks us to understand the 'others' practices as
they do, not as we as 'outsiders' do. What is anathema to us,
perhaps FGM or child marriage, may be totally unproblematic to them. They insist that we ask not whether we approve
a particular practice on the basis of our moral considerations,
but whether they are sanctioned by the relevant social understandings of the cultures within which they are practised. If
relativists were right, we could not condemn apartheid or
Nazism or slavery or caste. This is discussed further in relation to 'Asian values', below, p. 275.

The CRC is afraid to do more than dip its toe into
these dangerous waters. Article 24(3) mandates states to take

'all effective and appropriate measures with a view to abolishing traditional practices prejudicial to the health of children'. This is intended to impose a universal standard, but it does not specify the practices. We know, however, that FGM was the principal target. As an open-textured text it is open to interpretation, and some states are bound to interpret it so as to allow FGM to continue. There was no intention to tackle male circumcision. If the CRC draftsmen had wished to outlaw it, they would have inserted after 'traditional' or 'religious'. As it stands, Article 24(3) does not reach the Jewish practice of *brit milah*. However, this has not stopped the Committee on the Rights of the Child attacking ritualistic male circumcision in its latest investigation on Israel (UN Committee on the Rights of the Child, 2013). It may be argued that the development of jurisprudence is a function of the Committee. It is certainly a role it has adopted. Its legitimacy may be questioned (how representative a body is it?). Certainly, some of its lacuna-filling is generally acceptable, for example that 'violence' in Article 19 includes corporal punishment. The CRC must be a 'living instrument' if it is to retain relevance, and more than forty states have made it unlawful to hit children since 1989. But to include a religious practice like male circumcision within harmful practices would require a Protocol, and would invite debate as to whether it is a harmful practice. Since its benefits outweigh its harms, it may be argued that it is a therapeutic practice (Morris et al., 2016).

8

Interlude: What We Can Learn from the Sociology of Childhood

A number of disciplines have something to contribute to our understanding, and propagation of children's rights. Literary studies (Bowlby, 1969; Todres and Higinbotham, 2016) and environmental studies (Hayward, 2013) are but two examples. I look here at sociology in the belief that it can be especially valuable to advocates of children's rights. The academic discipline of the sociology of childhood, as part of childhood studies, should be seen not as a competitor, but as a fellow warrior in the battle to dismantle 'childism' (Young-Bruehl, 2012), and create a better world for children. Engagement through dialogue is called for. Hitherto, the initiative has been taken by childhood studies scholars, in particular Alanen (2010) and Mayall (2000, 2002) (see also Burman, 1995; Gallagher, 2008; Lenzer, 2002; Quennerstedt, 2013) though now contributions are being made too by children's rights scholars like Karl Hanson, thus beginning to redress this imbalance (see also Freeman, 2015; King and Piper, 1995).

Sociology of Childhood

Whilst conceding that there are differences of emphasis, even outlook, it is possible to categorise the starting points of the sociology of childhood as follows.

First, to understand the social order better. This is a goal of sociology generally. A study of adult-child relations will inevitably throw light on social organisation, and therefore on structure (and agency).

Secondly, to appreciate the ways in which childhood has been used as a strategy to propound visions of social cohesion. I think here of the work of Talcott Parsons (1951) and of Jean Piaget (1927), however marginalised their findings are now conceived.

Thirdly, to appreciate how (and why) the child has come to represent difference, and therefore, how what is constructed as childhood requires explanation, in a way that other forms of deviance also do.

Fourthly, to demonstrate, with the support of historical work (Ariès, 1962; Huttquist and Dahlberg, 2001; Pollock, 1983) that childhood is not a natural phenomenon and cannot be understood as such. Rather, it is a social construct, and the meaning of childhood is essentially contested. There are, however, signs that social constructionism is now being questioned (Editorial, 1998).

Fifthly, to grasp how childhood came to be seen as a stage, rather than as a social practice, with children spoken of as in the process of 'becoming', and therefore in terms of inadequacy, inexperience and immaturity. They were to be 'measured' against an unexplained, unproblematic, rational adult world, which is (so it is assumed) both complete and desirable, and, in contrast to childhood, is also static.

The 'sociology of childhood' involves moving beyond understandings of childhood as a period of socialisation (the study of what children are becoming) to a sociology that is interested in understanding how children experience their own lives in the 'here-and-now'. Berry Mayall has explored the links between sociology of childhood and children's rights in a series of articles (see also Freeman, 2005) and suggested that there is a 'need to remove children conceptually from parents, families, professionals to study the social conditions of childhood and write children into the script of the social order' (Mayall, 2000: 243). She has emphasised that:

> Childhood is a political issue. Theories about what children need, about how they develop and what input from adults is appropriate, are indeed theories or stories (rather than facts) and practices that derive exclusively from adult perspectives. They derive from adults' study of children, contextualised and structured by adults' social and economic goals in specific societies. Yet in the name of 'scientific' formulas about child development and children's needs, we tend to separate childhood from politics. (2000: 244–5)

More recently, she put forward the view that:

> studying childhood is about describing the character and status of childhood, and advancing arguments in favour of improving its character and status. If sociology is the study of social systems, about how social groups interrelate and how the social order works, with due attention to power issues, then the focus as regards children and childhood has to be as it is for adults and adulthood – a central focus on the social. (2000: 35)

For Mayall:

> sociology can be seen to have a discrete function in proposing other ways of understanding children: as agents

in the present tense, as competent, and as a social group. Sociology also presents potentially useful challenges. . .in proposing the crucial importance of processes within intergenerational relations, as structuring childhoods, and in seeing how they are lived and experienced. (2013: 36)

Some Common Ground

From these descriptions, some strands, some links (sometimes clear, sometimes more tenuous) emerge. I would suggest that common ground can be found in the following.

First, both sociologists of childhood and proponents of rights for children accept that, where once children were to be studied as passive beings structured by the social context of the family or the school, now research should focus on children's agency, on the ways that children construct their autonomous social worlds. Hardman wrote in 1973 (see Hardman, 2001) of the need for children to be studied as people 'in their own right, and not just as receptacles of adult teaching'. This has been grasped by courts (the *Gillick* decision in England is a paradigmatic case; *Williamson, Mabon* v. *Mabon* less so) and by legislators, both national, and international.

Secondly, there is recognition within the literature of both that children are persons, not property; subjects, not objects of social concern or control; participants in social processes, not social problems.

Thirdly, both are sensitive to the need to treat children as individuals rather than to categorise them as a collective and undifferentiated class. This means that gender, race, sexual orientation, disability and all cultural variables become significant.

In addition, both doubt whether (as is all too commonly assumed) adulthood is more important, and both deny that either difference or the well-entrenched belief in a golden age of childhood can explain why children were seen as rightless non-persons, or why rights for children were for so long thought of as unnecessary.

Both also accept that childhood has been constructed as, what Chris Jenks (1996) calls, a 'protectionist experience', as a period when there is an absence of responsibility and in which there are 'rights to protection and training but not to autonomy'.

There is also a general agreement that these ideas are particularly suspect where such notions are culturally irrelevant, for example, where young children have to work or where criminality by the young is treated no differently from that by adults, as graphically exemplified in England by the *James Bulger* case and its aftermath.

What Sociology Can Offer Children's Rights

Each of the two disciplines has much to offer the other. In what follows I will emphasise the contribution that sociologists of childhood can make to the development of children's rights. I do not, however, ignore what children's rights thinking can offer towards understanding of childhood. It is my belief that those who work within, and to propagate, children's rights can find much in sociological literature and research about children to assist them in their goal to improve children's lives, and it is to this I turn.

First, it is more than a striking coincidence, perhaps even a paradox, that with the growing institutional recognition that children have rights has come the assertion that childhood is a disappearing phenomenon. Indeed, Neil Postman believes that it is because of this that there exists a movement to recast the legal rights of children so that they are, as he sees it, more or less the same as adults. And he cites in evidence Richard Farson's *Birthrights* (1974). For Postman, the evidence for the disappearance of childhood comes from several sources:

> The evidence is displayed by the media themselves, for they not only promote the unseating of childhood through their form and context but reflect its decline in their content. There is evidence to be seen in the merging of the taste and style of children and adults, as well as in the changing perspectives of relevant social institutions, such as the law, schools and sport. And there is evidence of the 'hard' variety – figures about alcoholism, drug use, sexual activity, crime etc., that imply a fading distinction between childhood and adulthood. (Postman, 1996: 120)

It would be well to pretend that these trends do not exist, whether in the form of twelve-year-old waif-like models exploited by the advertising industry, or in the horrific examples of murders of young children by young children, of which the *Bulger* case is only the most notorious.

But the Postman thesis nevertheless lacks credence. Childhood was no more created by the printing press than it will be 'disappeared' by the spread and intrusion of electronic media. What we should take from Postman is not his prognosis, but his implication that childhood is a social construction – though this is demonstrated more obviously by others – and the consequences which follow from this. And it certainly does not lead to a denial that children have rights; indeed, quite the contrary.

It does, however, lead to the further recognition that childhood cannot be understood outside the context of other variables, such as class, gender, ethnicity and culture. If childhood is a social construction, then there are 'childhoods' rather than a single, universal, cross-cultural phenomenon (and see Chapter 10). The Convention on the Rights of the Child (CRC) adopts, by contrast, a universalist approach to children and to their rights. The sociology of childhood suggests this is wrong. Of course, it does not prescribe an answer – this would exceed its remit. But is the answer to be found in cultural relativism – unquestionably the orthodox view until recently – or in cultural pluralism? The Convention, it is true, says that 'due account' should be taken of the 'importance of the traditions and cultural values of each people for the protection and harmonious development of the child'. These traditions and cultural values are not problematised. There is clear recognition that the child's welfare (which, in the Convention, is a 'primary' consideration) may well be 'trumped' in certain situations (but which?) by 'cultural values and traditions'. And states parties are required (by CRC, Article 24(3)) to 'take effective and appropriate measures with a view to abolishing traditional practices prejudicial to the health of children', but this is in itself qualified by Article 24(4), which provides that states undertake to promote and encourage international cooperation with a view to achieving progressively the full realisation of the rights in Article 24.

A second insight which those concerned with children's rights may gain from studies in the sociology of childhood is an understanding of the child as social actor. Sociology enables us to see some of the ways in which the child constructs his/her social world. The world of children's rights has failed to grapple with this perspective. Thus, the Convention on Rights of the Child was drawn up by adults – many very committed to a better world for children, but it was a better world as they perceived it. Most commentators on the Convention believe that Article 12 is its linchpin. This, as is well-known, requires states parties to:

> assure to the child who is capable of forming his/her own views the right to express those views freely, on all matters affecting the child, the views of the child being given due consideration in accordance with the age and maturity of the child.

Yet, on the major 'matter' of the contents of the Convention itself, there is no evidence that children or children's groups as such participated or were consulted on drafting, or had any real influence in preliminary discussions. The Convention thus encodes a set of rights and takes an image of childhood from the perspective of the adult world, looking in almost as an external observer on the world(s) of children.

The Convention, had it used insights derived from the social world of children, might have made significant additions and amendments. Article 9, for example, gives the child the right not to be separated from parents against their will:

the child is given an opportunity to participate in separation proceedings and make views known. But there is no right to representation.

A second example is Article 24, which recognises the right of the child to enjoy the highest attainable standard of health, to have facilities for the treatment of illness and rehabilitation of health, but not as such the right to food, although malnutrition is to be combated.

Thirdly, and surprisingly in a Convention on the Rights of the Child, there is no reference to the issue of the consent of the child, relevant in a range of circumstances but particularly with reference to medical treatment (American Academy of Pediatrics, Committee on Bioethics, *Informed Consent in Decision-making in Pediatric Practice*, 2016: 138, arguing that children should be able to give informed consent at seven). The Convention is thus silent on one of the most controversial issues in relation to children in recent years in England, the question of whether a child – in the reported cases always an adolescent – can refuse consent to medical treatment. It is doubtful whether English judges understood, for example, the inner world of an anorexic and, had they been able to do so, whether they would have come to the conclusion they did in *Re W* in 1992 (Ross, 2009).

Fourthly, though a very strong case can be made for saying that the Convention makes corporal punishment, even in the context of the home, a practice states parties should eliminate, Article 19 does not say so directly. With greater understanding of, and greater input from, children, the Convention might well have contained a more explicit prohibition on corporal punishment.

Children should not be 'just passive subjects of social structural determinations', James and Prout, two leading sociologists of childhood remind us. It has thus become common to parrot the aphorism in the Butler-Sloss report into sexual abuse in Cleveland in North East England that children are social actors, subjects in their own right, not merely objects of social concern or the targets of social intervention. But the implications of this, even after Article 12, have not been properly thought through. The dissonance between children's own experiences of being a child and the institutional form which childhood takes is paralleled by a mismatch between the different understandings of childhood which have been emerging in the writings of sociologists, anthropologists and historians, and what so often finds its way into laws, institutions, policies and practices in relation to children.

The sociology of childhood also has much to offer those who fight for children's rights when they grapple, as they must, with such problems as dependency and capacity. The Convention has done little to reduce the equation that being dependent, as to a greater or lesser extent all young children must be, means being deprived of basic rights. Dependency implies a sufficient justification to suspend basic rights to privacy, respect and individual choice. Being dependent implies being legitimately subject to the often arbitrary and invasive authority of social service providers and other public and private administrators, in the education system, for example, who enforce rules with which the dependent must comply, and otherwise exercise power over the conditions of their lives. In meeting the needs of the dependent, often with the aid of social scientific disciplines, welfare agencies also construct those needs themselves. Medical and social service professionals know what is good for those they serve, and those who are dependent do not have the right to claim to know what is good for them. The lessons here go wider than debates about children's rights, but, without question, cast meaningful light on them.

Perhaps surprisingly, given the attention to the 'being' child, much research in childhood studies remains firmly rooted in the child as a 'becoming'. Where are the successors to Bluebond-Langner and to Alderson? What do children think about being deprived of the vote? Of the reproduction revolution (three parents? procreative beneficence? cloning? saviour siblings?). What is it like to be the child of a surrogate mother? Or an IVF child? There are PhDs crying out to be done.

What is also missing is any real theory of childhood. There are exceptions, of course. Alderson's recent work (2013, 2015) stands out. But having cast out Piaget, Mead, Parsons, etc., what do we have to put in their place? Childhood studies has surely something to offer us on the limits of children's rights, or on why the CRC has failed to turn children's lives round. On ways of making it more effective in practice. On the part children play in norm-creation when/if we come to revise the Convention, on whether we need to get beyond rights. On the relationship between rights and social justice. Can the indicators of children's well-being be fitted into a theory about children?

9

Childhoods and Rights

Is there one childhood or are there many? Were they over-ambitious or just naive in thinking they could draw up a single code for all the world's children? Those who drafted the CRC seemed to assume there was a universal understanding of childhood. They should have realised very soon that this was not so when they couldn't even agree when childhood began and when it ended. On the beginning of childhood, they sought refuge in an uncomfortable compromise which saw the Preamble recognising pre-natal life, and Article 1 on insisting on a definition of 'child' which says this begins on birth and not before. But without this compromise the Convention may have fallen at the first hurdle. Two interests, two dignities, are in conflict. One day, perhaps with ectogenesis (Alghrani, 2013), a solution which recognises both may become possible (McLean, 1990), but I will take this speculation no further, or I may fall at the first hurdle too!

It is clear that there are many childhoods and, for that matter, many adulthoods as well (Montgomery, 2009). And if agency is constrained by structure, it follows that the ability of children to shape their own lives is closely related to the social, economic and political conditions of their societies, to power, gender and to citizenship.

Put childhood into historical context and this becomes obvious. Even a cursory glance at Ariès' deeply-flawed

Centuries of Childhood (1962) will show this. Childhood (in the Global North) is different today from what it was a generation ago and certainly from what it was in Charles Dickens' time. But caution is called for, since we may be on our way back to the world of *Oliver Twist* (Waller, 2006) and Wackford Squeers (Dickens, in *Nicholas Nickleby* (1839)). It is all too easy to accept the Whig interpretation of history (Butterfield, 1931) and assume, or confuse, because there is development there is necessarily progress. An example is the way more and more attention is being paid to the agency of children, but at the same time more and more control is being exercised over their lives. Sixteen-year-olds may soon be able to vote, but it is dubious whether they may lawfully pet.

This is a reflection of an understanding of children as both autonomous and vulnerable, needing their rights to be protected as well as requiring them to be safeguarded, as both beings and becomings.

Children in the Global North are socialised today in a knowledge-based economy. One legacy of colonialism is that this model has been imposed on the Global South too (Bentley, 2005; Boyden, 1999; Burman, 1995). The work/education conundrum, as I described it (above, p. 168), can lead to a failure to recognise that for children of the Global South, work may be more important than education, particularly where the syllabus is modelled on the needs of a Western economy. Is the Bolivian model (see above, p. 176) the answer?

Even if it is, it is an accommodation to cultural difference that will not fit everywhere. Expressed more broadly, are pluralism and paternalism compatible? Can we give with one hand and take back with the other?

To compound our difficulties, I have throughout taken it as unproblematic that it is clear and uncontentious where the line between Global North and Global South is to be drawn. But it is not as easy as we might assume. Different parts of the same country may belong one to the 'north', the other to the 'south'. This can happen in the same city, as was revealed when Hurricane Katrina made landfall in New Orleans in 2005, with devastating consequences for the disadvantaged (Giroux, 2007). A country can change from one classification to the other in a relatively short time too, and this can happen in both directions. China, South Korea, Brazil and Turkey are examples of countries which have been 'promoted'. Nigeria has gone in the other direction. Peter Lewis (2007) compares it with Indonesia: in 1980, the percentage of the population below the poverty line was identical (28.6 per cent in Indonesia, 28.1 per cent in Nigeria). By 2003, it was 17.4 per cent in Indonesia and 70.2 in Nigeria. We can be sure that children will have felt the increase in poverty at least as much as adult society. These are big questions, beyond me to analyse satisfactorily (but see Fukuyama, 2014; Stiglitz, 2013), and beyond the immediate scope of this book. It is to this that I must now return.

Can we expect a Convention largely modelled on the culture, norms and concerns of the Global North to revolutionise the lives of children across the globe? Let us examine poverty. It is an example of violence against children, though it is not usually characterised as such.

The CRC is important if for no other reason than that it made the world think about children. It made the connection between children and respect and dignity, and thus drew attention to poverty, which undermines both these values. But legislative activity did not necessarily follow (Nolan, 2011). There has been some valuable judicial intervention in Latin America and in South Africa, but there are limits to what courts can do (Freeman, 2015).

New Thinking about Children and their Rights

Poverty Reduction Strategy

Accordingly, other strategies have been employed. There is the Poverty Reduction Strategy initiated by the IMF and the World Bank in 1999. This requires poor countries to report on their progress, but little has come of this.

Millennium Development Goals

The second strategy can be found in the Millennium Development Goals, adopted by the United Nations in 2000. One of its goals was to reduce poverty by half by 2015. This objective was presented as having been met, but this was only because of very large reductions in poverty in India and China. In Sub-Saharan Africa, by contrast, it increased. This is partly the result of aid failures and partly of corruption in the poor countries themselves, but also because of the absence of any coherent economic or social development strategy or a strategy for respecting human rights (UNCTAD, 2010; UNDP, 2010).

Both strategies have been criticised as not being taken seriously enough (Mestrum, 2011; Pogge, 2002).

Sustainable Development

The next phase in human rights, proclaimed in 2015, is sustainable development. This requires democratic development and respect for human rights. It is appropriate that we re-examine the UN Charter. This is based on the 'four pillars' of Peace, Justice, Freedom (i.e., Democracy), and Human Rights. The UDHR explains that human rights provide the base for the others, that is for freedom, justice and peace in the world. So, the realisation of human rights becomes a prerequisite for the achievement of global democracy, justice and peace. I maintain that this includes children's rights as well.

The CRC codifies a range of standards, for example the right to education, to health. Each standard identifies a desirable goal. Sustainable development and the realisation of human rights are integrally related: neither can be understood nor fully achieved without an appreciation of the other. Three of the four components of sustainable development reflect specific groups of human rights. Sustainable Social Development and social and cultural rights, Sustainable Economic Development and economic rights, Sustainable Political Development and Sustainable Environmental Development. As yet, Sustainable Environmental Development lacks a clear group of environmental rights, though there are some rights in the ICESCR, and in the International Covenant on Civil and Political Rights which relate to the environment. One searches in vain in the CRC for any meaningful reference to the environment.

That there is no reference there to climate change, given the impact this is going to have on children throughout the world, points to a lack of foresight in the 1980s, but perhaps also to the fact that it is likely to affect children in the Global South most seriously.

10

Regional Children's Rights

Children's Rights in Europe

An interesting, and largely neglected, development is the recognition by European institutions of children's rights. It is unlikely that the 'in-out debate' will be influenced by this. We should not ignore it. Potentially, the European development is more significant than the CRC. The CRC is not enforceable in the United Kingdom – this requires incorporation, discussed below, p. 407.

The ECHR has already been incorporated and individual petitions have been accepted since 1969. The United Kingdom has been taken to the ECtHR many times. It was a result of ECtHR rulings that corporal punishment was eventually banned in schools, Lord Denning memorably remarking that we should outlaw it before 'Europe took the inevitable decision away from us.'

The impact of the European Union may become greater, though not necessarily in the United Kingdom (Stalford and Schuurman, 2011). The context is the Lisbon Treaty. This raised the status of children in the EU in its constitutional order by announcing its commitment to the protection of children as one of its core objectives. It also affirmed commitment to the ECHR and the Charter of Fundamental Rights of the EU. In addition, it has embarked on a 'growth' programme for 'smart, sustainable and inclusive growth'. This 2020 strategy depends for its success, inter alia, on children's rights and well-being. Measures to tackle child poverty feature prominently. It has also published an EU Agenda for the rights of the child. This constructs various principles to ensure that EU action is consistent with the principles in the CRC.

Article 3 of Treaty of Lisbon lays down as a core objective of the EU:

> The Union. . .shall promote social justice and protection of the rights of the child, and in its relations with the wider world, the Union shall contribute to eradication of poverty and protection of human rights, in particular the rights of the child, as well as the strict observance and the development of international law.

This is highly significant. It sends out a number of important messages, notably, that children's rights are to be considered in both the development and application of all relevant policy areas. It creates an environment in which there is to be 'routine mainstreaming of children's rights into all legislation, policies and programmes for which the EU has competence' (Stalford and Schuurman, 2011: 400). The EU's guidelines on children in armed conflict are one example of this policy in practice.

A 'children's policy' emphasises children as a specific group in society. They are thus disaggregated from 'family'. The intention is to make children more visible when issues and directions of policy arise. The key elements of children's policy were identified in 1999 as:

- the 'best interests' of the child as a guiding principle;
- increasing investment in children and ensuring fair distribution of resources between social groups;

- overall coordination of policy, based on cross-departmental working to agreed strategies;
- policies addressing both the direct and indirect interests of children;
- the systematic collection of information on children to identify their needs and policy priorities;
- the establishment of independent bodies to monitor children's rights;
- the participation of children in decision-making, both within the family and beyond (Ruxton, 1999).

Children's Rights in Africa

African Charter on the Rights and Welfare of the African Child

The African Charter 1990 is the only regional code of substantive children's rights. It is close to the CRC in scope and in the concepts it uses, but there are important differences reflecting different conceptions of parent-child relationships (Lloyd, 2002; Sloth-Nielsen, 2008). Thus, it emphasises that children have responsibilities as well as rights. Article 31 sets out children's duties fully:

(1) To work for the cohesion of the family, to respect his parents at all times and to maintain in case of need;
(2) To serve his national community by placing his physical and intellectual abilities at its service;
(3) To preserve and strengthen social and national solidarity;
(4) To preserve and strengthen African cultural values in his relations with other members of the society, in the spirit

of tolerance, dialogue and consultation and to contribute to the well-being of society;

(5) To preserve and strengthen the independence and the integrity of his country;

(6) To contribute to the best of his abilities, at all times and at all levels, to the promotion and achievement of African Unity.

This emphasis on a child's responsibilities is a reflection of African values. It poses problems (Chirwa, 2002: 169). No correlativity seems to be expected: the rightless child is expected to carry out duties. Another more acceptable reading is that a child must exercise rights responsibly: for example, children have the right to dental treatment as an element of the right to the highest attainable standard of health, but can be expected to brush teeth regularly (at least where there is access to such rudimentary equipment). Another example is the link between a right to education and a duty to respect teachers. A third is the right to culture with the expectation that the cultural traditions of others will be respected. It is important that duties to parents and elders should not undermine children's rights to participate in decision-making in matters which affect the child specifically.

The Charter speaks to concerns which are specific to African culture. The plight of children living under apartheid is an example, though this racist institution was on its last legs. Another concern was gender inequality: many of the harmful practices, most obviously FGM, are directed at girls. It prohibits the betrothal of young girls, though it does not define what is 'young'. It requires marriage to be registered, thus turning its back on customary and other informal marriages. This has led to legislation, for example in Nigeria (Child Rights Act 2003), expressly endorsing eighteen as the minimum age for marriage.

The Charter has a provision like Article 12 of the CRC on child participation. This is even more innovative in the African context than in societies of the Global North. As Sloth-Nielsen et al. (2011) point out 'it runs contrary to traditional conceptions of children...grounded in children's respect for elders, which presupposes a hierarchical societal structure, in which children are regarded as having insufficient societal status to express useful opinions or views' (2011: 12). Despite this, there are children's parliaments, for example in Niger, one of the most traditionalist of African countries; it is said to constitute 'an environment of expression, concentration, and permanent exchange which allows the children to call out to the public authorities'.

Some other provisions which distinguish the African Charter from the CRC may be noted. The death penalty for crimes committed by children is prohibited, important because most of Africa still has the death penalty. Nothing, however, is said about life imprisonment. The right to health (Article 14) extends to spiritual health. It is the first international instrument to require resource allocation in respect of health: states parties are mandated to integrate basic health service programmes into national development plans. It is also the first to require 'the meaningful participation' of non-governmental organisations (NGOs), local communities and the local population in the planning and management of basic service programmes for children.

The African Charter deals with child abuse, sexual exploitation, trafficking and child abduction similarly to the CRC. It tackles begging, which the CRC does not do; indeed, it is the first international human rights instrument to do so. But it says nothing about street children, which is a little surprising. The Charter is also the first human rights instrument to provide a minimum age of marriage (it sets this at eighteen).

There is a straight age eighteen provision as far as participation in hostilities is concerned. The CRC drew the line at fifteen, which was extended to eighteen only in an Optional Protocol. There is some irony here, since Africa has been the site where most of the world's child soldiers have been involved, many of them much younger than fifteen.

Asian Values

Just as there are supposed to be universal human rights (Donnelly, 2003), so the CRC, ratified by all save the United States, purports to enact a universal code of children's rights. It offers scope for state interpretation and permits some derogation by means of reservations, and it could be better monitored (Johnson, 2015) and enforced, but it certainly lays down standards. However, it remains an essentially Western liberal document, a script emanating from European modernity. It is as if the Global South had come to be schooled by Northern pedagogy. It inevitably confronts so-called 'Asian values'.

It should be stressed that there were advocates for children's rights in Asia before they took root in the West. Bang Jung Whan (1899–1931) (Lee and Jung, 2015) set out 'Three Commitments' for children in Korea in 1923. These could have been written by Korczak, but neither of them could possibly have known of the work of the other.

It is difficult to summarise 'Asian values'. They are changing rapidly, nowhere more so than in China. And Asia is no monolith; Japan has nothing in common with Iran, nor India much with Malaysia. This would make an Asian Convention on the Rights of the Child difficult to formulate, though the obstacles are not insuperable. But when we refer to Asian values, we have reasonably clear images in our mind. Deferential, hierarchical, hardworking though reluctant to think outside the box.

Imagine if the United Kingdom were to introduce a 'one child' policy. China did (Greenhalgh, 2008; Naftali, 2016), and it was largely obeyed. It was abandoned in 2016. It had an impact on the population growth, but also unintended effects. Children had what Viviana Zelizer (1985: 211) called 'scarcity value'. It was reacted to differently in different parts of China. In urban areas girls came to enjoy better treatment and greater educational opportunities, but in rural areas there was sex selection, failure to register female births and even killing of baby girls.

What is the case, if any, for recognising Asian values, and what would be the implications for children's rights?

The case for rejecting the universal standards of the CRC in favour of Asian values is weak (Donnelly, 2003: ch. 7). It starts, most obviously, with a nod in the direction of Westphalia, with the sovereignty argument. 'The Right of each country to formulate its own policies should be respected and guaranteed' (China Information Office, quoted in Donnelly, 2003: 108).

Children's Rights and Devolution

The devolution process is a complex one, rendered all the more so because it has not been planned but has grown, and grown differently piecemeal in three jurisdictions. In addition, the prospect hangs over us of Scotland splitting from the United Kingdom if the UK votes to leave the European Union. Ireland poses even greater problems; Northern Ireland would exit but the Republic would remain part of the EU. But the border is seamless.

Some areas of children's rights have not devolved – immigration and asylum, child poverty, welfare and children in the military. Others have been devolved, and are the responsibility of the devolved governments. But, whether devolved or not, it is the UK government that is ultimately responsible for the implementation of the CRC across the United Kingdom, since it is the state signatory to the treaty. However, the devolution settlement has also placed duties on devolved governments. It did this through the Human Rights Act 1998. But this too, sadly, is under threat.

As the Joint Committee of the House of Lords and House of Commons noted in its report on the UK's compliance with the CRC (Joint Committee on Human Rights, 2015: para. 162):

> This has led to a patchwork of responsibilities and duties
> which sometimes overlap and in which there is also
> inevitably the possibility of gaps emerging in human right
> protection. It is therefore clearly important for all those
> across the UK with a national or UK-wide remit to
> maintain good lines of communication and remain

aware of their differing, and often complementary, responsibilities and powers.

As an example, examine the position of the four Children's Commissioners (see Rees and Williams, 2016), two of whom are Commissioners of Children and Young People. Non-devolved areas across the United Kingdom are within the remit of the Office of the Children's Commissioner for England. The Dunford Report (2014) said that this created confusion, inconsistencies and gaps in coverage. Children in Scotland, Wales and Northern Ireland are expected to contact the English Commissioner when it relates to a non-devolved matter, and certainly a question could arise which crossed jurisdictional boundaries, forcing the child to go to two Commissioners. There was an attempt to deal with this in the Children and Families Bill, but nothing came of it.

The four Children's Commissioners have different roles, remits and powers and a different relationship with their Parliaments and governments. This concerns the Committee on the Rights of the Child. There is concern that children do not get the same rights across the four countries. It has also meant that when the United Kingdom puts in its report to the Committee, it is not really able to present a coherent overarching view.

Clearly, a UK-wide examination of the impact of devolution on children's rights (indeed, human rights generally) is called for. The process of devolution will continue, and the problems will get more difficult. Before it goes any further, it should be looked at. In so far as children's rights are conceived of differently in the four different jurisdictions, it is to be hoped that a levelling up would take place, not a levelling down. Regression to the English model might result in weaker powers for the Commissioners, and a slowing of progress to more progressive legislation, for example, on outlawing corporal punishment within the home.

An Exit from the European Union?

It is important to draw attention to what an 'exit' would mean for children's rights in the United Kingdom. First, it should be stressed that children did not have the vote, despite having the largest stake in its result. Children's lives are affected by EU provisions on free movement, on immigration and asylum, on family law. There are norms on consumer protection which have implications for toy safety, paediatric drug development, etc.; there are also laws relating to sexual exploitation which directly affects the lives of adolescents in particular.

As important is the symbolism of UK withdrawal. Would it constitute yet further endorsement of pervasive neglect of children's rights by the UK government? We know that children have suffered most from the cuts in public services. 27 per cent of children are living in poverty, an increase of 3 per cent since 2008. Children's Rights Alliance for England (CRAE) predicts there will be 4.7 million children living in poverty in 2020, the year Blair promised there would be none. Resources to tackle child protection have not kept pace with the increased number of referrals. Youth services have been cut, as have budgets for child and adolescent mental health. The nadir of this blinkered parsimony has been to deny unaccompanied asylum-seeking children access to care leavers' support immediately they attain their eighteenth birthday. We have been warned that this and similar measures could plunge up to 120,000 irregular child migrants into destitution (Children's Society, 2016). So much for the best interests of children being a primary consideration (CRC, Article 3), and the emphasis on life, survival and development in Article 6. Perhaps matched only by Greece denying starving babies milk (*The Guardian*, 20 April 2016).

It is worth contrasting this record with that of the EU. The European Commission has published a preventative strategy, 'Investing in Children: Breaking the Cycle of Disadvantage', which targets child poverty and promotes child well-being. The aim is to ensure that children get access to adequate resources (including child and family benefits), as well as access to quality and inclusive services, including child care and education. The importance of real – not tokenistic – participation in decision-making is also emphasised.

The EU acts as a conduit, disseminating best practice as regards tackling poverty. The European Structural and Investment Funds are available to Member States to enhance cohesion and to reduce economic and social disparities. England is to receive £6.174 billion in regional development and social funding for the period 2014 to 2020, with children the primary beneficiaries. Wales, Scotland and Northern Ireland have invested much of their European social fund budget effecting improvements in care-leavers' education, the dental health of young children, and in enhancing affordable child care provision. The EU also has a fund to support the most deprived, providing essentials to the most materially deprived children and adults, subject to the state itself committing 15 per cent in co-funding. It has supported the development of breakfast clubs, vital for the very poorest in our society.

In conclusion, if Brexit were to succeed, the poorest children would lose out more than most. Child poverty and social exclusion will get worse. 'The EU plays a significant role in ensuring that optimum resources and opportunities are in place to enable children to develop to their fullest potential' (Stalford, 2016: 8).

This is inevitably being written at a time of great uncertainty. The UK government is committed to Brexit without being clear as to what this means or its implications. What is clear is that it hadn't realised the complexities of leaving the EU. It is possible that in the end the United Kingdom will not leave. Or is this mere fantasy by the author who is a committed European?

11

Child-Friendly Justice

Although it has only become a theme of children's rights very recently, child-friendly justice has motivated the movement for children's rights since the emergence of the child-saving movement in the mid-1880s: thus, there developed an institutional structure to target juvenile crime, the juvenile court in 1908, approved schools, borstal. It was not until 1907 that Parliament recognised the concept and value of probation (a terse summary of these developments can be found in Freeman 1983: 66–9). Most discussion even today centres on making criminal justice child-friendly, but there are now similar concerns in family dispute processes and elsewhere. In Wales there is even discussion of a 'play-friendly' Wales (Welsh Government, 2012).

Child-friendly justice was explained by the High Commissioner for Human Rights (2013) as 'the ability to obtain a just and timely remedy for violations of rights in national and international norms and standards, including the Convention on the Rights of the Child'. The report went on to emphasise that the 'concept of access to justice for children requires the legal empowerment of all children'. The importance of effective remedies to claim rights is also stressed. Also in 2013, the Council of Europe issued Guidelines. These explain that child-friendly justice refers to 'justice systems which guarantee the respect and the effective implementation of all children's rights at the highest attainable level'. Pinheiro (2015) adds that adults must do more than stand back and encourage children. They must act to secure justice for children, expose violations and pursue effective remedies.

Child-friendly justice is a continuation of the agenda set out by the CRC. Thus, Article 12 seen in a child-friendly way will ensure that children's voices are actually heard, and that they are interpreted consistently with current social psychological evidence and thinking. Cederborg (2015) emphasises the importance of high-quality interviews when trying to understand legal matters from children's perspectives. Fridriksdottir (2015) points to the concern to the need for a balance between participation and protection. 'Under-representation, over-representation and conflicting representation can silence the voice of the child and distort the interests of the child in the process' (2015: 72). There is focus on the best ways of getting evidence.

Child-Friendly Systems

The adoption of child-friendly systems is fast becoming a dominant theme. Thus, the Council of Europe Conference of Health Ministers in 2011 produced a Declaration on child-friendly health care. The United Kingdom is a signatory to this. It recognises 'children's rights as a guiding principle in the planning, delivery and monitoring of healthcare services for children'. The Lewis and Lenehan Committee in 2012 recommended that the NHS Constitution apply also to children, young people and their families, and that the Department of Health should produce a children's health charter based on the CRC.

It is important that children see themselves as addressees of the CRC. They should be encouraged to understand what rights they are supposed to have, what is the value of such rights, and what they are missing out on by not having a particular right. They should also be encouraged to appreciate that they have responsibilities too, some of which are correlative to the rights. This is brought out very well in a South African comic strip (and see Appendix 5). The Convention, as with laws everywhere, is not addressed to children, but rather to administrators, law-makers, judges and other adults, and it is expressed in language with which they are familiar. This is typical of the top-bottom approach. It is therefore important that the CRC is simplified and can be used in lessons/discussions. There are many examples of this, often produced by NGOs. UNICEF's reduction of the Convention is reproduced as Appendix 4.

How many schools currently teach human rights and/or children's rights? My hunch is that very few do. Just as 'war studies' (and cadet corps) are more likely to be found in syllabi than 'peace studies' and negotiation skills, so in a largely top-down environment it is hardly surprising that a subject which could lead to the boat being rocked is likely to be side-lined.

In 2011, African Guidelines on child-friendly justice were issued. The dominant aim of all these guidelines is to enhance children's access to, and treatment in, the justice system. On access, see below, p. 290.

Peter Newell (2015) has asked the pertinent question whether making children criminals can ever be child-friendly. Should we instead be promoting forms of diversion and restorative justice? We have an absurdly low minimum age at which criminal sanctions bite: children of primary school age can be convicted of criminal offences. In most other European countries even a crime like that of the murder of James Bulger would have been dealt with without invoking the full majesty of the criminal law (Freeman, 1997b). Although not contrary to the letter of the CRC – this leaves the minimum age to be fixed by each state party – it most certainly undermines its ideological message that children's best interests must be a primary consideration, that children have a right to maximum possible development (Article 6), and that states must establish laws, procedures, authorities and institutions specifically for children in conflict with the law (Article 40(3)).

It is imperative that the Committee grasps the nettle and makes a firm proposal that no state party should impose criminal sanctions on a child. This would not preclude fixing a minimum age below which a child would be presumed to lack the capacity to commit a crime. This could be pitched at fourteen, fifteen or sixteen, but certainly not ten (the English standard) or twelve (the Committee's current recommendation). In 2016, Egypt exceeded all expectations and convicted a four-year-old boy of an offence, allegedly committed when he was two, for which he was given life imprisonment!

Bulger *and a Norwegian Comparison*

The vast majority of children who offend are damaged and/or disadvantaged, the victims of abuse or neglect. Putting them through the criminal process serves principally to reinforce low self-esteem. Literacy rates are poor, employment prospects are dismal. There is alienation, and increasing radicalisation. I was fortunate to be present at a day of the trial in Preston Crown Court of James Bulger's killers. Anything less like 'child-friendly' justice it would be difficult to imagine. Many years ago we tried animals. This was little different. Neither boy participated in the trial process; one snoozed on a social worker's shoulder, the other doodled. They were bored and bewildered. Meanwhile, outside the court the crowd bayed for their blood. If *vox populi* had had anything to do with it, the boys would have been hanged. There was a gap of nine months between the killing and the trial, but there could be no therapeutic intervention during this time since this might lead to the evidence being contaminated. The trial made no concessions to the age of the defendants. It was conducted in a traditional court-room before a bewigged and robed judge, and in the presence of a jury, though hardly one of the boys' peers. The trial proceeded according to adult norms of behaviour, expression, procedure and style. The boys sat in a dock, with two male social workers in attendance. The judge clearly had no experience of youth delinquency. At times he addressed the boys as if they were Victorian urchins straight out of *Oliver Twist*. At one point he even adopted a mock scouse accent, as if conceding that the language of the trial was alien to the boys.

As said already, neither boy gave evidence. In a less formal setting they might have been quite revealing. As it was, they were psychologically traumatised. Their minds were confused, their memories blurred, they were fantasising in childish ways. One spoke (outside the trial) of James Bulger as a character in a chocolate factory and imagined that, as in some

286

Disneyesque scenario, he might be brought back to life. The other also talked of James being 'mended'. They might have been living on different planets.

A good comparison is with a case contemporaneous with the Bulger events in Norway.

In 1994, in Trondheim, Norway, five-year-old Silje Redergard was beaten to death by two boys. Today, the girl's family still suffers, and one of the boys is in trouble again – the echoes of the *Bulger* case are clear. So, why has the public reaction in Norway been so startlingly different?

The most significant difference was that, in Britain, the authorities decided to let the nation judge the child killers. Trying Thompson and Venables as adults and releasing names and mugshots unleashed a countrywide roar of anguish that can still be heard – much to the disadvantage of any damaged child who behaves badly to another, and who needs help rather than 'justice'. What Silje's story demonstrates is that it needn't have been that way.

'At first there was a lynch mob atmosphere (in the town)', her mother says. 'Everybody wanted to know who had done it. Once we got to know that it was these little boys who'd done it, that lynch mob mood died down'. Beathe Redergard says she 'felt bad' for the boys even in the middle of her grief, because they were 'just little kids'.

Why two little boys should have inflicted such terrible violence on a playmate will never be known. 'We beat her till she stopped crying', one of them later told the police, a clue perhaps as to why the viciousness of the attack escalated, but not as to why it should have occurred in the first place.

Everyone agreed that something must have been wrong psychologically. There were reports that one of the boys had been sexually abused before the attack. Nobody said the boys were evil. Neither were they branded criminal – and nor would they have been, even if they had been the same age as Thompson and Venables, who were both aged ten when they killed James. In Norway, the age of criminal responsibility is fifteen.

The death of a child at the hands of other children is rare, and of huge national interest wherever it occurs. In Trondheim, there had been just two murders in the previous six years. What happened to Silje Redergard could have been the news event of the decade. But in contrast to the vengeful rage of the popular press in the United Kingdom towards the Bulger killers, there was no sensational reporting of her death in the Norwegian press.

On the day after Silje's body was discovered there were no pictures or descriptions of her in Norwegian newspapers, nor did they give her name. The names of the boys, also, were never revealed to the public – and their anonymity has been protected and respected, even though many people (not least Silje's parents) know who they are. The efforts made to contain the tragedy were huge. Within a couple of weeks the two boys were enrolled in another local infants school. 'The parents of the other children accepted this situation and a lot of parents thought that these children needed to be in the kindergarten and needed to be taken care of.'

Aase Prytz Slettemoen, who managed the caseworker responsible for supervising the care of the boys for eight years after Silje's death is clear about Norway's policy of avoiding the criminalisation of the young. 'We don't believe in prison for youngsters', she says, 'so we think that if we can help them in any other way, that's what we should do'.

Great care was taken to ensure that the two boys were protected rather than punished. The boys are now adults. Prytz Slettemoen is adamant that there have been no serious problems. 'Neither of them have been involved in violence or criminal activities. They've done quite well', she says.

In Norway, child protection services maintain their relationship with troubled children until they reach majority. At that point they are given the choice of making their own way, or maintaining contact with the children's agency up to the age of twenty-three. After that they may choose to maintain a relationship with adult services.

The legacy of Silje's killing runs deep for her family, too. Not a day passes when they do not think about her, says Jorgen Barlaup, Silje's step-father. And what do they think of the two boys who killed her now? 'We've forgiven them for being children', he says, 'but we'll never forgive them for what they did, if that makes sense...If we'd gone around hating children afterward, we wouldn't be able to love our own children, and we remember Silje best by loving our kids. I mean, Silje won't come walking through the door.'

What is strange – at least to British eyes – is that the people of Norway appear to have forgiven and forgotten. The debate has been had and people have learned what they can. In Britain, the outcry over the *Bulger* case is still in full voice, with crowds baying for Venables' blood.

Access to Justice

One of the best known clauses in Magna Carta states:

> To no man will we delay or deny justice.

For more than 700 years we did just that routinely. The ordinary person had no opportunity to prosecute or defend a claim. A system of legal aid and advice did not exist. We had to wait until the Attlee government after the Second World War for legislation to introduce a rudimentary system. There was a means test and a merits test. The latter was to ensure that the State's money was not frittered away on unwinnable causes. Most litigants subsidised by legal aid won. Legal aid was not a great success. It assumed the barrier to using courts was exclusively economic, but the malaise goes deeper than that. There were geographical barriers: lawyer's offices tend to be congregated in middle-class enclaves or legal squares, places where the majority of the population fear to tread. There are socio-psychological barriers, which include a lack of legal socialisation. These were not the only barriers, but they were enough to ensure that the promise of Magna Carta was not fulfilled. The doors to justice opened ajar in 1949 have now been finally closed.

The latest developments have cast a shadow over the whole project. The Legal Aid, Sentencing and Punishment of Offenders (LASPO) Act 2012 had as one of its aims the saving of £350 million from the legal aid budget, then amounting to £2.1 billion. No ECHR memorandum was attached to the LASPO Bill, and it paid no attention to children's rights. Areas of life with major impact on children, such as welfare and asylum, were badly affected. The number of children granted legal aid for education fell by 84 per cent, and the number granted such support where parents have divorced or separated dropped by 69 per cent. But because it led to an increase in the number of litigants in person and consequently to cases taking more time, the money saved was less than anticipated.

An attempt to protect in exceptional cases where an absence of funding would lead to a clear breach of human rights has not been successful. There were many fewer applications than had been anticipated, and almost all the applications failed. As far as children are concerned, evidence by JustRights indicates that the number of children and young persons receiving Special Welfare legal aid and immigration and asylum legal aid have fallen by nearly two-thirds to below even the post-LASPO levels anticipated by the government. It also reports that only three children were granted legal aid under the Exceptional Case Funding scheme in the first twelve months for which there are available statistics.

As if LASPO were not a sufficient barrier frustrating access to justice, the government followed it by introducing a draft Legal Aid, Sentencing and Punishment of Offenders Act 2012 (Amendments of Schedule 1) Order 2014. This introduced a residence test and, in doing so, further restricted access. Under it, to be eligible an applicant would have to demonstrate a 'strong connection' to the United Kingdom. They needed to be 'lawfully resident in the UK' at the time of their application for legal aid, and to have resided lawfully in the UK for twelve months continuously prior to this. There were no exemptions for children. And children, particularly unaccompanied migrant children, refused asylum-seekers unable to return to their country of origin, age-disputed children, children abandoned by parents or carers, undocumented migrant children, and children lawfully resident for less than twelve months, forfeited any eligibility they might have had. This Order breached the CRC:

Article 2 because it discriminated against particular children within its jurisdiction;

Article 3 because it didn't treat children as a primary consideration;

Article 12 because a child has the right to be heard in any judicial or administrative process.

The High Court ruled that the residence test was illegal and discriminatory. It held that the Lord Chancellor had acted *ultra vires* in introducing the residence test through secondary legislation, and that the test was unjustifiably discriminatory in that it excluded access to legal aid on grounds that did not relate to need. This is the sort of high-handed action which led to the proclamation of Magna Carta 800 years earlier. The residence test showed scant regard for the welfare of vulnerable children. These legal aid reforms are said to be 'a significant black mark on the Coalition Government's human rights record' (Joint Committee on Human Rights, 2015: para. 118), there is no reason to anticipate things getting any better, with refugees now 'folk devils' (S. Cohen, 1972).

Children in Custody

It is good to be able to report that the number of children involved in the youth custody system has decreased substantially in recent years. The number of first time entrants in

2013/14 is 75 per cent less than it was ten years ago, and 2 per cent less than in 2012/13. But there has been a huge increase in the number of children in prison. We have the highest level of incarceration in Western Europe. The average length of time spent in prison by each child has increased. This should set alarm bells ringing, if only to alert us to the gross breach of our obligations under the CRC:

Article 39: no cruel, inhuman or degrading treatment or punishment. Reintegration in an environment which fosters the health, self-respect and dignity of the child.

Article 40: the right of every child to be treated in a manner consistent with the promotion of the child's sense of dignity and worth which reinforces the child's respect for the human rights of others, and which take a child's age into consideration.

In the light of these provisions, concern is raised by revelations about the use of force on children in custody. A graphic example is the *Panorama* investigation screened on BBC television in March 2016. This showed a level of violence which was in clear breach of these Articles, as well as Articles 3, 6, 19 and 27. New legislation only accentuates these concerns. The Criminal Justice and Courts Act 2014 establishes a new form of youth detention, in what are to be called secure colleges. The concept neatly combines the image of the educational establishment with the penal, as to be almost oxymoronic! However, the government has stressed that education is to be at the heart of detention.

Secure colleges can use force to restrain if 'authorized to do so by secure college rules'. These permit the use of reasonable force where necessary to secure good order and discipline. 'Good order and discipline' is both vague and value-laden. It would be better if force were to be triggered only where there was danger that significant harm to the inmate or others was likely if force were not used to restrain.

Access to justice for children in prison is of concern. In the light of the reforms already discussed, children will find it very difficult to get redress when victimised. Where remedies are absent, rights are meaningless.

Deaths in custody are of particular concern. The Committee on the Rights of the Child (2016) is concerned about the large numbers of children in custody, and with the disproportionate number of them who are from Afro-Caribbean communities. They are concerned also about the use of solitary confinement, which they think should be stopped, and with the use of deliberately painful restraint on children, a practice they believe should be abolished.

12

The World Twenty-Five Years On:
New Issues and Responses

The world has changed since 1989: the end of Communism and the rise of a 'capitalist' China, and of Islam. How many draftsmen of the Convention anticipated this? The World Wide Web: this only dates from 1989, though this seems difficult to believe so 'ordinary' has it become. The sexual abuse of children: the 'Cleveland Affair' (Butler-Sloss, 1988) had only just turned this into a recognisable social problem. Globalisation (Darian-Smith, 2013; Stiglitz, 2002) was not the force it is now. Only a few scientists spoke of global warming and climate change. Few, if any, spoke of biodiversity or sustainable development. The medically assisted revolution was still in its infancy. Human enhancement was science fiction, neuro-enhancement, fantasy, and discussion of cloning belonged to the world of fiction (*The Boys from Brazil* and such like). Islamophobia, like antisemitism, was embedded deep in the cultural heritage of Western civilisation, but hadn't yet boiled over – this only happened in the wake of 9/11 in the case of Islam, and Gaza in the case of antisemitism, and subsequently in 2016 in the British Labour Party (Ornstein, 2017).

These changes affect the world's children more than any other section of society. It is they who will live with the impact of global warming, the IT revolution, the reproductive revolution, neuroscience. It is they who are being groomed – and 'Jim Won't Fix It' (Davies, 2014; Furedi, 2013). They who

are being trafficked (O'Connell Davidson, 2005). They who
are being 'sexted', often for sexual slavery. They who have to
live with ageist policies.

Childhood Exploited

Childhood has always been exploited: now, there are new ways
of exploiting children (Giroux and Pollock, 2010). Subjected to
'corporate capture' (Nairn, 2013), children are becoming more
and more 'materialistic, overweight, stressed, depressed and
self-destructive' (Beder, Varney and Gosden, 2009: 223).

Girls' bodies are more commercialised than ever
(Carey, 2011; Orbach, 2013; Pilcher, 2011). *Vogue* can happily
publish seventeen pages of paedophile images of a ten-year-old
model, and it takes the *Daily Mail* (2011) to expose this. The
Internet has created a global market for child sexual abuse
(Girling, 2013). Childhood is said to be 'toxic' (Palmer, 2006),
'under siege' (Bakan, 2011), to suffer from 'nature-deficit disorder' (Louv, 2010). There has been a 'criminalisation' of natural play, and the rise of 'play' (Hawes, 2013; Louv, 2010). The
porn culture turns women (and therefore girls) into sex objects
(MacKinnon, 1992); the 'music' culture encourages misogyny
(Kistler and Moon, 2009; Warburton, 2013). It is not only boys
who are affected by this. Adolescent women exposed to 'rap
music' with lyrics about female subordination seem to accept
date violence towards women more than those not so subjected
(Johnson, Jackson and Gatto, 1995). Child abuse is barely
recognisable as even related to what Henry Kempe wrote
about fifty years ago (Kempe and Kempe, 1973). As an example,
look at the following, as reported by Joel Bakan:

In the spring of 2008 the video game *Grand Theft Auto IV* was released, selling in its first weeks six million units for a half billion dollars and thus smashing every entertainment industry record. It was now clear that brutal and sometimes sexual violence was a top entertainment choice for kids (*sic*). Tween and teenage boys loved the video game (nearly half of all thirteen-year-old boys reported it as their favourite), which like many other popular video games allows players to choose among and create different, and unusually violent, scenarios for a protagonist avatar.

In one possible *GTA IV* scenario, inspired by a promotional trailer for the game and posted on YouTube, protagonist Nick Bellic, a grizzled Balkan Wars vet, has sex with a female prostitute in his car and then murders her. The murder is brutal. Bellic beats her with a baseball bat and then, as she runs away, he throws a bomb at her. The bomb explodes, she catches fire, and falls to the ground, engulfed in flames, her body quivering. Bellic then sprays her with bullets from a machine gun. Once she stops moving, Bellic reaches into her pants pocket to retrieve the money he paid her for sex. He then saunters back to his car.

Despite its 'mature' rating (the industry's designation that a game is inappropriate for kids (*sic*) under the age of eighteen), *GTA IV*, like other mature-rated games, is often sold to underage kids who happily buy and play it. Nearly one half of all twelve-to sixteen-year-olds and a quarter of eight-to-eleven-year-olds own mature-rate games. (Bakan, 2011: 19)

So what of the future? Is it as good as it gets? Or can we still hope for a better deal for our children? Let's face it – the plight of children has got worse in the twenty-six years since the Convention. Laws can only achieve so much. I have said many times that rights require remedies, and remedies require the injection of resources. Much from which children suffer, such as a degraded environment, for example, can only be put right by a world committed to children and ultimately to humane world governance (Falk, 2013).

Post-1989 Developments

As UNICEF explained, 'investment in children is a fundamental means to eradicate poverty, and enhance inter-generational equity...Sustainable development starts and ends with safe, healthy and well-educated children' (UNICEF, 2013). It cannot be a substitution for children's rights. It is not a project which should allow us to bypass children's rights. As UNICEF admitted in 2004, 'A Child-Friendly City is a local system of good govern-ance committed to fulfilling children's rights' (UNICEF, 2004).

Millennium Development Goals and Sustainable Development Goals

More than a decade after the CRC, eight Millennium Development Goals (MDGs) were agreed at a UN Millennium Summit in 2000 where all UN member states agreed to work towards achieving these goals by 2015. They covered all aspects of human development, with the most relevant to children being Goal 2 'Achieve universal primary education by 2015'. Since the MDGs expired at the end of 2015, the United Nations introduced a new process to develop 'Sustainable Development

Goals' (SDGs), to be agreed by the world's governments as new targets for 2030.

Since Education for All (EFA) goals and MDGs/SDGs are often no more than restatements of legal obligations the same governments have already accepted when they ratified the ICESCR and CRC, and a monitoring mechanism is already in operation, the question arises as to why these additional processes are needed? Colclough (2005) points out that the EFA goals and MDGs do not represent legal obligations on governments like the provisions of human rights treaties, but are expressions of political will and commitment. States that have not successfully met their obligations, instead of being named and shamed as rights violators, can be recognised as, and supported in, working on an agreed plan to achieve firm targets by fixed dates. The legal and political processes are thus intended to be complementary and mutually supportive.

The 2013 UNICEF report identified three principles behind the post-2015 agenda for children:

> Sustainable development starts with safe, healthy and well-educated children. Safe and sustainable societies are, in turn, essential for children; and children's voices and participation are critical for the sustainable future we want.
> (UNICEF, 2013: 3)

This was emphasised too in UNICEF's *State of the World's Children Report* for 2012:

> Equity must be the guiding principle in efforts for all children in urban areas. The children of slums...will require particular attention. But this must not come at the

> expense of children elsewhere. The larger goal must remain in focus: fairer, more nurturing cities and societies for all people – starting with children. (UNICEF, 2012: 75)

One way the Child Friendly Cities Initiative can, at the same time, advance children's rights is by engaging with children and recognising that they can play a role in the rehabilitation of their environments. The UN Resolution 'The Future We Want' in 2012 made this clear:

> We stress the importance of the active participation of young people in decision-making processes, as the issues...have a deep impact on present and future generations and as the contribution of children and youth is vital to the achievement of sustainable development.

There are already examples of this, and there are positive results. In India, 'children's direct participation in local area planning and design for slum improvements...[was] a good step forward in creating child-friendly cities' (Chatterjee, 2012: 23). Children's needs and rights are thus inter-dependent with sustainable development (see also Y. Bradshaw, 1993).

Other Global Initiatives

The United Nations has also initiated a number of international mechanisms to further the realisation of education rights for the world's children. In 2012, UN Secretary-General Ban Ki-moon launched a Global Initiative on Education ('Education First'). The initiative's three priorities are to put every child in school; improve the quality of learning; and to foster global citizenship (United Nations, 2012).

Another well-established initiative is 'Education for All', an ongoing global process led by UNESCO in partnership with other UN agencies, launched in 1990 with a 'World Declaration on Education For All' (UNESCO, 1990), followed by an international 'Framework for Action' in 2000 (UNESCO, 2000). Annual Education for All Global Monitoring Reports provide data the goal of which is to inform and motivate stakeholders to achieve these goals (UNESCO, 2015).

As human-rights-based approaches gained influence in international cooperation and development in the 2000s (United Nations, 2003; UNDP, 2006), concern was expressed that the EFA process was taking the global education campaign away from its human rights base and regressing to needs-based thinking (Beiter, 2006; Tomaševski, 2001). To address these concerns, UNESCO and UNICEF produced a new framework document entitled 'A Human Rights-Based Approach to Education For All' (Lansdown et al., 2007) based on three key education rights; namely, the rights of access to education, the right to quality education, and the right to respect in the learning environment. A new Declaration was agreed, and draft Framework for Action proposed, at Incheon, South Korea, in May 2015, expressing the UN agencies' and participating states' shared commitment to move towards 'inclusive and equitable quality education and lifelong learning for all' by 2030 (UNESCO, 2015).

1989 and beyond has seen many new challenges. All affect children, some of them acutely. These range from financial instability to global warming; pandemics such as HIV/AIDS; widening disparities in wealth and well-being; cultural and religious conflicts (these are destined to surpass the notorious 'Thirty Years War' of the seventeenth century) (Wedgwood, 1947); the reproduction revolution; the Human Genome mapping; the possibility of human enhancement, even now neuro-enhancement; environmental degradation, including food scarcity; increasing migratory problems (the European election of 2014 was driven by moral panics about the consequences of these); threats to cyber security (Livingstone, 2009).

The generation of adults now engaged in production are the first to have grown up global (Fass, 2007; Katz, 2004). Globalisation will have had – and continue to have – a profound impact on their lives, more than the Convention of 1989 will have had though, of course, the CRC is itself an example of the inexorable drive towards globalisation (Nieuwenhuys, 2010).

Nor does the Convention do much to protect children from the 'slings and arrows' of globalisation. The effects of globalisation alone require many books. Perhaps this is what the writer of *Ecclesiastes* had in mind when he wisely observes that 'of the making of many books there is no end'! But he also thought there was nothing new under the sun, and there clearly is!

The Convention is, of course, an example of globalisation in action. So is the work of UNICEF and the World Bank and other international development agencies. UNICEF assumed a role to protect children worldwide (Burr, 2002). But the tendency is to impose a Western model of childhood on the developing world's children (R. Smith, 2010). Thus, Erica Burman argues that 'the concept of childhood on offer is a Western construction that is now being incorporated, as though it were universal, into aid and development policies'

(Burman, 1999: 178). The measuring-rod of all societies is the Western standard. Lewis puts it thus:

> The problems with the globalisation of Western models of childhood...is not a normative but a political one. By setting this standard southern childhood is not only effectively erased from international view, but the western model of childhood becomes the standard by which to judge southern societies...The southern child...becomes the object of Western Intervention either in the form of aid or nurture, or as a constraint and moral condemnation of southern societies as a whole. (Lewis, 1998: 95)

And Gareth Jones explains:

> The notion of the 'global child' as the holder of rights is a barely-obscure western-centric view of 'normal' child-adult and child-society relations that condemns 'other' styles of upbringing as 'outside' childhood. (G. Jones, 2005: 338, see also Jones and Thomas de Benitez, 2014)

It is difficult to know the best way to deal with this. One answer is to regionalise. But then there is already an African Charter, and it is remarkably close in content to the UN Convention. It is all very well having doubts about the application of Western norms to African children. But take a simple example. On the whole, the West condemns violence against children. In most Western societies, corporal punishment in schools (at least) is a thing of the past. Caning remains endemic in African schools. Are we wrong to want to rid African schools of the cane? In the same way, are we not right to condemn FGM? Should it survive censure just because it is one of Africa's cultural practices? (Twum-Danso, 2016).

The work/education balance is more difficult. It is easy to condemn child labour and advocate schooling for all children (including girls), but take away the income from work (and it is pathetically small – children are exploited), and children can starve. Children without jobs do not necessarily end up in schools. They may end up as street children or in the informal economy (in prostitution, for example). The application of Western standards may actually harm children (Kauffman, 2002). Is it an answer that it will benefit future generations of such children? That today's children must suffer to foster a cultural revolution? Also, we know there is often resistance to imposed change.

Rethinking Some Norms

It is inevitable that in a period of rapid change there will be different concerns. New problems will emerge or at least be recognised. The IT revolution, the reproductive revolution, radical movements, global warming, are just a few of the issues on our minds today, but not so back in 1989. And so, there is cyber bullying and sexting, there is international surrogacy and reprogenetics, there is radicalisation, there is breast ironing (or flattening) – as if we didn't have enough to cope with in the CRC, as formulated.

There are also practices now being questioned, which are not new, but which are now of concern for the first time. Male circumcision is a good example; the non-enfranchisement of children is another. The sexual abuse of children has always been with us, but in the United Kingdom it came into prominence only with the Cleveland revelations shortly before the CRC was finalised. This was not something that 'Jim' could fix. In the last quarter of a century we have been swamped by stories of sexual exploitation. Our eyes have been opened to sex tourism and to grooming. The courts have handed down some condign sentences – in 2016, a football idol was given six years for what would have passed relatively unnoticed a generation ago (*The Guardian*, 24 March 2016). This sets a standard, but uses him to do so. It is a form of judicial law-making; as such is it acceptable? And it treats the individual as a means to an end.

The IT revolution has brought with it problems that few can have anticipated. Those who drafted the CRC may therefore be exonerated. Bullying has always been a problem in schools, but the development of the Internet has exacerbated it. The bully now has immediate access to his victim, and not just in the school playground, but everywhere and at all times. Threats come online, via the Internet, by e-mail, through social media such as Facebook, by mobiles, messaging apps and games. US research (National Crime Prevention Council, 2014) suggests nearly half of teens experience cyber bullying. We know of suicides by adolescents. In the United States, it is said that 20 per cent of middle school students have thought about ending their lives because of bullying threats (Goodman, 2016: 116).

Sexting too has emerged as a form of cyber bullying. It is a particular variant of stalking but which is used to target mainly adult women, and sexting affects adolescents too. Sexting is undoubtedly a growing phenomenon: a recent US study suggests as many as 67 per cent of college-age students admitted to indulging in the practice (Drouin and Landgraff, 2012).

Bullying and grooming are both harmful to children and adolescents, and it is uncontroversial that they should be targeted, as indeed they are. A specific provision directed to each would be preferable: this could be affected by a Protocol. Sexting is more controversial. Where this is consensual, outlawing it denies willing participants autonomy. Does the harm, or the risk of harm, trump the choice we would otherwise be prepared to recognise?

A Magna Carta for Children

PART III

A Major Cure for Children

13

Rethinking Children's Rights

From Participation to Citizenship

As noted previously, discussion about, and research into, children's rights, has been ensnared by consensus. It is easy to take the Convention on the Rights of the Child (CRC) as the final victory for children, what we have long been aiming for and have now achieved. It is tempting to chorus 'Halleluiah'! But there are dangers in foreclosing critique. To get as far as we have it has been necessary to challenge the status quo, for example, to show that children are 'beings', not merely 'becomings'. But having achieved this, we must ask 'What are the implications of recognising this?' It is easy to rest on our laurels and to accept the Convention as the new status quo. Beethoven's first foray into symphonic writing broke new ground but it didn't stop him writing the 'Eroica' and ultimately the 'Choral'.

We must acknowledge that the CRC is a landmark in the history of childhood. In its day, 800 years ago, Magna Carta was a milestone on the way to a rule of law society and to democracy, and progress was slow thereafter. We had to fight for rights. None was given without a struggle. Think of the women's suffrage movement. Or the fight (still continuing) for the right of workers to organise collectively. (Ironically, children got the CRC without a fight.)

Children now have Article 12 (Daly, 2018). Back in 1998, I described this as the 'linchpin' of the Convention. And it is. Significantly, it has stimulated a huge volume of research, and much of it is valuable. We have greater insights into children's abilities; we know what they think of work, school, their parents' divorce, corporal punishment, abuse, than was the case a generation ago. Indeed, we have insights into what they think about children's rights (see e.g., Ruck, Abramovitch and Keating, 1998). Childhood studies have sharpened our understanding of the agency of children, made us appreciate that it is a social construction. A branch of childhood studies, child psychology, has enlightened us about development. Another branch of childhood studies – children's geographies – has shown us how children participate in changing the nature of social space (R. Hart, 2008: 13). Children's rights scholarship, by contrast, certainly until recently, remained firmly moored to the 'safe' ground of positivistic legal analysis. But even childhood studies has succumbed to being colonised by the 1989 Convention.

Let us take Article 12 as a test case. After all, there is a general agreement that it constitutes the most significant innovation in the Convention. But a careful examination of Article 12 reveals at once that it is not all that it is taken for.

Article 12(1) states:

> States parties shall assure to the child who is capable of forming his or her views the right to express those views freely in all matters affecting the child, the views of the child being given due weight in accordance with the age and maturity of the child.

We are told this gives children the right to participate, even, I loosely claimed, 'autonomy'! (Freeman, 1998). This is far from the truth.

First, note that before Article 12 can take off, the child must have been assessed (presumably by adults) as capable of forming his/her own views. Secondly, adults must allow the child to express views, but only where adults are of the opinion that the matter in question affects the child. Thirdly, these views are to be given the weight that adults believe they should have. This will be calibrated on an assessment of the child's development and maturity, the assessment also undertaken by adults. A similar process is used when an assessment is undertaken by a court in England to determine whether a child is *Gillick*-competent. And note that we have a Children Act (an Act about children), not a Children's Act (an Act *for* children) (Freeman, 1996a; Hough, 1995).

I have made the point often that children played no part in the drafting of the Convention. Negotiating states were represented by adults. Children were excluded from what has been called 'the social practice of active citizenship' (Percy-Smith, 2014). Is participation just a sham? Brian Milne comes close to such a conclusion. He writes:

> Child participation tends. . .to be a distraction and to move the issue away from citizenship. . .The contemporary pro-child participation view tends to suggest separatism. Accordingly, children generally make decisions addressing the issues of children and are allowed to have a degree of opinion but no real political influence. There is certainly no real decision making capability in the world generally

> where adults are best placed to decide for them. In other
> words, children are allowed only partial citizenship
> through a veneer of playing a role in their part of *civil
> society*. (Milne, 2013: 35)

Has the time come to transcend participation and move towards
the recognition of children as citizens? Children are citizens
from birth, if not before. Onora O'Neill, it will be remembered,
could not conceive of the growth of children's movements, and
I was critical of this myopia. When I was in Chile in 2008,
I witnessed large demonstrations by secondary school students,
demanding the right to work and rights in work. This can in no
way fit with Article 12's participatory rights. These demonstrations exposed the inequalities afflicting Chilean society in spite
of the macro-economic achievements and existing spaces of
freedom; this massive group of secondary school students managed to raise awareness and show the unrest which had grown
during the years of transition to democracy post-Pinochet.

There are many more examples in the recent past
(A-M. Smith, 2007; Cordero Arce, 2015) and in history
(Stammers, 2009). Does this mean that the Convention lacks
legitimacy amongst children? Jürgen Habermas certainly
thinks so. He wrote of the idea of 'self-legislation by citizens'
requiring that 'those subject to law as its addressees' at the
'same time understand(ing) themselves as authors of law'
(Habermas, 1996: 120). This has its roots in a fictional social
contract (Cockburn, 2013), first articulated in the seventeenth
century by the political philosopher, John Locke (1690).

The writings of Iris Marion Young (1990, 2000),
though she does not address children, are particularly

instructive. She argues that instead of a fictional contract, what is required are:

> real participatory structures in which actual people, with their geographical, ethnic, gender and occupational differences, assert their perspectives on social issues that encourage the representation of their distinct voices.
> (1990: 116)

She argues that oppressed groups should have a guaranteed role in policy formation. This group representation implies institutional mechanisms and public resources supporting three activities: (i) self-organisation to achieve collective empowerment; (ii) group analysis and group generation of policy proposals in institutionalised contexts where decision-makers are obliged to show that their deliberations have taken group perspectives into account; and (iii) group veto power regarding specific policies that affect a group directly (1990: 184). She does not develop the implications of these proposals for children, but they can be so considered. The concept of the impact statement can clearly be seen in the second of the items on her agenda.

Young writes also of oppression, more fully than any-one. She sees this as having five faces, all relevant to children. They are exploitation, marginalisation, powerlessness, cultural imperialism and violence. She does not discuss any of these specifically in relation to children, but each is relevant to children's lives. Briefly, examples are exploitation of young carers (there are nearly a quarter of a million in the United Kingdom, 29,000 of whom are under nine); marginalisation of 'racially marked groups'; powerlessness of all deprived of

313

voting rights; cultural imperialism, common to those stereo-
typed as 'the Other'; and violence, including institutional
racism, child abuse, being trafficked, corporal punishment.

Young offers us a partial characterisation of children
only. But, certainly in the late 1970s when the possibility of
a convention was first being mooted, there was no demand by
children for a code of children's rights. The initiative came
from enlightened adults whose actions may be described,
somewhat ironically, as paternalist (see also Cordero Arce,
2015: 15). As the Pole, Adam Lopatka, who had been Chair of
the UN Working Group on the CRC, recollected at
a conference in Jerusalem in 1990, children needed 'additional
human rights' because they were weaker than adults (Lopatka,
1992: 48–9). It is worthy of note that when Lopatka sum-
marises the CRC, he quotes Article 12(1) and refers to the
child's right to privacy (Article 16), but ignores the basic
freedoms in Articles 13–15 (expression, thought, conscience,
religion, association, peaceful assembly), which not only children but also adults lacked in the Communist bloc which had
just come to an end when he spoke. I recall asking him
whether he wished to revise his text for publication, but he
was steadfast in his refusal to do so. Of course, it is the Articles
following Article 12 – the very ones missing from Lopatka's
account – which point beyond participation towards citizenship. It is an interesting question why we emphasise participation, which is so vague and indeterminate that a whole
scholarship has grown up pouring content into it (see, for
example, R. Hart, 1997; Shier, 2002; Thomas, 2007), and at the
same time gloss over the very rights with which we
associate citizenship. And, more to the point, the freedoms

most likely to be articulated by older children, at least those in the Global North.

Article 12 is a beginning, perhaps the beginning of the end, but it is far from the end. Article 12 is a reflection of a dominant adultism. It is a long way from democracy. Perhaps, youth activism points the way. We saw an example of this earlier in the book; the radicalism of the Youth Liberation of Ann Arbor in the 1970s. There were judicial statements in that era too, albeit isolated, like Justice Abe Fortas in *Tinker*, supporting the right of school children to protest the Vietnam War. Today, much engagement for democracy in parts of the world where it is totally absent stems from youth activism.

But not only from youth activism. We should not forget the work of Janusz Korczak in running progressive orphanages in Poland 100 years ago. He designed them to be just communities. Look at the Declaration of Children's Rights constructed by Korczak (it is reproduced as Appendix 2). It includes the child's right to respect, the right to make mistakes and the right to be taken seriously. He was convinced that children were more capable than most adults think.

Patricia Williams (1991: 93) apropos of racism makes the point that:

> if women enter environments where men have only been talking to men, the conversation is bound to change. If blacks enter spaces where whites have only been talking to other whites, the conversation is bound to grow somewhat more encompassing.

There are important lessons here for including children in decision-only processes where they have something to offer, as will often be the case.

Roche comments (1999: 489):

> We need to think through the terms on which participation is being offered, to be aware of the context in which children are being 'invited in' and the risk of responsibility for making a decision being thrust upon children in circumstances not of their choosing.

It is obvious that children will participate more effectively with proper adult support.

There are many examples of youth engagement for social change outside the confines of traditional politics. A famous old example is the protest against the cane in 1911, which was not, of course, successful. The 'Newsboys' strike in New York in 1899 is another example, and this was successful (Woodhouse, 2008).

In the 1970s, youth were prominent in the fight to remove apartheid. The Soweto 'riots', which initially targeted the imposition of teaching in Afrikaans, the language of their oppressors, was a catalyst for the demise of apartheid (Sherrod, 2006).

Youth have taken leading roles in protests about war (Gordon, 2010) (they took to the streets to protest injustice), corruption, censorship, the undermining of democracy (in Hong Kong, for example, where the 'umbrella movement' against the force of the National People's Congress is led by students). In Iran, cultural policies have been challenged by young adults defying them and re-imagining Iranian reality (Khosravi, 2008). The 'Arab Spring' of the early 2010s had youth in the vanguard (Ahmari, 2012): its early successes have proved a chimera.

Political activism by the young can pass unnoticed when it takes place away from adult society, in school or more commonly today in social media. The latest (or the latest I have heard about) are Video blogging and the Indymedia (Independent Media Center). The Convention took it for granted that children would express their views in the same way as adults. But, as Philip Veerman (2010) points out, 'in the world of childhood.com, children communicate as much with their thumbs as with their tongues'. He argued that in a world dominated by the Internet, the CRC no longer fits children's lives. It may be that the problem is now not lack of input by children, but information overload.

All this transcends by far what the drafters of the Convention had in mind when Article 12 was being formulated. It is essentially the work of young citizens, where their citizenship is denied. It is a remarkable fact that neither the CRC nor any other human rights treaty recognises any right to citizenship. And just as remarkable is that this is hardly anywhere commented upon: can it really have escaped the notice of nearly the whole children's rights community? (Doek (2009) being the only exception.) The CRC does, it is true, stress in Article 7(1) that 'every child has the right to acquire a nationality'. Nationality is an element of citizenship, but it is far from its only content. As Leiter, McDonald and Jacobson (2006: 13) note:

317

> Children's citizenship has remained largely invisible until
> very recently and scholars have just begun to examine
> children's citizenship and how it relates to existing
> conceptions of citizenship regarding rights,
> responsibilities, identities and participation.

There are many challenges in deciding which elements of adult citizenship apply to children also. It is additionally necessary to decide in which contexts, and with what outcomes. Bulmer and Rees (1996) explain why children have 'partial citizenship' only since they have both legal and social dependence upon adults. Cockburn (1998, 2013) explains that children's civil citizenship is severely limited, but that they do have considerable social rights. For Lister, the case for recognising children as citizens is not so much extending to them adult rights and obligations, but rather the recognition that their citizenship practices constitute them as '*de facto*, even if not complete *de jure* citizens'. And she goes on to explain that this position 'points towards an understanding of citizenship which embraces but goes beyond that of a bundle of rights' (Lister, 2007: 693).

For most of history citizenship has functioned as an exclusionary device (Coady, 2008; Mitchell, 2015). Since women were excluded, there was feminist scholarship to tackle patriarchal definitions of citizenship. Lister (2007) thinks lessons may be learned from feminist critiques of mainstream constructions of citizenship paying particular attention to the question of capacity for citizenship. Bacon and Frankel (2014) explore the meanings of children's citizenship by emphasising children's capacities to generate and negotiate both their own and others' social meanings. It is clear, as Stasiulis (2002: 516) argued that 'the participation of children will always occur in dialogue that is fundamentally asymmetrical given the dependency of children'.

The reduction of the voting age in the United Kingdom was first seriously considered in 1999. A motion to do so was heavily defeated (434 to 36). In 2005 there was another vote, again to reduce the voting age to sixteen, and again it was defeated, this time by eight votes only. Two years later a Youth Citizenship Commission was established; one of its tasks was to examine the case for lowering the voting age. The Prime Minister, Gordon Brown, on its launch indicated that it was right as part of the debate to hear from young persons themselves 'whether lowering the age would increase participation'.

A study of young peoples' citizenship in the United Kingdom found that very few of them thought of citizenship in terms of rights (Lister et al., 2003). In the United Kingdom, and elsewhere in states which aspire to democratic principles, children have the entitlement to one symbol of citizenship (a passport), but not to another (the right to vote).

Writing in 2007, Ruth (now Baroness) Lister detected two approaches in the literature to children's citizenship (2007: 696–9). Much of it just ignored children, implicitly identifying citizenship with adulthood. So, children were citizens of the future, what Wyness et al. (2004: 82) called 'apprentice citizens'.

In the classic statement of citizenship, T. H. Marshall (1950: 25) referred to children and young people as 'citizens in the making', much as elsewhere at this time they were stigmatized as 'becomings'. This drew an angry riposte from a nineteen-year-old student: 'I am not a citizen in the making. I am a citizen today' (Burke, 2005: 53). Of course, as a nineteen-year-old he was, but his point is essentially right – just substitute seventeen for nineteen.

At the other end, is found the 'extreme' view that children were unquestionably citizens, so that there was nothing to debate. Thus, proclaimed the Carnegie Young People Initiative, children are 'citizens and should be treated as such' (Cutler and Frost, 2001: 2). But children are not a single homogenous category. They differ in age, gender, sexual orientation, ethnicity, etc. The amount of citizenship they may hold may be related to these variables. For obvious reasons I will concentrate on 'age'.

Inevitably, age comes into focus since capacity increases with age. The older the child, the more compelling is the case for recognising his/her input to the decision-making process (Roche, 1999). UNICEF argue that children's capacities are invariably underestimated by adults (Lansdown, 2005: 30–1).

But first we must unpack the relationship between children and citizenship. Are the two concepts compatible? (Hill and Tisdall, 1997). Or are children at best only semi-citizens? (E. Cohen, 2009). They do not vote, and they do not even have formal, systematic political representation. They are the 'largest group of unrepresented people in every liberal democracy in the world' (2009: 181).

Child citizenship goes beyond 'the political domain' (Biesta, 2011: 40). It is about also 'individuals having a sense of belonging to, and functioning in, communities'. An adult-centric list of the features of citizenship may emphasise the 'political', but from a child's perspective, as identified by Malala

Yousafzai (Yousafzai, 2013), education rights are more significant. And in today's fractured world, symbolised by the refugees trudging continents, 'every child, and not only those with a birth certificate and a nationality, should be treated as a citizen' (Doek, 2009: xvi). Jaap Doek, a former Chair of the Committee of the Rights of the Child, adds:

> This means. . .the full respect for and implementation of the rights of every child in order to allow her/him to live an individual and decent life in society and to facilitate his/her active and constructive participation in the community. (Doek, 2009)

Case for Enfranchisement

Should children be enfranchised? If so, should the vote be extended to all children and, if not, where should the line be drawn? In the majority of countries the minimum age to be allowed to exercise the vote is eighteen years of age. A generation ago it was twenty-one. There is an impetus towards lowering it to sixteen. In Scotland's referendum on independence in 2014, sixteen- and seventeen-year-olds could vote and a high percentage did. It was a manifesto commitment of the Liberal Democrats in 2001 to lower the age of voting to sixteen but the Electoral Commission in 2004 rejected such a reform. In its view, sixteen-year-olds had insufficient social responsibility and emotional maturity. The Commission feared that if the age at which people could vote were lowered, the percentage of those voting would also decrease (Electoral Commission, 2004). That, of course, assumes nothing changes, but a party pledged to promote the interests of the young might encourage greater participation by those currently disadvantaged, and disaffected. Widening the places at which votes can be cast, for example to schools, universities, factories, would also see greater participation. Only 37 per cent of eighteen- to twenty-four-year-olds had voted in the General Election of 2015, whereas 61 per cent of those who were aged between thirty-five and forty-four had voted. Evidence from the Scottish Independence referendum has shown that, with the encouragement of families and schools, sixteen- and seventeen-year-olds have higher turnout rates than eighteen- to thirty-four-year-olds. There have been a number of proposals since.

It is significant that the Convention (Article 12(2)) gives children 'the opportunity to be heard in any judicial and administrative proceedings affecting the child'. Legislative proceedings are not included. Adults, by contrast, have the power to hold a representative to account, albeit only by denying him/her their vote in the next general election, which may be five years away. This (preferably strengthened) is one element which we would regard as a precondition for a polity to be reasonably democratic.

It is common to put children's welfare first, to argue that it is more important than citizenship. I do not deny this. Giving the vote to young children is pointless if we do not protect them from abuse. But we must also not fail to see that when children become citizens they are less likely to be abused. If children had the vote in the United Kingdom today, a budget transferring assets from the poor, in particular children, to the wealthy, in particular well-heeled pensioners, would have fallen at the starting gate. In July 2015, such a redistribution passed through the House of Commons relatively easily.

Critics of 'votes for children' commonly cite lack of competence as the reason. But competence is not the test. If it were, a substantial number of adults would lose their right to vote. And anyway, when is someone competent enough to participate in democratic politics? What amounts to 'competence'? Is it 'political intelligence'? (Mill, 1865). 'Enlightenment'? (Dahl, 1989: 126, who argued that an eight-year-old child 'can hardly be enlightened enough to participate equally with adults in deciding on laws to be enforced by the government of the state'). An extensive study of the American electorate assessed their knowledge by summarising the results of a large sample of surveys between 1940 and 1994. In total, 448 factual questions about institutions, processes, people and players were included, as were domestic and foreign affairs; 43 per cent of the questions were answered correctly (Delli Carpini and Keeter, 1996). Should those who are particularly 'competent' have more than one vote? Oxbridge graduates did until 1948! (John Stuart Mill (1865) supported this, even arguing that employers should have extra votes.) If the test is pitched too high, not even some MPs would satisfy it.

Why is eighteen the standard minimum age? It was not stipulated because eighteen-year-olds have insights which seventeen-year-olds lack. It is not entirely arbitrary since it is also the age of majority, though this too can be said to be arbitrary. Even though eighteen is the age of majority, it is not an inflexible rule: for example, you can marry at sixteen. We could allow young people to vote at seventeen – they do in North Korea and it hasn't damaged the political fabric there! But if seventeen, why not sixteen, and if sixteen why not fifteen? The regression has infinite potential. So, does the line have to be drawn somewhere? Or not? What harm would be done to our polity or to civil society if the franchise were extended to the whole population? We would be giving the vote to 'know nothings', but there is nothing novel in that. And 'know nothing' Tories would, broadly speaking, cancel out those who voted Labour (Bennett, 1988, 1996). We would not expect many three-year-olds to vote, but if a few did (and some would be more capable than some thirty-three-year-olds and many eighty-three-year-olds), they are unlikely to affect the overall result.

Where the line is drawn is to some extent arbitrary. Unless the vote is given to everyone – there is a current debate about whether prisoners should be allowed to vote – then it must be given to all children or a line must be drawn somewhere.

To extend the franchise to fourteen-year-olds would not be acceptable to most people. Whether the age of criminal responsibility could be tinkered with without considering evidence from neuroscience is also contentious.

But a seventeen-year-old can legitimately complain that a democratic polity should take account of her views. Being a girl she may well have matured intellectually faster than the eighteen-year-old male. Reduce the age to seventeen, and sixteen-year-olds will contest their exclusion, to sixteen and fifteen-year-olds will consider they have a grievance. And so it goes on with infinite regress.

The most widely-quoted empirical study of children and politics suggests:

> By the age of nine, much of the political language of adult life has been acquired. By eleven, many children have as good a working vocabulary for politics as any adults could claim, and a framework of ideas which, even if developed no further, will enable them to grasp the facts of current affairs, understand something of relationships between principles and issues in politics and make their choices at general elections. (Stevens, 1982: 148)

If competence is not the test, is experience? Can we justify denying the vote to children because they lack life's experiences? This is not true; many children have experiences which adults may lack, of schooling today, of grooming, of insecurities, of fears. They may have concerns about a future which many voters today will not see, one dominated by the impact of climate change.

Giving children the vote will have important consequences. It will be more awkward to marginalise them. Politicians will have to take the best interests principle more seriously. Children's rights will be placed on the agenda more firmly; child poverty will be tackled speedily and coherently; abuse, exploitation, grooming, neglect will begin to be relegated to the history books.

A suggestion is to draw the voting age at the same place as we impose criminal responsibility on children. In England and Wales, that would mean allowing ten-year-olds to vote. This might encourage Parliament to increase the threshold for the imposition of criminal responsibility, but to where?

Could it raise the age of criminal responsibility to eighteen? This would fly in the face of public opinion. To impose it at fourteen would also not be a popular move. This might be one of those areas calling for the legislature to take the lead and mould popular sentiment (Dror, 1957) rather as it did in 1965 and 1968 when it passed race relations legislation (Freeman, 1974), and when it abolished the death penalty, and removed the criminal sanction from homosexuality.

Whether the age of criminal responsibility could be tinkered with without considering evidence from neuroscience is also contentious. As neuroscience hints at raising the mini-mum age of criminal responsibility, English law in effect low-ered it in 1998 when it disposed of 700 years of history and abolished the *doli incapax* presumption. It was motivated to do this by a moral panic caused by the *Bulger* case in 1993.

Politics is the art of the possible, and there is no like-lihood of all children being enfranchised in the foreseeable future. Extending the franchise to sixteen- and seventeen-year-olds is as far as we are likely to get now. We should take encouragement from the way the 'vote' was first extended to women, initially only to those of thirty and above. It is also worth reminding ourselves that the same arguments were used against allowing women to vote as opponents of votes for children use today. Many nasty things creep, but so can democracy!

There are compromises too. One is to extend the fran-chise but discount the value of the vote. For example, the vote of a sixteen- and seventeen-year-old could be worth 50 per cent of an adult's vote, that of fourteen- and fifteen-year-olds 25 per cent, and younger children's votes a token 10 per cent. Another model that has been mooted is to give a parent (usually the mother) an additional vote. This was proposed in Hungary, but not implemented. Another possibility is to base voting on constituencies of age rather than geography.

Impact of Neuroscience

We have begun to unwrap the mysteries of the human brain. This is the most complicated mechanism known. We live in an age of unprecedented discoveries and challenges as regards this. A generation ago we mapped the human genome and were promised all manner of progress. No shortage of enthusiasm greeted its earliest findings. We were told that there would soon be a 'genealyser' in every doctor's surgery. The Internet erupted with promises of ways of enhancing our lives. We were going to be able to improve our children's athletic performances – would this have fallen foul of the sport's authorities, like a banned drug? – we were going to discover the best diet suited to our genome, we were even promised we could identify through DNA analysis whom we should marry!

The same hype may well greet discoveries which emerge from the brain sciences. Hopefully not. From misunderstanding comes false expectation, and sadly exploitation of the vulnerable and the gullible. Commercial interests usually take the driving seat. One of the reasons why the Human Genome Project has not lived up to the early hype about it is that it failed to make the huge profits that were predicted.

Implications of Neuroscience

It is doubtful whether any of those who debated the Convention in the 1980s had any knowledge of the existence

327

of neuroscience, let alone whether it might impact on our understanding of adolescent behaviour. But by the mid-1990s, it was influencing decisions as important as whether the death penalty could be imposed on a person who committed the crime when under eighteen (*Roper* v. *Simmons*, 2005), and, subsequently, whether a life sentence without any possibility of parole could be given to an offender who had not yet reached the age of majority (*Graham* v. *Florida*, 2010). Heart-rending accounts of thirteen-year-olds not fitting into the electric chair, and of twelve-year-old Lionel Tate not comprehending that he would never be going home can be found in Stevenson, 2014 and Woodhouse, 2008, respectively (Woodhouse, 2008: ch. 13). It is salutary to be reminded of this when a child of fourteen was given a life sentence in Blackburn only very recently (*The Guardian*, October 2015).

Brain science has been developing for millennia (Freeman, 2010). But it is only since the late 1960s that the human brain has become the focus of medico-legal debates, first in relation to the definition of death, and now to attempt to negate free will in relation to criminal behaviour. (It's my brain what did it! (Gazzaniga, 2015).)

We should treat the development of what has been called 'neurolaw' with caution (Rose and Abi-Rached, 2013: 177). *Roper* v. *Simmons* in 2005 may, in the perspective of history, be seen as a landmark in our understanding of criminal responsibility, or a false alarm. It is too early to say. The age of criminal responsibility is arbitrary and contingent on culture and history and therefore is not uniform: when the age was lowered in England (to ten) it was based more on folklore than neurolaw. In *Roper* v. *Simmons*, the Supreme Court was presented with an *amicus* brief put together by a group of liberal New York lawyers containing evidence from American professional organisations, including the American Medical Association, the American Psychiatric Association, the American Society for Adolescent Psychiatry, and the National Mental Health Association (Haider, 2006). The brief argued that juvenile brains are anatomically different and that the frontal lobes:

> the part of the brain responsible for reasoning, impulse control, cost-benefit calculation and good judgment is not fully developed. This means that adolescents are inherently more prone to risk-taking behaviour, and less capable of governing impulses, than adults...These studies were presented to the Court as evidence that adolescents are biologically different. (Haider, 2006: 371–2)

We should, however, be careful not to read too much into this case. The judgment did not explicitly refer to neurobiological evidence, or the adolescent brain, although it did refer to some sociological research on adolescence as well as to common-sense knowledge about the impulsiveness of youth. The brief was submitted in the context of a fairly major mobilisation of liberal US academics, lawyers and medical professionals against the death penalty. Nonetheless, despite the well-known cultural and historical specificity of the notion of adolescence, and the relative novelty of the association of this stage in life with risk taking and poor impulse control, which would rule out any underlying evolutionary changes in the rate of brain development, a number of US researchers argue that such characteristics are a consequence of 'the developing brain' and the neural mechanisms responsible for processing emotions (Casey, Jones and Hare, 2008).

But even if it were possible to connect the theoretical dots between neuropathology and behaviour, this correlation may not be legally relevant. These complicated questions of responsibility and agency are far from being resolved. As yet, no brain image can identify thoughts or ascribe a motive. Neuroscience cannot distinguish thought from deed and has little, if any, predictive power (Baskin, Edersheim, and Price, 2007: 267). We continue to encounter the same moral and methodical problems predicting violence with neuroimaging as we do trying to predict violence with other clinical instruments. In most instances violence is a complex, multifactorial and socially driven behaviour that cannot be reduced to a unitary brain function or region (Baskin, Edersheim, and Price, 2007).

In *Roper* v. *Simmons* (2005) a man was found guilty of murdering a woman when he was seventeen years old. At the sentencing stage, the *amicus* brief used neuroimaging evidence to argue that he did not deserve the death penalty since adolescents are less blameworthy than adults.

Even when neuroscience evidence is deemed inadmissible, or is admitted but does not result in acquittal, it still could be relevant and admissible in sentencing, which by its very nature demands consideration of a broader range of information (Shuman and Gold, 2008: 732). Therefore, the use of neuroimaging evidence has generally been more successful in showing diminished culpability at the sentencing stage than in disproving criminal intents (Mobbs et al., 2007; Snead, 2007, 2008). The US federal sentencing guidelines make it clear that impulse control disorders can justify a downward departure from the recommended sentences and allow a lower threshold for reduced mental capacity if the defendant is unable either to absorb information normally or to exercise the power of reason, or if the person knows what he is doing and that it is wrong, but cannot control his compulsion. When a criminal court establishes that a defendant did commit the crime he is accused of, it must still determine criminal intent (*mens rea*) and, if this is found, whether there are any mitigating circumstances that make him less blameworthy (Arneson, 2010; Blank, 2013).

Implications for the Adolescent's Autonomy Rights

There are limits to medicine, limits to effective legal action (Pound, 1917), and certainly limits to what neuroscience can tell us. As if enhancement were not difficult enough (Savulescu and Bostrom, 2009), we are having to grapple with the science of brain imaging and one of its results, which suggests that people we now hold responsible for their actions have diminished moral responsibility and legal culpability because of the structure or function of their brain (Erickson, 2010: 36). A 'foundational premise of cognitive neuroscience is that all aspects of the mind are ultimately reducible to the structure and function of the brain' (Blank, 2013: 130).

Neuroimaging has been used in courts as evidence to show the defendant did not have the capacity to have the *mens rea*, and to show diminished culpability (Bennett and Hacker, 2008). It has tended to be more successful when used at the sentencing stage than in disproving criminal intent.

As discussed above, in *Roper* v. *Simmons* (2005) neuroscientific evidence (neuroimaging) was adduced to show that the brain development of adolescents showed them to be risk-seeking, to be more aggressive, and to have poorer decision-making ability than adults. This is explained by observing that the limbic system of the brain develops earlier than the prefrontal cortex. This means that the parts of the brain most involved in decision-making and self-control are not fully developed until about the age of twenty or even twenty-five. Simmons was spared the death penalty, but we are not spared unravelling the implications of the decision. All adolescents are not the same; their brains will develop at a different pace.

The vista is depicted of a future in which convicted juveniles are required to undergo brain scans to calculate the state of their brain development.

Neuroimaging evidence could at best only then be introduced at the sentencing stage. Would public opinion support this? And if such evidence becomes admissible, why should it be limited to those of twenty or twenty-five? There is equally evidence of a decline from about forty-five years of age. Are we to exonerate middle-aged offenders? And what of the gender difference? Brain maturation is linked to puberty, and girls reach puberty earlier than boys (Brizendine, 2006; Strauch, 2003). Girls on average experience early adolescence neural exuberance, particularly in the frontal lobes, at least a year before boys. Would it be morally right for the criminal justice system to treat them differently? It would, of course, be contrary to the non-discrimination provision in the CRC (Article 2). Afro-Caribbean girls tend to reach puberty before white British girls. Should the criminal justice system take cognisance of this? Should children of different races be subjected to different rules? It is bad enough that in practice police policies, for example to 'stop and search', are fundamentally racist.

Terry Mahoney (2009, 2011) puts the dilemmas which face us into a nutshell. She writes:

> Any argument that law's treatment of children should track developmental neuroscience must demonstrate why such inequality is not its logical outcome, and the only way to do this is to concede that neuroscience (and, for that matter, developmental science generally) must sometimes give way to other values. (Mahoney, 2011: 275)

What, then, are the implications of neuroscience for an adolescent's autonomy? The trend is to recognise this. The *Gillick* decision, the Children Act 1989 recognise 'evolving capacities' (see also CRC, Article 5).

14

Alternatives to Rights: Or Are They?

A number of alternatives to rights have been suggested. Five are briefly considered here:

(i) benevolence;
(ii) duties;
(iii) care;
(iv) happiness;
(v) well-being.

But first we must recognise that the case for rights does not limit us to the rights in the 1989 Convention.

Which Rights?

It tends to be assumed that a rights-based approach inevitably means resort to the CRC at the very least as a measuring rod. It is as if we are saying that after a long struggle we eventually got to our goal and that the norms in this are the only conclusions to which we could possibly have come. But, as Tobin (2013) points out:

> there is no logical impediment to a rights-based approach embracing alternative sources of human rights standards which could be drawn from regional or domestic human rights instruments (or indeed a moral or political theory of rights that has not been transformed into law).

So, when there is an appeal to rights, the obvious question is which rights, and whose rights. We might come up with a list of different rights to adopt in substitution for these in the CRC.

(i) Benevolence

Benevolence is great when it works, but there is no comeback when it doesn't. Rights enable us to stand with dignity, to demand that what is done to us, we are entitled to. Contrast life under a benevolent dictator: if he withdraws resources from us, we can protest, we can beg, we can grovel, we can pray he changes his mind. We can appeal to his good nature. But we cannot demand. Even if life is better under a benign dictatorship, most of us would prefer the security of a rights regime. And dictatorships rarely stay benign for very long.

(ii) Duties

Are duties an adequate substitute for rights? Do children need rights or is it sufficient that relevant adults have obligations to fulfil towards children? To be fair, it would be perfectly feasible for the Convention to be one about 'wrongs' rather than 'rights' (Simon, 2000), and to have enacted a code of duties owed by the state, parents and significant others to children. But this would be to adopt a dismally negative view of human nature of the character we associate with Hobbes (see above, p. 21). The individual thus described only responds to coercion, and so is totally lacking a sense of obligation. He may be obliged by the threat of sanctions, but obligated he is certainly not. This gendarme state is quite alien. The view that we should be emphasising duties rather than rights is particularly associated with the Kantian philosopher, Onora O'Neill (1988) (see above, p. 58), and has been restated recently and most fully by Lucinda Ferguson (2015).

Ferguson argues that 'duty' can have three roles:

> as a tool to give specificity and resolve conflicts in current rights and welfare-based decision-making; as a theoretical framework focused on the decision-maker; and as part of the justification for adopting a virtue-inspired understanding of the aim for legal decision-making affecting children – to enable children to flourish on their own terms. (2015: 142)

Ferguson argues the case for preferring duty fully and thoroughly. She gives seven reasons (2015: 171–5). I do not find them convincing.

(1) Looking initially to the decision-maker rather than the child 'more readily enables prioritisation of the child's position than adopting an ostensibly child-centred approach' (2015: 171). Those who dispute this use, it is claimed, do so for historical rather than conceptual reasons. It may be, Maitland (1920) observed in another context, that we are ruled by history from its grave, but this does not mean that we cannot break free of it. The so-called safe smack has its roots in history (*R* v. *Hopley*, 1860), but is now under attack from those espousing a rights model. It looks patently ridiculous to say a parent

336

is under a duty not to leave a mark. Try to express Article 12 of the CRC in duty-informed language: the emphasis is the child's right of participation. Or take an example from the intercices of criminal law and family law – the marital rape immunity, still in effect when the CRC was finalised (incredible to think it fell after the Berlin Wall!). Once defended in terms of a wife's duty – she was supposed to be on tap, he on top. It has been abolished because modern sensibilities dictate that wives have rights, from which it follows that husbands have duties (*R* v. *R*, 1991).

(2) A duty-based account 'more readily enables particularisation to the individual child' (2015: 172). But why should this be so? I do not see that it does, but nor do I see any real problem if it does do so.

(3) A 'duty-based approach reduces the potential for the reasoning to be vague', a 'smokescreen', etc. It is argued that from the premise of duty, the decision-maker is more likely to support his/her decision with detailed reasoning. I accept that detailed reasoning is the ideal, and note that no decision-maker gives more detailed reasoning than a judge, but why the reasoning should be more transparent it is difficult to follow.

(4) It is more likely that a 'better balance (will be) struck between competing concerns' (2015: 173). She says this will be better in cases of a child's refusal of consent to medical treatment. But, surely, this is only because competing concerns are being weighed, which is to treat mature adolescents differently from adults, which is not what Parliament intended in 1969 (see Family Law Reform Act 1969,

section 8) nor is it within the reasoning of the House of Lords in *Gillick* (1986).

(5) It is more likely to employ relevant empirical evidence and so reach 'empirically-grounded judgments' (2015: 173). Of course, empirical evidence is important. I think this claim is dubious. What is the evidence for it?

(6) 'A duty-based approach removes an unnecessary layer of complexity from the process of reasoning.' This is, she admits, counter-intuitive.

(7) 'A duty-based approach imposes positive obligations on those making decisions affecting children to do so virtuously and to take positive steps to benefit the child' (2015: 174–5). On the contrary, if a child has rights, the imperative to benefit the child will be even greater.

The question of whether rights or duties come first is one of importance. Do we have rights because others have duties towards us, or are duties the result of our being rights-bearers ? To put duties up front is to take a pessimistic view of the nature of those who bear the duties, to assume that they will only carry out their duties because they are compelled to do so. There is a distinct resemblance to the Austinian model of law (1832), which H. L. A. Hart so convincingly demolished in *The Concept of Law* (1961). Putting duties centre-stage also overlooks why the duties are deemed to exist. They are there because others have rights. To illustrate simply, if a child is entitled to an upbringing free from violence, his parents will be under a duty not to spank him. The duty arises because there is a right.

There are also rights where there is no, or no obvious, person or persons with any correlative obligation. The right to life (CRC, Article 6), freedom of expression (CRC, Article 13) are two examples. Interestingly, Wesley Hohfeld (1923) could find no word in legal literature to offer as a correlative, and invented the word 'no-right'. It has been argued that children have the right to be loved (Liao, 2006, 2015), but, even were this so, to say parents have a duty to love their children would reduce 'love' to a commodity (and see above, p. 156).

Children and Responsibilities

Children have duties, as well as rights. In law, they have very few. Obviously, from the age of ten, they are under an obligation not to break the criminal law. As we have seen, this is an internationally unacceptable low age, made even more so by the development of anti-social behaviour legislation. Strangely, children are not duty-bound to go to school. Few know this! Few also know the biblical injunction to honour/respect parents (Giordano, 2015). It is in the African Charter of Rights and Welfare of 1990 and also in the Israeli legal system (Bainham, 1998). But there is not strict correlativity: a child who behaves irresponsibly does not forfeit his/her rights.

A few examples may illustrate the type of responsibilities that children may be expected to bear. Together with the right to education, an entitlement and an expectation, children have the responsibility to respect teachers; together with the right to good dental care, the responsibility to brush their teeth regularly; together with the right to their own culture,

339

the responsibility to respect the culture of others (see further Appendix 5). But it should be stressed that reciprocity is not essential, so that a child does not forfeit rights because she/he reneges on a responsibility.

It is, of course, perfectly feasible to construct a code for children where the emphasis is on duties but this would be to take a rather negative view of human nature.

There is no reason why a Magna Carta for children should not reiterate children's responsibilities as well as affirming their rights.

Procreative Beneficence

We all want to give our children the best we can. But should this be a moral obligation? Perhaps even a legal obligation? Should children have a right to the fruits of procreative beneficence. The expression was coined by Julian Savulescu in 2005. He and Kahane argue that it would be a moral defect in parents when they do not take advantage of an opportunity to use procreative beneficence (PB) (Savulescu and Kahane, 2009). What is PB? At first encounter it looks suspiciously like the now totally discredited practice of eugenics (Trombley, 1988). But they are very different: eugenics aims at producing a better population, can be negative, and was coercive and penal, whereas PB's goal is to produce the best child.

First, can this be done? It is clear that we are not talking science fiction. There are a number of drugs which can achieve this. The neurotransmitter Oxytocin has been found to increase the level of trust and cooperation between people. Propranolol may reduce implicit racial bias (Archer, 2016).

A Duty to Have Children!

There is a burgeoning literature on whether we have a right to have children. Do the infertile, for example, have the right to expect access to IVF? There is also David Benatar's intriguing thesis that procreation is wrong (2008). Less attention has been given to whether we have a duty to have children. Smilansky (1995) wrote an article some twenty years ago, arguing against, and Christine Overall (2012) is also opposed on the good liberal grounds that to impose a duty conflicts with the emphasis on autonomy and integrity which liberals cherish. This is not a pressing question at the moment. The current problem is over-population, not under-population. There are projections of huge increases and doubts whether resources are sustainable. Nevertheless, as a hypothetical, the issue is important. In not all places nor at all times is there over-population: countries ravaged by war, disease, natural disasters or bad social policies (as in China with the one child policy) may wish to adopt pro-natalist policies to boost declining birth figures.

If there is such a duty it would be in the interests of existing persons, and not, or not necessarily, in the interest of the children born as a result. I assume that the prospective children can be expected to have at least acceptably fulfilling lives. Of course, the conventional view is that having children is a liberty (Hohfeld, 1923), a no-right (ibid.), and not a duty. Parents certainly have a duty not to harm their existing children by assuming additional burdens they cannot bear.

Of course, if no one had children society would crumble and ultimately cease to exist. This is a good reason for having children, but this does not mean that specific persons have a duty to procreate. In a society with a gender imbalance, likely to be weighted in favour of boys, having girls is a good idea, but clearly there can be no duty to produce girls. Pre-embryo genetic diagnosis makes this possible, though a dim view is taken of this way of proceeding by English law and many other legal systems.

Can a duty thus be justified? The main argument is put in this way. There are obligations which one assumes as a member of society by reason of a fictive social contract. An example is defence from state enemies. This explains why conscription into the armed forces is justified. But is conscription to become mothers analogous? Is this to accept a form of coercive pregnancy? Rape by the state almost? A more acceptable moral justification might be found in the 'carrot rather than the stick', in welfare payments, tax benefits, which nudge rather than coerce (Thaler and Sunstein, 2008). An objection, certainly from a children's rights perspective, is that a child is being produced as a means to achieve a goal; in no sense is that in the child's best interests (Kant, [1797] 1996). This is a problem we have previously encountered with the so-called 'saviour sibling' (Sheldon and Wilkinson, 2004), but there the concern was more easily overcome since clearly the new baby was loved and cherished, and not just seen as 'spare parts' (Freeman, 2004). There is evidence that children produced for the state in Communist Europe were not so well received, in the disturbing images of Romanian orphanages which troubled our conscious briefly in the early 1990s.

If such an obligation could be established, concerns would turn to how to enforce it (Gheaus, 2015: 95–100). In an area of intimate association such as this, monitoring would be unacceptable. There are precedents – pre-revolutionary France, Communist China to enforce its one child policy – but they do not easily fit within a democratic polity.

(iii) Care and its Ethics

Feminist ethics of care developed in the 1980s in response to the prevailing liberal rights model. Its most influential source is Carol Gilligan's *In a Different Voice* (1982). It offers a different approach to morality, one which emphasises care and responsibility rather than abstract rules and principles. Caring is central to children's well-being. Babies are totally dependent on adults' commitment to care. The liberal rights model sees individuals as autonomous subjects. It translates moral questions into conflicts over rights. The liberal rights model accepts the public/private dualism, with children joining women in Aristotle's *Oikos*. This has implications for our responses to many questions, including why the legal system has been so slow in challenging child abuse. The 'public' has a tendency to regard the 'private' as beyond its writ.

Instead of seeing women's moral reasoning as 'deficient', Gilligan showed that it was a different, but equally valid, way of approaching a moral problem, even if in a male-dominated world it was undervalued. Those committed to this ethical theory tend to ask not 'what is just?', but rather 'how are we to respond?'.

The theory has particular resonance in a discussion on children because it emphasises dependence: contrast other theories which see people, including children, as independent, autonomous interest-holders. It also recognises vulnerability and the importance of context. These may be particularly relevant where it is necessary to safeguard and promote the interests of those involved.

Ethics of care is a feminist ethic. It can, and has, been criticised for reinforcing sexist stereotypes (Bartky, 1990). Others (e.g., Tong, 2009) have adopted its ideology as a basis for care-focused feminism. Care-focused feminists see women's capacity for care as a 'human strength' (Tong, 2009: 162).

The ethics of care is not a single theory but, though there are differences, there are also common features. Relationships of care are central to ethical reflection. So, as opposed to the notion of a 'generalised' other it adheres to the principle of the 'concrete' other. It requires us to view every rational being as an individual with a concrete history, identity and affective-emotional constitution (Benhabib, 2012: 411).

Secondly, it operates on the principle of the 'relational self'; it is part of networks of care and dependence. Thirdly, it challenges the moral theory that views moral situations in terms of rights and responsibilities.

Care, though absolutely essential, is no substitute for rights. It suffers from the same defect as benevolence in that the putative recipient is dependent on the goodwill of person in charge.

Right to be Breast-Fed

Whether there is a right to be breast-fed is a subject which has not been discussed very much (but see Kent, 1997). If it is a right, it is unenforceable. It may be an example of a 'manifesto right' (Feinberg, 1980). If it is a right it is one of the clearest manifestations of the interest theory of rights, though this does not mean young babies cannot express a preference (see Alderson, Hawthorne and Killen, 2005).

Breast-feeding is the 'optimal' way of feeding and caring for young babies. Breastmilk contains the right mixture of protein, carbohydrate, fat, vitamins and minerals to provide ideal nutrition for a baby (Jelliffe and Jelliffe, 1989). It is also a living fluid with live cells which provide anti-infectious constituents which are of great value to the baby's health. It is important for the child's development, including mental development (Latham, 1997), that wherever possible young babies are breast-fed.

The CRC does not stipulate a right to be breast-fed as such. However, Article 24, in emphasising enjoyment to the highest attainable standard of health, refers to the provision of adequate nutritious foods. States parties also have the responsibility to ensure that all segments of society are informed and have access to education and are supported in the use of basic knowledge of child health and nutrition, and the advantages of breast-feeding. To attain the highest standard of health, it is necessary that babies be exclusively breast-fed for the first six months of life (UNICEF, 2013). In developed countries, formula-fed babies are three to five times more likely to be hospitalised during infancy than breast-fed babies (Quigley, Kelly and Sacker, 2007). It is common for feminists to oppose breast-feeding since it frustrates women's freedom, but a feminist case in favour of breast-feeding can also be made. It may be said to empower women. It confirms 'a women's power to control her own body and challenges both the male-dominated medical model and also business interests that promote formula feeding' (Latham, 1997: 404). It also opposes the projection of breasts as sex objects. Breast-feeding is also a woman's right; obstacles should not be put in the way of a lactating mother. Too many places remain out of bounds, including the House of Commons.

(iv) Happiness

Although no one would suggest that a child's happiness is a substitute for his/her rights, best interests or well-being, the value of happiness cannot altogether be discounted. Happiness is integral to standard greetings – 'Happy New Year', 'Happy Birthday'. As far as children are concerned, it is significant that our desire to advance their happiness is a relatively modern phenomenon. The jingle which accompanies 'Happy Birthday To You' was written in 1893, but not for its purpose; it initially accompanied the words 'Good morning to you. . .Good morning dear children'.

Childhood mortality rates were too high to aim for happy children. A Roman writer, Epictetus, understood this well: 'when you kiss your child, you say to yourself, it may be dead in the morning'. Childhood was not supposed to be a happy time. Christianity with its doctrine of original sin encouraged children to be obedient, not happy. The germ of the notion of happiness took root in eighteenth-century England with the Romantic writers. The idea of a happy home with innocent children as central belongs to the early nineteenth century; it is no coincidence that the practice of giving children gifts, notably at Christmas, emerges at the same time.

Stearns (2006: 172) points out that it is in the 1910s that in the parenting manuals 'happiness becomes a central purpose, a leading quality of childhood, and an essential obligation for parents'. Happiness is said to be as essential as food if the child is fully to develop. By the 1940s 'the equation of childhood and happiness even infused advice books' (2006: 174). Stearns sees the embrace of happy childhood as coinciding with four developments (2006: 175–6):

(1) it was part of a larger set of redefinitions about children stimulated by the growth of child professionals;
(2) a decline in the birth rate and with this the increasing pricelessness of children (and see Zelizer, 1985);
(3) 'The larger turn to a heightened plea for cheerfulness' (Stearns, 2006: 176);
(4) Consumerism, increasingly directed at children. Advertising to sell directly to children began in the later nineteenth century and so did pocket money.

(v) Well-being

Do children need more than a platter of rights? And, if so, what? Attention has begun to focus on improving children's lives by emphasising their well-being. Note well-being, not well-becoming. Kay Tisdall sees a 'tension' between children's well-being and children's rights. I prefer to think of the two running in tandem with each other.

Well-being scholarship is more cognisant of children's rights thinking than are children's rights advocates of the products of well-being research. This is a failing which must be addressed. The concept of 'well-being' is not found as such in the lengthy discussions which led to the CRC, but this is not surprising – well-being was not much discussed in 1989. The first article on well-being to appear in the *International Journal of Children's Rights*, by Camfield et al., was in 2009. It observed (Camfield et al., 2009: 65) that 'monitoring, promoting and protecting wellbeing is central to realisation of children's rights'.

It may well be that the failure of children's rights thinking to engage with well-being can be attributed, in part at least, to the marginalisation of the concept in the CRC itself. It appears substantively only in Article 3(2), which is a little-noted provision (Freeman, 2007a). It may also be because well-being is associated with goals for children which are 'manifesto rights' (Feinberg, 1980), no more, like the right to be loved (Liao, 2015); for babies to be breast-fed (Latham, 1997). And all the socio-economic rights in the CRC are confined to the maximum extent of a state's 'available resources' (Article 4).

Lundy (2014: 2442) points to one important difference between the two approaches to children, their source. The well-being movement has emerged from 'scholarly interest and activism'; the CRC is the product of government and grants children rights. Does this mean children would be better off if we took the well-being route? Or pursued them in tandem? Is there any reason to believe they are incompatible? On the contrary, the Convention offers an infrastructure upon which the well-being of children can be built.

But, as already noted, the CRC itself does not focus on children's well-being. Article 3(2) apart, there are only three mentions of well-being (in Articles 4, 17(e) and 9(4)). In the

348

General Comments issued by the Committee on the Rights of the Child, however, there is greater reference, perhaps a reflection of the development of well-being work in the years between the CRC and the writing of the Comments (twenty-two years in the case of the Comment on Violence Against Children (2011)).

There is very full analysis of the provisions of the Convention and their relationship to well-being by Lundy (2014). I will therefore be brief. Article 3 justifies a focus on children as the unit of analysis. To understand best interests, it is necessary to understand well-being. Article 6 emphasises two of the most important constituents of well-being, namely life and survival, but it is its reference to 'development' that is the more significant in the context of well-being. It clearly supports the shift in emphasis from the child as 'becoming' to a 'being', and so from well-becoming to well-being (see Camfield et al., 2009). It also recognises that childhood is not a static concept.

Article 12 is the linchpin of the CRC. What is its relevance for the well-being of the child? Lundy suggests two. First:

> children's ability to influence their own lives should be looked at in its own right as a core aspect of wellbeing, and secondly, any process purporting to measure outcomes from a child rights perspective should comply with it engaging with children from start to finish in a meaningful way. (2014: 2444)

All the substantive provisions of the Convention are about well-being even if the concept does not appear as such. So, to take

349

three obvious examples, Article 19 on protection against abuse, Article 24 on the highest attainable standard of health, and Article 28 on education could all be rewritten in the language of well-being.

The case for focusing on well-being has been proclaimed for many years by Asher Ben-Arieh. As Tisdall (2015: 782) explains, there are many advantages to taking this route to improving children's lives: 'it is maximizing, it can incorporate positive outcomes and it can consider what assists children's wellbeing as well as what hinders it'. And she adds it is a 'flexible concept, as it has no fixed definition, so it can be developed and adapted, debated and collectively agreed' (2015: 782).

Legislation passed in Scotland in 2014 imposed duties on local authorities and health boards to plan, and deliver services to 'better safeguard, support and promote the wellbeing of children in their area' (Children and Young People (Scotland) Act 2014, section 9(2)(a)(i)). What is meant by well-being is not defined. An understanding of this can be sought in research, of which there is now a substantial amount. This can be seen in the indicators measuring well-being, such as standard of living, health, the ability to have an annual holiday (Bradshaw, 2014). Children's own concerns are also calibrated (Ben-Arieh et al., 2005). So are relationships of friendship and of love.

Well-being indicators tend to focus on objective data, but it is recognised that this is not the whole story. Subjective indicators using individuals' self-reports are therefore particularly valuable too. For Statham and Chase (2010: 5) well-being can be measured by 'how people interact with the world around them'. They add 'it is not necessarily the same as being happy'. The focus is on the quality of lives. Obviously, it is 'intangible, difficult to define and even harder to measure' (Thomas, 2009: 11).

The two approaches to advancing the status and lives of children – rights and well-being – complement each other.

As far as children are concerned, there is an important distinction in the interaction between an understanding of childhood well-being from a developmental perspective and from the perspective of children's rights. The developmental perspective focuses on deficits (poverty, insurance, illness) and overlooks the strengths of children. The children's rights understanding looks more to factors which provide opportunities to enable children to reach their aspirations, and looks to the quality of their lives now and not just in the future (Morrow and Mayall, 2009).

There is general agreement that childhood well-being is 'multi-dimensional', that it needs to be contextualised and is concluded in a holistic way (Statham and Chase, 2010: 10). It can be looked at through different lenses (Axford, 2009).

A Local Index of Child Wellbeing was created by researchers at the Universities of York and Oxford for the Department for Communities and Local Government to provide a method for rating child well-being at small area level (Lower Super Output Area Level, LSOA). This can be used to inform local planning. It is made up of seven domains which are populated with existing data (including information on 'children in need') to produce a figure for each LSOA in England (Bradshaw et al., 2007).

Scotland has implemented a programme called Getting It Right for Every Child (GIRFEC), which revolves round children's well-being. There are eight well-being indicators as guidance for assessments. These are: Safe, Healthy, Achieving, Nurtured, Active, Respected, Responsive and Included (known best as SHANNARRI). The intention is to make Scotland 'the best place in the world to grow up' (Minister for Children and Young People). The Children and Young People (Scotland) Act 2014, which imposed a duty on local authorities and health boards to plan, and deliver services to 'better safeguard, support and promote the wellbeing of children' in their area, was discussed above.

The initial results from what has been described as 'the first national survey in England to take a broad and comprehensive view of children and young people's subjective well-being' (Rees et al., 2009) were publicised at an 'Understanding Children's Wellbeing' launch in London in January 2010. This National Survey of Young People's Wellbeing was undertaken as part of an ongoing programme of work on childhood well-being by the Children's Society. Nearly 7,000 young people (aged ten to fifteen) were surveyed in schools by Ipsos MORI in 2008. The questionnaire included three off-the-peg measures of subjective well-being: a measure of overall happiness with life, and two measures of overall life satisfaction, Cantril's Ladder and Huebner's Life Satisfaction Scale, plus additional indicators of subjective and psychological well-being. Under subjective well-being were included aspects of self (physical health, emotional health, time use); relationships (with

352

family, friends, people in local areas); and environments (material well-being, home, school, local areas, national and global issues). Psychological well-being was treated as distinct from subjective well-being and focused on aspects such as a sense of purpose; a sense of autonomy; competence; relatedness, focus of control; self-image, self-esteem; optimism and aspirations for the future (Statham and Chase, 2010: 9).

Children's own views on well-being are particularly significant and there is considerable evidence of this. This reveals the importance that children and young people place on their subjective well-being, and has highlighted some important differences in how children and adults view and define well-being. In Ireland, children's views were sought to inform the development of the set of national well-being indicators (Gabhainn and Sixsmith, 2005). Central to these eight- to twelve-year-old children's views of well-being were interpersonal relations with family and friends (including pets), and positive activities or things to do. There were notable differences between children's, parents' and teachers' views of what was most important for children's well-being (Sixsmith et al., 2007).

The Good Childhood Inquiry (Layard and Dunn, 2009) surveyed some 8,000 young people (fourteen to sixteen years) across sixteen areas in England and within school or educational establishments, asking them what they thought were the most important things that make for a good life for young people, and what in their view prevented young people from having a good life. An analysis of their replies revealed three overarching themes with respect to how young people perceived a 'good childhood': the quality of relationships they had with others, safety and freedom. Aside from these themes there were ten components identified as important for a 'good life': family; friends; leisure opportunities; school, education and learning; their own behaviour; their local (physical environment); their local community; money; their own attitudes; and health, particularly mental and emotional aspects of health (Layard and Dunn, 2009).

(i) Enhancement

Human enhancement has become somewhat rapidly a challenge for liberal democracies in the Global North. Controversy rages between transhumanists, who believe a wide range of enhancements should be developed and that people should use them to transform themselves in radical ways, and bioconservatives, who believe we should not alter the human condition. Pro-enhancers point to the ways we are already using enhancement and not questioning it – shoes enhance our feet, bras women's breasts. As Savulescu and Bostrom (2009: 3) note, 'tea, sleep, literacy, (most) prescription medicines "enhance"'. Would we ban these?

A severe critic of enhancement is George Annas (2005). Together with Lori Andrews and Rosario Lasi (2002) he proposed a new UN Convention on the Preservation of the Human Species.

One approach to human enhancement is through the framework of capabilities. The concept of capabilities tries to answer the question 'What is this person able to do and to be?' (Nussbaum, 2000: 18). Capabilities are basic goods of human flourishing, in the absence of which life would be seriously impoverished. Martha Nussbaum lists ten central capabilities:

- life;
- bodily health;
- bodily integrity;
- senses, imagination and thought;
- emotions;
- practical;
- affiliation;
- being able to live with other species;
- play;
- control over one's environment, both political and material (2000: 25).

One of the most controversial issues relating to enhancement centres on the Deaf community and the cochlear implant. The Deaf community is strongly opposed to cochlear implant surgery. They have three objections:

(i) deaf people have an equally high quality of life as hearing people: deafness is not a disability;

(ii) 'curing' deaf people through implant surgery conveys the message that deaf peoples' lives are less valuable, which exposes them to discrimination; and

(iii) deaf parents have the right to bring up their children in their own cultural tradition.

As far as the first argument is concerned, the simplest response is that it is not true. There is research which supports the Deaf claim (Albrecht and Devlieger, 1999), but none of it, as far as

I am aware has compared the same person before and after a cochlear implant. The Deaf lack one element of normal human functioning. Are they saying that this should not be the test? That they have (or believe they have) a high quality of life, which includes a rich cultural heritage and their own language. The second argument collapses when it is accepted that, whilst there may be some initial discrimination, this will disappear as society becomes habitualised and does not see the deaf with cochlear implants as any more strange than the blind with a white stick or a dog. As far as the third argument is concerned, there is no reason why the deaf child should not learn and use sign language as a second or supplementary language.

(vi) The Child's Right to an Open Future

As the case for children's rights has become more urgent, Joel Feinberg's article 'The Child's Right to an Open Future' was published (Feinberg, 1980). His premise is that children have rights even when they cannot presently exercise them, but will be able to do so in the future provided that such potentiality is preserved. Withdrawing a child from school at fourteen, as Amish parents purported to do (see *Wisconsin* v. *Yoder*, 1972), removed from these children a vast range of career opportunities, ensuring that they lived thereafter as Amish farmers. Not for them any possibility of a career as a concert pianist, an oceanographer or an astronaut, said Mr Justice Holmes (ibid.). A similar example is the impact that FGM has on the lives of young women. Sexual relationships become difficult, and childbirth painful. A third example is the impact that certain faith schools, with a narrow curriculum, are likely to have on employment prospects. As Feinberg notes, '(the) violating conduct guarantees now that when the child is an autonomous adult, certain key options will already be closed to him' (1980: 126). He maintains that children hold 'rights in trust' for their future interests. They are claim-rights, but they cannot be currently exercised because the capacity to do so is lacking. He describes them as 'anticipatory autonomy rights'. He envisages a future autonomous child with no constraints.

But what is meant by an 'open' future? Is such a thing possible? Does it entail giving the child as many opportunities or merely enough choices? Archard (2015: 76) says of the former that it is 'impossibly demanding', and of the latter that it is 'hard clearly to specify' (see also Mills, 2003). Arneson and Shapiro (1996), on the other hand are more positive; they interpret 'open future' as requiring an individual to make a choice between 'the widest possible variety of ways of life'.

It seems that Feinberg is also overlooking the fact that the present child has interests to uphold too. In the *Wisconsin* case the child may well have had an interest in being educated now, as well as what education might equip him to do in the future. John Eekelaar agrees that the right should not inhere in the future adult, but in today's child. He maintains that all children 'should have an equal opportunity to maximise the resources available to them' during their childhood (including abilities) so as to minimise the degree to which they enter adult life affected by avoidable prejudices incurred during childhood.

357

We must not over-emphasise the significance of decisions like *Roper* v. *Simmons* for questions like the termination of a pregnancy. Murder is often committed impulsively, whereas the decision to seek an abortion or to refuse medical treatment is usually taken after careful thought (for an example, see M. Freeman, 2004).

15

A Magna Carta for Children?

In giving this book and this chapter the title I have, in invoking the 'Great Charter', I am not to be taken literally. They did things differently 800 years ago (Carpenter, 2015; Holt, 1965). I am not advocating that we drag Theresa May or Boris Johnson to Runnymede's 'meadows', leading them 'beside the still waters' of the Thames (Psalm 23), or that we draw up a new code for children in Latin, in which Jacob Rees-Mogg is, we must presume, proficient. Anything more top-bottom, it would be difficult to imagine! Magna Carta was first drawn up in Latin, and subsequently in French in 1225, before an English text was produced in the sixteenth century. Invariably described as containing quintessential British values, it reflects rather the interests of Norman aristocracy. Runnymede is described in the Charter as between Windsor and Staines. Today, it is more apposite to note its proximity to Heathrow. On the direct flight path of planes leaving the airport, any negotiation would be drowned out by high decibel noise. The relevance of language might count for little.

Little of it remains, and only a couple of the clauses are of relevance today (clauses 39, 40). These provisions are 'sacrosanct' (Bingham, 2010), containing the building blocks of a rule of law society. Children do not feature prominently. They are relevant as heirs to property, and nothing else. Thus, Article 3 deals with the problem of the underage heir. There are more references to Jews than to children.

In the 800 years since 'Runnymede', Magna Carta has proved very influential. Its doctrines have spread far and wide, new groups have sought access to its provisions, for example women, black people (Nelson Mandela appealed to it during his treason trial), trade unionists, dissidents everywhere. But not, apparently, children. The anniversary exhibition at the British Library in 2015 featured children as learners ('becomings'). It did not show how Magna Carta could be used as a resource by children. The otherwise excellent exhibition guide (Breay and Harrison, 2015) is similarly remiss; it has room for '1066 and All That' (Sellar and Yeatman, 1930), which proclaimed it 'a good thing', and for a Tony Hancock script, in which Tony enquired 'Did she die in vain?'. But none for school strikes – there was an unsuccessful one against the cane in 1911 (see above, p. 316).

Magna Carta has sixty-two clauses, and I have no intention of matching its length. What follows is, as Magna Carta was, local rather than global, and top-down. I hope that much of what I say will be endorsed by advocates of children's rights in both the Global North and the Global South, and by children. At the very least it should offer space for dialogue and debate.

We need to start with a Preamble. This will recognise that children are human beings. This seems too obvious to state, were it not for the fact that for most of history they have not been so regarded. Nineteenth-century 'child savers' (Meyer, 1973; Platt, 1969) saw them as investments, though of lesser importance than animals (when Philip Mundella MP introduced a Bill in Parliament to outlaw cruelty to children in 1889, sixty-six years after it became a criminal offence to be cruel to a domestic animal, he had to concede that his Bill gave children *almost* the same protection as we bestowed on domestic animals). Ask yourself whether James Bulger would be alive today had he been a dog, rather than a toddler. Why do we have an RSPCA, but only an NSPCC! Isolated examples apart (Hutcheson, 1755; Spence, 1797), no one saw children as anything more than 'becomings' before Janusz Korczak 100 years ago.

As human beings, children will have human rights. They come within the Human Rights Act 1998 (Fortin, 2011) and are protected by the ECHR. (It seems we are not withdrawing from this, *The Guardian*, 18 May 2016). Their Magna Carta, as is the case with the CRC, is an addition to recognise the special position which children occupy in society, rather like CEDAW for women and the Disabilities Convention for those who suffer from disabilities. How is an additional package of rights for children to be morally justified? There are two arguments.

The first emphasises children's vulnerability. Dixon and Nussbaum (2012: 574) suggest that vulnerability is an important reason why. But they are more taken with a second argument, namely, that it is more cost-effective. This is, I believe, a subsidiary consideration only.

Preamble

The institution of rights upholds certain values. We have been recommended by Ronald Dworkin to 'take rights seriously' (Dworkin, 1977). For Dworkin, anyone who proposes to take rights seriously must accept the ideas of human dignity and potential equality. He argues in favour of a fundamental right to equal concern and respect, and against any general right to liberty. The advantage in so arguing, as John Mackie (1984) acknowledged, is that the right to equal concern and respect is a final and not merely 'a prima facie right', in the sense that one person's possession or enjoyment of it does not conflict with another's. Dworkin put this forward as a 'postulate of political morality' (1977: 272), that is, a fundamental political right, so that governments must treat citizens with equal concern and respect.

But why do we have the rights we have? Is this sufficient by itself to explain a right-based moral theory? This question is left open as to where do rights come from? Why do we have the rights we do? I am not talking here of legal rights. The answer to why we have these can be sought within the legal framework itself (the statute/convention says...), or historically by depicting the struggles (for the vote, trade union rights, to rid schools of the cane) and, of course, for children's rights.

What is there then when there 'are' rights? As Jan Narveson put it, there:

> must be certain features or properties of those who 'have' them such that we have good reason to acknowledge the obligation to refrain from interfering with, or possibly sometimes to help other bearers to do the things they are said to have the right to do, or have those things they are said to have a right to have. (Narveson, 1985: 164)

Rights, then, are dependent on reasoned argument, though this is not always clear. Thus, Robert Nozick can merely assert peremptorily that 'individuals have rights' (Nozick, 1973: ix), and leave it at that. Justifying principles can, and have, been sought.

One common answer links right with interests. This takes us part of the way, but not, I would suggest, far enough. Thus, as an example, Joel Feinberg tells us that the 'sort of beings who can have rights are precisely those who have (or can have) interests' (Feinberg, 1966). There is much that is in my interests but to which I can in no way make a justifiable claim. The same applies to other adults and to children too. This is rather different from Onora O'Neill's objection to finding rights where there are imperfect and non-institutionalised obligations only, but it creates a caveat at least against the indiscriminate use of the 'manifesto' sense in which rights are sometimes used (O'Neill, 1988).

Another argument often put forward is purely formal. It is that all persons ought to be treated alike unless there is a good reason for treating them differently. Dworkin, for one, accepts this. He envisages the right to treatment as an equal as a morally fundamental idea (Dworkin, 1977: 226–9). It is that which requires that each person be accorded the same degree of concern and respect as every other person. Though an attractive argument, this reasoning alone is not without its difficulties. A problem lies in deciding what constitutes a 'good reason' for treating people differently. Gender and race are now almost universally accepted to be indefensible distinctions, and sexual orientation is close to achieving this status – though on all three examples I am speaking of the liberal democratic world. Whether discrimination on grounds of age is justifiable is still controversial. But what of children?

We must accept that children, particularly young children, have needs that must be satisfied, and recognise also their vulnerability (Herring, 2014). These needs cannot be met by recognising that they have rights on a par with adults. Vulnerability may justify granting rights to children over and above those which adults have. An appealing argument has been advanced by William Frankena. He argues that humans are 'capable of enjoying a good life in the sense in which other animals are not'. And he continues: 'it is the fact that all men are similarly capable of enjoying a good life in the sense that justifies the prima-facie requirement that they be treated as equals' (Frankena, 1962). Superficially, this is an attractive argument. But it question-begs. Are all persons, even all adults, capable of enjoying a good life? All children are capable of so doing, even if their capacities during childhood are limited. But there are dangers in using an argument like this: it can backfire. It can lead to the deprivation of rights on the ground that it is meaningless to the person in question. And it has done: so, for example, it was common to sterilise the intellectually disabled (Trombley, 1988), and we say it is in the best interests of those in a persistent vegetative state to have nutrition and hydration withdrawn.

It can also be argued that, without more, it fails to show how factual similarity can be said to ground the obligation claimed by Frankena. Nor is it entirely clear how factual similarity should lead to egalitarian treatment, since it would be possible to argue that two persons were similar, and at the same time support useful treatment on the ground that the value of one person's happiness is greater than that of other persons. Ronald Dworkin himself attempts to identify the existence of a moral right against the state when, for 'some' reason, the state would 'do wrong' to treat a person in a certain way, 'even though it would be in the general interest to do so'. It is, however, clear that what is 'wrong' for the state to do is what the state has an obligation not to do. Dworkin, in other words, seems to be defining rights in terms of duties, But, why is it 'wrong' for the state to act in a particular way? It is because the individual has a 'right' on which state action of a particular sort would illegitimately trample. This suggests the argument is inherently circular.

Thus, Dworkin's arguments take us so far, but not far enough. Equality by itself cannot explain what Dworkin is trying to explain: namely, that rights as such 'trump' counter-vailing utilitarian considerations. Something more is needed. I believe this additional concept/value is autonomy. A plausible theory of rights – and this most emphatically includes rights for children – needs to take account not just of equality but also of the normative value of autonomy. It is important to recognise that persons as such have a set of capacities that enables them to make independent decisions regarding appropriate life choices. The deep structure of the rights thesis is this equality and autonomy. Kant recognised this, and it is also at the root of the Rawlsian contractarian conception (Rawls, 1971). To see persons as both equal and autonomous is to repudiate the moral claim of those who would allow utilitarian calculations of the greatest happiness of the greatest number to prevail over the range of significant life choices which the rights thesis both facilitates and enhances. Utilitarianism, by contrast, demands that the pattern of individual life choices be overridden if others are in this way made better off. The result of this is that life choices become in effect the judgement of one person, the sympathetic onlooker whose pleasure is maximised only when the utilitarian principle is upheld. But such an assimilation contradicts the central thesis of equality and autonomy – the fundamental tenet of ethics that people are equal and have the capacity to live as separate and independent beings. To treat persons as utilitarianism requires is to focus almost obsessively on aggregated pleasure as the only ethically significant goal, and to ignore the critical fact that persons experience pleasure, and that pleasure has human and moral significance only in the context of a life a person chooses to lead.

It is the rights thesis that protects the integrity of the person in leading his or her life. One of Dworkin's insights was to link Rawlsian contractarian theory to the language of rights. One of his failings was not to appreciate that both values at the root of Kantian moral theory (equality and autonomy) were equally morally significant. When we take both equality and autonomy seriously, we are back to the contractarian thinking which we find in Kant and in the contemporary constructivism of John Rawls. Equality is, I would argue, best expressed as an original position of equal beings, and autonomy is best understood as the putative choice of those beings under a 'veil of ignorance'.

To believe in autonomy is to believe that anyone's autonomy is as morally significant as anyone else's. And autonomy does not depend on the stage of life that a person has reached. Only human beings are 'persons'. A legal system may attribute 'personhood' to other entities, corporations or animals, for example, but these do not become 'persons' in the sense used here. What is it, then, about human beings that makes them 'persons'? A possible answer is critical competence or the capacity for reasoning. It is interesting that such a test is close to that posited by Lord Scarman in his ground-breaking judgment in the *Gillick* case in 1985. Lord Scarman offered no guidelines as to when a child reached '*Gillick*-competence' and, in terms of age, legal commentators have since assumed this was reached during adolescence, at perhaps fourteen or fifteen. However, there is clear and increasing evidence that it is achieved much earlier. Once criteria for personhood are examined this conclusion is supported. A good account of the criteria of personhood is found in Richard Lindley's account of autonomy. He argues:

> Certainly consciousness is a requirement. More specifically a person is a creature which has beliefs and desires, and acts on its desires in the light of its beliefs. However, this is insufficient for personhood. What is required in addition is the capacity to evaluate and structure one's beliefs and desires, and to act on the basis of these evaluations. (Lindley, 1986)

To respect a child's autonomy is to treat that child as a person and as a rights-holder. It is clear that we can do so to a much greater extent than has been assumed hitherto. But it is also clear that the exercising of autonomy by a child can harm that child's life chances. It is true that adults make mistakes too. And it is undoubtedly the case that they make mistakes when interfering with a child's autonomy. But having rights means being allowed to take risks and make choices. There is a reluctance to interfere with an adult's project. This is exemplified by the law's attitude to a competent adult's decision to refuse medical treatment. Such a person may do this for a reason that is quite irrational, or indeed for no reason at all. And the legal system has come out at last to recognise the institution of the advance directive. But this reluctance is tempered when the project pursuer is a child because of a belief that choice now may undermine the exercise of choice later. Lomasky puts it thus: 'what counts as damage...is determined by what will likely further or diminish its eventual success in living as a project pursuer' (Lomasky, 1987).

This is to recognise that children are different. Many of them have lesser abilities and capabilities. They are more vulnerable. They need protection. Without welfare rights – protection – they will not be in a position to exercise autonomy, to participate in decision-making. Of course, all of this is true, but it is not as true as we have come to believe. Children are different, but they are not all that different. Age is often a suspect classification. If we are to use a double standard, it needs to be justified. The onus lies on those who wish to discriminate. Hitherto, it has to be said that they have not discharged this burden very convincingly. How many of the structures, institutions and practices established to 'protect' children actually do so? It is much easier to assume abilities and capacities are absent than to take cognisance of children's choices. A recent example in the United Kingdom is the peremptory way in which the argument to include children within the remit of the Equality Act 2010 was dismissed.

If we are to make progress we have to recognise the moral integrity of children. We have to treat them as persons entitled to equal concern and equal respect, entitled to have both their present autonomy recognised and their capacity for future autonomy safeguarded. This is to recognise that children, particularly younger children, need nurture, care and protection. In other words, children have rights that adults do not have – additional rights.

In seeking to develop a children's rights prospective we must thus recognise the integrity of the child and his/her decision-making capacities, but at the same time note the dangers of complete liberation. The child liberation writers of the 1970s enlivened the debate, but they went too far. The writings of John Holt (1974), Richard Farson (1974), Howard Cohen (1980), and others – interestingly all Americans, since the United States has obstinately refused to ratify the CRC – need to be rediscovered and reassessed (see Byrne, 2016) but I doubt if the message they preached, in effect an adulthood for every child, would command respect today. When they wrote (to take just one example) sexual abuse of children had not been discovered.

Nevertheless, too often writers on children's rights have dichotomised: thus, there is either salvation or liberation, nurturance or self-determination – in Richard Farson's pithy phrase, the one protects children, the other protects their rights. But both are necessary. Thus, for example, we will be better able to tackle child abuse if we recognise that children have rights. To take children's rights more seriously requires us to take more seriously the protection of children and recognition of their autonomy, both actual and potential. This recognises that there is a need to respect both individual autonomy and to treat persons as equals. Actual autonomy is important, but it is as much the capacity for autonomy that is at the root of

369

this thinking. The constructivism of John Rawls' theory of justice (Rawls, 1971) is useful to this argument. It is the normative value of equality and autonomy which forms the substructure of the Rawlsian conception of the social contract. The principles of justice which Rawls believes we would choose in the 'original position' are equal liberty and opportunity, and an arrangement of social and economic inequalities so that they are both to the greatest benefit of the least advantaged, and attached to offices and positions open to all under conditions of fair equality and opportunity.

These principles confine paternalism – the philosophy at the root of protection – without totally eliminating it. Those who participate in a hypothetical social contract would know that some human beings are less capable than others. They would in turn know about variations in intelligence and strength, and they would know of the very limited capacities of small children and the rather fuller, if incomplete, capacities of adolescents. They would employ the insights of developmental psychology. They would also bear in mind how the actions of those with limited capacities might thwart their autonomy at a future time when their capacities were no longer as limited.

These considerations would lead to an acceptance of interventions in children's lives to protect them against irrational actions. But what is to be regarded as 'irrational' must be carefully monitored. It is, of course, both vague and value-laden. Is it irrational to refuse a clinically-indicated blood transfusion and does the reason for the refusal matter? Is it irrational to want to work rather than go to school? Does this depend on age, on the work involved, on the reasons for wanting to work? Is it irrational to want gender reassignment? (Spain, I note, allowed this to a sixteen-year-old boy: *The Guardian*, 13 January 2010.) Is it rational to want to die? The examples are legion. What is to be regarded as 'irrational' must be strictly confined. The subjective values of the would-be protector must not be allowed to intrude. But this is easier said than done. What is 'irrational' must be defined in terms of a neutral theory capable of accommodating pluralistic visions of the 'good'. We should not see an action as irrational unless it is manifestly so because it is obvious that it would undermine future life choices, impair interests in an irreversible way. And, we must tolerate mistakes: Dworkin notes 'someone may have the right to something that is wrong for him to do' (Dworkin, 1977: 188–9). He writes, of course, only about adults – nowhere does he consider the application of this argument to children. However, we cannot treat persons as equal without also respecting their capacity to take risks and make mistakes. We would not be taking rights seriously if we only respected autonomy when we considered the agent was doing the right thing. But we would also be failing to recognise a child's integrity if we allowed her to choose an action which could seriously and irreparably impair the attainment of a full personality and development subsequently.

The test of 'irrationality' must also be confined so that it justifies intervention only to the extent necessary to obviate the immediate harm, or to develop the capacities of rational choice by which the individual may have a reasonable chance of avoiding such harms.

It is not difficult to present a case for protecting children against actions which may lead to their death or serious injury. A straightforward example today is the use of dangerous drugs such as heroin. Another is protecting children from the worst form of labour. We did this in the nineteenth century when we stopped children going down coal mines and up chimneys. Of course, we cannot really believe that children were exercising any autonomy in undertaking these tasks. We would also wish to protect children from sexual exploitation and abuse and from trafficking.

What should legitimise such interferences with autonomy is what Gerald Dworkin has called 'future-oriented' consent (Dworkin, 1972). The question is: can the restrictions be justified in terms that the child would eventually come to appreciate? Looking back, would the child appreciate and accept the reason for the restriction imposed on him/her, given what she/he now understands as a rationally autonomous and mature person? This is far from an easy test to apply. It involves something akin to what Derek Parfit has called 'ideal deliberation' (1984). He explains it thus:

> What each of us has most to do is what would best achieve, not what he *actually* wants, but what he *would* want, at the time of acting, if he had undergone a process of 'ideal deliberation' – if he knew the relevant facts, was thinking clearly, and was free from distorting influences.

But what are 'relevant facts'? And how are hypothetical preferences to be considered? Can the distortion of values be eliminated? These are very real problems. We must recognise these before we can begin to disentangle them. The effort to do so is, I believe, worthwhile.

The dichotomy drawn between autonomy and protection is thus to a large extent a false divide. It should not divert us from the proposition that the true protection of children does also protect their rights. Thus, it is not a question of whether child-savers or liberationists are right. They have both grasped an essential truth in that they each emphasise part of what needs to be recognised. But both have also failed in that they do not address the claims of the other side.

16

Rethinking Principles and Concepts

Child Defined

The first concept to which thought must be given is 'child'. In 1989, the drafters of the CRC could not agree a definition and foisted upon us a compromise. The provision in Article 1 purports to define 'child' but fails to do so. It digs a hole with traps for the unwary, made all the more hazardous by the non-legally binding paragraph in the Preamble which tells us that the 'child' (note not the foetus) 'needs special safeguards and care, including appropriate legal protection, before as well as after birth'. Article 1 defines a child as any human being under the age of eighteen (and see Freeman, 2018). It imposes a uniform closure for childhood, unless the applicable law directs otherwise.

It has been generally assumed that the difficult question in getting to grips with the perimeters of childhood related to its beginning, but answering when it ends poses more complex questions (Gregg, 2016).

We must have a concept of 'child' before we can decide when 'childhood' ends (or for that matter begins). We also need to have an understanding of what being an adult involves. One assumes the existence of the other in this binary classification, rather as night follows day, and guilty presumes that there is a not guilty verdict. Naming in this way overlooks, but does not overcome, the difficulties in drawing the distinction between child and adult on the basis of age. It certainly does not explain why (in England) one can marry before one can buy a gerbil, and spend eight years in a penal institution before one is entitled to participate in the democratic process. A distinction based on age is simplistic; when there are a jumble of ages, lacking in coherence and rationality, largely the result of historical contingency, the result is untenable. One must have a better justification for a law than it was decided thus in the reign of Henry IV, as Holmes J remarked.

The law's legalism (Shklar, 1964) fits the binary break-down very well but it fits ill with developmental psychological knowledge and the evidence emerging from neuroscience. These suggest that there is a period of development which bridges childhood and adulthood. Although it was discovered at the very beginning of the twentieth century, it only began to make an impact at the end of that century when the US Supreme Court was challenged as to whether the death penalty might be imposed on a seventeen-year-old murderer (*Roper* v. *Simmons*, 2005, above, p. 81). We are now beginning to appreciate that the brain only reaches full maturity at some point between the ages of fourteen and twenty-five (and begins to decline at about the age of forty-five). This has led Steinberg (2014: 72) to conclude that legal systems which draw the line at eighteen have got it about right by fixing on eighteen, just under the half way point. But, in some cases, this means they will have got it horribly wrong. Coping with adolescence is a huge dilemma for a legal system structured round a binary split.

Should we give up on a clear dividing line between adults and children, reject it as a form of apartheid, an institution which it proved difficult to operate in practice? (Fuller,

1964). One response is to adopt individualised justice, to treat each case on its merits. On one level this leads to *Gillick*-type decision-making (see above, p. 183); on another to a conclusion that an MRI scan would become a prerequisite to every trial. *Gillick* was very promising but there has been a retreat from it; and even were it feasible, considerable caution would be needed before we put our faith in neuroscience (Morse, 2013).

It leaves open the conundrum as to when childhood begins. Though posed as a question of legal analysis we are really into the realm of political morality. Is a child *en ventre sa mère* a human being or just a human becoming? The conservative response is it is human life from conception; the liberal view sees it as becoming, and therefore not a human being. But whatever, it is certainly not nothing, and is clearly 'human'.

Defining a human being is even more difficult. We share 98 per cent of our DNA with chimpanzees and nearly half with cabbages. How many spare parts can an individual have before she/he is no longer human? The tests for classification as a human being are capacity and vulnerability. Machines can be built which are capable of performing activities which, until recently, could only be carried out by human beings. They are also vulnerable. Is it then possible that the CRC might apply to these machines (robots, computers) also?

Added to all this are the further complications in the Preamble. This recognises that the foetus (and indeed the embryo and the zygote) are vulnerable and need special protection. It is not clear what protection. In the United Kingdom, embryos are protected from experimentation after fourteen days, at which time the primitive streak is deemed to have developed. The law of abortion protects the foetus. The father has no rights (*Paton v. BPAS*, 1979), nor does the mother. The rights that exist inhere in the medical profession, which is immune from criminal sanctions if certain conditions are complied with. The structure of the abortion law – a legal defence to a crime – is clumsy, and the language in which the law is expressed is antiquated (the legislation is the Offences Against the Person Act 1861). Reform, at the very least reconstruction and modernisation, is urgently needed, but is no one's priority, and there is certainly no consensus as to what a modern law of abortion should look like. We permit abortion for a longer period of time than most other European countries, but that does not mean that our law is more liberal than theirs. On the contrary, it is less so. I argued this in 1988, in relation to the law then when terminations were permitted for twenty-eight weeks (Freeman, 1988a). It remains the case today.

Is there a way out of this impasse? Is there any room for compromise between two entrenched positions, two dignities? One appealing idea is to permit a woman to terminate her pregnancy as she wishes (full autonomy in other words), whilst at the same time preserving the life of the foetus. The way to this is to be found in ectogenesis (Alghrani, 2013; Mclean and Ramsey, 2002). There is not the space to consider all the implications of this here, but in brief it would involve the use of an artificial uterus to carry the baby to term and the availability of adoptive parents to take on the responsibility of rearing the child. Cost would be one consideration: who would meet it? It is unlikely that the state would take it on. There have already been large cutbacks in the IVF budget. The burden is likely to fall on those who adopt these orphans. In all probability, the wealthy. As is often the case they are advantaged in the fertility stakes. Would this be seen as yet another attempt to 'rescue' children of the poor by transferring them to 'good' homes?

I have concentrated on questions relating to the beginning of childhood because they raise the most issues and most acute controversies. But there are also questions about the end of childhood. Had the CRC been a generation earlier, twenty-one would have been the upper limit, not eighteen. Such are the contingencies of law-making. At earlier periods of history there would have been class and gender differences. The Convention is not completely consistent since it permits states parties to recruit fifteen-year-olds into its armed services. That there is now an Optional Protocol raising this age to eighteen only partially saves face. The United Kingdom still permits sixteen-year-olds to join the army, many of them disadvantaged youth straight from care.

There is evidence that childhood is getting longer. Youth dependency extends well into the twenties. It is common for twenty-somethings, who a generation ago would have married and set up home, to return or never have left the family nest. The causes are many, including house prices, unemployment and badly paid employment, and cuts in welfare, with the elderly being favoured to the detriment of the young (and children). Do we need to extend the CRC beyond eighteen? And, if so, to what? Twenty-one, twenty-five? Or should we be thinking of a Convention of the rights and responsibilities of (perhaps) eighteen to thirty-year-olds? Alderson (2015) has pointed to systems which draw the boundary at nineteen or twenty. We attach too much importance to chronological age. This is seen most clearly when claims of asylum seekers are being adjudicated. In much of the world, particularly in the Global South, births are not registered. About one-third of the world will not have a birth certificate or know how old they are. Childhood is a phase in the life cycle. As Morrow explains, 'the category "age"...can mean various things – not simply chronological age (which is the dominant understanding in western societies), but also functional age and relational age' (2013: 151). Age is more important to those involved in governance than to those who are the objects of social control.

Children have been increasingly defined in terms of age-related competencies. Age dictated when the child started school, as well as the school-leaving age. Age also governed when sexual intercourse was permitted, when marriage was allowed, when the young person could be convicted of a criminal offence, etc. Professionals (child experts) knew the answers to these questions. These experts could draw on developmental psychology to assist them in answering these questions. This psychological knowledge was constructed 'by adults for other adults to use in order to make sense of, regulate and promote children's lives and learning' (Woodhead and Faulkner, 2000: 11).

Non-Discrimination: Some Limits

The CRC (Article 2) targets discrimination on a wide range of grounds and concludes with the catch-all 'or other status'. The construction of a definitive list of grounds is both impossible and undesirable. An attempt has been made to do so by Hodgkin and Newell, 2007. Sexual orientation is omitted – not surprisingly in 1989 – but it is generally accepted now that it is covered by 'other status'. The grounds tend to expand as we become a more pluralistic society, more tolerant of difference. What is also omitted is age. Clearly, this cannot be embraced by this catch-all expression and despite the Convention, children are discriminated against when their status is compared to adults. To take the simplest of comparisons, adults have the vote but children do not. There is a strong case for permitting children to participate in the electoral process, and a case for enfranchising all children, in other words dispensing with a minimum age requirement (Cook, 2013). But other differences can be justified. We all accept the need for a minimum age requirement before a person can be held esponsible for a criminal act. We may differ as to what that age should be, as different legal systems do, but no one could sensibly argue that four-year-olds should be held criminally responsible for stealing smarties from the local supermarket, where anyway they are placed to tempt the young child. A child-friendly environment has its disadvantages too!

The children's liberationist programme cannot thus be accepted in its entirety. We know more about the dangers of drugs and more about the destructive force of paedophilia than we did in the 1970s. We have come to appreciate that children are capable of self-determination, but we also remain conscious of their vulnerability. For this reason I have long defended limited paternalism. I called it 'liberal paternalism', though this is oxymoronic (Freeman, 1983: 54–60). 'Limited paternalism' may be a preferable way of describing it. It is paternalism cut down to size, and the burden rests on the person who wishes to justify intervention to remove autonomy. It must be more than anything which will impose barriers to the pursuit of an 'open future'; opting for an arts diet at school will close off the possibility of becoming a doctor. I have argued, following Richards (1981: 16) that the action chosen by the child/adolescent must reach a level of irrationality which is 'severe and systematic and a severe and permanent impairment of interests is in prospect'. Further, intervention is justified only to the extent necessary to obviate the immediate harm or to develop the capacities of rational choice by which the individual may have a fair chance to avoid such harms on her or his own (Richards, 1981: 19–20).

In not treating children in the same way as we treat adults, we do not necessarily discriminate. As Lord Hoffmann explained in the *Carson* case (2007): 'there is obviously no discrimination when the cases are relevantly different'. As regards children, it is clearly necessary to distinguish between discrimination and reasonable measures of differentiation. Children may also be victims of economic and social discrimination, for example, because of where they live (Boyden and Holden, 1991). English courts are reluctant to grant relief in respect of social and economic discrimination (Nolan, 2011). Courts elsewhere, for example in South Africa and South America, have been much more interventionist (ibid.).

The Convention lumps all who are under eighteen years of age into one category. They are children. But it hardly needs more than a moment's contemplation to realise that childhood can be broken up into several categories; new-born, toddler, small child, pre-pubescent, adolescent, but the CRC does not distinguish between them. At least, that is so in its definition of childhood. It recognises difference in Article 5 (Freeman, 2015) on 'evolving capacities'. As does the common law, spearheaded by Lord Scarman (*Gillick* v. *West Norfolk and Wisbech AHA*, 1986). The evolving capacities thesis has the support of developmental psychology, psychoanalysis and neuroscience. Neuroscientific research establishes that the first few years of life are crucial for cognitive development and that early experiences can influence the emerging architecture of the brain (Ryan, 2012: 50). Further, there is data showing that language learning is one of the 'behavioural systems whose development is altered – neurobiologically and behaviourally – by caregiving experience' (Thompson, 2014: 1451). Anne Dailey (2014: 12) believes 'the most important insight psychoanalysis brings is that the skills of adult autonomy derive from children's earliest relationships with caregivers'. The Equality Act 2010 is clear: discrimination on more or less every ground is banned, except discrimination against those under eighteen years of age. There was evidence that 43 per cent of under eighteen-year-olds considered that they had been treated unfairly because of their age.

There are many examples of age discrimination which, I would argue, are caught by the CRC. Anti-social behaviour legislation applies only to children. Behaviour that is normal for children may annoy adults and be deemed anti-social. Play may be seen as noise and attract sanctions. Adults also play and create noise but are more likely to do so in private. Children's space is controlled by adults. One control technique employed against children is the 'mosquito'. This emits a sound which is painful to young ears, but cannot be heard at all by adults. It is sold as an anti-loitering device, and can be used, it would seem, perfectly lawfully against children who congregate in public places. The use of the mosquito has been attacked by, amongst others, the Committee on the Rights of the Child, but it remains a weapon in the battery of police forces and presumably anyone else who wishes to control child movements.

It can be a lot worse than this. Street children – 'children out of place' – have not many years ago been subjected to police extermination squads. This was a common practice in Latin America, and was particularly prevalent in Brazil. There was some concern that the streets might be 'cleansed' in the run up to Rio's Olympics in 2016. The President of the Philippines has threatened to introduce this policy there too. There are precedents; examples of wealthy entrepreneurs using the police force to clear an area abutting their store of children who do not have the money to shop but who wish to use the area to window-shop, or to play football, or skate-board.

Children's space is also controlled by civil society, for example, by shopkeepers who regulate the entry of children to two at a time (though to be fair there was a left-wing bookshop in London which restricted entry to two MPs at a time). Shopping malls operate similar policies – as regards children, not I assume MPs! One in Sydney is discussed by Malcolm Voyce (2005).

The development of 'curfew' laws is a further example of a discriminatory practice. The Anti-social Behaviour Act 2003 permitted the creation of dispersal zones. Anyone under sixteen could be removed from one of these zones if found there between 9 pm and 6 am, unless accompanied by an adult. No distinction is made between those who were misbehaving and those who were innocent of any offence. As a fifteen-year-old,

I regularly used my local reference library until it closed at 10 pm; today I might be forced to return home! This would have delighted my parents but infuriated me. My feelings would have counted for nought. It is hardly surprising that the curfew law angered many adolescents. It was challenged in the courts by Liberty acting on behalf of a fourteen-year-old boy 'W' in the *Richmond* case in 2013. The Court of Appeal held that the law could only be applied where there was actual bad behaviour, or such behaviour was imminently anticipated.

There are also status offences. A notorious victim was Gerald Gault, though he was rescued by the US Supreme Court (1967; see above, p. 151). An example is truancy from school; truancy from employment tends to be labelled as 'taking a sickie'.

Best Interests: An Overworked Concept

Best interests is an overworked concept, but this does not necessarily mean it should be pensioned off. It labours under serious difficulties. The judge cannot apply it without a vast amount of information-gathering. Without full grasp of the facts, a weighing of utilities is impossible. Even with possession of all the data – and it is dubious whether this is attainable – the decision-maker needs predictive ability. She/he has in a typical case to fast forward six, eight, ten or more years to determine what is in a child's best interests. It will sometimes be in the child's best interests now, but more often it is some time in the future.

Psychology can offer insights but no scientific discipline can account for the impact of divorce, death, serious illness or unemployment. Such external events may well have an impact on happiness, and thus on best interests. And what interests are we examining? Attachment bonds, where best interests may favour the residential status quo? (Bowlby, 1969). Material welfare? Emotional security? A stimulating educational environment? Concern for spiritual well-being? It is inevitable that different judges will have different hier-archies of values. They may not state these explicitly, but a careful reading of their reasoning may reveal what has motivated their conclusion: a reference perhaps to one party being on legal aid, endorsement of regular church attendance by the other. For an excellent example look at Justice Stewart's judgment in the Iowa case *Painter* v. *Bannister* (1966).

It is difficult to eliminate values, easier to see through prejudices, though it is not always easy to separate one from the other. Decisions which invoked the mother's lesbianism to deny her custody were clear examples of prejudice, but were cloaked in supposedly rational reasoning, employing arguments such as that her children would be bullied at school, and might 'catch' homosexuality from contact with a gay parent. The law reports are littered with cases where judicial values are difficult to defend. Thus, an English judge could find a naturist lifestyle harmful to children (*Re W*, 1999), but another in the same era could order supervised contact to a father with a history of psychiatric illness, alcohol and drug abuse, who had Nazi sympathies and dressed his sons (five and eight) in Nazi uniforms, before marching them round the house to Nazi salutes (*Re P*, 1996).

There are alternatives to the 'best interests' standard (Melli, 1993). It is rare for a child who is the subject of contested litigation not to have already forfeited his/her best interests.

So, it may be preferable to follow Goldstein, Freud and Solnit (1979), who argue that the decision-maker is seeking, not the best interests of the child, but what is in effect the 'least detrimental alternative' to this (Eekelaar, 2002: 243–4). Least detrimental alternative conveys to the decision-maker that the child is already a victim, that she/he is at risk and needs speedy action to avoid further harm (2002: 54). Thus, a court confronted with the dilemma of conjoined twins, where only one can survive, may conclude, as the Court of Appeal did in *Re A* (2000), that the weaker twin must be sacrificed. This decision was, and remains, highly controversial (see, e.g., Harris, 2013). Were not the judges approving murder? Could it possibly be in the best interests of the weaker twin to die? The decision – an application of least detrimental alternative – is utilitarian. The weaker twin's rights were obliterated. It is significant that the judges gave short shrift to human rights arguments.

There are other alternative standards. The judgment of Solomon (see 1 *Kings*) could be invoked. A dispute between two women over maternity was solved by awarding custody of a child to the woman who was prepared to give up the child, and not to the one who was happy to see the child cut in two. It was obvious who was the true mother. There is a variant on this approach in Brecht's *Caucasian Chalk Circle* (Freeman, 1998). As a solution to a real-life problem, this is unlikely to attract much support. Nor is Jon Elster's plaintive cry of despair, which would solve disputes by the toss of a coin (Elster, 1987). What will they think of next? A penalty shoot-out? A duel?

More sensibly, there is a case for decisions reflecting the lives of children being governed by a class rule. Hence the importance of the primary caretaker rule. This is based on the presumption that it is good for children that there should be continuity of care. This is undoubtedly true but will not be so in every case. The primary caretaker may have been abusive. Courts need to deal with this dilemma. They may find themselves balancing attachment and abuse. (For a case where they had this dilemma, see *Re B*, 1990; the judge came down in favour of continuity.)

It is arguable that there are better ways of deciding these disputes (over contact, for example). Mediation is one answer, but the parties inevitably 'bargain in the shadow of the law' (Mnookin, 1975). Another non-legal approach, both less of a drain on resources and more effective, is to treat the dispute therapeutically, rather than through the family justice system (see Thorpe LJ in *Re L (A Child) Contact: Domestic Violence*, 2000, at 439).

The discussion has looked at these disputes through the prism of welfare. But is there any reason why the child should not decide the question for him or herself? The evidence is to the effect that children want to be listened to, but that most do not want the burden of being compelled to decide between their parents (Cantwell and Scott, 1995). Indeed, it is arguable that children have a right not to be asked; it was so argued in *M* v. *M* in 1977 and doubtless many times since.

There are good reasons for not making children the decision-makers. In many cases they are the true victims of divorce. Whilst this is contested, what cannot be questioned is that exposure to parental conflict is bad for children and that the legal system should do whatever it can to minimise this (Kaganas and Diduck, 2004). It is also now clear that the children who come best out of divorce are those able to maintain a good relationship with both parents after divorce (Wallerstein and Kelly, 1980). There is also clear evidence of a negative association between divorce and the development of children and young adults (Richards, 1997). For example, there are on average lower levels of academic achievement and self-esteem, and higher incidence of problems of psychological adjustment. But there may be other factors at play, such as welfare provision, housing policies, availability of child care, minimum living wage legislation and also societal attitudes to divorce (Richards, Hardy and Wadsworth, 1997: 544).

But bold statements such as that children are the victims of divorce can turn the public debate into one about the welfare of these children rather than about their rights. As Smart, Neale and Wade put it (2001: 366), 'as objects of concern, rather than as persons'. Back in 1983, I wrote (Freeman, 1983: 192):

> What rights should children have in relation to divorce?
> A right to choose which parent they prefer to remain with?
> Or should they have a right not to be asked? To express
> a preference? A right to be separately represented in custody
> proceedings? But who is to represent the child and what is
> she to represent? A right to see the parent with whom they
> are not living? But how is such a right to be enforced?

Remove the word 'custody' and, a third of a century on, the questions posed remain as they were.

What rights do children have when their parents divorce? First, let's dispose of the obvious. An increasing number of children have parents who are not married. Secondly, many parents separate but do not divorce. Thirdly, in the majority of cases there is no dispute and therefore no need for a court order. It should also be noted that despite media panic children cannot divorce parents (Freeman, 1997a: 213). The result of this is that children are largely marginalised. There have been suggestions at various times that there ought to be different categories of marriage and that one where there were to be children should be virtually indissoluble. Mia Kellmer-Pringle (1980: 127–9) was one advocate of this. But, even were this desirable, it is not easy to imagine it being put into operation.

Participation: Gaps in our Thinking

Article 12 of the CRC is generally regarded as the linchpin of the Convention. We parrot positive cosy sentiments about it, equating its meaning with agency, autonomy and, above all, participation. And yet none of these words appears in Article 12. In fact, the article, though of great importance, is dependent entirely on adult cooperation. It is adults who decide whether a child meets the requirements of Article 12. It is clear that the article is regularly violated. Children themselves say this, and they are supported by the Committee on the Rights of the Child in its reports: for example, in 1995 the United Kingdom was criticised for failures to take children's views into account on sex education and on school exclusions.

There are a number of reasons why Article 12 is not working as well as it might. Those who need to cooperate with children are not necessarily aware of this obligation. There is general ignorance of what is expected by the Convention. Laura

Lundy (2007: 930) describes Article 12 as the 'most widely cited yet commonly misunderstood' of all the provisions in the CRC. For example, it is not always appreciated that the child's rights to express views extends to all matters affecting the child, and not merely to the rights enunciated in the Convention itself. On the other hand, it is sometimes assumed that children must express views. But this would turn a right (a privilege) into a duty, and nothing of the sort is intended. Indeed, children have the right to opt out of the decision-making process, for example, to express no view as to which parent they wish to live with.

Decision-making in the presence of adults is not a daily experience for children. It is therefore important that the context be as child-friendly as possible. Formality should be reduced to an absolute minimum. It should be explained to the child that she/he only has to participate if she/he wishes to do so. It is important to note the significance of the verb 'assure' in Article 12(1). It is a powerful endorsement of the value of the child's voice. Weaker, less compulsory language could equally well have been used, as it is elsewhere in the CRC. It is important that the space offered to children to contribute should be a safe one. Hence the importance of Article 19. This is especially important within the context of a school, where the child may be seen to be challenging the authority of the teacher. Sometimes children will need the help of adults to be able to formulate a view: Article 5 is thus important in that it gives children the right to receive guidance and direction from adults in the exercise of their Convention rights. This guidance extends to encouraging all forms of expression: Article 13 of the CRC states that the child's right to freedom of expression includes the right to impart information, 'either orally, in writing or print, in the form of art, or through any other media of the child's choice'.

End of Childhood

Neuroscience also gives us the opportunity to reconsider the appropriate terminus for childhood. Most legal systems, in line with the CRC, say childhood ends at eighteen. But this is relatively recent: it was commonly twenty-one until the 1970s. Should we build on what we now know about brain development and reassess the cut-off point?

There are at least four possible answers to this.

(1) Abandon a fixed age and operate on a case by case basis. This is very much the approach adopted by the House of Lords by a three to two majority in *Gillick* thirty years ago. It also reflects the legislative response, both in the United States and in the United Kingdom. So, in both countries, although the norm is eighteen, the age at which certain activities are permitted varies according to the activity in question and can be completely irrational. But *Gillick* has not had the anticipated impact. A conservative judiciary has resisted using it over much to advance children's rights. Indeed, there has been a retreat from it (Freeman, 2007b).

(2) We could shift from a classification based on a dualism in which everybody is deemed either a child or an adult to a regime which recognises three categories, one for children, one for adolescents, one for adults. Legal systems have been slow to acknowledge the existence of adolescence

and there is the problem of knowing exactly where to fix the boundaries.

(3) We could acknowledge that there is variation in brain development amongst persons of the same chronological age, and would accordingly make individualised decisions rather than drawing categorical age boundaries.

(4) We could stipulate a boundary age based on our experiences of the difference between adults and children. This would probably hit on an age somewhere between puberty and adulthood, drawing the boundary line about fifteen or sixteen.

17

Conclusion

Rights are important moral coinage. Without them we are impoverished. Benevolence is no substitute. This can be seen strikingly in the case of children. Children's rights thus becomes an interesting test-case for rights generally (MacCormick, [1982] 1984). In examining the case for children's rights and the values such rights uphold, we are thus engaged in a wider enterprise of explaining rights, their rationale and their role. We are also finding a way of evaluating society.

I first started writing about children's rights nearly forty years ago. Children's rights were then said to be 'a slogan in search of a definition' (Rodham, 1973). The CRC was then a distant prospect. The child's voice was silent, or at least silenced. We hadn't yet awakened to sexual abuse or child slavery, even less so to child poverty. There was no discussion of participation or autonomy, or of child-friendly justice. The idea of children voting was not even contemplated. We have come a long way since, but much more progress needs to be made. There is always a concern that we may go backwards, that we may have witnessed a false dawn. Part of the way forward lies in reiterating the case for children's rights and exploring the values such rights embody. This book is part of, what I hope will continue to be, a healthy and constructive debate.

Rethinking children's rights does not mean jettisoning them. The significance of the CRC cannot be overestimated. It is a landmark in the history of childhood. It may be looked back at in centuries to come as being as significant as Magna Carta, or even more so. Or it may be viewed as a ham-fisted and abortive attempt to raise the profile of children, an exercise in symbolic politics and nothing more. That depends upon us, on whether we take children's rights seriously, press for improvements and do not allow the rights conferred thus far to be frozen in time. Duties are no substitute. Without rights there would never have been duties, and duties would soon evaporate were the emphasis on rights to be diminished.

But rights themselves are insufficient. There must be effective remedies too. These were not questions particularly addressed by the drafters of the 1989 Convention. The Third Protocol is a start, but what is really needed is a court. It is also important that children be efficiently and effectively represented by well-trained personnel (lawyers and other professionals), and that resources are available. It is important that here, as elsewhere, child-friendly justice operates.

More attention must be paid to neglected groups of children, particularly those who slipped through the net in the 1980s. Our empathies do not remain constant. The gay no longer offend, but the refugee is now seen as a potential terrorist. We are more aware of the plight of girl children than we were: we have Malala and Boko Haram to thank for this. Our reaction to FGM is more condemnatory than it was a generation ago. As our insights into children's lives increase with the large amount of research being published, so our understanding of their rights, and the lack thereof, challenges us to rethink. How different would the CRC have looked had there been child input? Or a greater contribution from the Global South?

There is a need to liberate 'suppressed narratives and voices drowned out by univocal projections of master narratives' to 'illuminate the underside of master narratives, thereby exposing the subordination and marginality of alternative social visions whose relegation to the status of exception to the rule, counter-tradition or minority perspective can no longer be objectively justified' (Cook, 1992). A major theme in postmodernism is subversion, the commitment to undermine dominant discourse. The potential for subversive struggle is particularly propitious given the discrediting of Marxism, the instabilities of late capitalism and the contradiction of the bureaucratic Welfare State. These faults and fissures are seen as a source of resistance and freedom. We must 'look to new forms of politics that go beyond emancipation because the "enemies", if they exist at all, are no longer the bourgeoisie or the boss so much as the bureaucracy, centralized government and "democratically" elected representatives' (Rosenau, 1991: 146).

It is argued that change will be brought about through small-scale transformation. J. Boyle (1985) maintains that, by increasing the plasticity of social structures, the state itself will be converted from a source of stability to a source of change: equality and rights discourse play a fundamental role in reconstructing collective identities. Once the principle of equality is accepted in one sphere, there will be a demand for it in other areas too and the structures of late capitalism will be subverted from within. By 'within' is meant from 'below'. The goals of postmodern politics are stated in terms of a radical and a plural democracy. According to Aronowitz (1988) the contemporary state, reflecting the logic of modernity, is characterised by extreme centralising tendencies: it is colonising, totalising, bureaucratic. By way of contrast, the postmodern state is minimalist because radical democracy depends on the proliferation of public spaces where social agents become increasingly capable of self-management.

There is no question: to get the Convention was an achievement. But the litmus test must ultimately be whether it effects any improvements in the lives of children. There is no doubt that there has been an increase in rights-based advocacy on behalf of children. Children are gaining rights but is their overall welfare getting better? It would be churlish not to recognise that there have been important gains.

We talk of children as agents and their participation in decision-making processes is valued more than can have been envisaged a generation ago. We are more conscious of the problems confronting children than we were, children are more visible. But they continue to be vulnerable. They remain second-class 'semi-citizens' (E. Cohen, 2009). They continue to be disenfranchised nearly everywhere – a debate in the UK Parliament in December 2015 said it all, with the government rejecting votes for sixteen-year-olds in the Referendum on membership in the EU on financial grounds – it would apparently have cost £6 million, about the same as a widget for Trident!

Grugel (2013) explains:

> Rights claims work by framing injustices in ways that train the gaze on individuals who have been deprived of their rights and to whom restitution must be made...but...they can also serve to distract attention

away from underlying political practices and structures that shape and contribute to structural inequalities and their reproduction. (2013: 20)

In addition, because of the need to achieve consensus (Sunstein, 1995), rights are often vague and/or open-ended.

Until recently, we (in the United Kingdom) aimed to better the lives of children not through a rights regime (the Human Rights Act 1998 was nearly a decade later than the CRC) but by the state reinventing itself as a welfare state (Esping-Andersen, 1990).

This started during the Second World War. Most of it was constructed on the initiative of the 1945 Labour government. The establishment of the National Health Service in 1948 met opposition from the vested interests of the medical profession's 'union', the BMA. This was overcome. For many years the NHS was the admiration of the world.

The post-war Labour government also introduced family allowances which were paid to the mother for the second and subsequent child. The sum involved was small, but being paid to the mother and not the father it was assumed would promote children's welfare rather than augment beer money. There were education reforms too; the school-leaving age was raised from fourteen to fifteen. Free school meals had been introduced by the Liberal government in 1906.

Sustaining the full welfare state ideal proved difficult, and it began to be rolled back very soon. The first breach was the introduction of prescription charges for medicines. This proved to be the precedent for further attacks on the welfare state ideal; most dentistry had to be paid for. Eventually, it became inevitable that another strategy would be employed. It took sustained effort to see this as lying in human rights, but this model was eventually superimposed upon the remnants of the welfare state. Children's rights followed, but only after equal opportunities legislation had targeted women and ethnic minorities. Persons with disabilities came a poor fourth.

Where Next?

There are many reforms which would follow if we were prepared to take children's rights more seriously. Some of these are easy to effect – outlawing corporal punishment, raising the minimum age of criminal responsibility; others are much more difficult to make – ending child poverty, enfranchising children are examples. But the most difficult change of all is the cultural revolution without which we may get only superficial reform of the sort which is unlikely to survive and even less likely to penetrate our consciences – even committing the promise to end child poverty by 2020 in legislation did not save it from the austerity axe, by which time anyway it had increased. The cultural revolution, as I am calling it, looks forward to the end of 'childism' (Young-Bruehl, 2012). We cannot look forward to the end of child abuse in its many manifestations, we cannot look to a future in which children are genuinely offered the best they can be given, to paraphrase the Geneva Declaration of 1924, until we understand the acts which harm them and the prejudices which structure and delegitimate them.

What kind of society do we want our children to grow up in? In a nutshell, a healthy democracy. A healthy democracy needs actively involved citizens, and this includes children. It is important that we give our children opportunities to participate, to challenge, to protest. There is, however, no point doing this if we are not prepared to listen to their concerns. We must be open to change. Hayward asks:

> What is moral about encouraging children to take personal
> responsibility for their lives and the future of the planet
> while the community passes the costs of escalating carbon
> emissions, superannuation and unsustainable resource use
> onto this generation and the ones that follow through
> a complex series of investment decisions with short-term
> benefits that exacerbate long-term vulnerability in
> a changing world? (2013: 140)

And she comments:

> Young citizens cannot live sustainable lives in
> communities where the institutional structures and
> processes of decision-making are discriminatory,
> exploitative or unjust. (Hayward, 2013)

How are we to stimulate our children's capabilities for ecological citizenship? We must not silence their imagination; rather encourage them to question existing structures, become aware of injustices. Orr (cited in Hayward, 2013: 143) envisages new models of citizenship which employ hand, head and heart to encourage young citizens to reflect on their values (heart), to think critically as they develop their ideas (head), and to take actions (hand).

Some Important Reforms

There follows a discussion of some of the most important reforms on the agenda. The list is far from exhaustive.

(1) Citizenship

Debates have revolved around citizenship since the Greeks, but it remains a contested concept. If we did not categorise children differently from adults, the question would not arise as acutely as it does. If there were no refugees or asylum seekers, the question would throw up fewer difficulties. If we applied a *ius soli* rule, as we did until 1981, the citizenship of babies born to refugee mothers would be clear, though in today's world many would be uncomfortable with the conclusion.

Children in the United Kingdom today are 'semi-citizens' (E. Cohen, 2009). They are 'subjects'; they are nationals; they are entitled to a passport; they are entitled to have their births registered. But they do not have voting rights in general or local elections, or in referenda, even when (as was the case with the 2016 Brexit referendum) it may have a greater impact on them than it does on the adult population (and see above, p. 279).

(2) Minimum Age or Votes for All?

There is a view that the age should be the same as the minimum age of criminal responsibility (MACR). This would enfranchise ten-year-olds. This conclusion might encourage the raising of MACR to an age closer to other European states. Would public opinion support fourteen as the age for both criminal responsibility and voting? I doubt it. And fourteen would be an arbitrary choice. It is more likely that the minimum age for exercising the vote be reduced to sixteen. But there is nothing significant about the age of sixteen. If sixteen, why not fifteen? And if fifteen, why not fourteen? We reach a conclusion that there is no case for a minimum age, and that accordingly all children should have the vote (and see Cook, 2013). It is not anticipated that many three-year-olds will vote, but, save in the rarest of constituencies, it is not likely to affect the result.

Equally important are changes to facilitate high or at least higher turnout rates. There is no reason why the traditional polling booth should not be supplemented by virtual voting. This is likely to replace the time-honoured but labour-intensive infrastructure in the not too distant future anyway. But an obvious starting point is to permit the young to exercise the vote using the latest IT. If this is a step too far, children could be encouraged to vote in their schools. But politics being the art of the possible, we should be content if initially we were able to enfranchise sixteen-year-olds. Recall when women were given the vote, it was first limited to those over thirty; and remember too the arguments against women voting were suspiciously like those used today to deny the vote to children.

(3) Minimum Age of Criminal Responsibility

The minimum age of criminal responsibility in England today is ten. This means that criminal sanctions can be imposed on primary school children. The CRC does not lay down a minimum age, nor do the Beijing Rules. The latter stipulate that this should not be too low, but offer no guidance as to where to draw the line. The abolition of the *doli incapax* presumption in 1998 in effect reduced MACR from fourteen to ten. Judged against the standards of comparable nations, the English MACR is indefensible. There is no reason to believe that our ten-year-olds require the threat of criminalisation to conform when French and German children do not.

In fixing MACR it is suggested that the following considerations be borne in mind:

- the best interests principle in CRC, Article 3 (see above, p. 98);
- the desirability of rehabilitation of the offender and his reintegration into society;
- the importance of restorative justice (Gal, 2011);
- the dissonance between MACR at ten and the inability to buy a gerbil until one is eighteen (and countless other similar examples);
- the evidence from neuroscience that the brain is not fully developed until the age of twenty-five;
- juvenile crime is in decline: it is 72 per cent down on its peak in 2007–8; the moral panic provoked by the *Bulger* case was unfortunate – it was a one-off;
- we imprison far too many people: one way of reducing the prison population would be to raise MACR; there are about 1,000 under-eighteens in penal institutions today, forty-four of them being aged twelve or thirteen;
- the example of neighbouring states which typically have a MACR of fourteen or fifteen (see Cipriani, 2009); even Scotland, where it was set at eight until 2011, now stipulates a threshold of twelve;

- a Bill was presented in the House of Lords in June 2016 to raise MACR; even if it passes in the Lords, it stands no chance of becoming law – the spectre will be raised of twelve-year-old terrorists and crimes committed by radicalised young teens.

(4) An End to the Hitting of Children

Fifty-two countries have made it unlawful to hit children, the latest being Mongolia and Montenegro. In England this reform has been resisted. We've settled on a compromise, which provides a defence when moderate chastisement amounts to no more than an assault – in lay language does not leave a mark (Children Act 2004, section 58). Corporal punishment is no longer permitted in schools or against children in most other environments. Only children are still exposed to legalised violence: it was abolished in prisons and the armed services long ago. One irony/paradox which remains is the child in care, who becomes exposed to physical punishment when adopted. Children in children's homes and children who are fostered are legally immune from corporal punishment.

We must follow the trend, which has accelerated, and put a full stop to this legalised violence. The case hardly needs to be put. In brief, there are five reasons:

(1) It is morally wrong; hitting people is wrong and children are people too (Newell, 1989a). It is an affront to dignity, a violation of the rights of the child.

(2) It does not work and it teaches the wrong lesson, that violence is an answer, which it is definitely not. On the contrary, it breeds violence. Children who are spanked

may develop lower IQs than their peers whose behaviour is challenged verbally (and see the work of Murray Straus et al., 2014).

(3) It is arguably child abuse, and if not, there is the danger that it can lead to child abuse. In many of the most notorious cases child abuse has started as discipline and escalated. Parents may not intend to hurt their child but underestimate their strength and do not appreciate the damage they can do.

(4) Though the CRC is not explicit – there is no mention of corporal chastisement as such – it is generally accepted that the reference to 'violence' in Article 19 embraces physical punishment. This is also as the Committee on the Rights of the Child interprets it.

(5) The best interests of the child should never be a justification.

It must be outlawed immediately. We now have zero tolerance of domestic violence, a policy inconceivable ten years ago. We can achieve this in the case of child abuse too, but only if this goal is pursued in conjunction with a raft of policies using education, the media, etc. This will be unashamedly social engineering. We know that such legislation encounters resistance, and that this is more difficult to undermine in the domain of the family (Aubert, 1959; Dror, 1957) (see further, Freeman, 1974: ch. 3).

Anti-spanking legislation will be judged as successful if it changes attitudes towards children, if it valorises the status of childhood and if it defeats childism (Young-Bruehl, 2012). If it leads to an increase in care proceedings and prosecutions of parents it will have failed in its principal aim. Getting rid of legalised violence will also have a positive impact on society (see, further, Freeman, 2000a, 2007b; Freeman and Saunders, 2014).

(5) Right to Work

Should children have the right to work?

This is a most difficult question to answer. Note must be taken of the following:

(1) in much of the world they already do;

(2) in the United Kingdom there is an informal economy;

(3) a major part of the informal economy are the many carers, looking after parents and other family members;

(4) there is currently a disparity in the 'living wage' paid to children and to adults; this discrimination is difficult to justify, but perhaps can be where a genuine apprentice-ship scheme is in operation;

(5) in the 'black economy' there is exploitation of the type that wishful thinking encouraged us to believe was abol-ished in the nineteenth century;

(6) children can easily disappear: insufficient attention is paid to home-schooling (it is questionable whether this should be allowed) and to enrolled children who slip through the net, go to unregistered schools, or abroad, some to be radicalised;

(7) there are positive models of children in work; the Bolivian example, above, p. 176, stands out;

(8) there are health and safety concerns;

(9) restrictions are, it seems, difficult to enforce (Pond and Searle, 1991);

(10) most protective legislation has been repealed (Deakin, 1990); and

(11) the school leaving age has periodically been raised, and is now eighteen.

A tension exists between liberationalists, who would deregulate totally, giving children the freedom to work; and the protectionists, who believe children should have the right not to work. There is no reason why children should not possess both of these freedoms.

(6) Right to Trial by Peers?

One of the best known provisions of Magna Carta provided for trial by one's peers, in effect for trial by jury. The historical context is important: trial by jury was about to emerge as the replacement for trial by ordeal. Children in England have never had trial by their peers, that is, by other children. They have, of course, experienced jury trial in adult courts. There has been no demand for child decision-makers to determine guilt in adult courts. In the United States, by contrast, in the aftermath of *Re Gault*, an attempt was made to rule it unconstitutional to deny jury trial to an underage defendant (see *McKeiver v. Pennsylvania*, 1971), and trials of juveniles by juveniles took place, inter alia, in California. The State of Kansas has extended to juveniles the constitutional right to jury trial.

Trial by one's peers must not be taken too literally. It could lead to burglars insisting on being tried by burglars and bankers by bankers. It is important that the jury system retains the confidence of the public if it is to cling to its fragile legitimacy (Freeman, 1983). A jury of fifteen-year-olds is unlikely to convince members of the public. It might be better to select, presumably at random, just one under eighteen-year-old. Another approach would be to use a shadow jury of children to test their behaviour against that of the 'real' jury.

A lot depends on what is conceived to be the function of the jury. Orthodox jurisprudence limits its role to fact-finding but this may be, and has been, questioned. There is a concept of the jury as a judge of the law as well. Those who hold this view see the jury as more than a rubber-stamp of judicial directions. After all, why have a jury if it is merely there to agree with the judge?

A child jury, even if it is only a shadow jury, might well be able to judge laws which undermine the interests of children, and, in doing so, act as a catalyst for change: laws like those which criminalise normal adolescent sexual behaviour (see above, p. 147), and those which control children's space (curfew laws and anti-social behaviour legislation, for example).

(7) The Case for Incorporation

The United Kingdom has not incorporated the Convention and it is unlikely to do so. Should it?

(1) It would make the CRC more widely known.
(2) Its provisions could be 'directly invoked' in the courts and applied.

(3) It would make it easier to argue that socio-economic rights are justiciable (Nolan, 2011).

(4) With incorporation, the CRC becomes a clear standard against which 'all law, policy and practice' can be judged (Save the Children, 2011: 16).

(5) The Human Rights Act 1998 is a precedent. This incorporated the ECHR into UK law. It applies to children as well as adults. But there are no child-specific provisions in the ECHR. This means it is easier to enforce some children's rights than others.

(6) There is evidence that where there has been incorporation, children are perceived as rights-holders and there is a culture of respect for children and their rights (Lundy et al., 2012: 100).

(7) Further, it gives policy-makers 'leverage' (Lundy et al., 2012: 101) when they seek support for rights-focused policies for children.

(8) It is also of significance that there is greater impact, so it seems, where a deliberate and calculated decision is taken to incorporate, as contrasted with the lesser impact when this happens automatically.

It is clear that we must incorporate the CRC and its Protocols.

Research: The Future

There has been more research about children in the years since the CRC than in the previous 1,000 years. And, to be fair, more of it has emanated from a children's rights perspective than ever before. But too little research today is informed by children's rights. The dominant image remains the child as a problem who one day will become an adult and a citizen, rather than the child as participant now as agent and as social actor. Twelve years ago, the IJCR published an article by Terry Dobbs, Anne Smith and Nicola Taylor (2006). It was surprisingly innovative because it actually looked at the disciplining of children from the perspective of children themselves. Children were asked to explain to an alien how parents disciplined children on earth. What emerged from this research was a picture of children's feelings and their perceptions of being physically punished. This study is a model of child research, but despite the huge amount of publications on punishment since Dobbs et al., the article has had a low profile. I can only assume it has been marginalised because it deviates from standard research which sees the child as an object, an adult in the making, rather than as a subject. As a test case, I examined the four issues of *Childhood*, 2005. There are thirty-six articles and only two of them are informed by a rights perspective (by Ruth Gasson, see p. 45, and Ana Vergaria del Solar). But, perhaps this is not so surprising if Judith Ennew is right in her belief that some researchers have an 'almost wayward academic ignorance of children's rights' (2011: 136).

Right to Development

The right to development was formulated in 1996 in a UN Declaration (General Assembly Resolution 41/128). Its importance should not be overlooked, even if it has been rather marginalised. It aimed at laying down a duty to provide international assistance to put into operation the plan of action of the World Summit for Children, We the Children and A World Fit For Children, thought to be essential to ensure that the CRC was universally implemented.

At least as significant was that it saw human development as the basis for human rights. The important connection between development and children's rights was recognised in the Geneva Declaration in 1924, and subsequently in the 1959 UN Declaration. The CRC itself emphasises 'development' throughout (see Article 27, recognition of need for moral and social development). It stresses also 'happiness, love and understanding' (Preamble, para. 6), and enrichment of traditions and cultural values (Preamble, para. 12).

Child development is a precondition to human development more generally, an example, if one be needed, of the value to the wider society of recognising children's rights. Note O'Manique's observation (1990) that the moral foundation for a right is 'the virtually universal belief that development is good, ought to develop, and have or do what is required to develop'.

This human development approach to human rights maintains that all have a claim to the rights recognised in the UDHR and the major human rights treaties, since the enjoyment of those rights is essential for the 'integral development' (Ensalaco, 2005: 23) of all dimensions of the human person, though it hasn't yet totally reached children.

The 1986 Declaration reinforces this. It insists that the right to development is an 'inalienable human right' (Article 1), that the 'human person is the central subject of development' (Article 2), and that respect for human rights is necessary to ensure free and complete fulfilment of the human being (Article 2). The human development approach is an advance on traditional development theory in that it stresses the realisation of an individual's freedoms and enhancement of an individual's capabilities. This sees economic growth as necessary but not sufficient.

The Development Declaration and the CRC are in agreement on (to quote the CRC) 'the importance of international cooperation for improving the living conditions of all children' (CRC, Preamble, paras 12 and 13).

There hinges on both the Declaration and the CRC the question of the extent to which they impose an obligation for international cooperation. The Declaration is just that: it is not a Convention. The CRC uses weak language, hardly suggestive of imposing an obligation.

Is there then a right to development? Donnelly (1984) argues against affirming 'a right not to be economically underdeveloped'. However, we cannot overlook the numerous occasions on which the right to development has been restated by official bodies: in 1993, 1995 and 2000. As an example, examine the UN Millennium Declaration of 2000. This called upon world leaders to make the right to development 'a reality for everyone'. Everyone clearly includes children. But what does 'development' mean? A careful reading of UN Committee material (Peleg, 2012) suggests that in the eyes of those who interpret the CRC it amounts to nothing more than the right to become an adult (Abi-Saab, 1980).

The Binary Classification

Adolescence is a twentieth-century discovery. The law has long operated with a binary classification of adults and children, in effect squeezing out those who do not readily fit into either category, or stretching a category to accommodate a problematic case. The mature minor doctrine in the United States, the reasoning in the *Gillick* decision in the House of Lords, Article 5 of the CRC and its emphasis on 'evolving capacities', are all attempts to get to grips with the difficult case.

Are there better answers than drawing a boundary line at eighteen? Do we need to separate children from adults? And, if we do, can we avoid adopting a purely arbitrary event like attainment of eighteenth birthday? Why should so much hinge on the number of times our planet has circumnavigated the sun? Are we engaged in a form of calendar worship? People of few years can be more vulnerable than others who have more experience of life, but this is not an invariable truth: many six-year-olds are more competent than many sixty-six-year-olds. It is easier to defend a child's right to 'an open future' than to propose such a right for senior citizens. Paternalism is easier to defend where young persons are involved: I have long justified a form of limited paternalism that I call 'liberal paternalism'. It is not discrimination and therefore not the target of Article 2 if there are genuine differences between two cases. But with only the simple dichotomy of adults and children, it is difficult to sustain differential treatment. Sixteen-year-olds are not very different from eighteen-year-olds, who are adults.

In the light of this, ought we to consider replacing the current binary classification by one which divides the first third of lifespan into three, with a new intermediary category of adolescence? One consequence of this would be that it would by no means follow that adulthood began at eighteen. Much would depend upon what were conceived to be the standard elements of the developmental paradigm. Childhood/Adolescence in the Global North seems, paradoxically, to be getting both longer and shorter at the same time. If, for example, one looks at sexuality or fashion, then there is a lot of truth in the comment that eleven is the new sixteen. If, on the other hand, one focuses on questions of dependency, childhood could be extended to twenty-five or even further. Neuroscientific evidence indicates that the brain is not fully developed until the age of twenty-five, and, furthermore, that it declines from about forty-five years.

A tripartite division would result in cutting back on childhood, and extending minority, though it would by no means follow that changes would take place at both ends. A possible threefold split would see childhood as ending at ten, adolescence at sixteen or eighteen, or possibly even at twenty-five. If this were to be implemented, we would need to replace the CRC by two Conventions, one for children, another for adolescents. Learning from the experiences of the 1989 'experiment', greater input could be expected from the two categories of the 'young', and from the Global South. There would still be controversies over when life begins. There would be demands to break up the categories further: nine-year-olds do not have much in common with children of five; nor do five-year-olds with toddlers of two.

413

Changes like these mooted here would not command public support, and I do not therefore advocate that we rush into them. But the binary classification is ripe for a considered rethink. It makes no sense to treat six-year-olds and sixteen-year-olds as if they had more in common than divided them.

18

Coda: A Child of Our Time

The Convention on the Rights of the Child is not set in stone. As I write, it is twenty-eight years old and there have been many changes in the world. A generation ago we were pulling down walls; today we are about to rebuild them. In the twenty-eight years since the CRC, development has gone from being a goal of the Global South to a contributor to global warming and climate change. China has shown us it is possible to combine Communism and capitalism, but not, it seems, to recognise human rights at the same time. The rich have got richer (the so-called 1 per cent, Dorling, 2013), and the poor poorer. The refugee crisis is set to reconfigure Europe, as parts of the Global South self-destruct. The seeds of colonialism no longer bear fruit but return to haunt old colonial powers. The world seems to be peopled by bigots and isolationists in ways that were not predictable in 1989. Religion both threatens world order yet remains in terminal decline. In an age of human rights, Guantánamo still stands. In an age of women's rights, girls are still genitally mutilated (many more than was thought, see *The Guardian*, 8 February 2016, p. 2), forced into marriage and deprived of an education. And in an age of children's rights – let us not forget Ellen Key's prediction that the twentieth century would be the 'century of the child' – we achieved the Convention but failed to improve the well-being of many children. There are still child slaves (more than 6 million), child soldiers, child labourers, child sex workers, child refugees, many of them unaccompanied, many more than there were in 1989. Children are the principal victims of war, particularly civil war like that being waged in Syria. A large percentage of births are not registered: these children do not exist, they do not have rights, nor even the right to claim rights (Arendt, 1964). Children 'disappear' and acquire new identities, as happened in Argentina in the 1970s and 1980s, and may now be happening with ISIS. They are kidnapped, as occurred in Nigeria when Boko Haram descended on a girls' dormitory and swept up nearly 300 girls many of, whom are unlikely to be seen again. Children still die from preventable diseases. Child poverty remains rife. So does child malnutrition. Children remain the only group disenfranchised in those parts of the world where the ballot box has a meaningful existence. Children's badge of inferiority leaves them as the only group against whom violence is legitimately inflicted in the name of discipline. And so the litany continues. And it will continue.

Global Order

The 1989 Convention is an example of international integration, a new global legal order. It is an attempt to get beyond sovereignty. In its day, beginning with the Treaty of Westphalia (1648) and climaxing in the twentieth century, it was an instrument of modernity and of development. Today, as Domingo points out (2010: 65), 'it has become a hindrance that must be roused out of its noxious lethargy or risk disappearing altogether'. And, he adds, 'its usefulness is in doubt in an era of globalization, in which...daily life has been globalized, creating a dense web of human interaction and an interdependence of relations incompatible with its theoretical assumptions' (Domingo, 2010). The ineluctable pluralism that we associate with a global society undermines the nation-state's pretence of exclusivity.

But we must pause to rethink. This was yesterday's narrative, before the shutters were pulled down on asylum seekers fleeing Syria, and Greece returning refugees to Turkey, and economic migrants from Pakistan and Afghanistan battering at Europe's fences, and doubtless soon Mexicans at the 2,000 mile wall which is promised to divide the United States from its southern neighbour.

So, where do we go next? Back to Westphalia? Or to a new model of global politics? To hyperglobalisation (Steger, 2013)? Or do we join the globalisation sceptics, who endorse the continued relevance of the nation-state? It is, I believe, probable that the globalisation thrust is accentuating a people's sense of nationhood and nurturing the growth of isolationist parties such as UKIP.

It is commonly held that the scope of obligations of justice extend no further than membership in a common political community. This understanding can be traced back to Thomas Hobbes (1651), or earlier. It retains currency today. Hobbes argued that, whilst the principles of justice could be found by moral reasoning, actual justice could not be achieved except within a sovereign state. Rawls in *The Law of Peoples* (1999) came to the same conclusion, and this led him to endorse a laissez-faire global economic order and, in the international context, to a conception of justice little different from that of Nozick (1973).

The facts of global injustice are well known. For children under ten, the main causes of death in the Global South are diarrhoea and measles; 300 die every hour because of malnutrition.

Rawls' views are of course, influential, 'but if individuals have basic rights in virtue of their humanity', surely they should hold against the whole world? (Kukathas, 2006: 1). One who thinks they do not is Thomas Nagel (2006). He argues people are in a justice relationship only if they belong to the same state. He adds he owes 'nothing beyond humanitarianism to those with whom he shares no state'. He explains:

> What creates the link between justice and sovereignty is something common to a wide range of conceptions of justice: they all depend on the coordinated conduct of large numbers of people, which cannot be achieved without law backed up by a monopoly of force. At least among sizable populations, it cannot be provided by voluntary conventions supported solely by the mutual recognition of a common interest. (2006: 165)

But what this overlooks is that, although states are essential, rule-making tends to emanate from international bodies; the United Nations, International Labour Organization, World Trade Organization, World Health Organisation, and, of course, the Committee on the Rights of the Child. Cohen and Sabel (2006: 186) point to the fact that global politics is not merely 'an occasional matter of sparse agreements', but is 'enduring and institutionally dense'. Nagel's response is to see such treaties as 'pure' contracts, with nothing guaranteeing the justice of their results. They offer no assurance of socio-economic justice. It is sad to have to admit that the CRC is an example of this.

None of these philosophers directs their mind to obligations toward children. As 'semi-citizens' at best, they would appear to occupy the status of the outsider to whom nothing more than humanitarianism (charity) is owed. This is so obviously counter-intuitive as to cast doubt on what Rawls and Nagel argue about global obligations. But my concern here is not with the poor Brazilian who picks the coffee beans to enable me to enjoy an expresso in London, unless she/he is a child, but with our obligations to children worldwide.

In a global economy, new human rights problems may emerge as markets are integrated, states are shrunk, there are transnational flows such as migration, the spread of cultures of intolerance, and the decision-making processes of new or growing global institutions (Brysk, 2002: 3). And, she adds, 'The same Internet that empowers human rights activists increases government monitoring, instructs neo-Nazis, and carries transnational death threats against dissenters' (ibid.). The World Bank, to pick out one institution amongst many, increasingly controls the lives of the most powerless citizens of weak states.

Is the answer some form of world government? This is, of course, to swim against the tide. As I write, the European Union may be about to break up, and even European government seems doomed. We need to defeat the challenges confronting humanity. What is required is 'a coordinated, compassionate and equitable response to global warming' and (Falk adds, 2013), a dramatic reduction in the likelihood of 'apocalyptic warfare'. A danger it would be necessary to overcome is the inevitable freezing of the inequities of present world order.

How then do we move forward? We need to understand that justice, and accordingly injustice, has a number of dimensions. There are first order questions of substance. This is well-understood. How much economic inequality does justice accept? 'Injustice' tends to be neglected; the legal and political theoretical literature focuses on justice rather than its absence. Thinking about children offers us the incentive to correct this bias. And, secondly, there are 'second-order, meta-level questions' (Fraser, 2013). Nancy Fraser (ibid.) explains that beyond these questions of substance, there are 'above and beyond' arguments about the proper frame within which to consider these questions of justice. Most obviously, who are the relevant subjects entitled to a just distribution or reciprocal recognition in the given case?

So is what has been called 'professional engagement' (Williams, 2013: 4). This imposes obligations on all professionals, not just lawyers, to employ their skills to further the children's cause. This engagement extends beyond professionals to judges to create child-friendly courts which encourage child participation. When contact with the law is an alienating experience, legal socialisation can be frustrated. Children must not be made to feel they are like items of property. They are 'beings' and as such should be entitled to participate in processes which affect their lives, unless doing so is likely to harm them irreparably.

Engagement should not be seen as merely the prerogative of the professional NGOs: local communities, civil society organizations, even the private business sector all have a part to play. This is recognised by the Committee on the Rights of the Child (CRC Committee, 2003).

This is particularly so when the interests of children are deliberately kicked into touch. The best recent example of this was the refusal, allegedly on grounds of cost, to permit sixteen-year-olds to vote in the Referendum to decide whether the United Kingdom should stay in the European Union. Children constitute one-quarter of the population, the part of the population most affected by the decision. But there was no dissent. Imagine if the Referendum vote had not been extended to pensioners! There would have been riots. The press wasn't interested. You will comb the media and not find a serious article expressing concern for this failure of democracy. Where were the lawyers, the political scientists, the childhood studies academics? There clearly remains a gulf between the children's rights advocates and those who labour in the sociology of childhood.

We have always been more concerned with child offending than with offences against children. They impact more on the lives of the adult world. This may explain why child abuse, and especially child sexual abuse and exploitation, remained hidden for so long. And why corporal punishment survived for so long in schools, and why we remain almost the only country in Europe not to have made it unlawful for parents to hit their children. It may even go part of the way to explaining why we were so slow in getting to grips with climate change and environmental pollution – these are problems which will impact upon our children more than us. UNICEF's *Unless We Act Now* (2015) highlighted this (see above, p. 208).

Emma Hamlyn, it seems, had a very positive view of the law. If it is the case, and I believe it is, that a society can be judged by the way it treats its weakest members, then we do not come out very well. But as lawyers we should not overlook the ability of law to help construct a better world. It has been done before, and it can be done again. It needs a government with a vision, adequate resources and good state-subsidised legal services to encourage innovative challenges – and a creative judiciary. But how long will we have to wait?

Appendices

The Rights of Infants by Thomas Spence, 1797[*]

Open thy mouth for the dumb.

Proverbs xxxi.8

'AND pray what are the Rights of Infants?' cry the haughty Aristocracy, sneering and tossing up their noses.

WOMAN. Ask the she-bears, and every she-monster, and they will tell you what the rights of every species of young are. They will tell you, in resolute language and actions too, that their rights extend to a full participation of the fruits of the earth. They will tell you, and vindicate it likewise by deeds, that mothers have a right, at the peril of all opposers, to provide from the elements the proper nourishments of their young. And seeing this, shall we be asked what the Rights of Infants are? As if they had no rights? As if they were excrescences and abortions of nature? As if they had not a right to the milk of our breasts? Nor we a right to any food to make milk of? As if they had not a right to good nursing, to cleanliness, to comfortable cloathing and lodging? Villains! Why do you ask that aggravating question? Have not the foxes holes, and the birds of the air nests, and shall the children of men have not where to lay their heads? Have brute-mothers a right to eat grass, and the food they like best, to engender milk in their dugs, for the nourishment

---

[*] See at: www.thomas-spence-society.co.uk/rights-of-infants.

of their young and shall the mothers of infants be denied such a right? Is not this earth our common also, as well as it is the common of brutes? May we not eat herbs, berries, or nuts as well as other creatures? Have we not a right to hunt and prowl for prey with she-wolves? And have we not a right to fish with she-otters? Or may we not dig coals or cut wood for fuel? Nay, does nature provide a luxuriant and abundant feast for all her numerous tribes of animals except us? As if sorrow were our portion alone, and as if we and our helpless babes came into this world only to weep over each other?

ARISTOCRACY (SNEERING). And is your sex also set up for pleaders of rights?

WOMAN. Yes, Molochs! Our sex were defenders of rights from the beginning. And though men, like other he-brutes, sink calmly into apathy respecting their offspring, you shall find nature, as it never was, so it never shall be extinguished in us. You shall find that we not only know our rights, but have spirit to assert them, to the downfall of you and all tyrants. And since it is so that the men, like he-asses, suffer themselves to be laden with as many pair of panyers of rents, tythes, etc., as your tender consciences please to lay upon them, we, even we, the females, will vindicate the rights of the species, and throw you and all your panyers in the dirt.

ARISTOCRACY. So you wish to turn the cultivated world into a wilderness, that you may eat wild fruits and game like Indians?

WOMAN. No, Sophists, we do not want to be as Indians. But the natural fruits of the earth being the fruits of our undoubted common, we have an indefeasible right to, and we will no longer be deprived of them, without an equivalent.

Aristocracy. Do you not, in lieu of those wild productions, get bread, and mutton, and beef, and garden stuff, and all the refined productions and luxuries of art and labour; what reason then have you to complain?

WOMAN. Are you serious? Would you really persuade us that we have no reason to complain? Would you make us believe that we receive these productions of art and culture as a fair compensation for the natural produce of our common, which you deprive us of? Have we not to purchase these things before we enjoy them?

ARISTOCRACY. Sure, woman, you do not expect the fruits of men's labours and ingenuity for nothing! Do not the farmers, in the first place, pay very high rents for their farms; and, in the next place, are they not at great trouble and expence in tilling and manuring the ground, and in breeding cattle; and surely you cannot expect that these men will work and toil, and lay out their money for you, for nothing.

WOMAN. And pray, ladies and gentlemen, who ever dreamt of hurting the farmers, or taking their provisions for nothing, except yourselves? It is only the privileged orders, and their humble imitators on the highway, who have the impudence to deprive men of their labours for nothing. No; if it please your noblenesses and gentlenesses, it is you, and not the farmers, that we have to reckon with. And pray now, your highnesses, who is it that receive those rents which you speak of from the farmers?

ARISTOCRACY. We, to be sure; we receive the rents.

WOMAN. You, to be sure! Who the D-v-l are you? Who gave you a right to receive the rents from our common?

Aristocracy. Woman! Our fathers either fought for or purchased our estates.

WOMAN. Well confessed, villains! Now out of your own mouths will I condemn you, you wicked Molochs! And so you have the impudence to own yourselves the cursed brood of ruffians, who by slaughter and oppression, usurped the lordship and dominion of the earth, to the exclusion and starvation of weeping infants and their poor mothers? Or, at the best, the purchasers of those ill-got domains? O worse than Molochs! Now let the blood of the millions of innocent babes who have perished through your vile usurpations be upon your murderous heads! You have deprived the mothers of nature's gifts, and farmed them out to farmers, and pocketed the money, as you audaciously confess. Yes, villains! You have treasured up the tears and groans of dumb, helpless, perishing, dying infants. O, you bloody landed interest! You band of robbers! Why do you call yourselves ladies and gentlemen? Why do you assume soft names, you beasts of prey? Too well do your emblazoned arms and escutcheons witness the ferocity of your bloody and barbarous origin! But soon shall those audacious Gothic emblems of rapine cease to offend the eyes of an enlightened people, and no more make an odious distinction between the spoilers and the spoiled. But, ladies and gentlemen, is it necessary, in order that we eat bread and mutton, that the rents should be received by you? Might not the farmers as well pay their rents to us, who are the natural and rightful proprietors?

If, for the sake of cultivation, we are content to give up to farmers our wild fruits, our hunting grounds, our fish and game; our coalmines, and our forests, is it not equitable that we should have the rents in lieu thereof? If not, how can the farmers have the face to sell us again the produce of our own land?

Hear me! Ye oppressors! Ye who live sumptuously every day! Ye, for whom the sun seems to shine, and the seasons change, ye for whom alone all human and brute creatures toil, sighing, but in vain, for the crumbs which fall from your overcharged tables; ye, for whom alone the heavens drop fatness, and the earth yields her encrease; hearken to me, I say, ye who are not satisfied with usurping all that nature can yield; ye, who are insatiable as the grave; ye who would deprive every heart of joy but your own, I say hearken to me! Your horrid tyranny, your infanticide is at an end! Your grinding the faces of the poor, and your drinking the blood of infants, is at an end! The groans of the prisons, the groans of the camp, and the groans of the cottage, excited by your infernal policy, are at an end! And behold the whole earth breaks forth into singing at the new creation, at the breaking of the iron rod of aristocratic sway, and at the rising of the everlasting sun of righteousness!

And did you really think, my good gentlefolk, that you were the pillars that upheld the universe? Did you think that we would never have the wit to do without you? Did you conceive that we should never be able to procure bread and beef, and fuel, without your agency? Ah! my dear creatures, the magic spell is broke. Your sorceries, your witchcrafts, your priestcrafts, and all your juggling crafts, are at an end; and the Meridian Sun of Liberty bursts forth upon the astonished world, dispelling the accumulated mists of dreary ages, and leaves us the glorious blue expanse, of serene unclouded reason.

Well then, since you have compelled, since you have driven us, through your cruel bondage, to emancipate ourselves, we will even try to do without you, and deal with the honest farmers ourselves, who will find no difference, unless for the better, between paying their rents to us and to you. And whereas we have found our husbands, to their indelible shame, woefully negligent and deficient about their own rights, as well as those of their wives and infants, we women, mean to take up the business ourselves, and let us see if any of our husbands dare hinder us. Wherefore, you will find the business much more seriously and effectually managed in our hands than ever it has been yet. You may smile, tyrants, but you have juster cause to weep. For, as nature has implanted into the breasts of all mothers the most pure and unequivocal concern for their young, which no bribes can buy, nor threats annihilate, be assured we will stand true to the interest of our babes, and shame, woe, and destruction be to the pitiful varlet that dare obstruct us. For their sakes we will no longer make brick without straw, but will draw the produce of our estate. If we deprive ourselves of our common, in order that it may be cultivated, we ourselves will have the price thereof, that we may buy therewith, as far as it will go, the farmer's produce. And so far as our respective shares of the rent may be inadequate to the comfortable and elegant support of ourselves and infants, so far will we chearfully, by our honest endeavours, in our several callings, make up the deficiency, and render life worth enjoying. To labour for ourselves and infants we do not decline; but we are sick of labouring for an insatiable aristocracy.

To convince your highnesses that our plan is well digested, I will lay it before you. You will find it very simple, but that is the sign of the greater perfection. As I said before, we women (because the men are not to be depended on) will appoint, in every parish, a committee of our own sex (which we presume our gallant lock-jawed spouses and paramours will at least, for their own interest, not oppose) to receive the rents of the houses and lands already tenanted, and also to let, to the best bidders, on seven years leases, such farms and tenements as may, from time to time, become vacant. Out of those rents we can remit to government so much per pound, according to the exigencies of the state, in lieu of all taxes; so that we may no longer have taxes nor tax-gatherers. Out of these rents we shall next pay all our builders and workmen that build or repair our houses; pave, cleanse, or light our streets; pay the salaries of our magistrates and other public officers. And all this we women shall do quarterly, without a bank or bank-notes, in ready money, when the rents are paid in; thus suffering neither state nor parish to run in debt. And as to the overplus, after all public expences are defrayed, we shall divide it fairly and equally among all the living souls in the parish, whether male or female; married or single; legitimate or illegitimate; from a day old to the extremest age; making no distinction between the families of rich farmers and merchants, who pay much rent for their extensive farms or premises, and the families of poor labourers and mechanics, who pay but little for their small apartments, cottages and gardens, but giving to the head of every family a full and equal share for every name under his roof.

And whereas births and funerals, and consequent sicknesses, are attended with expence, it seems requisite to allow, at quarter-day, to the head of every family, a full share for every child that may have been born in his house since the former quarter-day, though the infant may be then but a day old, and also, for every person who may have died since the former quarter-day, though the death should have happened but a day after it.

This surplus, which is to be dealt out again among the living souls in a parish every quarter-day, may be reasonably supposed to amount to full two-thirds of the whole sum of rents collected. But whatever it may amount to, such share of the surplus rents is the imprescriptible right of every human being in civilized society, as an equivalent for the natural materials of their common estate, which by letting to rent, for the sake of cultivation and improvement, they are deprived of.

Wherefore, now ladies and gentlemen, you see the glorious work is done! and the rights of the human species built on so broad and solid a basis, that all your malice will not be able to prevail against them! Moreover, when we begin with you, we will make a full end of your power at once. We will not impoliticly tamper with the lion, and pluck out a tooth now and then, as some propose to melt down your strength by degrees, which would only irritate you to oppose us with all the power you had remaining. No; we will begin where we mean to end, by depriving you instantaneously, as by an elective shock, of every species of revenue from lands, which will universally, and at once, be given to the parishes, to be disposed of by and for the use of the inhabitants, as said before.

But yet be not cast down, my good ladies and gentlemen, all this is done for the sake of system, not revenge or retaliation, for we wish not to reduce you to beggary, as you do us, for we will leave you all your moveable riches and wealth, all your gold and silver, your rich clothes and furniture; your corn and cattle, and every thing that does not appertain to the land as a fixture, for these, you know, must come to the parish with our estates. So that you see you will still be the richest part of the community, and may, by your chearful acquiescence, be much more happy than you are now under the existing unjust system of things. But if, by foolish and wicked opposition, you should compel us, in our own defence, to confiscate even your moveables, and perhaps also to cut you off, then let your blood be upon your own heads, for we shall be guiltless. It will therefore be your interest and wisdom to submit peaceably, and fraternize chearfully with us as fellow-citizens. For, instead of you then having the revenues of the country to carry on war against us, as you have now, the parishes will then have these revenues to carry on the war against you. And as to your moveable property, we are not afraid of it, for it would soon melt away in supporting you in a state of hostility against the strength and standing revenues of the country, unburthened with debts and pensions. So prepare yourselves peaceably to acquiesce in the new system of things, which is fast approaching. And when you shall hear of the blessed decree being passed by the people, that the land is from that day forth parochial property, join chorus with your glad fellow-creatures, and joyfully partake in the universal happiness.

The Golden Age, so fam'd by men of yore,
Shall now be counted fabulous no more.
The tyrant lion like an ox shall feed,
And lisping Infants shall tam'd tygers lead:
With deadly asps shall sportive sucklings play,
Nor ought obnoxious blight the blithesome day.
Yes, all that prophets e'er of bliss foretold,
And all that poets ever feign'd of old,
As yielding joy to man, shall now be seen,
And ever flourish like an evergreen.
Then, Mortals, join to hail great Nature's plan,
That fully gives to Babes those Rights it gives to Man.

Chorus horusully gives t'Sally in our Alley'

Then let us all join heart in hand,
Through country, town, and city; Of every sex and
    every age,
Young men and maidens pretty. To haste this Golden
    Age's reign,
On every hill and valley, Then Paradise shall greet our eyes,
Through every street and alley.

Conclusion

BUT stop, don't let us reckon without our host; for Mr Paine
will object to such an equal distribution of the rents. For says he,
in his Agrarian Justice, the public can claim but a *Tenth Part* of
the value of the landed property as it now exists, with its vast
improvements of cultivation and building. But why are we to be
put off now with but a Tenth Share? Because, says Mr Paine, it
has so improved in the hands of private proprietors as to be of

ten times the value it was of in its natural state. But may we not ask who improved the land? Did the proprietors alone work and toil at this improvement? And did we labourers and our fore-fathers stand, like Indians and Hottentots, idle spectators of so much public-spirited industry? I suppose not. Nay, on the contrary, it is evident to the most superficial enquirer that the labouring classes ought principally to be thanked for every improvement.

Indeed, if there had never been any slaves, any vassals, or any day-labourers employed in building and tillage, then the proprietors might have boasted of having themselves created all this gay scene of things. But the case alters amaz-ingly, when we consider that the earth has been cultivated either by slaves, compelled, like beasts, to labour, or by the indigent objects whom they first exclude from a share in the soil, that want may compel them to sell their labour for daily bread. In short, the great may as well boast of fighting their battles as of cultivating the earth.

The toil of the labouring classes first produces provi-sions, and then the demand of their families creates a market for them. Therefore it will be found that it is the markets made by the labouring and mechanical tribes that have improved the earth. And once take away these markets, or let all the labour-ing people, like the Israelites, leave the country in a body, and you would immediately see from what cause the country had been cultivated, and so many goodly towns and villages built.

You may suppose that after the emigration of all these beggarly people, every thing would go on as well as before: that the farmer would continue to plough, and the town landlord to build as formerly. I tell you nay; for the farmer could neither proceed without labourers nor find purchasers for his corn and cattle. It would be just the same with the building landlord, for he could neither procure workmen to build, nor tenants to pay him rent.

Behold then your grand, voluptuous nobility and gentry, the arch cultivators of the earth; obliged, for lack of servants, again to turn Gothic hunters, like their savage forefathers. Behold their palaces, temples, and towns, mouldering into dust, and affording shelter only to wild beasts; and their boasted, cultivated fields and garden, degenerated into a howling wilderness.

Thus we see that the consumption created by the mouths, and the backs, of the poor despised multitude, contributes to the cultivation of the earth, as well as their hands. And it is also the rents that they pay that builds the towns, and not the racking building landlord. Therefore, let us not in weak commiseration be biassed by the pretended philanthropy of the great, to the resignation of our dearest rights. And if our estates have improved in their hands, during their officious guardianship, the D-v-l thank them; for it was done for their own sakes, not for ours, and can be no just bar against us recovering our rights.

Declaration of Children's Rights by Janusz Korczak[*]

- The child has the right to love.
  'Love the child, not just your own.'
- The child has the right to respect.
  'Let us demand respect for shining eyes, smooth foreheads, youthful effort and confidence, Why should dulled eyes, a wrinkled brow, untidy gray hair, or tired resignation command greater respect?'
- The child has the right to optimal conditions in which to grow and develop.
  'We demand: do away with hunger, cold, dampness, stench, overcrowding, overpopulation.'
- The child has the right to live in the present.
  'Children are not people of tomorrow; they are people today.'
- The child has the right to be himself or herself.
  'A child is not a lottery ticket, marked to win the main prize.'
- The child has the right to make mistakes.
  'There are no more fools among children than among adults.'
- The child has the right to fail.
  'We renounce the deceptive longing for perfect children.'
- The child has the right to be taken seriously.
  'Who asks the child for his opinion and consent?'
- The child has the right to be appreciated for what he is.
  'The child, being small, has little market value.'

[*] See www.fortrefuge.com/korczak-declaration-of-childrens-rights.php.

- The child has the right to desire, to claim, to ask.
  'As the years pass, the gap between adult demands and children's desires becomes progressively wider.'
- The child has the right to have secrets.
  'Respect their secrets.'
- The child has the right to a lie, a deception, a theft.
  'This doesn't mean that he always has the right to lie, out-wit, coerce and steal. If a person didn't have a single chance as a child to pick out the raisins in a cake and pinch them a bit in secret, then he isn't honest; he won't be honest when his character has been formed.' 'It is your duty to raise human beings, not sheep, workers, preachers but physically and morally healthy human beings.'
- The child has the right to respect for his possessions and budget.
  'Everyone has the right to his property, no matter how insignificant or valueless.'
- The child has the right to education.
- The child has the right to resist educational influence that conflicts with his or her own beliefs.
  'It is fortunate for mankind that we are unable to force children to yield to assaults upon their common sense and humanity.'
- The child has the right to protest an injustice.
  'We must end despotism.'
- The child has the right to a Children's Court where he can judge and be judged by his peers.
  'We are the sole judges of the child's actions, movements, thoughts, and plans...I know that a Children's Court is

essential, that in fifty years there will not be a single school, not a single institution without one.'

- The child has the right to be defended in the juvenile-justice court system.
'The delinquent child is still a child. . .Unfortunately, suffering bred of poverty spreads like lice: sadism, crime, uncouthness, and brutality are nurtured on it.'
- The child has the right to respect for his grief.
'Even though it be for the loss of a pebble.'
- The child has the right to commune with God.
- The child has the right to die prematurely.
'The mother's profound love for her child must give him the right to premature death, to ending his life cycle in only one or two springs. . .Not every bush grows into a tree.'

Youth Liberation of Ann Arbor, 1973[*]

YOUTH LIBERATION PROGRAM LIST OF WANTS – 'We must liberate ourselves from the death trip of corporate America.'

1. We want the power to determine our own destiny.
2. We want the immediate end of adult chauvinism.
3. We want full civil and human rights.
4. We want the right to form our education according to our needs.
5. We want the freedom to form into communal families.
6. We want the end of male chauvinism and sexism.
7. We want the opportunity to create an authentic culture with institutions of our own making.
8. We want sexual self-determination. We believe all people must have the unhindered right to be heterosexual, homosexual, bisexual, or transsexual.
9. We want the end of class antagonism among young people.
10. We want the end of racism and colonialism in the United States and the world.
11. We want freedom for all unjustly imprisoned people.
12. We want the right to be economically independent of adults.

---

[*] See https://en.wikipedia.org/wiki/Youth_Liberation_of_Ann_Arbor.

13. We want the right to live in harmony with nature.
14. We want to rehumanize existence.
15. We want to develop communication and solidarity with the young people of the world in our common struggle for freedom and peace.

UNICEF, Our Rights[*]

In 1989, governments across the world promised all children the same rights by adopting the UN Convention on the Rights of the Child. The Convention says what countries must do so that all children grow as healthy as possible, can learn at school, are protected, have their views listened to, and are treated fairly.

These are our rights.

Article 1

Everyone under the age of 18 has all the rights in this Convention.

Article 2

The Convention applies to everyone whatever their race, religion, abilities, whatever they think or say, no matter what type of family they come from.

Article 3

All organisations concerned with children should work towards what is best for you.

Article 4

Governments should make these rights available to you.

Article 5

Governments should respect the rights and responsibilities of families to direct and guide their children so that, as they grow, they learn to use their rights properly.

---

[*] See www.unicef.org/rightsite/files/Know_your_rights_and_responsibiliti es.pdf.

Article 6
You have the right to life. Governments should ensure that children survive and develop healthily.

Article 7
You have the right to a legally registered name and nationality. You also have the right to know and, as far as possible, to be cared for by your parents.

Article 8
Governments should respect children's right to a name, a nationality and family ties.

Article 9
You should not be separated from your parents unless it is for your own good – for example, if a parent is mistreating or neglecting you. If your parents have separated, you have the right to stay in contact with both parents, unless this might harm you.

Article 10
Families who live in different countries should be allowed to move between those countries so that parents and children can stay in contact or get back together as a family.

Article 11
Governments should take steps to stop children being taken out of their own country illegally.

Article 12
You have the right to say what you think should happen when adults are making decisions that affect you, and to have your opinions taken into account.

Article 13
You have the right to get, and to share, information as long as the information is not damaging to yourself or others.

Article 14

You have the right to think and believe what you want and to practise your religion, as long as you are not stopping other people from enjoying their rights. Parents should guide children on these matters.

Article 15

You have the right to meet with other children and young people and to join groups and organisations, as long as this does not stop other people from enjoying their rights.

Article 16

You have the right to privacy. The law should protect you from attacks against your way of life, your good name, your family and your home.

Article 17

You have the right to reliable information from the mass media. Television, radio, and newspapers should provide information that you can understand, and should not promote materials that could harm you.

Article 18

Both parents share responsibility for bringing up their children, and should always consider what is best for each child. Governments should help parents by providing services to support them, especially if both parents work.

Article 19

Governments should ensure that children are properly cared for, and protect them from violence, abuse and neglect by their parents or anyone else who looks after them.

Article 20

If you cannot be looked after by your own family, you must be looked after properly, by people who respect your religion, culture and language.

Article 21

If you are adopted, the first concern must be what is best for you. The same rules should apply whether the adoption takes place in the country where you were born or if you move to another country.

Article 22

If you are a child who has come into a country as a refugee, you should have the same rights as children born in that country.

Article 23

If you have a disability, you should receive special care and support so that you can live a full and independent life.

Article 24

You have the right to good quality health care and to clean water, nutritious food and a clean environment so that you can stay healthy. Rich countries should help poorer countries achieve this.

Article 25

If you are looked after by your local authority rather than your parents, you should have your situation reviewed regularly.

Article 26

The government should provide extra money for the children of families in need.

Article 27

You have a right to a standard of living that is good enough to meet your physical and mental needs. The government should help families who cannot afford to provide this.

Article 28

You have a right to an education. Discipline in schools should respect children's human dignity. Primary education should be free. Wealthy countries should help poorer countries achieve this.

Article 29

Education should develop your personality and talents to the full. It should encourage you to respect your parents, your own and other cultures.

Article 30

You have a right to learn and use the language and customs of your family whether or not these are shared by the majority of the people in the country where you live.

Article 31

You have a right to relax, play and join in a wide range of activities.

Article 32

The government should protect you from work that is dangerous or might harm your health or education.

Article 33

The government should provide ways of protecting you from dangerous drugs.

Article 34

The government should protect you from sexual abuse.

Article 35

The government should ensure that you are not abducted or sold.

Article 36

You should be protected from any activities that could harm your development.

Article 37

If you break the law, you should not be treated cruelly. You should not be put in a prison with adults and you should be able to keep in contact with your family.

Article 38

Governments should not allow children under 16 to join the army. In war zones, you should receive special protection.

Article 39

If you have been neglected or abused, you should receive special help to restore your self-respect.

Article 40

If you are accused of breaking the law, you should receive legal help. Prison sentences for children should only be used for the most serious offences.

Article 41

If the laws of a particular country protect you better than the articles of the Convention, then those laws should stay.

Article 42

The government should make the Convention known to all parents and children.

Articles 43–54 are about how adults and governments should work together to make sure all children get all their rights.

Children's Rights and Responsibilities

From an illustrated guide issued by the National Children's Rights Committee, South Africa.[*]

- Children have the right to be taken seriously...and the responsibility to listen to others.
- Children have the right to quality medical care...and the responsibility to take care of themselves.
- Children have the right to a good education...and the responsibility to study and respect their teachers.
- Children have the right to be loved and protected from harm...and the responsibility to show love and caring to others.
- Children have the right to special care for special needs...and the responsibility to be the best people they can be.
- Children have the right to be proud of their heritage and beliefs...and the responsibility to respect the origins and beliefs of others.
- Children have the right to a safe and comfortable home...and the responsibility to share in keeping it neat and clean.

---

[*] See www.cyc-net.org/cyc-online/cycol-0101-rights.html.

- Children have the right to make mistakes. . .and the responsibility to learn from those mistakes.
- Children have the right to be adequately fed. . .and the responsibility not to waste food.

APPENDIX 6

The Rights of the Dying Child: Trieste Charter Proposal[*]

- To be considered a person until death irrespective of age, location, illness, and care setting.
- To receive effective treatment for pain, and physical and psychological symptoms causing suffering through qualified, comprehensive, and continuous care.
- To be listened to and properly informed about his or her illness with consideration for his or her wishes, age, and ability to understand.
- To participate, on the basis of his or her abilities, values and wishes, in care choices about his or her life, illness, and death.
- To express and, whenever possible, have his or her feelings, wishes, and expectations taken into account.
- To have his or her cultural, spiritual, and religious beliefs respected and receive spiritual care and support in accordance with his or her wishes and choices.
- To have a social and relational life suitable to his or her age, illness, and expectations.
- To be surrounded by family members and loved ones who are adequately supported and protected from the burden of the child's illness.

---

[*] See www.thelancet.com/journals/lancet/article/PIIS0140-6736(14)60746-7/fulltext?rss=yes.

450

- To be cared for in a setting appropriate for his or her age, needs, and wishes and that allows the proximity of the family.
- To have access to child-specific palliative-care programmes that avoid futile or excessively burdensome practices and therapeutic abandonment.

Abebe, T. and Ofusu-Kusi, Y. (2016), 'Beyond Pluralizing African Childhoods', *Childhood* 23: 303–16.

Abi-Saab, G. (1980), 'The Legal Formulation of a Right to Development', *Hague Academy of International Law* 163.

Abramson, B. (1996a), 'The Invisibility of Children and Adolescents: the Need to Monitor Our Rhetoric and Our Attitudes', in E. Verhellen (ed.), *Monitoring Children's Rights*, Leiden: Martinus Nijhoff, 393–402.

(1996b), *Article 2*, Leiden: Martinus Nijhoff.

Abramson, P. A. (2015), 'Smells like Teens Spirit: the Conundrum of Kids, Sex and the Law', in S. Coupet and E. Marrus (eds), *Children, Sexuality and the Law*, New York University Press, 6–29.

Adams, P. (1971), *Children's Rights: Towards the Liberation of the Child*, New York: Praeger.

Adler, P. (2016), 'Draft CDC Circumcision Recommendations', *International Journal of Children's Rights* 24: 239–64.

Ahmari, S. (2012), *Arab Spring Dreams: the Next Generation Speaks Out for Freedom and Justice from North Africa to Iran*, Basingstoke: Palgrave Macmillan.

Aitken, S. C. (2001), 'Global Crisis of Childhood: Rights, Justice and the Unchildlike Child', *Area* 33(2): 119–27.

Alcock, A. (1971), *History of the International Labour Organisation*, London: Macmillan.

Alanen, L. (1994), 'Gender and Generation: Feminism and the "Child Question"', in J. Qvortup, M. Bardy, G. Sgritta and

H. Wintersberger (eds), *Childhood Matters: Social Theory, Practice and Politics*, Aldershot: Avebury.

(2010), 'Taking Children's Rights Seriously', Editorial, *Childhood* 7(1): 5–8.

(2011), 'Critical Childhood Studies?', *Childhood* 18(2): 147–50.

(2015), 'Are We All Constructionists Now?', Editorial, *Childhood* 22(2): 149–53.

Albrecht, G. L. and Devlieger, P. J. (1999), 'The Disability Paradox: High Quality of Life Against All Odds', *Social Science & Medicine* 48: 977–88.

Alcock, A. (1971), *History of the International Labour Organisation*, London: Macmillan.

Alderson, P. (1990), *Children's Consent to Surgery*, Buckingham: Open University Press.

(2000), 'UN Convention on the Rights of the Child: Some Common Criticisms and Suggested Responses', *Child Abuse Review* 9: 439–43.

(2003), *Institutional Rites and Rights: A Century of Childhood*, London: Institute of Education.

(2008), *Young Children's Rights*, London: Jessica Kingsley.

(2012), 'Young Children's Human Rights: A Sociological Analysis', *International Journal of Children's Rights* 20(2): 177–98.

(2013), *Childhoods: Real and Imagined*, London: Routledge.

(2014), 'Research by Children', *Ethics and Research in Inclusive Education: Values into Practice*: 61–75.

(2015),*The Politics of Childhoods Real and Imagined*, vol. 2, London: Routledge.

(2016), 'Children's Rights and Violence', *International Journal of Children's Rights* 24(2): 915–23.

Alderson, P. and Goodwin, M. (1993), 'Contradictions within Concepts of Children's Competence', *International Journal of Children's Rights* 1: 303–13.

Alderson, P., Hawthorne, J. and Killen, M. (2005), 'The Participation Rights of Premature Babies', *International Journal of Children's Rights* 13: 31–50.

Alfieri, A. V. (1990), 'The Policies of Clinical Knowledge', *New York Law School Law Review* 35: 7.

Alghrani, A. (2013), 'Assisted Reproductive Technologies and Family Formation: Womb Transplant Technology and the Allocation of Family Responsibilities', in Keating, H. (ed) *Taking Responsibility, Law and the Changing Family*, London: Routledge: 221–36.

Allan, J. (2010), 'Questions of Inclusion in Scotland and Europe', *European Journal of Special Needs Education* 25 (2): 199–208.

Allbrecht, G. and Devlieger, P. (1999), 'The Disability Paradox: High Quality of Life Against All Odds', *Social Science and Medicine* 48(8): 977–88.

Alston, P. (1990), 'The Unborn Child and Abortion under the Draft Convention on the Rights of the Child', *Human Rights Quarterly* 12(1): 156–78.

(1992), 'The Legal Framework of the Convention on the Rights of the Child', *Bulletin of Human Rights* 91(2): 1–15.

(1994), 'The Best Interests Principle: Towards a Reconciliation of Culture and Human Rights', *International Journal of Law and the Family* 8: 1–25.

Alston, P. and Gilmour-Walsh, B. (1996), *The Best Interests of the Child*, Florence: UNICEF.

Alston, P., Parker, S. and Seymour, J. (eds) (1992), *Children, Rights and the Law*, Oxford: Clarendon Press.

American Bar Association (1979), *Standards Relating to Rights of Minors*, Cambridge, MA: Ballinger Publishing.

Andrews, C. (1980), 'Is Blood Thicker than Local Authorities?' *Social Work Today* 12(1): 19–21.

Annas, G. (2005), *American Bioethics: Crossing Human Rights and Health Law Boundaries*, New York: Oxford University Press.

Appadurai, A. (2006), *Fear of Small Numbers: An Essay on the Geography of Anger*, Durham, NC: Duke University Press.

Appell, A. R. (2006), 'Children's Voice and Justice: Lawyering for Children in 21st Century', *Nevada Law Journal* 6: 692–723.

(2009), 'The Pre-political Child of Child-Centred Jurisprudence', *Houston Law Review*, 46: 703.

Archard, D. (1993), *Children: Rights and Childhood*, London: Routledge.

(2015), *Children, Rights and Childhood*, 3rd edn, London: Routledge.

Archard, D. and Macleod, C. (2002), *The Moral and Political Status of Children*, Oxford University Press.

Archard, D. and Skivenes, M. (2001), 'Balancing a Child's Best Interests and a Child's Views', *International Journal of Children's Rights* 17: 1–21.

Archer, A. (2016), 'Moral Enhancement and Those Left Behind', *Bioethics* 30: 500–10

Arendt, H. (1964), *The Origins of Totalitarianism*, London: Andre Deutsch.

Arieli, I. (2002), 'On the Necessary and Sufficient Conditions for the Emergence of the Doctrine of the Dignity of Man and His Rights', in D. Kretzmer and E. Klein (eds), *The Concept of Human Dignity in Human Rights Discourse*, The Hague: Kluwer Law.

Ariès, P. (1962), *Centuries of Childhood*, London: Jonathan Cape.

Armstrong, A. (1994), 'School and Sadza: Custody and the Best Interests of the Child in Zimbabwe', *International Journal of Law and the Family* 8: 151.

Armstrong, C. (2013), *Global Distributive Justice*, Cambridge University Press.

Arneson, G. (2010), 'Neuroimaging, Uncertainty and the Problem of Dispositions', *Cambridge Quarterly of Healthcare Ethics* 19: 183–95.

Arneson, R. J. and Shapiro, I. (1996), 'Democratic Autonomy and Religious Freedom', in I. Shapiro and R. Hardin (eds), *Political Order*, New York University Press, 112.

Aronowitz, S. (1988), 'Postmodernism and Politics', in A. Ross (ed.), *Universal Abandon?: The Politics of Postmodernism*, Minneapolis, MN: University of Minnesota Press, 48.

Ashenden, S. (2003) *Governing Child Sexual Abuse*, London: Routledge.

Asquith, S. (1996), *Children and Young People in Conflict with the Law*, London: Jessica Kingsley.

Aubert, V. (1959), 'Chance in Social Affairs', *Inquiry*, 2: 1–24.

Auroque, D. and Wiesing, U. (2005), 'German Law on Circumcision', *Bioethics* 29: 203–20.

Axford, N. (2009), Child Well-being through Different Lenses: Why Concept Matters', *Child and Family Social Work* 14: 372–83.

Bacon, K. and Frankel, S. (2014), 'Rethinking Children's Citizenship', *International Journal of Children's Rights* 22: 21–42.

Bailey, A. and McCabe, S. (1979), 'Reforming the Law of Incest', *Criminal Law Review*: 749–64.

Bainham, A. (1998), 'Changing Families and Changing Concepts: Reforming the Language of Family Law', *Child and Family Law Quarterly* 10(1): 1.

Bainhaim, A. (2006), *International Survey of Family Law*, Bristol: Jordan Publishing.

Bainham, A. and Gilmore, S. (2013), *Children: The Modern Law*, 4th edn, Bristol: Jordan.

Bakan, J. (2011), *Childhood Under Siege: How Big Business Targets Children*, New York: Free Press.

Bandman, B. (1973), 'Do Children have Any Natural Rights?', *Proceedings of 29th Annual Meeting of Philosophy of Education Society*, 212.

Bartky, S. (1990), *Femininity and Domination: Studies in the Phenomenology of Oppression*, London: Routledge.

Baskin, J. H., Edersheim., J. G. and Price, B. H. (2007), 'Is a Picture Worth a Thousand Words? Neuroimaging in the Courtroom', *American Journal of Law and Medicine* 33(2/3): 239–69.

Beaumont, P. and McEleavy, P. (1999), *The Hague Convention on International Child Abduction*, Oxford University Press.

Becker, H. (1963), *Outsiders*, New York: Free Press.

Beder, S., Varney, W. and Gosden, R. (2009), *This Little Piggy Went to Market*, London: Pluto Press.

Beeckman, K. (2004), 'Measuring the Implementation of the Right to Education: Educational versus Human Rights Indicators', *International Journal of Children's Rights* 12: 71–84.

Behlmer, G. K. (1982), *Child Abuse and Moral Reform in England, 1870–1908*, Stanford University Press.

Beiter, K. D. (2006), *The Protection of the Right to Education by International Law*, Dordrecht: Martinus Nijhoff.

Beitz, C. (2011), *The Idea of Human Rights*, Oxford University Press.

Bell, C. and Newby, H. (1976), 'Husbands and Wives: The Dynamics of the Deferential Dialectic', in D. Barker and S. Allen (eds), *Dependence and Exploitation in Work and Marriage*, Harlow: Longman, 154–64.

Bell, S. (1988), *When Salem Came to the Boro: The True Story of the Cleveland Child Crisis*, London: Pan Books.

Bellow, G. (1996), 'Steady Work: a Practitioner's Reflections on Political Lawyering', *Harvard Civil Rights: Civil Liberties Law Review* 31(2): 297–302.

457

Ben-Arieh, A. et al. (2005), 'Where are the Children? Children's Role in Measuring and Monitoring their Well-being', *Social Indicators Research* 74: 573–96.

(2014), 'Multifaceted Concept of Child Well-Being', in A. Ben-Arieh et al. (eds.), *Handbook of Child Well-Being*, Dordrecht: Springer.

Benatar, D. (2008), *Better Never to Have Been Born*, Oxford University Press.

(2015), 'The Misanthropic Argument for Anti-Natalism', in S. Hannan, S. Brennan and R. Vernon (eds), *Permissible Progeny?* New York: Oxford University Press, 34–64.

Benhabib, S. (2012), *The Rights of Others*, Cambridge University Press.

Benjamin, W. (1927), 'Moscow', in M. W. Jennings et al. (eds), *Walter Benjamin: Selected Writings, vol. 2, Pt 1: 1927–1930*, Cambridge, MA: Harvard University Press, 22–49.

Benjet, C. and Kazdin, A. E. (2003), 'Spanking Children: The Controversies, Findings, and New Directions', *Clinical Psychology Review* 23: 197–224.

Bennett, M. R. and Hacker, P. M. S. (2008), *History of Cognitive Neuroscience, Chichester*, West Sussex: Wiley-Blackwell.

Bennett, R. W. (2000), 'Should Parents be Given Extra Votes on Account of Their Children?: Toward a Conversational Understanding of American Democracy', *Northwestern Law Review* 94(2): 503–66.

(2014), 'When Intuition is Not Enough: Why the Principle of Procreative Beneficence Must Work', *Bioethics* 28: 447–53.

Bennett, S. E. (1988), '"Know-Nothings" Revisited: The Meaning of Political Ignorance Today', *Social Science Quarterly* 69: 476–90.

(1996), '"Know-Nothings" Revisited Again', *Political Behaviour* 18 (3): 219–33.

Bentley, K. A. (2005), 'Can There be Any Universal Children's Rights?' *International Journal of Human Rights* 9: 107–23.

Benvenisti, E. (1999), 'Margin of Appreciation: Consensus and Universal Standards', *NYULR International Law and Policy* 843.

Berganza, C. (2005), 'Children's Right to Mental Health. How Adults Have Failed Youth Worldwide: The Latin America Case', *World Psychiatry* 4: 157–8.

Berman, H. (2003), 'Getting Critical with Children. Empowering Approaches with a Disempowered Group', *Advances in Nursing Science* 26(2): 102–13.

Besson, S. (2005), 'The Principle of Non-Discrimination in the Convention on the Rights of the Child', *International Journal of Children's Rights* 13(4): 433–61.

Bhabha, J. (2011), *Children Without a State*, Cambridge, MA: MIT Press.

(2014), *Human Rights and Adolescence*, Philadelphia, PA: University of Pennsylvania Press.

Bhabha, J. and Crock, M. (2007), *Seeking Asylum Alone: A Comparative Study of Laws, Policy and Practice in Australia, the UK. and the US*, Sydney: Themis Press.

Biesta, G. (2011), *Learning Democracy in School and Society: Education, Lifelong Learning, and the Politics of Citizenship*, Rotterdam: Sense Publishers.

Biggeri, M., Ballet, J. and Conim, F. (2011), *Children and the Capability Approach*, Basingstoke: Palgrave Macmillan.

Bingham, T. (2010), *The Rule of Law*, London: Penguin.

Bissell, S. (2005), 'Earning and Learning: Tension and Compatibility', in B. H. Weston (ed.), *Child Labor and Human Rights*, Boulder, CO: Lynne Rienner.

Bissett-Johnson, A. (1994), 'What did States Really Agree To? Qualifications of Signatories to the United Nations

Convention on the Rights of the Child', *International Journal of Children's Rights* 2: 399–411.

Bitensky, S. (2006), *Corporal Punishment of Children: a Human Rights Violation*, Ardsley, NY: Transnational.

Blackstone, W. (1765), *Blackstone's Commentaries on the Laws of England*, Bk One, ch. 16, available at: http://lonang.com/lib rary/reference/blackstone-commentaries-law-england/bla-11 6, last accessed 24 April 2017.

Blackwell, A. and Dawe, F. (2003), *Non-resident Parent Contact*, London: Office for National Statistics.

Blanchet-Cohen, N. (2015), 'Igniting Citizen Participation in Creating Healthy Built Environments: The Role of Community Organizations', *Community Development Journal* 50(4): 264–79.

Blank, R. (2013), *Intervention in the Brain*, Cambridge, MA: MIT Press.

Bluebond-Langner, M. (1978), *The Private Worlds of Dying Children*, Princeton University Press.

Bonnett, A. and Armstrong, K. (2014), *Thomas Spence: the Poor Man's Revolutionary*, London: Breviary Stuff Publications.

Bosteels, S. and Blume, S. (2014), 'The Making and Unmaking of Deaf Children', in M. Ellers, K. Gruber and C. Rehmann-Sutter (eds), *The Human Debate and Disability: New Bodies for a Better Life*, Basingstoke: Palgrave Macmillan, 81–100.

Bourdillon, M., Levison, D., Myers, W. and White, B. (2010), *Rights and Wrongs of Children's Work*, New Brunswick, NJ: Rutgers University Press.

Bowlby, J. (1969), *Child Care and the Growth of Love*, Harmondsworth: Penguin.

Bowles, B. and Gintis, H. (1976), *Schooling in Capitalist America*, London: Routledge.

Boyden, J. (1999), 'Childhood and the Policymakers: a Comparative Perspective on the Globalization of Childhood', in A. James and A. Prout (eds), *Constructing and Reconstructing Childhood*, London: Falmer Press, 184–229.

Boyden, J. and Holden, P. (1991), *Children of the Cities*, London: Zed Books.

Boyle, E. H. (2002), *Female Genital Cutting*, Baltimore, MD: Johns Hopkins University Press.

Boyle, J. (1985), Review: 'Modernist Social Theory: Robert Unger's "Passion"', *Harvard Law Review* 98: 1066–83.

Bradshaw, J. (2001), 'Child Poverty under Labour', in G. Fimister (ed.), *An End in Sight? Tackling Child Poverty in the UK*, London: Child Poverty Action Group, 9–27.

(ed.) (2002), *The Well-being of Children*, London: Save the Children.

(2014), 'Subjective Well-being and Social Policy: Can Nations Make their Children Happier?' *Child Indicators Research* 8(1): 227–41.

Bradshaw, J., Hoelscher, P. and Richardson, D. (2007), 'An Index of Child Well-Being in the European Union', *Social Indicators Research* 80(1): 133–77.

Bradshaw, Y. (1993), 'New Directions in International Development Research: a Focus on Children', *Childhood* 1: 134–42.

Breay, C. and Harrison, J. (2015), *Magna Carta: Law, Liberty, Legacy*, London: British Library.

Breen, C. (2006), *Age Discrimination and Children's Rights: Ensuring Equality and Acknowledging Difference*, Leiden: Martinus Nijhoff.

Bremner, R. et al. (1970), *Children and Youth in America, a Documentary History, 1600–1865*, Cambridge, MA: Harvard University Press.

Brems, E. (2001), *Human Rights: Universality and Diversity*, Dordrecht: Martinus Nijhoff.

(2006), *Article 14: the Right to Freedom of Thought, Conscience and Religion*, Leiden: Martinus Nijhoff.

Brennan, S. and Noggle, R. (1997), 'The Moral Status of Children: Children's Rights, Parents' Rights, and Family Justice', *Social Theory and Practice* 23(1): 1–26.

Brighouse, H. (2002), 'What Rights (if any) do Children Have?' in D. Archard and D. Macleod (eds), *The Moral and Political Status of Children*, Oxford University Press, 31–52.

(2003), 'How Should Children Be Heard?', *Arizona Law Review*, 45: 691.

Brinton, C. (1936), *Revolutionary Laws on Illegitimacy*, Cambridge, MA: Harvard University Press.

Brizendine, L. (2006), *The Female Brain*, New York: Morgan Road Books.

Brock, D. W. (2001), 'Children's Rights to Health Care', *Journal of Medicine and Philosophy* 26: 163–77.

Brooks, S. (1990), 'When a Child Needs a Lawyer', *Creighton Law Review* 23: 737.

(1999), 'Therapeutic and Preventive Approaches to School Safety', *New England Law Review* 34: 615.

(2006), 'Representing Children in Families', *Nevada Law Journal* 6(3): 13.

Browning, D. (2006), 'The United Nations Convention on the Rights of the Child: Should it be Ratified?' *Emory International Law Review* 20: 157.

Brysk, A. (2002), *Globalisation and Human Rights*, Berkeley, CA: California University Press.

Buchanan, A. (2009), 'Human Nature and Enhancement', *Bioethics* 23: 141–50.

(2015), *The Heart of Human Rights*, New York: Oxford University Press.

Bulmer, M. and Rees, A. (1996), *Citizenship Today*, London: UCL Press.

Burgess, J. (2010), 'Could a Zygote be a Human Being?', *Bioethics* 24: 61–70.

Burke, T. (2005), 'Postscript on Citizenship', in Monica Barry (ed.), *Youth Policy and Social Inclusion: Critical Debates with Young People*, London: Routledge, 51–4.

Burman, E. (1995), 'Local, Global or Globalized? Child Development and International Child Rights Legislation', *Childhood* 3: 45–66.

(1999), 'Morality and the Goals of Development', in M. Woodhead et al. (eds), *Making Sense of Social Development*, London: Routledge.

(2008), *Deconstructing Developmental Psychology*, London: Routledge.

Burman, E. and Stacey, J. (2010), 'The Child and Childhood in Feminist Theory', *Feminist Theory* 11(3): 227–40.

Burr, R. (2002), 'Global and Local Approaches to Children's Rights in Vietnam', *Childhood* 9(1): 49–61.

Burton, P. (2008), *National Primary School Violence Survey 2007*, Cape Town: Centre for Justice and Crime Prevention.

Buss, E. (1996), 'You're My What? The Problem of Children's Misperceptions of Their Lawyers Roles', *Fordham Law Review* 64: 1699.

(1999), 'Confronting Developmental Barriers to the Empowerment of Child Clients', *Cornell Law Review* 84: 895.

(2009), 'What the Law Should (and Should Not) Learn from Child Development Research', *Hofstra Law Review* 38: 13–68.

Butler-Sloss, E. (1988), *Report of Inquiry into Child Abuse in Cleveland*, London: HMSO.

Butterfield, H. (1931), *The Whig Interpretation of History*, London: G. Bell.

Byrne, B. (2016), 'Do Children Still Need to Escape Childhood? A Reassessment of John Holt and his Vision for Children's Rights', *International Journal of Children's Rights* 24 (1): 113–34.

Byrne, B. and Lundy, I. (2015), 'Reconciling Policy and Children's Rights', *Children and Society* 29: 266–76.

Cahill-O'Callaghan, R. J. (2013), 'The Influence of Personal Values on Legal Judgments', *Journal of Law and Society* 40(4): 596–623.

Camfield, L., Streuli, N. and Woodhead, M. (2009), 'What's the Use of "Well-Being" in Contexts of Child Poverty? Approaches to Research, Monitoring and Children's Participation', *International Journal of Children's Rights* 17(1): 65–109.

Campbell, T. (1992), 'The Rights of the Minor: as Person, as Child, as Juvenile, as Future Adult', *International Journal of Law and the Family* 6: 1–23.

(1994), 'Really Equal Rights? Some Philosophical Comments on "Why Children Shouldn't Have Equal Rights" by Laura M. Purdy', *International Journal of Children's Rights* 2: 259–63.

Cantwell, B. and Scott, S. (1995), 'Children's Wishes, Children's Burdens', *Journal of Social Welfare and Family Law* 17(3): 337–54.

Cantwell, N. (2011), 'Are Children's Rights Still Human?', in A. Invernizzi and J. Williams (eds), *The Human Rights of Children: From Visions to Implementation*, Aldershot: Ashgate, 37–59.

Carbone, J. (2011), 'Neuroscience and Ideology?' in M. Freeman (ed.), *Law and Neuroscience*, Oxford University Press, 231–54.

Carey, T. (2011), *Where Has My Little Girl Gone?* Oxford: Lion Hudson.

Carlin, J., Howard, J. and Messinger, S. (1966), 'Civil Justice and the Poor: Issues for Sociological Research', *Law & Society Review* 1 (1): 9–90.

Carpenter, D. (2015), *Magna Carta*, London: Penguin.

Casey, B., Jones, R. M. and Hare, T. A. (2008), 'The Adolescent Brain', *Annals of the New York Academy of Sciences* 1124(1): 111–26.

Casey, B., Jones, R. and Somerville, L. (2011), 'Braking and Accelerating of the Adolescent Brain', *Journal of Research and Adolescence* 21(1): 21–33.

Cederborg, A. C. (2015), 'Children's Rights to be Heard from Their Unique Perspectives', in S. Mahmoudi (ed.), *Child-Friendly Justice*, Leiden: Brill, 73–84.

Chakrabortty, A. (2014), 'Today's Britain: Where Poor are Forced to Steal or Beg from Food Banks', *The Guardian*, 28 October, 37.

(2015), 'This Battle Will Define Us. We Must Protect Our Children from Austerity', *The Guardian*, May 25.

Chapman, A. R. (2009), 'Towards an Understanding of the Right to Enjoy the Benefits of Scientific Progress and its Applications', *Journal of Human Rights* 8(1): 1–36.

Chatterjee, S. (2012), 'Children Growing Up in Indian Slums: Challenges and Opportunities for New Urban Imaginations', *Early Childhood Matters* 118: 17–23.

Cheung, A. (2012), 'Tackling Cyber-Bullying From a Children's Rights Perspective', in M. Freeman (ed.), *Law and Childhood Studies*, Oxford University Press, 281–301.

Children's Rights Alliance for England (CRAE) (2016), *Children Speak Out on Transgender Issues*, London: CRAE.

Chirwa, D. M. (2002), 'The Merits and Demerits of the African Charter on the Rights and Welfare of the Child', *International Journal of Children's Rights* 10: 157–77.

Choudhry, S. and Fenwick, H. (2005), 'Taking the Rights of Parents and Children Seriously: Confronting the Welfare Principle under the Human Rights Act', *Oxford Journal of Legal Studies* 25(3): 453–92.

Cipriani, D. (2009), *Children's Rights and the Minimum Age of Criminal Responsibility: A Global Perspective*, Aldershot: Ashgate.

Coady, M. (2008), 'Beings and Becomings: Historical and Philosophical Considerations of the Child as Citizen', in G. MacNaughton, P. Hughes and K. Smith (eds), *Young Children as Active Citizens: Principles, Policies and Pedagogies*, Newcastle: Cambridge Scholars, 2–14.

Cockburn, T. (1998), 'Children and Citizenship in Britain', *Childhood* 5(1): 99–117.

(2005a), 'Children and the Feminist Ethic of Care', *Childhood* 12 (1): 71–89.

(2005b), 'Children's Participation in Social Policy: Inclusion, Chimera or Authenticity', *Social Policy and Society* 4: 109–19.

(2013), 'Authors of Their Own Lives? Children, Contracts, their Responsibilities, Rights and Citizenship', *International Journal of Children's Rights* 21: 372–84.

Cohen, A. (2016), *Imbeciles*, Princeton University Press.

Cohen, C. P. (1984), 'Freedom from Corporal Punishment: One of the Human Rights of Children', *NYL School of Human Rights* 2: 111.

(1997), 'The United Nations Convention on the Rights of the Child: A Feminist Landmark', *William and Mary Journal of Women and the Law* 3: 29–78.

(2006), 'Role of the United States in the Drafting of the Convention on the Rights of the Child', *Emory International Law Review* 20: 185.

Cohen, E. (2009), *Semi-citizenship in Democratic Politics*, Cambridge University Press, 20.

Cohen, H. (1980), *Equal Rights for Children*, Totowa, NJ: Littlefield, Adams.

466

Cohen, J. and Sabel, C. (2006), 'Extra Rempublicam Nulla Justitia', *Philosophy and Public Affairs* 34: 147–75.

Cohen, S. (1972), *Folk Devils and Moral Panics*, London: MacGibbon & Kee.

Coigney, V. (1975), *Children are People Too: How We Fail Our Children and How We Can Love Them*, New York: Morrow.

Colclough, C. (2005), 'Rights, Goals and Targets: How Do Those for Education Add Up?', *Journal of International Development* 17 (1): 101–11.

Coleman, D., Dodge, K. and Campbell, S. (2010), 'Where and How to Draw the Line Between Reasonable Corporal Punishment and Abuse', *Law and Contemporary Problems* 73: 107–65.

Collins, T. (2015), 'Child Participation in Monitoring the CRC' in T. Gal and B. Duramy, *International Perspectives and Empirical Findings on Child Participation*, New York: Oxford University Press.

Colón, P. and Colón, A. R. (2001), *A History of Children: A Socio-Cultural Survey Across Millennia*, Westport, CT: Greenwood Press.

Committee of Ministers of the Council of Europe (2001), Recommendation 13 on Developing a Methodology for Drawing up Guidelines on Best Medical Practices and Explanatory Memorandum of the Council of Europe, Council of Europe, Strasbourg.

Committee of Ministers of the Council of Europe (2010), *Guidelines on Child-friendly Justice*, adopted on 17 November 2010 at the 1098th meeting of the Ministers' Deputies.

Connolly, H. (2015), 'Seeing the Relationship between the UNCRC and the Asylum System', *International Journal of Children's Rights* 23: 52–77.

Coombes, B. (2001), 'Linking Children's and Women's Rights: An Early Childhood Perspective', *Development* 44: 35–40.

467

Cook, A. E. (1992), 'Reflections on Postmodernism', *New England Law Review* 26: 751.

Cook, P. (2013), 'Against a Minimum Voting Age', *Critical Review of International, Social and Political Philosophy* 11: 439–53.

Cooper, D. (2013), *Everyday Utopias: The Conceptual Life of Promising Spaces*, Durham, NC: Duke University Press.

Cordero Arce, M. (2012), 'Towards an Emancipatory Discourse of Children's Rights', *International Journal of Children's Rights* 20: 365–421.

(2015), 'Maturing Children's Rights Theory: From Children, With Children, Of Children', *International Journal of Children's Rights* 23: 283.

Cornell, D. and Limber, S. (2015), 'Law and Policy on the Concept of Bullying at School', *American Psychologist* 70 (4): 333–43.

Cornock, M. and Montgomery, H. (2011), 'Children's Rights In and Out of the Womb', *International Journal of Children's Rights* 19 (1): 3–19.

(1997), *The Sociology of Childhood*, Thousand Oaks, CA: Pine Forge Press.

Corsaro, W. A. (2005), *The Sociology of Childhood*, rev. edn, Thousand Oaks, CA: Pine Forge Press.

Cowden, M. (2012), 'What's Love Got to Do With It? Why a Child Does Not Have a Right to be Loved?' *Critical Review of International Social and Political Philosophy* 15(3): 325–45.

(2016), *Children's Rights*, Basingstoke: Palgrave Macmillan.

Cox, R. (1996), *Shaping Childhood*, London: Routledge.

Cregan, K. and Cuthbert, D. (2014), *Global Childhoods*, London: Sage.

Crenshaw, K. (1988), 'Race, Reform, and Retrenchment: Transformation and Legitimation in Antidiscrimination Law', *Harvard Law Review* 101(7): 1331–87.

Crock, M. (2006), *Seeking Asylum Alone: A Study of Australian Law, Policy and Practice Regarding Unaccompanied and Separated Children*, Sydney: Themis Press.

Crofts, Th., Lee, M., McGovern, A. and Milivojevic, S. (2015), *Sexting and Young People*, Basingstoke: Palgrave Macmillan.

Crowley, A. (2015), 'Anyone Listening? The Impact of Children's Participation on Public Policy', *International Journal of Children's Rights* 23: 602–21.

Crown, H. (2014), 'Terrorism Bill Means Nurseries "Must Understand Risk of Radicalisation"', *Nursery World*, available at: www.nurseryworld.co.uk/nursery-world/news/1148935/ter rorism-means-nurseries-understand-risk-radicalisation.

Cullen, H. (2007), *The Role of International Law in the Elimination of Child Labor*, Leiden: Martinus Nijhoff.

Cullet, P. (2003), 'Patents and Medicines: the Relationship between TRIPS and the Human Right to Health', *International Affairs* 79(1): 139–60.

Cunningham, H. (2005), *Children and Childhood in Western Society Since 1500*, Harlow: Pearson-Longman.

Curtis, B. (2014), 'A Zygote Could be A Human', *Bioethics* 26(3): 136–42.

Cutler, D. and Frost, R. (2001), *Taking the Initiative: Promoting Young People's Involvement in Public Decision Making in the UK*, London: Carnegie Young People's Initiative.

Cutner, L. P. (1985), 'Female Genital Mutilation', *Obstetrical and Gynaecological Survey*, 40(7): 152–9.

Dahl, R. (1989), *Democracy and its Critics*, New Haven, CT: Yale University Press.

Dailey, A. (2014), 'Children's Transitional Rights', *Law, Culture and the Humanities*, 1–17.

Daly, A. (2011), 'The Right of Children to be Heard in Civil Proceedings and the Emerging Law of the European Court of

Human Rights', *International Journal of Human Rights* 15(3): 441–61.

Daly, A. (2018), *Children, Autonomy and the Courts*, Leiden, The Netherlands: Brill | Nijhoff.

Darby, R. (2013), 'The Child's Right to an Open Future: Is the Principle Applicable to Non-Therapeutic Circumcisions?', *Journal of Medical Ethics* 39: 463–8.

Darian-Smith, E. (2013), *Laws and Societies in Global Contexts*, New York: Cambridge University Press.

Davey, C. and Lundy, L. (2009), 'Towards Greater Recognition of Right to Play', *Children and Society* 25: 3–14.

Davies, D. (2014), *In Plain Sight,* London: Quercus.

Davis, D. (2001), *Genetic Dilemmas*, New York: Routledge.

Davis, J. (2007), 'Analysing Participation and Social Exclusion with Children and Young People', *International Journal of Children's Rights* 15: 121–46.

Dawson, A. (2005), 'The Determination of the Best Interests in Relation to Childhood Immunization', *Bioethics* 19: 72.

De Berry, J. (2001), 'Child Soldiers and the Convention on the Rights of the Child', *Annals of the American Academy of Political and Social Science* 575: 92–105.

De Feyter, K. (2007), 'Localising Human Rights', in W. Benedek, K. De Feyter and F. Marrella (eds), *Economic Globalisation and Human Rights*, Cambridge University Press, 67–92.

De Gaay Fortman, B. (2011), *Political Economy of Human Rights: Rights, Realities and Realization*, London: Routledge.

De la Cava, A. R. (2015), 'The Elian Gonzalez Case: The World's Most Watched and Politically-Charged Custody Battle that Reached the US Supreme Court and Determined a Presidential Election', *Harvard Law Review* 18: 151.

De Melo-Martin, I. (2004), 'On Our Obligation to Choose the Best Children', *Bioethics* 18: 72–82.

(2011), 'Human Dignity in International Policy Documents', *Bioethics* 25: 37–45.

Deakin, S. (1990), 'Equality under a Market Order: The Employment Acts 1989 (Great Britain)', *Industrial Law Journal* 19: 1–19.

Dean, H. (2002), *Welfare Rights and Social Policy*, Harlow: Prentice Hall.

(2007), 'Social Policy and Human Rights: Re-Thinking the Engagement', *Social Policy and Society*, 7(1): 1–12.

(2009), 'Critiquing Capabilities: The Distractions of a Beguiling Concept', *Critical Social Policy* 29(2): 261–78.

Dekker, J. (2000), 'The Century of the Child Revisited', *International Journal of Children's Rights* 8: 133.

Delli Carpini, M. X. and Keeter, S. (1996), *What Americans Know about Politics and Why it Matters*, New Haven, CT: Yale University Press.

Dellavalle, S. (2013), 'From Imago Dei to Mutual Recognition' in C. McCrudden (ed.), *Understanding Human Dignity*, Oxford University Press, 435–56.

Desmet, E. (2012), 'Implementing the Convention on the Rights of the Child for "Youth": Who and How?', *International Journal of Children's Rights* 20: 3–23.

Desmet, E., Lembrechts, S., Reynaert, D. and Vandenhole, W. (2015), 'Conclusions: Towards a Field of Critical Children's Rights Studies', in W. Vandenhole, E. Desmet, D. Reynaert and S. Lembrechts (eds), *Routledge International Handbook of Children's Rights Studies*, London: Routledge, 1–23.

(1992), *The United Nations Convention on the Rights of the Child: A Guide to the Travaux Préparatoires*, Dordrecht: Martinus Nijhoff.

Detrick, S. (1999), *A Commentary on the United Nations Convention on the Rights of the Child*, The Hague: Kluwer Academic.

Devine, D. (2003), 'Children's Citizenship and the Structuring of Adult–Child Relations in School', *Childhood* 9: 303–20.

Devlin, P. (1965), *The Enforcement of Morals*, Oxford University Press.

Diduck, A., Peleg, N. and Reece, H. (2015), *Law in Society: Reflections on Children, Family, Culture and Philosophy*, The Netherlands: Brill – Nijhoff.

Dines, G. (2013), 'Grooming Our Girls', in J. Wild (ed.), *Exploiting Children*, London: Jessica Kingsley, 116–29.

Dixon, R. and Nussbaum, M. (2012), 'Children's Rights and a Capabilities Approach: the Question of Special Priority', *Cornell Law Review* 97: 549–94.

Dobbs, T., Smith, A. B. and Taylor, N. (2006), 'No, We Don't Get a Say, Just Suffer the Consequences: Children Talk about Family Discipline', *International Journal of Children's Rights* 14: 137–56.

Doek, J. E. (2009), 'CRC 20 Years: An Overview of Major Achievements and Remaining Challenges', *Child Abuse and Neglect* 33: 771–82.

(2011), 'The CRC: Dynamics and Directions of Monitoring its Implementation', in A. Invernizzi and J. Williams (eds), *The Human Rights of Children: From Visions to Implementation*, Farnham: Ashgate.

(2014), 'Child Well-being: Children's Rights Perspective', in A. Ben-Arieh et al. (eds), *Handbook of Child Well-Being*, Dordrecht: Springer.

Domingo, R. (2010), *The New Global Law*, New York: Cambridge University Press.

Donne, J. (1633), *Poems, by J. D. With elegies on the authors death*, London: John Marriot.

Donnelly, J. (1984), 'In Search of the Unicorn: the Jurisprudence and Politics of the Right to Development', *Californian Western International Law Journal* 15: 473.

(2003), *Universal Human Rights in Theory and Practice*, Ithaca, NY: Cornell University Press.

Donner, L. A. (1994), 'Gender Bias in Drafting International Discrimination Conventions: the 1979 Women's Convention Compared with the 1965 Racial Convention', *California Western International Law Journal* 24: 241–54.

Donzelot, J. (1979), *The Policing of Families*, New York: Pantheon Books.

Dorling, D. (2013), *The 1%*, London: Pluto Press.

Dorscheidt, J. H. H. M. (1999), 'The Unborn Child and the UN Convention on Children's Rights: the Dutch Perspective as a Guideline', *International Journal of Children's Rights* 7(4): 303–47.

Dottridge, M. (2004), *Kids as Commodities? Child Trafficking and What to Do About It*, Lausanne: International Federation Terre des Hommes.

Doughty, J. (2013), 'Re B (A Child) (Care order) (2013) UKSC 33', *Journal of Social Welfare and Family Law* 35(4): 491–501.

Douglas, H. and Walsh, T. (2013), 'Continuing the Stolen Generations: Child Protection Interventions and Indigenous Peoples', *International Journal of Children's Rights* 21: 59–87.

Douzinas, C. (2000), *The End of Human Rights*, Oxford University Press.

Drabble, M. (1965), *The Millstone*, London: Weidenfeld & Nicolson.

Dror, Y. (1957), 'Essays in Legal Sociology', PhD dissertation, SJD Harvard Law School.

Drouin, M. and Landgraff, C. (2012), 'Texting, Sexting, and Attachment in College Students' Romantic Relationships', *Computers in Human Behavior* 28(2): 444–9.

Dupre, A. P. (2009), *The Unintended Costs of Free Speech in the Public Schools*, Cambridge, MA: Harvard University Press.

Duquette, D. N. and Ramsey, S. H. (1987), 'Representation of Children in Child Abuse and Neglect Cases: An Empirical Look at What Constitutes Effective Representation', *University of Michigan Journal of Law Reform* 20: 341.

Durkheim, E. (1890), 'Les Principes de 1789 et la sociologie', *Revue international de l'enseignement* 19: 450–6, available at: http://durkheim.uchicago.edu/Bibliography/Bib01.html.

  (1979), 'Childhood: 1911', in W. F. Pickering (ed.), *Durkheim: Essays on Morals and Education*, London: Routledge.

Durrant, J. E. (1999), 'Evaluating the Success of Sweden's Corporal Punishment Ban', *Child Abuse and Neglect* 21(5): 435–48.

  (2003), 'Legal Reform and Attitudes toward Physical Punishment in Sweden', *International Journal of Children's Rights* 11(2): 147–73.

Dwork, D. (1991), *Children with a Star*, New Haven, CT: Yale University Press.

Dworkin, G. (1972), 'Paternalism', in R. Wasserstrom (ed.), *Morality and the Law*, Belmont, CA: Wadsworth, 107–26.

Dworkin, R. (1977), *Taking Rights Seriously*, London: Duckworth.

  (1986), *Law's Empire*, Cambridge, MA: Harvard University Press.

Dwyer, J. (1994), 'Parents' Religion and Children's Welfare: Debunking the Doctrine of Parents' Rights', *California Law Review* 82: 1386.

  (1998), *Religious Schools v Children's Rights*, Ithaca, NY: Cornell University Press.

  (2010), *Moral Status and Human Life: The Case for Children's Superiority*, Cambridge University Press.

Earls, E. (2011), 'Children: From Rights to Citizenship', *AAPSS* 61: 6–16.

Ebenstein, J. (2011), 'Estimating a Dynamic Model of Sex Selection in China', *Demography* 48: 783.

Editorial (1998), 'Editorial: The Social Construction of Childhood – and its Limits', *Childhood: A Journal of Global Child Research* 5: 131–2.

Eekelaar, J. (1986), 'The Emergence of Children's Rights', *Oxford Journal of Legal Studies* 6: 161–82.

—— (1992), 'The Importance of Thinking that Children Have Rights', *International Journal of Law and the Family* 6: 221–35.

—— (1994), 'The Interests of the Child and the Child's Wishes: The Role of Dynamic Self-Determination', *International Journal of Law and the Family* 8: 42–61.

—— (2002), 'Beyond the Welfare Principle', *Child and Family Law Quarterly* 14(3): 237–49.

—— (2015), 'The Role of the Best Interests Principle in Decisions about Children and Decisions Affecting Children', *International Journal of Children's Rights* 23: 3–26.

Egan, S. (2014), 'The New Complaints Mechanism for the Convention on the Rights of the Child: A Mini Step Forward for Children?', *International Journal of Children's Rights* 22(1): 205–25.

Eide, B. and Eide, T. (2006), 'The Mislabeled Child', *The New Atlantis* 12: 46–59.

Elder, G. (1994), 'Time, Human Agency, and Social Change: Perspectives on the Life Course', *Social Psychology Quarterly* 57: 4–15.

Electoral Commission (2004), *Age of Electoral Majority: Report and Recommendations*, Electoral Commission of the United Kingdom, London.

Elliston, S. (2007), *The Best Interests of the Child in Health Care*, London: Routledge-Cavendish.

Elster, J. (1987), 'Solomonic Judgments: Against the Best Interests of the Child', *University of Chicago Law Review* 54: 1–46.

Ennew, J. (1986), *The Sexual Exploitation of Children*, Cambridge: Polity Press.

—— (2000), 'Why the Convention is Not About Street Children', in D. Fottrell (ed.), *Children's Rights for the Twenty-First Century*, The Hague: Kluwer Law, 169–82.

—— (2002), 'Outside Childhood: Street Children's Rights', in B. Franklin (ed.), *The New Handbook of Children's Rights*, London: Routledge, 388–403.

—— (2003), 'Difficult Circumstances: Some Reflections on Street Children in Africa', *Children, Youth and Environments* 13 (1): 120.

—— (2008), 'Children as "Citizens" of the United Nations (UN)', in A. Invernizzi and J. Williams (eds), *Children and Citizenship*, London: Sage.

—— (2011), 'Has Research Improved the Lives of Children?' in A. Invernizzi and J. Williams (eds), *The Human Rights of Children: From Visions to Implementation*, Farnham: Ashgate.

Ensalaco, M. (2005), 'The Right of the Child to Development?' in M. Ensalaco and L. Majka (eds), *Children's Human Rights*, Lanham, MD: Rowman & Littlefield, 9–29.

Erickson, S. (2010), 'Blaming the Brain', *Minnesota Journal of Law, Science and Technology* 11: 27.

Erickson, S. et al. (2000), 'Are Overweight Children Unhappy?', *Archives of Pediatrics and Adolescent Medicine* 154(9): 931–5.

Erlings, E. (2016), 'Is Anything Left of Children's Rights? How Parental Responsibility Erodes Children's Rights under English Law', *The International Journal of Children's Rights* 24: 624–56.

Esping-Andersen, G. (1990), *The Three Worlds of Welfare Capitalism*, Cambridge: Polity Press.

European Parliament (2009), European Parliament Resolution 2008/2071(INI), 24 March 2009, on Combating Female Genital Mutilation in the EU, Strasbourg.

Evans, G. W. (2004), 'The Environment of Childhood Poverty', *American Psychologist* 59: 77–92.

Ezra, D. (1994), 'Sticks and Stones May Break My Bones but Tobacco Smoke can Kill Me', *St Louis University Public Law Review* 13(2): 547.

Fahmy, M. (2011), 'On the Supposed Moral Harm of Selecting for Deafness', *Bioethics* 25: 128–36.

Falk, R. (2013), *[Re]imagining Humane Global Governance*, New York: Routledge.

Farris, M. (2012), 'Nannies with Blue Berets: The UN Convention and the Invasion of National and Family Sovereignty', in C. Butler (ed.), *Child Rights*, West Lafayette, IN: Purdue University Press, 95–114.

Farson, R. (1974), *Birthrights*, London: Macmillan.

Fass, P. (2007), *Children of a New World: Society, Culture, and Globalization*, New York University Press.

Federle, K. H. (1993), 'On the Road to Reconceiving Rights for Children: A Post-Feminist Analysis of the Capacity Principle', *De Paul Law Review*, 983.

(1994), 'Rights Flow Downhill', *International Journal of Children's Rights* 2(4): 343–68.

(1995), 'Looking Ahead: An Empowerment Perspective on the Rights of Children', *Temple Law Review* 68(4): 1585.

(1996), 'The Ethics of Empowerment: Rethinking the Role of Lawyers in Interviewing and Counselling the Child Client', *Fordham Law Review* 64: 1655.

(2009), 'Rights, Not Wrongs', *International Journal of Children's Rights* 17: 321–9.

(2017), 'Do Rights Still Flow Downhill?', *International Journal of Children's Rights* 25(2): 273–84.

Feinberg, J. (1966), 'Duties, Rights and Claims', *American Philosophical Quarterly* 3: 137.

(1970), 'The Nature and Value of Rights', *Journal of Value Inquiry* 4: 243–57.

(1980), 'The Child's Right to an Open Future', in W. Aiken and H. LaFollette (eds), *Whose Child? Parental Rights, Parental Authority and State Power*, Totowa, NJ: Rowman & Littlefield, 124–53.

(1992), 'The Child's Right to an Open Future', in *Freedom and Fulfilment: Philosophical Essays*, Princeton University Press, 76–89.

Felders, B. (2006), 'Coming Out for Kids: Recognising, Respecting and Representing LGBTQ Youth', *Nevada Law Journal* 6: 274

Fenton-Glynn, C. (2014), 'The Child's Voice in Adoption Proceedings', *International Journal of Children's Rights* 22: 135–63.

Ferguson, L. (2013), 'Not Merely Rights for Children But Children's Rights: the Theory Gap and the Assumption of the Importance of Children's Rights', *International Journal of Children's Rights* 21: 177–208.

(2015), 'The Jurisprudence of Making Decisions Affecting Children', in A. Diduck, N. Peleg and H. Reece (eds), *Law in Society*, Leiden: Brill, 142–59.

Fergusson, D. M., Horwood, L. J. and Boden, J. M. (2008), 'The Transmission of Social Inequality: Examination of the Linkages Between Family Socioeconomic Status in Childhood and Educational Achievement in Young Adulthood', *Research in Social Stratification and Mobility* 26(3): 277–95.

Field-Fisher, T. (1974), *Report of the Committee of Inquiry into the Care and Supervision Provided by Local Authorities and Other*

Agencies in Relation to Maria Colwell and the Co-ordination between Them, London: Her Majesty's Stationery Office.

Figes, O. (2007), *The Whisperers*, London: Allen Lane.

Fineman, M. and Worthington, K. (eds) (2009), *What is Right for Children?* Farnham: Ashgate.

Finnis, J. ([1980] 2011), *Natural Law and Natural Rights*, Oxford: Clarendon Press.

Firestone, S. (1970), *The Dialectic of Sex*, New York: William Morrow.

Fitz, J. (1981), 'The Child as Legal Subject', in R. Dale et al. (eds), *Education and the State, Politics, Patriarchy and Practice 2*, London/Buckingham: Falmer Press/Open University Press, 301.

Flekkøy, M. (1991), *A Voice for Children*, London: Jessica Kingsley.

Fodella, A. (2008), 'Freedom from Child Labour as a Human Right: the Role of the UN System in Implementing ILO Child Labour Standards', in G. Nesi, L. Nogler and M. Pertile (eds), *Child Labour in a Globalized World: a Legal Analysis of ILO Action*, New York: Routledge.

Ford, N. (2005), 'Communication for Abandonment of Female Genital Cutting', *International Journal of Children's Rights* 13: 183–99.

Fordham Conference (1996), 'Recommendations of the Conference on Ethical Issues in the Legal Representation of Children', *Fordham Law Review* 65: 1301–24.

Fortin, J. (2009), *Children's Rights and the Developing Law*, 3rd edn, Cambridge University Press.

— (2011), 'A Decade of the Human Rights Act and its Impact on Children's Rights', *Family Law* 41: 176–83.

Fortuyn, M-D. and De Langen, M. (eds) (1992), *Towards the Realization of Human Rights of Children*, Amsterdam: Children's Ombudswork Foundation.

479

Fox, M. and Thomson, M. (2005), 'Short Changed? The Law and Ethics of Male Circumcision', *International Journal of Children's Rights* 13: 161–82.

Fox Harding, L. (1991a), *Perspectives in Child Care Policy*, London: Longman.

(1991b), 'The Children Act 1989 in Context: Four Perspectives in Child Care Law and Policy', *Journal of Social Welfare and Family Law*, 13(4): 140.

Frankena, W. (1962), 'The Concept of Social Justice', in R. Brandt (ed.), *Social Justice*, Englewood Cliffs, NJ: Prentice Hall, 1–29.

Franklin, B. (1986), *The Rights of Children*, Oxford: Blackwell.

Fraser, N. (2013), *The Fortunes of Feminism: From Women's Liberation to Identity Politics to Anti-capitalism*, London: Verso.

Freeman, H. (2012), 'I Dream of Being a Mother, Now I Feel Like a Murderer', *Daily Mail*, 25 October, 42.

Freeman, M. (1974), *The Legal Structure*, Harlow: Longman.

(1975), 'Towards a Critical Theory of Family Law', *Current Legal Problems* 38: 153–85.

(1979) *Violence in the Home*, Farnborough: Saxon House.

(1980), 'The Rights of Children in the International Year of the Child', *Current Legal Problems* 33: 1–32.

(1983), *The Rights and Wrongs of Children*, London: Frances Pinter.

(1988a), 'Abortion: What Do Other Countries Do?', *New Law Journal* 138: 233.

(1988b), 'Sterilizing the Mentally Handicapped', in M. Freeman (ed.), *Medicine, Ethics and Law*, London: Stevens, 55–84.

(1992a), *Children, Their Families and the Law*, Basingstoke: Macmillan.

Freeman, M. (1992b), 'Taking Children's Rights More Seriously', *International Journal of Law and the Family* 6: 52–71.

(1995), 'The Morality of Cultural Pluralism', *International Journal of Children's Rights* 3: 1–17.

(1996a), 'Children's Education: A Test Case for Best Interests and Autonomy', in R. Davie and D. Galloway (eds), *Listening to Children in Education*, London: David Fulton, 29–48.

(1996b), *Children's Rights: A Comparative Perspective*, Aldershot: Dartmouth.

(1997a), 'The Best Interests of the Child? Is the *Best Interests of the Child* in the Best Interests of Children?', *International Journal of Law, Policy and the Family* 11(3): 360–88.

(1997b), 'The James Bulger Tragedy: Childish Innocence and the Construction of Guilt', in M. Freeman (ed.), *The Moral Status of Children*, The Hague: Martinus Nijhoff, 235–53.

(1997c), *The Moral Status of Children: Essays on the Rights of the Child*, The Hague: Martinus Nijhoff.

(1998), 'The Sociology of Childhood and Children's Rights', *International Journal of Children's Rights* 6: 433–44.

(2000a), 'Disputing Children', in S. Katz, J. Eekelaar and M. Maclean (eds), *Cross Currents*, Oxford University Press, 44.

(2000b), 'Children and Cultural Diversity', in D. Fottrell (ed.), *Revisiting Children's Rights*, The Hague: Kluwer Law, 15–30.

(2000c), 'The Future of Children's Rights', *Children and Society* 14: 277–93.

(2001), 'Whose Life is It Anyway?', *Medical Law Review* 9: 259.

(2004), 'Medically Assisted Reproduction', in Laing, J. and McHale, J. (eds) *Principles of Medical Law*, Oxford University Press: 639–738.

(2005), 'Rethinking Gillick', *International Journal of Children's Rights* 13: 201.

(2006a), 'Saviour Siblings', in S. A. M. McLean (ed.), *First Do No Harm: Law, Ethics and Healthcare*, Aldershot: Ashgate, 389–406.

(2006b), 'What's Right with Rights for Children, Review Essay', *International Journal of Law in Context* 2(1): 89–98.

(2007a), 'Article 3: the Best Interests of the Child', in A. Alen et al. (eds), *A Commentary on the United Nations Convention on the Rights of the Child*, Leiden: Martinus Nijhoff.

(2007b), 'Why it Remains Important to Take Children's Rights Seriously', *International Journal of Children's Rights* 15: 5–23.

(2010), 'The Human Rights of Children', *Current Legal Problems* 63(1): 44.

(2011a), 'Children's Rights as Human Rights: Reading the UNCRC', in J. Qvortrup, W. A. Corsaro and M-S. Honig (eds), *The Palgrave Handbook of Childhood Studies*, New York: Palgrave Macmillan.

(2011b), 'The Value and Values of Children's Rights', in A. Invernizzi and J. Williams (eds), *The Human Rights of Children: From Vision to Implementation*, Farnham: Ashgate.

(2012a), 'Towards a Sociology of Children's Rights', in M. Freeman (ed.), *Law and Childhood Studies, Current Legal Issues*, vol. 14, Oxford University Press.

(2012b), 'Introduction', in M. Freeman (ed.), *Law and Childhood Studies: Current Legal Issues*, vol 14.

(2014), *Future of Children's Rights*, Leiden: Brill Nijhoff.

(2015), 'Thinking about Children's Rights Sociologically?' in A. Diduck, N. Peleg and H. Reece (eds), *Law in Society*, Leiden: Brill.

(2018), *The Definition of a Child*, Leiden: Brill.

Freeman, M. and Saunders, B. (2014), 'Can We Conquer Child Abuse if We Don't Outlaw the Physical Punishment of Children?' *International Journal of Children's Rights* 22: 681–709.

Freeman, M. and Veerman, P. (1992), *The Ideologies of Children's Rights*, Dordrecht: Martinus Nijhoff.

Fridriksdottir, H. (2015), 'Relational Representation: the Empowerment of Children in Justice Systems', in S. Mahmoudi (ed.), *Child-Friendly Justice*, Leiden: Brill, 55–72.

Friedman, L. (1971), 'The Idea of Right as a Social and Legal Concept', *Journal of Social Issues* 27(2), available at: http://law.stanford.edu/wp-content/uploads/sites/default/files/person/166209/doc/slspublic/friedman_cv.pdf.

Fruilli, M. (2008), 'Advancing International Criminal Law', *Journal of International Criminal Justice* 6: 1033–42.

Fukuyama, F. (2002), *Our Posthuman Future*, London: Profile Books.

(2011), *The Origins of Political Order: From Prehuman Times to the French Revolution*, New York: Farrar, Straus & Giroux.

(2014), *Political Order and Political Decay: From the Industrial Revolution to the Globalisation of Democracy*, London: Profile Books.

Fuller, L. (1964), *The Morality of Law*, New Haven, CT: Yale University Press.

Furedi, F. (2013), *Moral Crusades in an Age of Mistrust: the Jimmy Savile Scandal*, Basingstoke: Palgrave Macmillan.

Gabhainn, S. N. and Sixsmith, J. (2005), *Children's Understandings of Well-being*, The National Children's Office: Department of Health and Children, Government of Ireland.

Gal, T. (2011), *Child Victims and Restorative Justice*, New York: Oxford University Press.

Gallagher, M. (2008), 'Foucault, Power and Participation', *International Journal of Children's Rights* 16(3): 395–406.

Garbarino, J. (1998), 'The Stress of Being a Poor Child in America', *Child and Adolescent Psychiatric Clinics of North America* 7(1): 105–19.

Garrison, E. (1991), 'Children's Competence to Participate in Divorce Custody Decision-making', *Journal of Clinical Child Psychology* 20(1): 78–87.

Gasson, N. R. (2015), 'Young People's Employment: Protection or Participation?', *Childhood* 22: 154–70.

Gazzaniga, M. (2015), *The Ethical Brain*, New York: Dana.

Gearty, C. (2011), 'Putting Lawyers in their Place: the Role of Human Rights in the Struggle against Poverty', in A. Walker, A. Sinfield and C. Walker (eds), *Fighting Poverty, Inequality and Injustice*, Bristol: Policy Press.

Geldenhuys, J. and Doubell, H. (2011), 'South African Children's Voice on School Discipline: A Case Study', *International Journal of Children's Rights* 19: 321–37.

Gelles, R. J. (1979), 'The Social Construction of Child Abuse', in R. J. Gelles (ed.), *Family Violence*, Beverly Hills, CA: Sage.

Gershoff, E. (2010), 'More Harm Than Good: A Summary of Scientific Research on the Intended and Unintended Effects of Corporal Punishment of Children', *Law and Contemporary Problems* 73(2): 33–56.

(2013), 'Spanking and Child Development: We Know Enough Now to Stop Hitting Our Children', *Child Development Perspectives*, 7(3): 133–7.

(2016), 'Should Parents' Physical Punishment of Children be Considered a Source of Toxic Stress that Affects Brain Development?' *Family Relations* 65(1): 151–62.

Gerzon, M. (1973), *A Childhood for Every Child: the Politics of Parenthood*, New York: Outerbridge & Lazard.

Gheaus, A. (2015), 'Should there Ever be a Duty to Have Children?' in S. Hannan, S. Brennan and R. Vernon (eds), *Permissible Progeny*, New York: Oxford University Press, 87–106.

Gil, D. G. (1970), *Violence against Children: Physical Child Abuse in the United States*, Cambridge, MA: Harvard University Press.

Gillespie, A. (2004), 'The Sexual Offences Act 2003: Tinkering with "Child Pornography"', *Criminal Law Review*, 361–68.

(2010), 'Legal Definitions of Child Pornography', *Journal of Sexual Aggression* 16(1): 19–31.

Gilliam, J. (2004), 'Toward Providing a Welcoming Home for All', *Los Angeles Loyola Law Review* 37: 1037.

Gilligan, C. (1982), *In A Different Voice: Psychological Theory and Women's Development*, Cambridge, MA: Harvard University Press.

Gilmore, S. (2017), 'Use of the UNCRC in Family Law Cases in England and Wales', *International Journal of Children's Rights* 25: 500–18.

Gilmore, S. and Herring, J. (2011), '"No" is the Hardest Word: Consent and Children's Autonomy', *Children and Family Law Quarterly* 23(1): 3–25.

Giordano, S. (2015), 'The Fifth Commandment', *International Journal of Children's Rights* 23: 27–51.

Girling, S. (2013), 'The Internet: A Global Market for Child Sexual Abuse', in J. Wild (ed.), *Exploiting Childhood: How Fast Food, Material Obsession and Porn Culture are Creating New Forms of Child Abuse*, London: Jessica Kingsley.

Giroux, H. A. (2007), 'Violence, Katrina and the Biopolitics of Disposability', *Theory, Culture and Society* 24: 305–9.

Giroux, H. and Pollock, G. (2010), *The Mouse that Roared*, Lanham, MD: Rowman & Littlefield.

Gittins, D. (1998), *The Child in Question*, Basingstoke: Macmillan.

Glanzer, P. L. (2012), 'Educational Freedom and Human Rights', in C. Butler (ed.), *Child Rights*, West Lafayette, IN: Purdue University Press, 118–40.

Goldman, F. (2012), 'Children of the Dirty War: Argentina's Stolen Orphans', *The New Yorker*, 19 March.

485

Goldson, B. (1997), 'Children, Crime, Policy and Practice: Neither Welfare nor Justice', *Children and Society* 11: 77–88.

Goldson, B. and Kilkelly, U. (2013), 'International Human Rights Standards and Child Imprisonment: Potentialities and Limitations', *International Journal of Children's Rights* 21: 345–71.

Goldstein, J., Freud, A. and Solnit, A. ([1967] 1979), *Beyond the Best Interests of the Child*, New York: Free Press.

(1986), *In the Best Interest of the Child*, New York: Free Press.

Goodman, M. (2016), *Future Crimes*, New York: Anchor Books.

Gordon, H. R. (2010), *We Fight to Win: Inequality and the Politics of Youth Activism*, New Brunswick, NJ: Rutgers University Press.

Gostin, L. (2014), *Global Health Law*, Cambridge, MA: Harvard University Press.

Gottlieb, D. (ed.) (1973), *Children's Liberation*, Englewood Cliffs, NJ: Prentice Hall.

Gould, C. (2004), *Globalising Democracy and Human Rights*, Cambridge University Press.

Gran, B. and Aliberti, D. (2003), 'The Office of the Children's Ombudsperson: Children's Rights and Social-Policy Innovation', *International Journal of the Sociology of Law* 31 (2): 89–106.

Gran, B., Waltz, M. and Renzhofer, H. (2013), 'A Child's Right to Enjoy the Benefits of Scientific Progress and its Applications', *International Journal of Children's Rights* 21: 323–44.

Green, B. and Dohrn, B. (1996), 'Foreword: Children and the Ethical Practice of Law', *Fordham Law Review* 64: 1281.

Greenhalgh, S. (2008), *Just One Child*, Berkeley, CA: University of California Press.

Gregg, B. (2016), *The Human Rights State*, Philadelphia, PA: University of Pennsylvania Press.

Greven, P. (1992), *Spare the Child*, New York: Vintage Books.

Gribble, K. and Gallagher, M. (2014), 'Rights of Children in Relation to Breastfeeding in Child Protection Cases', *British Journal of Social Work* 44(2): 434–60.

Griffin, J. (2002), 'Do Children Have Rights?' in D. Archard and C. Macleod (eds), *The Moral and Political Status of Children*, Oxford University Press, 19–30.

(2008), *On Human Rights*, Oxford University Press.

Gross, B. and Gross, R. (eds) (1977), *The Children's Rights Movement: Overcoming the Oppression of Young People*, New York: Anchor Press/Doubleday.

Grover, S. (2004), 'Why Won't They Listen to Us? On Giving Power and Voice to Children Participating in Social Research', *Childhood* 11(1): 81–93.

(2005), 'Advocacy by Children as a Causal Factor in Promoting Resilience', *Childhood* 12(4): 527–38.

Grugel, J. (2013), 'Children's Rights and Children's Welfare after the Convention on the Rights of the Child', *Progress in Development Studies* 13(1): 19–30.

Grugel, J. and Piper, N. (2011), 'Global Governance, Economic Migration and the Difficulties of Social Activism', *International Sociology* 26(4): 433–54.

Guggenheim, M. (1999), 'Matter of Ethics: Counselling Counsel for Children', *Michigan Law Review* 97: 1488.

(2005), *What's Wrong with Children's Rights*, Cambridge, MA: Harvard University Press.

Gunn, T. (2006), 'The Religious Right and the Opposition to US Ratification of the Convention on the Rights of the Child', *Emory International Law Review* 20(1): 111–28.

Guru, S. (2013), *Curriculum Guide: Migration and Refugees*, College of Social Work, London.

Gusfield, J. (1963), *Symbolic Crusade*, Urbana, IL: University of Illinois Press.

Gutmann, A. (1993), 'The Challenge of Multiculturalism in Political Ethics', *Philosophy and Public Affairs* 22: 171–206.

Gwirayi, P. and Shumba, A. (2011), 'Children's Rights: How Much Do Zimbabwe Urban Secondary School Pupils Know?', *International Journal of Children's Rights* 19: 195–204.

Habermas, J. (1996), *Between Facts and Norms: Contributions to a Discourse Theory of Law and Democracy*, Cambridge, MA: MIT Press.

(2010), 'The Concept of Human Dignity and the Realistic Utopia of Human Rights', *Metaphilosophy* 41: 464–80.

Hacking. I. (2000), *The Social Construct of What?* Cambridge, MA: Harvard University Press.

Hafner-Burton, E. M. and Tsutsui, K. (2005), 'Human Rights in a Globalizing World: the Paradox of Empty Promises', *American Journal of Sociology* 110(5): 1373–411.

Hagger, L. (2003), 'Some Implications of the Human Rights Act 1998 for the Medical Treatment of Children', *Medical Law International* 6(1): 25–51.

Haider, A. (2006), 'Roper v. Simmons: the Role of the Science Brief', *Ohio State Journal of Criminal Law* 3: 369.

Hainz, T. (2015), 'The Enhancement of Children versus Circumcision: A Case of Double Moral Standards?', *Bioethics* 29: 507–15.

Hale, B. (2000), 'In Defence of the Children Act', *Archives of Disease in Childhood* 83(6): 463–7.

Hammarberg, T. (1990), 'The UN Convention on the Rights of the Child – and How to Make it Work', *Human Rights Quarterly* 12 (1): 97–105.

(1997), 'Children, the UN Convention and the Media', *International Journal of Children's Rights* 5(2): 243–61.

(1998), *A School for Children with Rights: The Significance of the United Nations Convention on the Rights of the Child for*

Modern Education Policy, Florence: UNICEF Innocenti Research Centre.

Hampshire County Council (2009), *Rights, Respect and Responsibility (RRR)*, Winchester: Hampshire County Council.

Handsley, E., et al. (2014), 'A Children's Rights Perspective on Food Advertising to Children', *The International Journal of Children's Rights* 22: 93–134.

Hanson, K. (2007), 'Concluding Remarks: Does the Practice also Work in Theory?' in *The UN Children's Rights Convention: Theory Meets Practice*, Proceedings of the International Interdisciplinary Conference on Children's Rights, Ghent.

(2011), 'International Children's Rights and Armed Conflict', *Human Rights and International Legal Discourse* 5(1): 40–62.

(2012), 'Schools of Thought in Children's Rights', in M. Liebel (ed.), *Children's Rights from Below: Cross-cultural Perspectives*, Basingstoke: Palgrave Macmillan, 63–79.

(2014), '"Killed by Charity": Towards Interdisciplinary Children's Rights Studies, Editorial', *Childhood* 21(4): 441–5.

(2015), 'International Legal Procedures and Children's Conceptual Autonomy', *Childhood* 22: 427–31.

Hanson, K. and Lundy, L (2017), 'Does Exactly What it Says on the Tin? A Critical Analysis and Alternative Conceptualisation of the So-called "General Principles" of the Convention on the Rights of the Child', *The International Journal of Children's Rights* 25: 285–306.

Hanson, K. and Nieuwenhuys, O. (2012), 'Living Rights, Social Justice, Translations', in K. Hanson and O. Nieuwenhuys (eds), *Reconceptualizing Children's Rights in International Development: Living Rights, Social Justice, Translations*, Cambridge University Press, 3–26.

489

(eds) (2013), *Reconceptualizing Children's Rights in International Development: Living Rights, Social Justice, Translations*, Cambridge University Press.

Hanson, K. and Vandaele, A. (2013), 'Translating Working Children's Rights into International Labour Law', in K. Hanson and C. Nieuwenhuys (eds), *Reconceptualizing Children's Rights in International Development: Living Rights, Social Justice, Translations*, Cambridge University Press, 250–74.

Haralambie, A. M. (1993), *The Child's Attorney: A Guide to Representing Children in Custody, Adoption and Protection Cases*, Chicago, IL: American Bar Association.

Hardman, C. (1973), 'Can There be an Anthropology of Children?', *Journal of the Anthropological Society of Oxford*, 85–99 (also in 2001 in *Childhood* 8: 501–17).

Harman, L. (1990), 'Falling Off the Vine: Legal Fictions and the Doctrine of Substituted Judgment', *Yale Law Journal* 100: 1.

Harris, J. (2013), 'In Search of Blue Skies: Science, Ethics, and Advances in Technology', *Medical Law Review* 21(3): 131–45.

Harris-Short, S. (2003), 'International Human Rights Law: Imperialist, Inept and Ineffective? Cultural Relativism and the UN Convention on the Rights of the Child', *Human Rights Quarterly* 25(1): 130–81.

Hart, H. L. A. (1963), *Law, Liberty and Morality*, Oxford University Press.

(1968), *Punishment and Responsibility*, Oxford University Press.

(1994), *The Concept of Law*, 2nd edn, Oxford: Clarendon Press.

Hart, J. (2008), 'Children's Participation and International Development', *International Journal of Children's Rights* 16: 407–18.

Hart, R. A. (1992), *Children's Participation: From Tokenism to Citizenship*, Innocenti Essays No. 4, Florence: UNICEF.

(1997), *Children's Participation*, London: Earthscan.

Hart, R. (2008), 'Stepping Back from "The ladder": Reflections on a Model of Participatory Work with Children', in A. Reid et al. (eds), *Participation and Learning: Perspectives on Education and the Environment, Health and Sustainability*, Dordrecht: Springer, 19–31.

Hartas, D. (2008), *The Right To Childhoods Critical Perspectives on Rights, Difference and Knowledge in a Transient World*, London: Bloomsbury.

Hasson, K. J. (2003), 'Religious Liberty and Human Dignity: a Tale of Two Declarations', *Harvard Journal of Law and Public Policy* 27: 83.

Hathaway, J. (2007), 'Forced Migration Studies: Could We Agree Just to "Date"?' *Journal of Refugee Studies* 20(3): 349–69.

Hawes, J. (1991), *The Children's Rights Movement*, Boston, MA: Twayne.

(2013), 'Changing Childhoods: Nature Deficit', in J. Wild (ed.), *Exploiting Childhood: How Fast Food, Material Obsession and Porn Culture are Creating New Forms of Child Abuse*, London: Jessica Kingsley.

Hay, C. (1995), 'Mobilization Through Interpretation: James Bulger, Juvenile Crime and the Construction of a Moral Panic', *Social and Legal Studies* 4: 197–324.

Hays, S. (1996), *The Cultural Contradictions of Motherhood*, New Haven, CT: Yale University Press.

Hayles, M. (ed.) (1979), *Changing Childhood*, London: London Writers and Readers Cooperative.

Hayward, B. (2013), *Children. Citizenship, and Environment: Nurturing a Democratic Imagination in a Changing World*, London: Taylor & Francis.

Hecht, T. (1998), *At Home in the Street: Street Children of Northeast Brazil*, Cambridge University Press.

Heersterman, W. (2005), 'An Assessment of the Impact of Youth Submissions to the United Nations Committee on the Rights of the Child', *International Journal of Children's Rights* 13(3): 351–78.

Helmholz, R. (1993), 'And Were There Children's Rights in Early Modern England? The Canon Law and Intra-Family Violence in England, 1400–1640', *International Journal of Children's Rights* 1: 23–32.

Henkin, L. (1990), *The Age of Rights*, New York: Columbia University Press.

Herczog, M. (2012), 'Rights of the Child and Early Childhood Education and Care in Europe', *European Journal of Education* 47(4): 542–55.

Herring, J. (2012), 'Vulnerability, Children and the Law', in M. Freeman (ed.), *Law and Childhood Studies*, Oxford University Press, 243–63.

(2014) 'The Welfare Principle and the Children Act: Presumably It's About Welfare?' *Journal of Social Welfare and Family Law* 36(1): 14–25.

Herzog, K. (2005), *Children and Our Global Future*, Cleveland, OH: Pilgrim.

Heywood, C. (2001), *A History of Childhood: Children and Childhood in the West from Medieval to Modern Times*, Cambridge: Polity Press.

Hill, M., Davis, J., Prout, A. and Tisdall, K. (2004), 'Moving the Participation Agenda Forward', *Children and Society* 18: 77–96.

Hill, M. and Tisdall, E. K. M. (1997), *Children and Society*, Harlow: Addison Wesley Longman.

Hinduja, S. and Patchin, J. W. (2011), 'Cyberbullying: A Review of the Legal Issues Facing Educators', *Preventing School Failure: Alternative Education for Children and Youth* 55(2): 71–8.

Hine, J. (2004), *Children and Citizenship*, London: Home Office Research and Development and Statistics Directorate.

Hiner, N. R. and Hawes, J. (1985), *Growing Up in America: Children in Historical Perspective*, Urbana, IL: University of Illinois Press.

Hing, B. (1983), 'Raising Personal Identification Issues of Class, Race, Ethnicity, Gender, Sexual Orientation, Physical Disability, and Age in Lawyering Courses', *Stanford Law Review* 45: 1807.

HM Government (2013), *Working Together to Safeguard Children: A Guide to Inter-agency Working to Safeguard and Promote the Welfare of Children*, London: Department for Education.

Hobbes, T. (1651), *Leviathan*, London: Printed for Andrew Crooke, available at: www.gutenberg.org/files/3207/3207-h/3207-h.htm.

Hodgkin, R. and Newell, P. (2007), Implementation Handbook for the Convention on the Rights of the Child, 3rd edn, New York: Unicef.

Hohfeld, W. N. (1923), *Fundamental Legal Conceptions as Applied in Judicial Reasoning*, New Haven, CT: Yale University Press.

Holland, A. (2015), 'The Case Against the Case for Procreative Beneficence', *Bioethics* 30: 490–509.

Hollingsworth, K. (2013), 'Theorising Children's Rights in Youth Justice: the Significance of Autonomy and Foundational Rights', *Modern Law Review* 76(6): 1046–69.

(2014), 'Assuming Responsibility for Incarcerated Children', *Current Legal Problems* 67: 99–134.

Holt, J. (1974), *Escape from Childhood: The Needs and Rights of Children*, Harmondsworth: Penguin.

Holt, J. C. (1965), *Magna Carta*, Cambridge University Press.

Holzscheiter, A. (2010), *Children's Rights in International Politics: The Transformative Power of Discourse*, Basingstoke: Palgrave Macmillan.

Honwana, A. (2005), 'Innocent and Guilty: Child-Soldiers as Interstitial and Tactical Agents', in A. Honwana and F. De

Boeck (eds), *Makers and Breakers: Children and Youth in Postcolonial Africa*, Oxford: James Currey, 31–52.

House of Lords/House of Commons (2015), *The UK's Compliance with the UN Convention on the Rights of the Child*, 8th report, HL 144, HC 1015.

Hough, J. (1995) 'Why Isn't It The Children's Act?', in Dalrymple, J. and Hough, J. *Having a Voice: An Exploration of Children's Rights and Advocacy*, Birmingham: Venture Press.

Howe, R. B. and Covell, K. (2010), 'Miseducating Children about their Rights', *Education, Citizenship and Social Justice* 5(2): 91–102.

Howells, J. (1974), *Remember Maria*, London: Butterworths.

Hoyano, L. C. H. and Keenan, C. ([2007] 2010), *Child Abuse Law and Policy Across Boundaries*, Oxford University Press.

Hulme, D. (2009), *The Millennium Development Goals (MDGs): A Short History of the World's Biggest Promise*, Brooks World Poverty Institute, University of Manchester, Manchester.

Hultqvist, K. and Dahlberg, G. (2001), *Governing the Child in the New Millennium*, London and New York: Routledge.

Hume, D. ([1740] 1968), *A Treatise on Human Nature*, Oxford: Clarendon Press.

Hungerland, B., Liebel, M., Liesecke, A. and Wihstutz, A. (2007), 'Paths to Participatory Autonomy: The Meanings of Work for Children in Germany', *Childhood* 14(2): 257–77.

Hungerland, B., Liebel, M., Milne, B. and Wihstutz, A. (eds) (2007), *Working to be Someone: Child Focused Research and Practice with Working Children*, London: Jessica Kingsley.

Hunt, A. (1990), 'Rights and Social Movements: Counter-Hegemonic Strategies', *Journal of Law in Society* 17: 309.

Hunt, L. (2007), *Inventing Human Rights: A History*, New York: W. W. Norton.

Hunter, R. (2007), 'Close Encounters of a Judicial Kind: "Hearing" Children's "Voices" in Family Law Proceedings', *Child and Family Law Quarterly* 19(3): 283–303.

Huntington, C. (2006), 'Rights Myopia in Child Welfare', *UCLA Law Review* 53(3): 637–99.

Hutcheson, F. (1755), *A System of Moral Philosophy*, Glasgow: University of Glasgow, available at: https://archive.org/detail s/systemmoralphiloo1hutc/page/n6.

Hymowitz, K. (2003), *Liberation's Children*, Chicago, IL: Ivan R. Dee.

Illich, I. (1973), *Deschooling Society*, Harmondsworth: Penguin.

International Labour Organisation (ILO) (2006), *The End of Child Labour: Within Reach*, ILO Global Report on Child Labour, London: ILO.

Invernizzi, A. (2003), 'Street-Working Children and Adolescents in Lima: Work as an Agent of Socialisation', *Childhood* 10: 319.

(2008), 'Everyday Lives of Working Children and Notions of Citizenship', in A. Invernizzi and J. Williams (eds), *Children and Citizenship*, London: Sage.

Invernizzi, A. and Milne, B. (2002), 'Are Children Entitled to Contribute to International Policy Making? A Critical View of Children's Participation in the International Campaign for the Elimination of Child Labour', *International Journal of Children's Rights* 10(4): 403–31.

Invernizzi, A. and Williams, J. (eds) (2001), *Human Rights of Children: from Visions to Implementation*, Farnham: Ashgate.

Ishay, M. R. (2008), *The History of Human Rights: From Ancient Times to the Globalization Era*, Berkeley, CA: University of California Press.

Israel, J. (2011), *Revolutionary Ideas*, Princeton University Press.

Iversen, C. (2014), 'Predetermined Participation', *Childhood* 21: 274–89.

Jackson, E. (2013), *Medical Law: Text, Cases, and Materials*, Oxford University Press.

James, A., Jenks, C. and Prout, A. ([1998] 2002), *Theorizing Childhood*, Cambridge: Polity Press.

James, A. and Prout, A. (eds) (1997), *Constructing and Reconstructing Childhood: Contemporary Issues in the Sociological Study of Childhood*, London: Falmer Press.

James, A. L. ([2009] 2011), 'Agency', in J. Qvortrup, W. A. Corsaro and M-S. Honig (eds), *The Palgrave Handbook of Childhood Studies*, Basingstoke: Palgrave Macmillan.

James, E. and MacDougall, I. (2010), 'The Norway Town that Forgave and Forgot its Child Killers', *The Guardian*, 20 March.

Jebb, E. and Buxton, D. F. (1929), *Save the Child!: A Posthumous Essay*, London: Weardale Press.

Jelliffe, D. B. N. and Jelliffe, E. F. P. (1989), 'Breastfeeding: General Review', in D. B. N. Jelliffe and E. F. P. Jelliffe (eds), *Programmes to Promote Breastfeeding*, Oxford: Oxford Medical Publications.

Jenkins, S. (1988), 'Theory Base and Practice Link', in C. Jacobs and D. D. Bowles (eds), *Ethnicity and Race: Critical Concepts in Social Work*, Silver Spring, MD: NASW.

Jenks, C. (1996), *Childhood*, London: Routledge.

Jerome, L., Emerson, L., Lundy, L. and Orr, K. (2015), *Teaching and Learning about Child Rights: A Study of Implementation in 26 Countries*, Geneva: UNICEF.

John, M. (2003), *Children's Rights and Power*, London: Jessica Kingsley.

Johnson, D. (1992), 'Cultural and Regional Pluralism in the Drafting of the UN Convention on the Rights of the Child', in M. Freeman and P. Veerman (eds), *The Ideologies of Children's Rights*, Dordrecht: Martinus Nijhoff, 95–114.

Johnson, J. (1997), *The Struggle for Student Rights*, Lawrence, KS: University Press of Kansas.

Johnson, J., Jackson, L. and Gatto, L. (1995), 'Violent Attitudes and Deferred Academic Aspirations: Deleterious Effects of Exposure to Rap Music', *Basic and Applied Social Psychology* 16: 1–2.

Johnson, R. (2015), 'Strengthening the Monitoring of and Compliance with the Rights of the African Child', *International Journal of Children's Rights* 23: 365–90.

Jones, G. (2005), 'Children and Development Rights: Globalisation and Poverty', *Progress in Development Studies* 5: 336–42.

Jones, G. and Thomas de Benitez, S. (2014), 'Lost Opportunity: the Lydia Cacho Case and Civil Rights in Mexico', *International Journal of Children's Rights* 22: 313–18.

Jones, M. and Basser Marks, L. A. B. (1997), 'Beyond the Convention on the Rights of the Child: The Right of Children with Disabilities in International Law', *International Journal of Children's Rights* 5(2): 177–92.

Jones, R. (2014), *The Story of Baby P: Setting the Record Straight*, Bristol: Policy Press.

Jonsson, U. (1996), 'Nutrition and the Convention on the Rights of the Child', *Food Policy* 21(1): 41–55.

Joseph, R. (2009), *Human Rights and the Unborn Child*, Leiden: Martinus Nijhoff.

Kaganas, F. and Diduck, A. (2004), 'Incomplete Citizens: Changing Images of Post-Separation Children', *Modern Law Review* 67 (6): 959–81.

Kahane, G. and Savulescu, J. (2015), 'Normal Human Variation: Refocusing the Enhancement Debate', *Bioethics* 29(2): 133–45.

Kant, I. ([1797] 1996) *Groundwork of the Metaphysics of Morals*, Cambridge University Press.

Kateb, G. (2014), *Human Dignity*, Cambridge, MA: Harvard University Press.

Katz, C. (2004), *Growing Up Global, Economic Restructuring and Children's Everyday Lives*, Minneapolis, MN: University of Minnesota Press.

Katz, M. (1986), 'Child-Saving', *History of Education* 26: 423–4.

Kauffman, N. H. (2002), 'The Status of Children in International Law', in N. Kauffman and L. Rizzini (eds), *Globalisation and Children*, Leiden: Kluwer.

Keating, H. (2012), 'When the Kissing Has to Stop', in M. Freeman (ed.), *Law and Childhood Studies*, Oxford University Press, 254–80.

Keck, M. and Sikkink, K. (1998), *Activist Beyond Borders: Advocacy Networks in International Politics*, New York: Cornell University Press.

Kell, W. (1998), 'Voices Lost and Found: Training Ethics Lawyers for Children', *Indiana Law Journal* 73: 635.

Kellmer-Pringle, M. (1980), *The Needs of Children*, London: Hutchinson.

Kelly, J. B. (1998), 'Marital Conflict, Divorce, and Children's Adjustment', in K. D. Pruett and M. K. Pruett (eds), *Child Custody Issues*, New York: W. B. Saunders, 259–72.

Kelly, R. and Ramsey, S. (1983), 'Do Attorneys for Children in Protection Proceedings Make A Difference? A Study of the Impact of Representation Under Conditions of High Judicial Intervention', *Journal of Family Law* 21: 405.

Kempe, C. H. and Kempe, R. S. (1973), 'Practical Approach to the Protection of the Abused Child and Rehabilitation of the Abusing Parent', *Pediatrics* 51: 804–12.

Kennedy, D. (2006), *The Well of Being: Childhood, Subjectivity and Education*, Albany, NY: State University of New York Press.

Kent, G. (1997), 'Realizing International Children's Rights through Implementation of National Law', *International Journal of Children's Rights* 5(4): 439–56.

Kerber-Ganse, W. (2015), 'Eglantyne Jebb: A Pioneer of the CRC', *International Journal of Children's Rights* 23: 272–82.

Key, E. (1909), *The Century of the Child*, New York: Putnam; originally published in Swedish as *Barnets Arhundrade*, Stockholm: Albert Bonniers, 1900.

Khadka, S. (2013), 'Social Rights and the United Nations: Child Rights Convention – is the CRC a Help or Hindrance for Developing Universal and Egalitarian Social Policies for Children's Wellbeing in the "Developing World"?' *International Journal of Children's Rights* 21(4): 616–28.

Khosravi, S. (2008), *Young and Defiant in Tehran*, Philadelphia, PA: University of Pennsylvania Press.

Khoury-Kassabri, M. (2012), 'The Relationship between Teacher Self-efficacy and Violence towards Students as Mediated by Teacher's Attitude', *Social Work Research* 36(2): 127–39.

Khoury-Kassabri, M. and Ben-Harush, A. (2012), 'Discipline Methods within the Israeli Education System : Arab and Jewish Teachers' Attitudes', *International Journal of Children's Rights* 20: 265–78.

Kiddle, C. (1999), *Traveller Children: A Voice for Themselves*, London: Jessica Kingsley.

Kilkelly, U. (2001), 'The Best of Both Worlds for Children's Rights? Interpreting the European Convention on Human Rights in the Light of the UN Convention on the Rights of the Child', *Human Rights Quarterly* 23: 308–26.

Kilkelly, U. and Donnelly, M. (2011), 'Participation in Healthcare: the Views and Experiences of Children and Young People', *International Journal of Children's Rights* 19(1): 107–25.

Kim, D. H., Kim, K. I., Park, Y. C., Zhang, L. D., Lu, M. K. and Li, D. G. (2000), 'Children's Experience of Violence in China and Korea: A Transcultural Study', *Child Abuse & Neglect* 24(9): 1163–73.

King, M. (1981), *The Framework of Criminal Justice*, London: Croom Helm.

(1982), 'Children's Rights in Education: More than a Slogan?', *Educational Studies* 8(3): 227–38.

(1995), 'The James Bulger Murder Trial: Moral Dilemmas and Social Solutions', *International Journal of Children's Rights* 3: 167.

(1997), *A Better World for Children*, London: Routledge.

King, M. (2004) *Y diritti dei bambini in un mondo incerto*, Rome: Donzelli.

King, M. and Piper, C. (1995), *How the Law Thinks about Children*, Aldershot: Ashgate.

Kistler, M. and Moon, L. (2009), 'Does Exposure to Sexual Hip-Hop Music Videos Influence the Sexual Attitudes of College Students?' *Mass Communication and Society* 13(1): 67–86.

Kitson, E. (2016), 'Whose Foot is in the Tight Shoe? Negotiating Inclusive Pathways for the Eradication of Child Marriage in West Africa', *International Journal of Children's Rights* 24(4): 718–40.

Klug, F. (2015), *A Magna Carta for All Humanity: Homing in on Human Rights*, Oxford: Routledge.

Kolstrein, A. and Toledo, I. (2013), 'Bullying', *International Journal of Children's Rights* 21: 46–58.

Konner, M. (2010), *The Evolution of Childhood*, Cambridge, MA: Harvard/Belknap.

Koops, W. and Zuckerman, M. (2003), *The Century of the Child Revisited*, Philadelphia, PA: University of Pennsylvania Press.

Korczak, J. (1920), 'How to Love a Child', in M. Wolins (ed.), *Selected Works of Janusz Korczak*, Warsaw.

([1928] 2009), *The Child's Right to Respect*, Strasbourg: Council of Europe.

(2007), *Loving Every Child*, Chapel Hill, NC: Algonquin Books.

Kuhn, T. (1962), *The Structure of Scientific Revolutions*, University of Chicago Press.

Kukathas, C. (2006), 'The Mirage of Global Justice', *Social Philosophy and Policy* 23(1): 1–28.

L'Anson, J. and Allan, J. (2006), 'Children's Rights in Practice: A Study of Change Within a Primary School', *International Journal of Children's Spirituality* 11(2): 265–79.

LaFollette, H. (1980), 'Licensing Parents', *Philosophy and Public Affairs* 9(2): 182–97.

(1989), 'Freedom of Religion and Children', *Philosophy and Public Affairs* 1: 75–87.

Lake, K. (2011), 'Character Education from a Children's Rights Perspective: An Examination of Elementary Students' Perspectives and Experiences', *International Journal of Children's Rights* 19: 6769–90.

Lamb, C. (1823), *Essays of Elia*, London: Macmillan.

Lancy, D. (2015), *The Anthropology of Childhood: Cherubs, Chattel, Changelings*, Cambridge University Press.

Lane, M. (2014), *Greek and Roman Political Ideas*, Pelican: 277–84.

Langford, M. (2009), 'Domestic Adjudication and Economic, Social and Cultural Rights: a Socio-legal Review', *Sur. Revista Internacional de Direitos Humanos* 6(11).

Langlaude, S. (2007), *The Right of a Child to Religious Freedom in International Law*, Leiden: Martinus Nijhoff.

Lansdown, G. (1994), 'Children's Rights', in B. Mayall (ed.), *Children's Childhoods: Observed and Experienced*, London: Falmer.

(2001), 'Children's Welfare and Children's Rights', in P. Foley, J. Roche and S. Tucker (eds), *Children in Society: Contemporary Theatre, Policy and Practice*, Basingstoke: Palgrave, 87–97.

(2005), *The Evolving Capacities of the Child*, Florence: UNICEF.

Lansdown, G., Clark, M., Craissati, D., et al. (2007), *A Human Rights Approach to Education for All: A Framework for the Realization of Children's Right to Education and Rights within Education*, New York: UNICEF.

(2010), 'The Realisation of Children's Participation Rights: Critical Reflections', in B. Percy-Smith and N. Thomas (eds), *A Handbook of Children's Participation: Perspectives from Theory and Practice*, Abingdon: Routledge, 11–23.

Larkins, C. (2014), 'Enabling Children's Citizenship', *Childhood* 21: 9–21.

Lasch, C. (1977), *Haven in a Heartless World: the Family Besieged*, New York: Basic Books.

Lassonde, S. (2012), 'Ten is the New Fourteen', in P. Fass and M. Grossberg (eds), *Reinventing Childhood After World War 2*, Philadelphia, PA: University of Pennsylvania Press, 51–67.

Latham, M. (1997), 'Breastfeeding: A Human Rights Issue?', *International Journal of Children's Rights* 5(4): 397–417.

Layard, R. and Dunn, J. (2009), *A Good Childhood*, London: Penguin.

Leach, P. (1994), *Children First*, London: Michael Joseph.

Ledogar, R. (1993), 'Implementing the Convention on the Rights of the Child through National Programmes of Action for Children', *International Journal of Children's Rights* 1(3–4): 377–91.

Lee, N. (1999), 'The Challenge of Childhood: Distributions of Childhood's Ambiguity in Adult Institutions', *Childhood* 6 (4): 455–74.

(2001), *Childhood and Society: Growing Up in an Age of Uncertainty*, Maidenhead: Open University Press.

Lee, Y. (2010), 'Communications Procedure Under the Convention on the Rights of the Child: 3rd Optional Protocol', *International Journal of Children's Rights* 18(4): 567–83.

Lee, Y. (2013), 'Address: Creating New Futures for All Children: The Promise of International Human Rights Law', *Australian International Law Journal* 20: 3–16.

Lee, Y. and Jung, B. (2015), 'Bang Jung Whan – the Korean Pioneer of Children's Rights', *International Journal of Children's Rights* 23: 261–71.

Leece, S. (2009), 'Should Democracy Grow up? Children and Voting Rights', *Intergenerational Justice Review* 9(4): 133–9.

Leiter, V., McDonald, J. L. and Jacobson, H. T. (2006), 'Challenges to Children's Independent Citizenship: Immigration, Family and the State', *Childhood* 13(1): 11–27.

Lenzer, G. (1991), 'Is There Sufficient Interest to Establish a Sociology of Children?' *Footnotes of the American Sociological Assn* 19(6): 8.

(2002), 'Children's Studies and the Human Rights of Children: Toward a Unified Approach', in K. Alaimo and B. Klug (eds), *Children as Equals: Exploring the Rights of the Child*, Lanham, MD: University Press of America, 207–25.

(2015), 'The Vicissitudes of Childhood', *International Journal of Children's Rights* 3(1): 243–51.

Leonard, M. (2004), 'Children's Views on Children's Right to Work: Reflections from Belfast', *Childhood* 11(1): 45–61.

(2016), *The Sociology of Children, Childhood and Generation*, London: Sage.

Levine, M. (2003), *Children for Hire*. Westport, CT: Praeger.

Lewis, C. E. (1983), 'Decision-making Related to Health: When Could/Should Children Act Responsibly?' in G. B. Melton, G. P. Koocher and M. J. Saks (eds), *Competence to Consent*, New York: Plenum, 75–91.

Lewis, N. (1998), 'Human Rights, Law and Democracy in an Unfree World' in *Tony Evans, Human Rights 50 Years on: An Appraisal*, Manchester University Press.

Lewis, P. (2007), *Growing Apart: Oil, Politics and Economic Change in Indonesia and Nigeria*, Ann Arbor, MI: University of Michigan Press.

Liao, M. (2006), 'The Right of Children to be Loved', *Journal of Applied Philosophy* 14(4): 420–40.

(2015), *The Right to be Loved*, New York: Oxford University Press.

Libesman, T. (2007), 'Can International Law Imagine the World of Indigenous Children?', *International Journal of Children's Rights* 15: 283–309.

Liden, H. and Rusten, H. (2007), 'Asylum, Participation and the Best Interests of the Child: Lessons from Norway', *Children and Society* 21: 273–83.

Liebel, M. (2003), 'Working Children as Social Subjects: the Contribution of Social Children's Organisations to Social Transformation', *Childhood* 10: 265–85.

(2004), *A Will of their Own: Cross-Cultural Perspectives on Working Children*, London: Zed Books.

(2007), 'Opinion, Dialogue, Review: The New ILO Report on Child Labour: A Success Story, or the ILO Still at a Loss?', *Childhood* 14: 279.

(2008), 'Citizenship from Below: Children's Rights and Social Movements', in A. Invernizzi and J. Williams (eds), *Children and Citizenship*, London: Sage.

(2012a), *Children's Rights from Below: Cross-Cultural Perspectives* (with contributions by Karl Hanson, Iven Saadi and Wouter Vandenhole), Basingstoke: Palgrave Macmillan.

(2012b), 'Children's Work, Education and Agency: the African Movement of Working Children and Youth', in G. Spittler and M. Bourdillon (eds), *African Children at Work: Working and Learning Up for Life*, Berlin: LIT, 303–32.

(2013), 'Do Children Have a Right to Work? Working Children's Movements in the Struggle for Social Justice', in K. Hanson and O. Nieuwenhuys (eds), *Reconceptualizing Children's Rights in International Development: Living Rights, Social Justice, Translations*, Cambridge University Press, 225–49.

(2014), 'From Evolving Capacities to Evolving Capabilities: Contextualizing Children's Rights', in D. Stoecklin and J-M. Bonvin (eds), *Children's Rights and the Capability Approach*, Dordrecht: Springer, 67–84.

(2015), 'Prioritising the Rights of Working Children Instead of Banning Child Labour', *International Journal of Children's Rights* 23: 529–47.

(2016), 'The Moscow Declaration on the Rights of the Child (1918): A Contribution from the Hidden History of Children's Rights', *International Journal of Children's Rights* 24: 3–24.

Liebel, M., Overwien, B. and Recknagel, A. (eds) (2001), *Working Children's Protagonism: Social Movements and Empowerment in Latin America, Africa and India*, Frankfurt: IKO.

Liebel, M. and Saadi, I. (2012), 'Children's Rights and the Responsibilities of States: Thoughts on Understanding Children's Rights as Subjective Rights', in M. Liebel (ed.), *Children's Rights from Below: Cross-Cultural Perspectives*, Basingstoke: Palgrave Macmillan, 108–22.

Lieden, H. and Rusen, H. (2007), 'Asylum Participation and Best Interests of the Child', *Children and Society* 21: 273–83.

Lifton, B. J. (1988), *The King of Children*, London: Chatto & Windus.

Lim, H. and Roche, J. (2000), 'Feminism and Children's Rights' in J. Bridgeman and D. Monk (eds), *Feminist Perspectives on Child Law*, London: Cavendish, 238.

Lindley, R. (1986), *Autonomy*, London: Macmillan.

Lister, R. (2004), *Poverty*, Cambridge: Polity Press.

(2007), 'Why Citizenship: Where, When and How Children?', *Theoretical Inquiries in Law* 8: 693–718.

Lister, R. et al. (2003), 'Young People Talk About Citizenship: Empirical Perspectives on Theoretical and Political Debates', *Citizenship Studies* 7: 235.

Lister, R. and Beresford, P. (2000), 'Where are the Poor in the Future of Poverty Research?', in J. Bradshaw and R. Sainsbury (eds), *Researching Poverty*, Aldershot: Ashgate.

Livingstone, S. (2009), *Children and the Internet*, Cambridge: Polity Press.

Livingstone, S. and O'Neill, B. (2014), 'Children's Rights Online: Challenges, Dilemmas and Emerging Directions', in S. van der Hof, B. van den Berg and B. Schermer (eds), *Minding Minors Wandering the Web: Regulating Online Child Safety*, Information Technology and Law Series, 24, The Hague: Springer/T. M. C. Asser, 19–38.

Lloyd, A. (2002), 'Evolution of the African Charter of the Child and the African Committee of Experts', *International Journal of Children's Rights* 10: 179–88.

Lobstein, T. (2013), 'Childhood Obesity and the Junk Food Marketers', in J. Wild (ed.), *Exploiting Children*, London: Jessica Kingsley, 49–64.

Locke, J. (1690), *Second Treatise of Government*, available from the Gutenberg Project, London, available at: www.gutenberg.org/files/7370/7370-h/7370-h.htm.

Lomasky, L. (1987), *Persons, Rights and the Moral Community*, New York: Oxford University Press.

Lopatka, A. (1992), 'The Rights of the Child are Universal: the Perspective of the UN Convention on the Rights of the Child', in M. Freeman and P. Veerman (eds), *The Ideologies of Children's Rights*, Dordrecht: Martinus Nijhoff.

Lopez, G. (1989), 'Training Future Lawyers to Work with the Politically and Socially Subordinated', *West Virginia Law Review* 91: 305.

(2005), 'Living and Lawyering Rebelliously', *Fordham Law Review* 73(5): 2041.

Louv, R. (2010), *Last Child in the Woods: Saving Our Children from Nature-Deficit Disorder*, London: Atlantic Books.

Lowe, N. and Juss, S. (1993), 'Medical Treatment: Pragmatism and the Search for Principle', *Modern Law Review*, 56: 865.

Lücker-Babel, M. F. (1995), 'The Right of the Child to Express Views and Be Heard', *International Journal of Children's Rights* 3: 391–404.

Lukes, S. (1974), *Power: A Radical View*, London: Macmillan.

Lundy, L. (2005), 'Family Values in the Classroom? Reconciling Parental Wishes and Children's Rights in State Schools', *International Journal of Law, Policy and the Family* 19(3): 346–72.

—— (2007), '"Voice" is Not Enough: Conceptualising Article 12 of the United Nations Convention on the Rights of the Child', *British Educational Research Journal* 33(6): 927–42.

—— (2012), 'Children's Rights and Educational Policy in Europe: the Implementation of the United Nations Convention on the Rights of the Child', *Oxford Review of Education* 38(4): 393–411.

—— (2014), 'United Nations Convention on the Rights of the Child and Child Well-being', in A. Ben-Arieh et al. (eds), *Handbook of Child Well-Being*, Dordrecht: Springer.

Lundy, L. et al. (2012), *The UN Convention on the Rights of the Child: A Study of Legal Implementation in 12 Countries*, London: UNICEF UK.

Lundy, L., Kilkelly, U. and Byrne, B. (2013), 'Incorporation of the United Nations Convention on the Rights of the Child in Law: A Comparative Review', *International Journal of Children's Rights* 21(3): 442–63.

Lundy, L. and McEvoy, L. (2012), 'Children's Rights and Research Processes: Assisting Children to Informed Views', *Childhood* 19: 129–45.

Lundy, L., Orr, K. and Marshall, C. (2015), *Towards Better Investment in the Rights of the Child: the Views of Children*, Belfast: Queen's University.

Lyon, R-M. (1987), 'Speaking for a Child: the Role of Independent Counsel for Minors', *California Law Review* 75: 681–93.

MacCormick, N. ([1982] 1984), 'Children's Rights: A Test Case for Theories of Rights', in N. MacCormick (ed.), *Legal Rights and Social Democracy: Essays in Legal and Political Philosophy*, Oxford: Clarendon Press, 154–66.

MacKenzie, M. J., Nicklas, E., Waldfogel, J. and Brooks-Gunn, J. (2013), 'Spanking and Child Development Across the First Decade of Life', *Pediatrics* 132(5): e1118–25.

Mackie, J. (1984), 'Can There be a Rights-based Moral Theory?' in J. Waldron (ed.), *Theories of Rights*, Oxford University Press, 169–80.

MacKinnon, C. (1992), 'Pornography, Civil Rights, and Speech', in C. Itzin (ed.), *Pornography: Women, Violence, and Civil Liberties*, New York: Oxford University Press.

(2006), *Are Women Human? And Other International Dialogues*, Cambridge, MA: Harvard University Press.

Macleod C. (2015) Agency, Authority and the Vulnerability of Children, in A. Bagattini and C. Macleod (eds) *The Nature of Children's Well-Being. Children's Well-Being: Indicators and Research, vol 9*. Springer, Dordrecht.

Mahmoudi, S. (2015), *Child-Friendly Justice*, Leiden: Brill.

Mahoney, J. (2007), *The Challenge of Human Rights: Origin, Development and Significance*, Oxford: Blackwell.

Mahoney, T. (2009), 'The False Promise of Adolescent Brain Science in Juvenile Justice', *Notre Dame Law Review* 85: 89.

(2011), 'Adolescent Brain Science and Juvenile Justice', in M. Freeman (ed.), *Law and Neuroscience*, Oxford University Press, 255–82.

Maitland, F. (1920), *The Forms of Action at Common Law*, Cambridge University Press.

Mandelbaum, R. (2000), 'Revisiting the Question of Whether Young Children in Child Protection Proceedings Should be Represented by Lawyers', *Loyola University Chicago Law Journal* 32(1): 1.

(2002), 'Representing Children in Child Protection Proceedings', *Loyola Law Journal* 32: 86.

Mapp, S. (2011), *Global Child Welfare and Well-Being*, New York: Oxford University Press.

Marshall, D. (1999), 'The Construction of Children as an Object of International Relations: The Declaration of Children's Rights and the Child Welfare Committee of the League of Nations, 1900–1924', *International Journal of Children's Rights* 7: 103–47.

(2004), 'Children's Rights in Imperial Political Cultures: Missionary and Humanitarian Contributions to the Conference on the African Child of 1931', *International Journal of Children's Rights* 12(3): 273–318.

Marshall, T. (1950), *Citizenship and Social Class: And Other Essays*, Cambridge University Press.

(1965), *Class, Citizenship, and Social Development*, Garden City, NY: Doubleday & Co.

Martin, K. (2005), 'William Wants a Doll. Can He Have One? Feminists, Child Care Advisors, and Gender-Neutral Child Rearing', *Gender and Society* 19(4): 457–79.

Marx, K. (1843), *On the Jewish Question*, Deutsch-Französische Jahrbücher: Paris.

Mason, M. A. (1994), *From Father's Property to Children's Rights*, New York: Columbia University Press.

Masson, J. (2014), 'The Quality of Care Proceedings Reform', *Journal of Social Welfare and Family Law* 36(1): 82–4.

Matsuda, M. (1987), 'Looking to the Bottom: Critical Legal Studies and Reparations', *Harvard Civil Rights: Civil Liberties Law Review* 22: 323.

Max, L. (1990), *Children: Endangered Species?* Auckland: Penguin.

May, V. and Smart, C. (2004), 'Silence in Court? Hearing Children in Residence and Contact Disputes', *Child and Family Law Quarterly* 16(3): 305–15.

Mayall, B. (ed.) (1994), *Children's Childhoods: Observed and Experienced*, London: Falmer Press.

(2000), 'The Sociology of Childhood in relation to Children's Rights', *International Journal of Children's Rights* 8: 243–59.

(2002), *Towards a Sociology of Childhood: Thinking from Children's Lives*, Buckingham: Open University Press.

(2003), 'Sociology Can Further Children's Rights', *Education Journal* 72: 7.

(2013), *A History of the Sociology of Childhood*, London: IOE Press.

McCowan, T. (2010), 'Reframing the Universal Right to Education', *Comparative Education* 46(4): 509–25.

(2012), 'Is There a Universal Right to Higher Education?' *British Journal of Educational Studies* 60(2): 118–28.

McCrory, S. (2007), 'The International Convention for the Protection of All Persons from Enforced Disappearance', *Human Rights Law Review* 7: 545–66.

McCrudden, C. (ed.) (2013), *Understanding Human Dignity*, Oxford University Press.

McDougall, R. (2007), 'The Morality of Reproductive Actions', *Bioethics* 21: 181–90.

McEwan, I. (2014), *The Children Act*, London: Chatto & Windus.

McGillivray, A. (1994), 'Why Children Do Have Equal Rights: In Reply to Laura Purdy', *International Journal of Children's Rights* 2: 243–58.

(1997), '"He'll Learn it on His Body": Disciplining Childhood in Canadian Law', *International Journal of Children's Rights* 5: 193–242.

McGrath, H. (2009), 'Young People and Technology: A Review of the Current Literature', Alannah and Madeline Foundation, Melbourne.

McLean, S. A. M. (1990), 'Abortion Law: is Consensual Reform Possible?' *Journal of Law and Society* 19: 106–23.

McLean, S. A. M. and Ramsey, J. (2002), 'Human Rights, Reproductive Freedom, Medicine and the Law', *Medical Law International* 5: 239–58.

Mead, M. (1969), 'We Face Generational Gap', *Tribune*, 17 February.

Melli, M. (1993), 'Towards Restructuring of Custody Decision-making at Divorce', in J. Eekelaar and P. Šarčević (eds), *Parenthood in Modern Society*, Leiden: Martinus Nijhoff.

Melton, G. (1984), 'Child Witnesses and the First Amendment: A Psycholegal Dilemma', *Journal of Social Issues* 40(2): 51–67.

Melton, G. B. (1991), 'Preserving the Dignity of Children Around the World: the UN Convention on the Rights of the Child', *Child Abuse and Neglect* 15(4): 343–50.

(1991), 'Lessons from Norway: The Children's Ombudsman as a Voice for Children', *Case Western Reserve Journal of International Law* 23: 197.

(2005a), 'Building Humane Communities Respectful of Children: the Significance of the Convention on the Rights of the Child', *American Psychologist* 60(8): 918–26.

(2005b), 'Treating Children like People: A Framework for Research and Advocacy', *Journal of Clinical Child and Adolescent Psychology* 34(4): 646–57.

(2014), 'Because it's the Right (or Wrong) Thing to Do: When Children's Well-being is the Wrong Outcome', in A. Ben-Arieh et al. (eds), *Handbook of Child Well-Being*, Dordrecht: Springer.

Melton, G. and Wong, W. (2015), 'Young People as Leaders (and Sometimes Victims) of Political and Social Change', in

A. B. Smith (ed.), *Enhancing Children's Rights*, Basingstoke: Palgrave Macmillan, 197–213.

Mendez, P. K. (2007), 'Moving from Words to Action in the Modern Era of Application: A New Approach to Realising Children's Rights in Armed Conflicts', *International Journal of Children's Rights* 15: 219–49.

Menke, C. (2014), 'Dignity as the Right to Have Rights: Human Dignity', in H. Arendt, M. Duwell et al. (eds), *The Cambridge Handbook of Human Dignity: Interdisciplinary Perspectives*, Cambridge University Press, 332–43.

Menkel-Meadow, C. (1987), 'Excluded Voices: New Voices in the Legal Profession Making New Voices in the Law', *University of Miami Law Review* 42: 29–53.

Mentha, S., Church, A. and Page, J. (2015), 'Teachers as Brokers: Perceptions of Participation and Agency in Early Childhood Education and Care', *International Journal of Children's Rights* 23: 623–37.

Merry, S. (2006), *Human Rights and Gender Violence: Translating International Law into Local Justice*, University of Chicago Press.

Mestrum, F. (2011), 'Child Poverty: A Critical Perspective', *Social Work and Society* 9(1): 161–8.

Meyer, A. (2007), 'The Moral Rhetoric of Childhood', *Childhood* 14: 85–104.

Meyer, P. (1973), 'The Exploitation of the American Growing Class', in D. Gottlieb (ed.), *Children's Liberation*, Englewood Cliffs, NJ: Prentice Hall, 35–52.

Mezmur, B. (2012), 'Acting Like a Rich Bully', *International Journal of Children's Rights* 20: 24–56.

Middleton, S., Ashworth, K. and Braithwaite, I. (1997), *Small Fortunes: Spending on Children, Childhood Poverty and Parental Sacrifice*, York: Joseph Rowntree Foundation.

Milbank, J. (2013), 'Dignity Rather than Rights', in C. McCrudden (ed.), *Understanding Human Dignity*, Oxford University Press, 189–206.

Mill, J. S. ([1859] 1989), *On Liberty*, Cambridge University Press.

(1865), *Considerations on Representative Government*, London: Longman, Green.

Miller, D. (2009), 'Global Justice and Climate Change: How Should Responsibilities be Distributed?' in G. B. Peterson (ed.), *Tanner Lectures on Human Values 28*, Salt Lake City, UT: University of Utah Press, 119–56.

Miller, H. (2010), 'From "Rights-Based" to "Rights-Framed" Approaches: A Social Construction View of Human Rights Practice', *International Journal of Human Rights* 14(6): 915–31.

Miller, P. (2005), 'Useful and Priceless: Children in Contemporary Welfare States', *Social Politics* 12: 3–41.

Mills, C. Wright (1967), *The Sociological Imagination*, Oxford University Press.

Mills, C. M. (2003), 'The Child's Right to an Open Future', *Journal of Social Philosophy* 34(4): 499–509.

(2013), 'Knowing When to Doubt: Developing a Critical Stance When Learning from Others', *Developmental Psychology* 49: 404–18.

Milne, B. (2005), 'Is "participation" as it is described by the United Nations Convention on the Rights of the Child the key to children's citizenship?' in A. Invernizzi and B. Milne (eds), *Children's Citizenship: An Emergent Discourse on the Rights of the Child?*, special vol. *Journal of Social Sciences* 9: 31–42.

(2008), 'From Chattels to Citizens: Jebb's Legacy', in A. Invernizzi and J. Williams (eds), *Children's Citizenship*, London: Sage, 44–54.

(2013), *The History and Theory of Children's Citizenship in Contemporary Societies*, Dordrecht: Springer.

Minow, M. (1986), 'Rights for the Next Generation: A Feminist Approach to Children's Rights', *Harvard Women's Law Journal* 9(1): 1–24.

(1987), 'Are Rights for Children Right?', *American Bar Foundation Research Journal* 203–23.

(1990), *Making All the Difference: Inclusion, Exclusion, and American Law*, New York: Cornell University Press.

Minow, M. and Shanley, M. L. (1996), 'Relational Rights and Responsibilities: Revisioning the Family', *Liberal Political Theory and Law: Hypatia* 11(1): 4–29.

Mintz, S. (2004), *Huck's Raft: A History of American Childhood*, Cambridge, MA: Harvard University Press.

Mirandola, P. della (1486, 1998), *On the Dignity of Man*, trans. C. Wallis, Indianapolis, IN: Hackett.

Mitchell, R. C. (2015), 'Re-theorizing Child Citizenship through Transdisciplinarity', in W. Vandenhole, E. Desmet, D. Reynaert and S. Lembrechts (eds), *New Handbook on Children's Rights*, London: Routledge.

Mizen, P. and Ofosu-Kusi, Y. (2013), 'Agency as Vulnerability: Accounting for Children's Movement to the Streets of Accra', *Sociological Review* 61(2): 363–82.

Mnookin, R. (1975), 'Child-Custody Adjudication: Judicial Functions in the Face of Indeterminacy', *Law and Contemporary Problems* 39: 226–93.

Mobbs, D., Lau, H. C., Jones, O. D. and Frith, C. D. (2007), 'Responsibility and the Brain', *P LoS Biology* 5: 693–700.

Mohan, G. and Holland, J. (2001), 'Human Rights and Development in Africa: Moral Intrusion or Empowering Opportunity?', *Review of African Political Economy* 28(8): 177–96.

Monk, D. (2002), 'Children's Rights in Education: Making Sense of Contradictions', *Child and Family Law Quarterly* 14(1): 45–56.

Montgomery, H. (2001), *Modern Babylon?: Prostituting Children in Thailand*, New York: Berghahn.

(2009), *An Introduction to Childhood*, Chichester: Wiley-Blackwell.

More, H. (1799), *Strictures on the Modern System of Female Education*, London.

Morgan, R. (2011), *Younger Children's Views: a Report by the Children's Rights Director for England*, London: Ofsted.

Morris, B. et al. (2016), 'Critical Evaluation of Adler's Challenge to CDC Male Circumcision Recommendations', *International Journal of Children's Rights* 24: 265–303.

Morrison, W. (2001), *Blackstone's Commentaries on the Laws of England*, Volumes I–IV, London: Routledge Cavendish.

Morrow, V. (1999), 'We are People Too: Children's and Young People's Perspectives on Children's Rights and Decision-Making in England', *International Journal of Children's Rights* 7(2): 149–70.

(2010), 'Should the World Really be Free of "Child Labour"? Some Reflections', *Childhood* 17: 435–40.

(2012), 'The Ethics of Social Research with Children and Families in Young Lives: Practical Experiences', in M. Bourdillon and J. Boyden (eds), *Childhood Poverty, Multidisciplinary Approaches*, Basingstoke: Palgrave Macmillan, 24–42.

(2013), 'What's in a Number? Unsettling the Boundaries of Age', *Childhood* 20: 151–5.

Morrow, V. and Mayall, B. (2009), 'What is Wrong with Children's Well-Being in the UK? Questions of Meaning and Measurement', *Journal of Social Welfare and Family Law* 31 (3): 217–29.

Morrow, V. and Pells, K. (2012), 'Integrating Children's Human Rights and Child Poverty Debates: Examples from Young Lives in Ethiopia and India', *Sociology* 46(5): 906–20.

Morse, S. (2013), 'Lost in Translation?: an Essay on Law and Neuroscience', in M. Freeman (ed.), *Law and Neuroscience*, Oxford University Press, 529–65.

Morss, J. R. (2002), 'The Several Social Constructions of James, Jenks and Prout: A Contribution to the Sociological Theorization of Childhood', *International Journal of Children's Rights* 20(16): 39–54.

Moyn, S. (2012), *The Last Utopia: Human Rights in History*, Cambridge, MA: Harvard University Press.

Mulley, C. (2009), *The Woman Who Saved the Children*, Oxford: Oneworld Publications.

Muncie, J. (2002), 'Children's Rights and Youth Justice', in B. Franklin (ed.), *The New Handbook of Children's Rights*, London: Routledge.

Muryaba, R. (2011), 'Early Marriage: a Violation for Girls' Fundamental Human Rights in Africa', *International Journal of Children's Rights*, 339–55.

Mweru, M. (2010), Why are Kenyan Teachers Still Using Corporal Punishment Eight Years after a Ban on Corporal Punishment? *Child Abuse Review*, 19: 248–258.

Myers, W. (2001), 'The Right Rights? Child Labour in a Globalizing World', *Annals of the American Academy of Political and Social Science* 575(1): 38.

Naftali, O. (2014), *Children, Rights and Modernity in China*, Basingstoke: Palgrave Macmillan.

(2016), *Children in China*, Cambridge: Polity Press.

Nagel, T. (2006), 'The Problem of Global Justice', *Philosophy and Public Affairs* 33: 113–47.

Nairn, A. (2013), 'Arguments, Bullies and Feeling Poor: How Consumer Culture Affects Children's Relationships', in J. Wild (ed.), *Exploiting Childhood: How Fast Food, Material*

Obsession and Porn Culture are Creating New Forms of Child Abuse, London: Jessica Kingsley, 34–48.

Narveson, J. (1985), 'Contractarian Rights', in R. Frey (ed.), *Utility and Rights*, Oxford: Blackwell, 161–74.

(2009), 'On Dworkinian Equality', *Social Philosophy and Policy* 1 (1): 1–23.

National Commission of Inquiry into the Prevention of Child Abuse (1996), *Childhood Matters*, vols 1 and 2, London: HMSO.

Nauert, C. (1995), *Humanism and the Culture of Renaissance Europe*, New York: Cambridge University Press.

Ncube, W. (1998), 'Prospects and Challenges in Eastern and Southern Africa: The Interplay Between International Human Rights Norms and Domestic Law, Tradition and Culture', in *Law, Culture, Tradition and Children's Rights in Eastern and Southern Africa*, Aldershot: Ashgate, 5.

Nedelsky, J. (1993), 'Reconceiving Rights as Relationship', *Review of Constitutional Studies* 1(1): 1–26.

Neill, A. (1968), *Summerhill*, Harmondsworth: Penguin.

Neill, A. S. (1973), *Neill! Neill! Orange Peel! A Personal View of Ninety Years*, London: Weidenfeld & Nicolson.

Nelson, L., Horath, M., Laci, L. and Mestano, K. (2009), 'Corporal Punishment of Children in Thailand', *Child Legal Research Journal* 29(2): 9–33.

Newell, P. (1972), *The Last Resort*, London: Bedford Square Press.

(1989a), *Children are People Too*, London: Bedford Square Press.

(1989b), 'The Thin Line between Punishment and Child Abuse', *The Independent*, 16 July.

(2015), 'It is not Child-friendly to Make Children Criminals', in S. Mahmoudi (ed.), *Child-Friendly Justice*, Leiden: Brill, 137–51.

Nickel, J. (2007), *Making Sense of Human Rights*, Berkeley, CA: University of California Press.

Nielssen, O. B., Large, M. M., Westmore, B. D. and Lackersteen, S. M. (2009), 'Child Homicide in New South Wales from 1991 to 2005', *Medical Journal of Australia* 190 (1): 7–11.

Nieuwenhuys, O. (1994), *Children's Lifeworlds: Gender, Welfare and Labour in the Developing World*, New York: Routledge.

(2007), 'Embedding the Global Womb: Global Child Labour and the New Policy Agenda', *Children's Geographies* 5(1/2): 149–63.

(2009), 'From Child Labour to Working Children's Movements', in J. Qvortrup, W. A. Corsaro and M. S. Honig (eds), *The Palgrave Handbook of Childhood Studies*, Basingstoke: Palgrave Macmillan, 289–300.

(2010), 'Keep Asking: Why Childhood? Why Children? Why Global?' *Childhood* 17(3): 291–6.

Nolan, A. (2011), *Children's Socio-Economic Rights, Democracy and the Courts*, Oxford: Hart.

(2013), *Human Rights and Public Finance: Budgets and the Promotion of Economic and Social Rights*, Oxford: Hart.

Nozick, R. (1973), *Anarchy, State and Utopia*, Oxford: Blackwell.

Nsamenang, A. B. (2006), 'Cultures in Early Childhood Care and Education', Background paper for EFA Global Monitoring Report 2007, *Strong Foundations: Early Childhood Care and Education*, Paris: UNESCO.

Nussbaum, M. (2000), *Women and Human Development: the Capabilities Approach*, Cambridge University Press.

O'Byrne, D. (2012), 'On the Sociology of Human Rights: Theorising the Language-Structure of Rights', *Sociology* 46(5): 829–43.

Ochaita, E. and Espinosa, M. A. (2001), 'Needs of Children and Adolescents as a Basis for the Justification of their Rights', *International Journal of Children's Rights* 9: 313–37.

O'Connell Davidson, J. (2005), *Children in the Global Sex Trade*, Cambridge: Polity Press.

OECD (2015), *Doing Better for Children*, Paris: OECD Publishing.

Ohmae, K. (1990), *The Borderless World*, New York: Harper Business.

Okin, S. M. (1979), *Justice, Gender and the Family*, New York: Free Press.

Olsaretti, S. (2013), 'Children as Public Goods?', *Philosophy and Public Affairs* 41: 226–58.

Olsen, F. (1985), 'The Myth of State Intervention in the Family', *University of Michigan Journal of Law Reform* 18: 835.

(1992), 'Children's Rights: Some Feminist Approaches to the United Nations Convention on the Rights of the Child', *International Journal of Law, Policy and the Family* 6(1): 192–220.

O'Manique, J. (1990), 'Universal and Inalienable Rights: A Search for Foundation', *Human Rights Quarterly* 12: 465–85.

O'Neill, O. (1988), 'Children's Rights and Children's Lives', *Ethics* 98: 445.

Ong Hing, B. (1983), 'Raising Personal Identification Issues of Class, Race, Ethnicity, Gender, Sexual Orientation, Physical Disability, and Age in Lawyering Courses', *Stanford Law Review* 45: 1807.

Ongay, L. (2010), 'Glocalists in Tijuana: Youth, Cultural Citizenship and Cosmopolitan Identity', *Children's Geographies* 8(4): 373–80.

Orbach, S. (2009), *Bodies*, London: Profile Books.

(2013), 'Commercialisation of Girls' Bodies', in J. Wild (ed.), *Exploiting Childhood: How Fast Food, Material Obsession and Porn Culture are Creating New Forms of Child Abuse*, London: Jessica Kingsley.

Orbinski, J. (2008), *An Inperfect Offering: Dispatches from the Medical Frontline*, London: Random House.

Ornstein, J. (2017), *Whitewashed: Antisemitism in the Labour Party*, London: Kitty Hawk Press Ltd.

Orr, D. (2014), 'The Story of Nigeria's Stolen Girls Fell Through the Cracks of Traditional Journalism', *The Guardian*, 16 May.

Osler, A. (2000), 'Children's Rights, Responsibilities and Understandings of School Discipline', *Research Papers in Education* 15(1): 49–67.

Osler, A. and Starkey, H., 'Children's Rights and Citizenship: Some Implications for the Management of Schools', *International Journal of Children's Rights* 6: 313–33.

Oswell, D. (2013), *The Agency of Children*, New York: Cambridge University Press.

Owen, R. D. (1824), *An Outline of the System of Education at New Lanark*, Glasgow: Glasgow University Press.

Overall, C. (2012), *Why Have Children? The Ethical Debate*, Cambridge, MA: MIT Press.

(2015), 'Reproductive? Surrogacy and Parental Licencing', *Bioethics* 29: 353–61.

Packer, H. (1968), *The Limits of the Criminal Sanction*, Stanford University Press.

Pahl, J. (1989), *Money and Marriage*, London: Macmillan.

Pais, M. (1992), 'The UNCRC on the Rights of the Child', *Bulletin of Human Rights* 91: 75–82.

Palmer, S. (2006), *Toxic Childhood*, London: Orion Books.

Panter-Brick, C. and Smith, M. (2000), *Abandoned Children*, Cambridge University Press.

Pare, M. and Collins, T. (2016), 'Government Efforts to Address Bullying in Canada: Any Place for Children's Rights?', *Journal of Law and Social Policy* 25: 54–77.

Parfit, D. (1984), *Persons and Reasons*, Oxford University Press.

Parker, S. (1994), 'Best Interests of the Child: Principles and Problem', *International Journal of Law Policy and the Family* 8(1): 26–41.

Parkinson, P. and Cashmore, J. (2009), *The Voice of the Child in Family Law Disputes*, Oxford University Press.

Parsons, T. (1951), *The Social System*, London: RKP.

Parton, N. (1986), 'The Beckford Report: A Critical Appraisal', *British Journal of Social Work* 16: 511–30.

Pearson, G. (1983), *Hooligan: A History of Respectable Fears*, London: Macmillan.

Peleg, N. (2012), 'Time to Grow Up: UN and Right to Development', in M. Freeman (ed.), *Law and Childhood Studies*, Oxford University Press, 371–91.

Peleg, N. (2013), 'Reconceptualising the Child's Right to Development: Children and the Capability Approach', *International Journal of Children's Rights* 21: 523–42.

(2017), 'Developing the Right to Development', *International Journal of Children's Rights* 25: 380–95.

(2019), *The Child's Right to Development*, Cambridge University Press.

Percy-Smith, B. (2014), 'Reclaiming Children's Participation as an Empowering Social Process', in C. Burke and K. Jones (eds), *Education, Childhood and Anarchism*, London: Routledge, 209–20.

Persson, I. and Savulescu, J. (2013), 'Getting Moral Enhancement Right: the Desirability of Moral Bioenhancement', *Bioethics* 27 (124): 131.

Peters, J-K. (1996), 'The Roles and Content of Best Interests in Children Directed Lawyering for Children in Child Protective Proceedings', *Fordham Law Review* 64: 1505.

(2007), *Representing Children in Child Protective Proceedings: Ethical and Practical Dimensions*, Newark, NJ: Lexis Law.

Peterson-Badali, M. and Abramovitch, R. (1992), 'Children's Knowledge of the Legal System: Are They Competent to

Instruct Legal Counsel?' *Canadian Journal of Criminology* 34: 139–60.

(1993), 'Grade-related Changes in Young People's Reasoning about Plea Decisions', *Law and Human Behavior* 17(5): 537–52.

Phiri, D. and Abebe, T. (2016), 'Suffering and Thriving: Children's Perspectives and Interpretations of Poverty and Wellbeing in Rural Zambia', *Childhood* 23: 378–93.

Piaget, J. (1927), *The Child's Conception of the World*, London: Routledge & Kegan Paul.

(1955), *The Construction of Reality in the Child*, London: Routledge & Kegan Paul.

Pigot, T. (1989), *Report of the Advisory Group on Video Evidence*, London: Home Office.

Pilcher, J. (2011), 'No Logo: Children's Consumption of Fashion', *Childhood* 18: 128–41.

Pinheiro, P. S. (2015), 'Reflections on Child-friendly Justice', in S. Mahmoudi (ed.), *Child-Friendly Justice*, Leiden: Brill, 27–9.

Piper, C. (2000), 'Assumptions about Children's Best Interests', *Journal of Social Welfare and Family Law* 22: 261.

(2010), 'Investing in a Child's Future: Too Risky?', *Child and Family Law Quarterly* 22: 1–20.

Pitts, J. (2005), 'The Recent History of Youth Justice in England and Wales', in T. Bateman and J. Pitts (eds), *RHP Companion to Youth Justice*, Lyme Regis: Russell House, 2–11.

Platt, A. (1969), *The Child Savers: the Invention of Delinquency*, University of Chicago Press.

Pogge, T. (2002), *World Poverty and Human Rights*, Cambridge: Polity Press.

(2008), 'Recognized and Violated by International Law: The Human Rights of the Very Poor', available at: www2
.ohchr.org/english/issues/poverty/expert/docs/ThomasPogge_
new.pdf.

Pollard, A. and Filer, A. (1996), *The Social World of Children's Learning*, London: Cassell.

Pollock, L. (1983), *Forgotten Children: Parent–Child Relations from 1500–1900*, Cambridge University Press.

Pond, C. and Searle, A. (1991), *The Hidden Army: Children at Work in the 1990s*, London: Low Pay Unit.

Poretti, M. et al. (2014), 'The Rise and Fall of Icons of Stolen Childhood', *Childhood* 21: 22–38.

Porter, G. (2011), '"I Think a Woman Who Travels a Lot is Befriending Other Men and that's Why She Travels": Mobility Constraints and their Implications for Rural Women and Girls in sub-Saharan Africa', *Gender, Place and Culture*, 18(1): 65–81.

Posner, E. (2014), *The Twilight of Human Rights Law*, New York: Oxford University Press.

Postman, N. (1996), *The Disappearance of Childhood*, New York: Vintage Books.

Pound, R. (1917), 'The Limits of Effective Legal Action', *International Journal of Ethics* 27(2): 150–67.

Prout, A. (2005), *The Future of Childhood*, Oxford: Routledge Falmer.

Prout, A. and James, A. (1997), 'A New Paradigm for the Sociology of Childhood? Provenance, Promise and Problems', in A. Prout and A. James (eds), *Constructing and Reconstructing Childhood*, London: Routledge Falmer, 7–33.

Pupavac, V. (1998), 'The Infantilisation of the South and the UN Convention on the Rights of the Child', *Human Rights Law Review* 3: 1–6.

—— (2001), 'Misanthropy Without Borders: The International Children's Rights Regime', *Disasters* 25(2): 95–112.

—— (2011), 'Punishing Childhoods: Contradictions in Children's Rights and Global Governance', *Journal of Intervention and State Building* 5(3): 285–312.

Purdy, L. (1992), *In Their Best Interest?* Ithaca, NY: Cornell University Press.

(1994), 'Why Children Shouldn't Have Equal Rights', *International Journal of Children's Rights* 2: 223.

Purves, L. (1993), 'Child Victims of Divorce', *The Times*, 7 December.

Quennerstedt, A. (2010), 'Children, But Not Really Humans? Critical Reflections on the Hampering Effect of the 3 "Ps"', *International Journal of Children's Rights* 18: 619–35.

(2011), 'The Construction of Children's Rights in Education: a Research Synthesis', *International Journal of Children's Rights* 19(4): 661–78.

(2013), 'Children's Rights Research Moving into the Future: Challenges on the Way Forward', *International Journal of Children's Rights* 21: 233–47.

Quigley, M. A., Kelly, Y. J. and Sacker, A. (2007), 'Breastfeeding and Hospitalization for Diarrheal and Respiratory Infection in the United Kingdom Millennium Cohort Study', *Pediatrics* 119: e837–e842.

Qvortrup, J. (1991), *Childhood as a Social Phenomenon: An Introduction to a Series of National Reports*, Eurosocial Report 36/1991, 2nd edn, Vienna: European Centre for Social Welfare Policy and Research.

(1996), 'Monitoring Childhood: Its Social, Economic and Political Features', in E. Verhellen (ed.), *Monitoring Children's Rights*, The Hague: Martinus Nijhoff.

(2009), 'Are Children Human Beings or Human Becomings? A Critical Assessment of Outcome Thinking', *Rivista Internazionale Di Scienze Sociali* 117, (3/4): 631–53.

Qvortrup, J., Corsaro, W. A. and Honig, M. S. (eds) (2013), *The Palgrave Handbook of Childhood Studies*, Basingstoke: Palgrave Macmillan.

Raes, K. (1997), 'Children's Rights and Modern Culture: the Politics of Justification and its Limits', in E. Vehellen (ed.), *Understanding Children's Rights*, Ghent: Ghent University Children's Rights Center, 9–26.

Rafferty, Y. (2007), 'Children for Sale: Child Trafficking in Southeast Asia', *Child Abuse Review* 16: 401–22.

Raj, L. (2011), 'Understanding Corporal Punishment in India', *Career Educator: An Interdisciplinary Education Journal* 1 (1): 3–18.

Rajagopal, B. (2003), *International Law from Below: Development, Social Movements and Resistance*, Cambridge University Press.

Rao, S. (2013), *Trafficking of Children for Sexual Exploitation: Public International Law 1864–1950*, New Delhi: Oxford University Press.

Ratpan, M. (2012), 'Reframing the Practice of "Son Preference" Through the Millennium Development Goals', *Law and Childhood Studies: Current Legal Issues* 14: 357–70.

Rawls, J. (1971), *A Theory of Justice*, Cambridge, MA: Harvard University Press.

(1999), *The Law of Peoples*, Cambridge, MA: Harvard University Press.

Reading, R. et al. (2009), 'Promotion of Children's Rights and Prevention of Child Maltreatment', *Lancet* 373: 332–43.

Reder, P. and Fitzpatrick, G. (1998), 'What is Sufficient Understanding?' *Clinical Child Psychology and Psychiatry* 3: 103–13.

Redmond, G. (2008), 'Child Poverty and Child Rights: Edging Towards a Definition', *Journal of Children and Poverty* 14(1): 63–82.

Reece, H. (1996), 'The Paramountcy Principle: Consensus or Construct?', *Current Legal Problems* 49: 267–302.

Rees, G., Bradshaw, J., Goswami, H. and Keung, A. (2009), *Understanding Children's Well-Being: A National Survey of Young People's Well-being*, London, Children's Society.

Rees, O. (2010), 'Dealing with Individual Cases: An Essential Role for National Human Rights Institutions for Children', *International Journal of Children's Rights* 21: 415–36.

Rees, O. and Williams, J. (2016), 'Framing Asymmetry: Devolution and UK's Four Children's Commissioners', *International Journal of Children's Rights* 24: 434–68.

Reif, L. C. (2015), 'The Future of Thematic Children's Rights Institutions in a National Human Rights Institution World: The Paris Principles and the UN Committee on the Rights of the Child', *Houston Journal of International Law* 37: 434–90.

Renteln, A. D. (2010), 'Corporal Punishment and the Cultural Defense', *Law and Contemporary Problems* 73(2): 253–80.

Reynaert, D., Bouverne-De Bie, M. and Vandevelde, S. (2009), 'A Review of Children's Rights Literature Since the Adoption of the United Nations Convention on the Rights of the Child', *Childhood* 16(4): 518–34.

(2010a), 'Children, Rights and Social Work: Rethinking Children's Rights Education', *Social Work and Society* 8(1): 60–9.

(2010b), 'Children's Rights Education and Social Work: Contrasting Models and Understandings', *International Social Work* 53(4): 443–56.

(2012), 'Between "Believers" and "Opponents": Critical Discussions on Children's Rights', *International Journal of Children's Rights* 20(1): 155–68.

Reynaert, D. and Roose, R. (2014), 'Children's Rights and the Capability Approach: Discussing Children's Agency Against the Horizon of the Institutionalised Youth Land', in D. Stoeklin and J-M. Bonvin (eds), *Children's Rights and the Capability Approach*, Dordrecht: Springer, 175–93.

Richards, D. (1981), 'Rights and Autonomy', *Ethics* 92: 3.

Richards, D. (1981), 'The Individual, the Family, and the Constitution: A Jurisprudential Perspective', *New York University Law Review* 55: 1–60.

Richards, M., Hardy, R. and Wadsworth, M. (1997). 'The Effects of Divorce and Separation on Mental Health in a National UK Birth Cohort', *Psychological Medicine* 27(5): 1121–8.

Ridge, T. (2002), *Childhood Poverty and Social Exclusion: From a Child's Perspective*, Bristol: Policy Press.

Risse, M. (2012), *On Global Justice*, University of Princeton Press.

Rizzini, I. and Butler, U. (2003), 'Life Trajectories of Children and Adolescents Living on the Streets of Rio de Janeiro', *Children, Youth and Environments* 13(1): 1–20.

Roberts, C., Alexander, K. and Davis, J. (1991), 'Children's Rights to Physical and Mental Health Care: A Case for Advocacy', *Journal of Clinical Child and Adolescent Psychology* 20: 18–27.

Roberts, J. V. (2000), 'Changing Public Attitudes Towards Corporal Punishment: the Effects of Statutory Reform in Sweden', *Child Abuse and Neglect* 24(8): 1027–35.

Robeyns, I. (2005), 'The Capability Approach: A Theoretical Survey', *Journal of Human Development* 6(1): 93–117.

Roche, J. (1999), 'Children: Rights, Participation and Citizenship', *Childhood* 6: 475–93.

Rodham, H. (1973), 'Children under the Law', *Harvard Educational Review* 43: 487–514.

Roker, D. and Coleman, J. (2000), *'The Invisible Poor': Young People Growing Up in Family Poverty*, London: The Children's Society.

Roose, R. and Bouverne-De Bie, M. (2007), 'Do Children Have Rights or Do Their Rights Have to be Realised? The United Nations Convention on the Rights of the Child as a Frame of Reference for Pedagogical Action', *Journal of Philosophy of Education* 41(3): 431–43.

(2008), 'Children's Rights: A Challenge for Social Work', *International Social Work* 5(1): 37–46.

Roose, R., Roets, G., Van Houte, S., Vandenhole, W. and Reynaert, D. (2013), 'From Parental Engagement to the Engagement of Social Work Services: Discussing Reductionist and Democratic Forms of Partnership with Families', *Child and Family Social Work* 18(4): 449–57.

Rose, N. (1990), *Governing the Soul: The Shaping of the Private Self*, London: Routledge.

Rose, N. and Abi-Rached, J. (2013), *Neuro: The New Brain Sciences and the Management of the Mind*, Princeton University Press.

Rosen, D. (2007), 'Child Soldiers, International Humanitarian Law, and the Globalization of Childhood', *American Anthropologist* 109: 296–306.

Rosen, M. (2012), *Dignity: Its History and Meaning*, Cambridge, MA: Harvard University Press.

(2013), 'Dignity: The Case Against', in C. McCrudden (ed.), *Understanding Human Dignity*, Oxford University Press, 143–54.

Rosenau, P. (1991), *Post-Modernism and the Social Sciences*, Princeton University Press.

Ross, C. (2015), *Lessons in Censorship*, Cambridge, MA: Harvard University Press.

Ross, E. M. (1996), 'Learning to Listen to Children', in R. Davie, G. Upton and V. Varma (eds), *The Voice of the Child: A Handbook for Professionals*, London: Falmer Press.

Ross, L. F. (2009), 'Against the Tide: Arguments Against Respecting a Minor's Refusal of Efficacious Life-Saving Treatment', *Cambridge Quarterly of Healthcare Ethics* 18: 302–15.

Roszak, T. (1968), *The Making of a Counter Culture: Reflections on the Technocratic Society and Its Youthful Opposition*, New York: Doubleday.

Roth, B. (2008), 'Marxist Insights for the Human Rights Project', in S. Marks (ed.), *International Law on the Left*, Cambridge University Press, 220–51.

Rousseau, J-J. (1762) *Emile*, Geneva.

Royal College of Paediatrics and Child Health, Ethics Advisory Committee (2000), 'Guidelines for the Ethical Conduct of Medical Research Involving Children', *Arch. Dis. Child.* 82: 177–82.

Ruck, M., Abramovitch, R. and Keating, D. (1998), 'Children's and Adolescents' Understanding of their Rights: Balancing Nurturance and Self-Determination', *Child Development* 64: 404–17.

Rudkin, O. D. (1927), *Thomas Spence and his Connections: Bibliography of Spence's Writings*, London: Allen & Unwin, 205–51.

Ruxton, S. (1998), *Implementing Children's Rights*, London: Save the Children.

(1999), *A Children's Policy for 21st Century Europe: First Steps*, European Children's Network: EURONET.

(2001), 'Towards a Children's Policy for the European Union', in P. Foley, J. Roche and S. Tucker (eds), *Children in Society*, Basingstoke: Palgrave Macmillan, 65–75.

Ruxton, S. and Bennett, F. (2002), *Including Children? Developing a Coherent Approach to Child Poverty and Social Exclusion across Europe*, Brussels: Euronet.

Ryan, R. A. (2012), *The Oxford Handbook of Human Motivation*, Oxford University Press.

Ryan, W. (1976), *Blaming the Victim*, New York: Vintage Books.

Sabatello, M. (2013), 'Children with Disabilities: a Critical Appraisal', *International Journal of Children's Rights* 21: 464–87.

Sabatello, M. and Appelbaum, P. (2016), 'Psychiatric Genetics in Child Custody Proceedings', *Current Genetic Medicine Reports* 4(3): 98–106.

Sacramento, L. F. and Pessoa, A. M. (1996), 'Implementation of the Rights of the Child in the Mozambique Context', in M. Freeman (ed.), *Children's Rights: A Comparative Perspective*, Aldershot: Dartmouth, 145–64.

Saito, M. (2003), 'Amartya Sen's Capability Approach to Education: A Critical Exploration', *Journal of Philosophy of Education* 37 (3): 17–33.

Sánchez-Eppler, K. (2005), *Dependent States*, University of Chicago Press.

Sartorius, P. (1975), 'Social-Psychological Concepts and the Rights of Children', in V. Haubrich and M. Apple (eds), *Schooling and the Rights of Children*, Berkeley, CA: McCutchan Pub. Corp., 64–91.

Saunders, B. (2013), 'Ending the Physical Punishment of Children by Parents in the English-Speaking World: the Impact of Language, Tradition and Law', *International Journal of Children's Rights* 21: 278–304.

(2015), 'Ending Corporal Punishment in Childhood: Advancing Children's Rights to Dignity and Respectful Treatment', in A. Diduck, N. Peleg and H. Reece (eds), *Law in Society*, Leiden: Brill, 127–43.

Saunders, B. and Goddard, C. (2008), 'Some Australian Children's Perceptions of Physical Punishment in Childhood', *Children & Society* 22: 405–17.

(2010), *Physical Punishment in Childhood: The Rights of the Child*, Chichester: John Wiley.

Saunders, K. (2003), *Saving Our Children from the First Amendment*, New York University Press.

Save the Children (2011), *Governance Fit for Children*, London: Save the Children.

Savolainen, M. (1986–7), 'Finland: More Rights for Children', *Journal of Family Law* 25: 113–26.

Savulescu, J. (2001), 'Procreative Beneficence: Why We Should Select the Best Children', *Bioethics* 15: 411–26.

Savulescu, J. and Bostrom, N (2009), *Human Enhancement*, Oxford University Press.

Savulescu, J. and Kahane, G. (2009), 'The Moral Obligation to Create Children with the Best Chance of the Best Life', *Bioethics* 23: 274–90.

Schabas, W. A. (2007), 'Study of the Right to Enjoy the Benefits of Scientific and Technological Progress and its Application', in Y. Donders and V. Volodin (eds), *Human Rights in Education, Science and Culture: Legal Developments and Challenges*, Paris/ Aldershot: UNESCO/Ashgate, 273–308.

Schabas, W. and Sax, H. (2006), *A Commentary on the United Nations Convention on the Rights of the Child, Article 37: Prohibition of Torture, Death Penalty, Life Imprisonment and Deprivation of Liberty*, Boston, MA: Martinus Nijhoff.

Scharff-Smith, P. (2014), *When the Innocent are Punished*, Basingstoke: Palgrave Macmillan.

Schechter, M. and Roberge, L. (1976), 'Child Sexual Abuse', in R. Helfer and C. Kempe (eds), *Child Abuse and Neglect: The Family and the Community*, Cambridge: Ballinger.

Scheinen, M. (1998), 'The Right to Social Security', in A. Eide et al. (eds), *Economic, Social and Cultural Rights: A Textbook*, Boston, MA: Martinus Nijhoff.

Scherer, L. P. and Hart, S. N. (1999), 'Reporting to the UN Committee on the Rights of the Child: Analyses of the First 49 State Party Reports on the Education Articles of the Convention on the Rights of the Child and a Proposition for an Experimental Reporting System for Education', *International Journal of Children's Rights* 7(4): 349–63.

Schmidt, E. (2007), 'The Parental Obligation to Expand a Child's Range of Open Futures', *Bioethics* 21: 191–7.

Schrag, F. (1973), 'Rights over Children', *Journal of Value Inquiry* 7: 96–105.

(1976), 'The Child's Status in a Democratic State', *Political Theory* 3: 341.

Schur, E. M. (1965), *Crimes Without Victims*, Englewood Cliffs, NJ: Prentice-Hall.

Schuz, R. (2013), *The Hague Child Abduction Convention: A Critical Analysis*, Oxford: Hart.

(2015), '30 Years of the Hague Child Abduction Convention: A Children's Rights Perspective', in A. Diduck, N. Peleg and H. Reece (eds), *Law in Society*, Leiden: Brill, 607–33.

Scolnicov, A. (2011), *The Right to Religious Freedom in International Law*, Abingdon: Routledge.

Scott, E. (2000–1), 'The Legal Construction of Adolescents', *Hofstra Law Review* 29: 547–98.

(2006), 'Keynote Address at Temple University James E. Beasley School of Law, Law and Adolescence Symposium: Adolescence and the Regulation of Youth Crime', *Temple Law Review* 79: 337–51.

Scottish Parliament (2013), *Official Report 21.11.13*, Scottish Parliament, Edinburgh.

(2014), *Official Report 19.2.14*, Scottish Parliament, Edinburgh.

Seccombe, K. (2002), '"Beating the Odds" versus "Changing the Odds": Poverty, Resilience, and Family Policy', *Journal of Marriage and Family* 64: 384–94.

Sellar, W. C. and Yeatman, R. J. (1930), *1066 and All That*, London: Methuen.

Sellars, K. (2002), *The Rise and Rise of Human Rights*, Stroud: Sutton.

Sen, A. (1999), *Development as Freedom*, Oxford University Press.

Sensen, O. (2011), 'Human Dignity in Historical Perspective: the Contemporary and Traditional Paradigms', *European Journal of Political Theory* 10: 71.

Shariff, S. and Johnny, L. (2008), 'Child's Rights in Cyber Space, Participation and Privacy', in T. O'Neill and D. Zinga (eds), *Children's Rights*, University of Toronto Press, 219–44.

Shaw, D. (2003), 'Deaf by Design: Disability and Impartiality', *Bioethics* 22: 407–13.

Sheldon, S. and Wilkinson, S. (2004), 'Should Selecting Siblings be Banned?', *Journal of Medical Ethics* 30: 533–7.

Shepherd, R. and England, S. (1996), 'I Know the Child is My Client, But Who am I?', *Fordham Law Review* 64(4): 1917.

Sherrod, L. R. (2006), *Youth Activism: An International Encyclopedia*, Westport Connecticut, CT: Greenwood Press.

Shier, H. (2002), 'Pathways to Participation: Openings, Opportunities and Obligations: A New Model for Enhancing Children's Participation in Decision-making, in line with Article 12.1 of the United Nations Convention on the Rights of the Child', *Children and Society* 15: 107–17.

—— (2010), 'Children as Public Actors: Navigating the Tensions', *Children and Society* 24: 24–37.

Shklar, J. (1964), *Legalism*, Cambridge, MA: Harvard University Press.

Shonkoff, J. and Phillips, D. (eds) (2000), *From Neurons to Neighborhoods: The Science of Early Childhood Development*, Washington DC: National Academy Press.

Shuman, D. W. and Gold, L. H. (2008), 'Without Thinking: Impulsive Aggression and Criminal Responsibility', *Behavioural Sciences and the Law* 26: 723–34.

Siberman, L. (2003), 'Patching Up the Abduction Convention: A Call for a New International Protocol and a Suggestion for Amendments to ICARA', *Texas International Law Journal* 38 (1): 41.

Siegel, R. (2010), 'Roe's Roots: The Women's Rights Claims that Engendered Roe', *Boston University Law Review* 90: 1875–1907.

(2012), 'Dignity and Sexuality: Claims on Dignity in Transnational Debates Over Abortion and Same-Sex Marriage', *International Journal of Constitutional Law* 10: 335–79.

(2014), 'Dignity and the Duty to Protect Unborn Life', in C. McCrudden (ed.), *Understanding Human Dignity*, Oxford University Press, 509–23.

Silverman, P. (1978), *Who Speaks for the Children: The Plight of the Battered Child*, Toronto: Musson.

Simmons, W. P. (2011), *Human Rights Law and the Marginalized Other*, New York: Cambridge University Press.

Simon, W. (2000), 'The Wrongs of Children', *International Journal of Children's Rights* 8: 1–13.

Siogvolk, P. (1852), 'The Rights of Children', *Knickerbocker* 39: 489–90.

Sixsmith, J., Gabhainn, N., Fleming, S. C. and O'Higgins, S. (2007), 'Children's, Parents' and Teachers' Perceptions of Child Wellbeing', *Health Education* 107(6): 511–23.

Slack, A. (1988), 'Female Circumcision: A Critical Appraisal', *Human Rights Quarterly* 10(4): 437–86.

Sloth-Nielsen, J. (2008), 'Children's Rights and the Law in Africa', in J. Sloth-Nielsen (ed.), *Children's Rights in Africa*, Aldershot: Ashgate, 1–12.

Sloth-Nielsen, J. and Mezmur, B. (2008), 'A Dutiful Child: The Implications of Article 31 of the African Children's Charter', *Journal of African Law* 52(2): 159–89.

Sloth-Nielsen, J., Murungi, N. and Wakefield, W. (2011), 'Does the Differential Criterion for Vesting Parental Rights and Responsibilities of Unmarried Parents Violate International Law? A Legislative and Social Study of Three African Countries', *Journal of African Law* 55: 203–29.

Smart, C. (1999), 'A History of Ambivalence and Conflict in the Discursive Construction of the "Child Victim" of Sexual Abuse', *Social and Legal Studies* 8: 391–409.

Smart, C. and Neale, B. (1999), *Family Fragments*, Cambridge: Polity Press.

Smart, C., Neale, B. and Wade, A. (2001), *The Changing Experience of Childhood*, Cambridge: Polity Press.

Smilansky, S. (1995), 'Is There a Moral Obligation to Have Children?', *Journal of Applied Philosophy* 12: 41–53.

Smith, A. B. (2002), 'Interpreting and Supporting Participation Rights', *Children and Society* 10: 73–88.

(2007), 'Children and Young People's Participation Rights in Education', *International Journal of Children's Rights* 15(1): 147–64.

Smith, A-M. (2007), 'The Children of Loxicha, Mexico: Exploring Ideas of Childhood and the Rules of Participation', *Children, Youth and Environments* 17(2): 33–55.

Smith, C. (1997a), 'Children's Rights: Have Carers Abandoned Values?', *Children and Society*, 11: 3–15.

(1997b), 'Children's Rights: Judicial Ambivalence and Social Resistance', *International Journal of Law, Policy and the Family* 11: 103.

Smith, Dame J. (2016), The Dame Janet Smith Review Report, *An Independent Review into the BBC's Culture and Practise during the Jimmy Savile and Stuart Hall Years*.

Smith, R. (2010), *A Universal Child?*, Basingstoke: Palgrave Macmillan.

(2013), 'The Third Optional Protocol to the UN Convention on the Rights of the Child? Challenges Arising Transforming the Rhetoric into Reality', *International Journal of Children's Rights* 21: 305–22.

Smolin, D. M. (2006), 'Overcoming Religious Objections to the Convention on the Rights of the Child', *Emory International Law Review* 20: 81–110.

Snead, O. C. (2007), 'Neuroimaging and the "Complexity" of Capital Punishment', *New York University Law Review* 82(5): 1265–339.

(2008), 'Neuroimaging and Capital Punishment', *New Atlantis* 19: 35–64.

Sommerville, C. (1990), *The Rise and Fall of Childhood*, New York: Vintage Books.

Sparrow, R. (2012), 'Human Enhancement and Sexual Dimorphism', *Bioethics* 26(9): 464–75.

Spence, T. (1797), *The Rights of Infants* London, available at: www.thomas-spence-society.co.uk/rights-of-infants.

Spencer, J. R. (2004), 'Child and Family Offences', *Criminal Law Review*, 347.

Sperber, J. (2013), *Karl Marx: A Nineteenth Century Life*, New York: W. W. Norton.

Spronk-Van der Meer, S. (2014), *The Right to Health of the Child*, Antwerp: Intersentia.

Spyrou, S. (2011), 'The Limits of Children's Voices: From Authenticity to Critical, Reflective Representation', *Childhood* 18: 151–65.

Srivastava, A., Gamble, R. H. and Boey, J. (2013), 'Cyberbullying in Australia: Clarifying the Problem, Considering the Solutions', *International Journal of Children's Rights* 21: 25–45.

Stalford, H. (2016), 'Not seen, not heard: the implications of Brexit for children', *openDemocracy*.

Stalford, H. and Schuurman, M. (2011), 'Are We There Yet?: The Impact of the Lisbon Treaty on the EU Children's Rights Agenda', *International Journal of Children's Rights* 19: 381–403.

Stammers, N. (2009), *Human Rights and Social Movements*, London: Pluto Press.

Stanley, T. and Guru, S. (2015), 'Childhood Radicalisation Risk', *Practice*, 1–15.

Stasiulis, D. (2002), 'The Active Child Citizen: Lessons from Canadian Policy and the Children's Movement', *Citizenship Studies* 6(4): 507–38.

Statham, J. and Chase, E. (2010), *Childhood Wellbeing: A Brief Overview*, Loughborough: Childhood Wellbeing Research Centre.

Stearns, Peter N. (2006), *Childhood in World History*, New York: Routledge.

(2012), *Human Rights in World History*, Themes in World History, Abingdon: Routledge.

(2016) *Childhood in World History*, London: Taylor & Francis.

Steger, M. (2013), *The Rise of the Global Imaginary*, New York: Oxford University Press.

Steinberg, L. (2014), 'Should the Science of Adolescent Brain Development Inform Public Policy?' *Court Review*, 50: 70–7.

(2014), 'The Science of Adolescent Brain Development, and Its Implications for Adolescent Rights,' in J. Bhaba (ed.), *Human Rights and Adolescence*, University of Philadelphia Press, 59–76.

Steinberg, L. and Scott, E. (2003), 'Less Guilty by Reason of Adolescence', *American Psychologist* 5: 1011.

Steinberg, S. (2011), *Kinderculture*, Boulder, CO: Westview Press.

Steinbock, B. (1992), *Life Before Birth*, New York: Oxford University Press.

Stephens, V. and Lowe, N. (2012), 'Children's Welfare and Human Rights under the 1980 Hague Abduction Convention: the Ruling in Re E', *Journal of Social Welfare and Family Law* 34(1): 125–35.

Stevens, O. (1982), *Children Talking Politics*, Oxford: Martin Robertson.

Stevenson, B. (2014), *Just Mercy*, Victoria: Scribe, Brunswick.

Stiglitz, J. (2002), *Globalization and Its Discontents*, London: Penguin.

(2013), *The Price of Inequality*, London: Penguin.

Stoecklin, D. and Bonvin, J-M. (2014), *Children's Rights and the Capability Approach*, Dordrecht: Springer.

Stoll, C. S. (1968), 'Images of Man and Social Control', *Social Forces* 47: 119–27.

Stott, A. (2003), *Hannah More, The First Victorian*, Oxford University Press.

Strauch, B. (2003), *The Primal Teen: What the New Discoveries about the Teenage Brain Tell Us about Our Kids*, New York: Doubleday.

Straus, M. A. (2000), 'Corporal Punishment and Primary Prevention of Physical Abuse', *Child Abuse & Neglect* 24(9): 1109–14.

Straus, M. et al. (2014), *The Primordial Violence: Spanking Children, Psychological Development, Violence, and Crime*, New York: Routledge.

Strauss, R. (2000), 'Childhood Obesity and Self-Esteem', *Pediatrics* 105(1): 15.

Such, E. and Walker, R. (2005), 'Young Citizens or Policy Objects? Children in the "Rights and Responsibilities" Debate', *Journal of Social Policy* 34: 39–57.

Sunstein, C. (1995/6), 'The Expressive Function of Law', *University of Pennsylvania Law Review* 144(1): 2012–53.

Swanson, K. (2010), *Begging as a Path to Progress: Indigenous Women and Children and the Struggle for Ecuador's Urban Spaces*, Athens, GA: University of Georgia Press.

Syrota, G. (1996), 'Consensual Fist Fights and Other Brawls: Are They a Crime?', *University of Western Australia Law Review* 26: 169–89.

Taefi, N. (2009), 'The Synthesis of Age and Gender: Intersectionality, International Human Rights Law and the Marginalisation of the Girl-child', *International Journal of Children's Rights* 17(3): 345–76.

Taylor, A. (2011), 'Reconceptualizing the "Nature of Childhood"', *Childhood* 18(4): 420–33.

Taylor, N. and Smith, A. B. (2009), *Children as Citizens*, Dunedin: Otago University Press.

Taylor, R. (2009), 'Parental Responsibility and Religion', in R. Probert, S. Gilmore and J. Herring (eds), *Responsible Parents and Parental Responsibility*, Oxford: Hart, 123–42.

Teitelbaum, L. (1980), 'The Meaning of Rights to Children', *New Mexico Law Review* 10: 235–53.

Thaler, R. and Sunstein, C. (2008), *Nudge*, New Haven, CT: Yale University Press.

Théry, I. (1989), 'The Interest of the Child and the Regulation of the Post-Divorce Family', in C. Smart and S. Sevenhuijsen (eds), *Child Custody and the Politics of Gender*, London: Routledge.

Thomas, J. (2009), Working Paper, 'Current Measures and the Challenges of Measuring Children's Wellbeing', Household, Labour Market and Social Wellbeing, Office for National Statistics, Newport, 7.

Thomas, N. (2001), 'Listening to Children', in P. Foley, J. Roche and S. Tucker (eds), *Children in Society*, Basingstoke: Palgrave Macmillan, 104–11.

(2007), 'Towards a Theory of Children's Participation', *International Journal of Children's Rights* 15: 199–218.

(2011), 'The Role and Impact of Independent Children's Rights Institutions in the UK and Europe', *Journal of Social Welfare and Family Law* 33: 279–88.

Thomas, N., Gran, B. and Hanson, K. (2011), 'An Independent Voice for Children's Rights in Europe? The Role of Independent Children's Rights Institutions in the EU', *International Journal of Children's Rights* 19: 429–49.

Thomas, N. and O'Kane, C. (1998), 'When Children's Wishes and Feelings Clash with Their "Best Interests"', *International Journal of Children's Rights* 6(2): 137–54.

Thompson, N. (1992), *Child Abuse: The Existential Dimension*, Norwich: New Social Work Monographs.

Thompson, R. (2014), 'Stress and Child Development', *The Future of Children* 24: 41–59.

Thorgeirsdóttir, H. (2006), *Article 13: The Right to Freedom of Expression*, Leiden: Martinus Nijhoff.

Thorne, B. (1987), 'Re-visioning Women and Social Change: Where are the Children?' *Gender and Society* 1(1): 85–109.

Tiboris, M. (2014), 'Blaming the Kids: Children's Agency and Diminished Responsibility', *Journal of Applied Philosophy* 31: 77–90.

Tiffin, S. (1982), *In Whose Best Interest: Child Welfare Reform in the Progressive Era*, Westport, CT: Greenwood Press.

Tisdall, E. K. M. (2014), 'Children Should be Seen and Heard? Children and Young People's Participation in the UK', in E. K. M. Tisdall, A. M. Gadda and U. M. Butler (eds), *Children and Young People's Participation and its Transformative Potential: Learning from Across Countries*, Basingstoke: Palgrave Macmillan.

(2015), 'Children's Wellbeing and Children's Rights in Tension?', *International Journal of Children's Rights* 23: 769–89.

Tisdall, E. K. M. and Davis, J. M. (2015), 'Children's Rights and Wellbeing: Tensions within the Children and Young People (Scotland) Act 2014', in A. Smith (ed.), *Enhancing the Rights and Wellbeing of Children: Connecting Research, Policy and Practice*, Basingstoke: Palgrave Macmillan.

Tisdall, E. K. M. and Hill, M. (2011), 'Policy Change Under Devolution: the Prism of Children's Policy', *Social Policy and Society* 10(1): 29–40.

Tobin, J. (2013), 'Justifying Children's Rights', *International Journal of Children's Rights* 21: 395–441.

(2015), 'Taking Children's Rights Seriously', in A. Diduck, N. Peleg and H. Reece (eds.), *Law in Society*, Leiden: Brill, 127–43.

Todres, J. (2012), 'Maturity', *Houston Law Review* 48: 1107.

(2014), 'A Child Rights Framework for Addressing Trafficking of Children', *Michigan State International Law Review* 22: 557–93.

Todres, J. and Higinbotham, S. (2016), *Human Rights in Children's Literature*, New York: Oxford University Press.

Tomaševski, K. (2001), 'Human Rights in Education as Prerequisite for Human Rights Education', *Right to Education Primers* 4.

(2004), 'The Right to Education', Report submitted by Katarina Tomaševski, Special Rapporteur, Addendum: Mission to Colombia, 1–10 October 2003, United Nations.

Tong, R. (2009), *Feminist Thought: A More Comprehensive Introduction*, Boulder, CO: Westview.

Trombley, S. (1988), *The Right to Reproduce*, London: Weidenfeld & Nicolson.

Tucker, B. (1998), 'Deaf Culture, Cochlear Implants and Elective Disability', *Hastings Center Report* 28(4): 6–14.

Tufte, B. and Rasmussen, J. (2010), 'Children and the Internet', in D. Marshall (ed.), *Children as Consumers*, London: Sage.

Twum-Danso, A. (2003), 'Children's Perceptions of Physical Punishment in Ghana and Implications for Children's Rights', *Childhood* 20: 550–65.

(2016), 'Tackling the Physical Punishment of Children in Resource Poor Contexts', *International Journal of Children's Rights* 24: 469–87.

UK Government Child Exploitation Centre (2015), 'Sexting Becoming "the Norm" for Teens, Warn Child Protection Experts', *The Guardian*, 10 November.

United Nations (2000), *The Millennium Goals*, United Nations Millennium Declaration A/RES/55/2, New York: United Nations.

(2003), *World Youth Report 2003: The Global Situation of Young People*, New York: United Nations Publications.

(2007a), *The Employment Imperative*, Report on the World Social Situation E.07.IV.9, New York: UN Publications.

(2007b), *The Millennium Development Goals Report 2007*, E.07. I.15, New York: UN Publications.

(2012), *The Future of What We Want*, New York: UN Publications.

UN Committee on Rights of the Child (CRC Committee) (2003), *General Comment No. 5, General Measures of Implementation of the Convention on the Rights of the Child* CRC/GC/2003/5.

(2007), *General Comment No. 10, Children's Rights in Juvenile Justice*, CRC/C/GC/10.

(2009), *General Comment No. 12, The Right of the Child to be Heard* CRC/C/GC/12.

(2013), *Concluding Observations on the Second to Fourth Periodic Reports of Israel, Adopted by the Committee at its Sixty-Third Session (27 May–14 June 2013)*, CRC/C/ISR/CO/2-4.

(2013), General Comment No. 15, *On the Right of the Child to the Enjoyment of the Highest Attainable Standard of Health*, available at: www2.ohchr.org/english/bodies/crc/docs/GC/CRC-C-GC-15en.doc.

(2016), *Committee on the Rights of the Child Reviews the Concluding Comments on 5th Report of United Kingdom*, available at: www.ohchr.org/EN/NewsEvents/Pages/DisplayNews.aspx?NewsID=20007&LangID=E.

UNDP (2006), *Beyond Scarcity: Power, Poverty and the Global Water Crisis*, Human Development Report, New York: UNDP.

UNCTAD (2010), *World Investment Report: Investing in Low-Carbon Economy*, New York: UNCTAD.

UN Human Rights Council (2013), *Annual Report of the United Nations High Commissioner for Human Rights*, Geneva: United Nations.

UNESCO (1990), *World Declaration on Education for All*, New York: UNESCO.

(2000), *The Dakar Framework for Action. Education for All: Meeting our Collective Commitments*, Paris: UNESCO.

(2014), *Education for All Global Monitoring Report: Teaching and Learning: Achieving Quality for All*, Paris: UNESCO.

(2015), *Education for All Global Monitoring Report: Education for All 2000–2015: Achievements and Challenges*, Paris: UNESCO.

UNICEF (2004), *Building Child Friendly Cities: A Framework for Action*, Florence: Innocenti Research Centre.

(2010), *The Right to a Childhood*, London: UNICEF UK.

(2012), *Championing Children's Rights: A Global Studies of Independent Human Rights Institutions for Children*, Florence: UNICEF.

(2013), *The Evidence and Rationale for the UNICEF UK Baby Friendly Initiative Standard*, London: UNICEF.

(2014a), *The State of the World's Children in Numbers 2014: Every Child Counts, Revealing Disparities, Advancing Children's Rights*, Florence: UNICEF.

(2014b), *Children in Danger: Act to End Violence Against Children*, Florence: UNICEF.

(2015), *Unless We Act Now*, Geneva: UNICEF.

(2016), *Uprooted: the Growing Crisis for Refugee and Migrant Children*, Geneva: UNICEF.

Uprichard, E. (2008), 'Children as Beings and Becomings', *Children and Society* 22: 303–13.

Valentine, G. (2004), *Public Space and the Culture of Childhood*, Aldershot: Ashgate.

Vallès, J. (2007), *L'Enfant (The Child)*, New York Book Reviews.

Van Bueren, G. (1995), *The International Law on the Rights of the Child*, The Hague: Martinus Nijhoff.

(2006), *Article 40: Child Criminal Justice in A Commentary on the United Nations Convention on the Rights of the Child*, Leiden: Martinus Nijhoff.

(2016), 'A Right to Housing Should be Part of UK Law: With Homelessness on the Increase, the UK Should Follow the Netherlands, Ireland, Brazil and India where a Right to Housing is Enshrined in Law', *The Guardian*, 1 March.

Van Esterik, P. (1989), *Beyond the Breast-Bottle Controversy*, New Brunswick, NJ: Rutgers University Press.

Vandenhole, W. (2012), 'Localizing the Human Rights of Children', in M. Liebel, K. Hanson, I. Saadi and W. Vandenhole (eds), *Children's Rights from Below: Cross-Cultural Perspectives*, Basingstoke: Palgrave Macmillan, 80–93.

Vandenhole, W. et al. (2011), 'Undocumented Children and the Right to Education: Illusory Right or Empowering Lever?' *International Journal of Children's Rights* 19(4): 613–39.

Veerman, P. (1992), *Rights of a Child and the Changing Image of Childhood*, Dordrecht: Martinus Nijhoff.

(2010), 'The Ageing of the UN Convention on the Rights of the Child', *International Journal of Children's Rights* 18(4): 585–618.

Verhellen, E. and Spiesschaert, F. (eds) (1988), *Ombudswork for Children*, Louvain: Acco.

Voigt, K., Nicholls, S. and Williams, G. (2014), *Childhood Obesity: Ethical and Policy Issues*, New York: Oxford University Press.

Vuckivic Sahovic, N. (2012), *ENOC Study Report on National Human Rights Institutions and Child/Juvenile Delinquency*, Strasbourg: Council of Europe.

Voyce, M. (2005), 'Up Against the Mall', *The Big issue*, 22725(04): 17–18.

(2012), *ENOC Study Report on National Human Rights Institutions and Child/Juvenile Delinquency*, Strasbourg: Council of Europe.

Wadsworth, M. E., Wolff, B., Santiago, C. and Moran, E. G. (2008), 'Adolescent Coping with Poverty-Related Stress', *Prevention Researcher* 15: 13–16.

Wald, M. (1979), 'Children's Rights: A Framework for Analysis', *University of California Davis Law Review* 12: 255.

Wall, J. (2010), *Ethics in the Light of Childhood*, Washington, DC: Georgetown University Press.

Wall, J. (2012), 'Can Democracy Represent Children?', *Childhood* 19: 86–100.

Wall, J. and Dar, A. (2011), 'Children's Political Representation: the Right to Make a Difference', *International Journal of Children's Rights* 19: 595–612.

Waller, J. (2006), *The Real Oliver Twist*, Cambridge: Icon Books.

Wallerstein, J. and Kelly, J. (1980), *Surviving the Break-Up*, London: Grant McIntyre.

Wang, W. (2005), 'Son Preference and Educational Opportunities of Children in China – "I Wish You Were a Boy!"', *Gender Issues* 22(2): 3–30.

Warburton, J. (2016), 'Preventing the Sexual Exploitation of Children: A Mapping of Practice and Interventions', *ECPAT International Journal No. 11*, Bangkok: ECPAT.

Warburton, W. (2013), 'The Science of Violent Entertainment', in J. Wild (ed.), *Exploiting Children*, London: Jessica Kingsley, 65–85.

Wasserstrom, W. (1964), 'Rights, Human Rights, and Racial Discrimination', *Journal of Philosophy* 61(20): 628–41.

Wedgwood, C. V. (1947), *The Thirty Years War*, London: Jonathan Cape.

Weinstein, J. (1997), 'And Never the Twain Shall Meet: the Best Interests of Children and the Adversary System', *University of Miami Law Review* 52: 79.

Weisbrodt, D., Hansen, J. C. and Nesbitt, N. (2011), 'The Role of the Committee on the Rights of the Child in Interpreting and Developing International Humanitarian Law', *Harvard Human Rights Journal* 24: 115–53.

Weithorn, L. and Campbell, T. (1982), 'The Competency of Children and Adolescents to Make Informed Treatment Decisions', *Child Development* 53: 1589.

Wells, K. (2009), *Childhood in a Global Perspective*, Cambridge: Polity Press.

Weston, B. H. (2007), *Child Labor and Human Rights*, Boulder, CO: Lynne Reinner.

White, B. (1999), 'Defining the Intolerable: Global Standards, Child Welfare and Cultural Relativism', *Childhood* 6(1): 133–44.

Wiggin, K. D. (1892), *Children's Rights: A Book of Nursery Logic*, Boston, MA: Houghton Mifflin.

Wild, J. (2013), *Exploiting Children*, London: Jessica Kingsley.

Wilkenson, A. (ed.) (1973), *The Rights of Children: Emergent Concepts in Law and Society*, Philadelphia, PA: Temple University Press.

Willems, J. (2002), *Developmental and Autonomy Rights of Children*, Antwerp: Intersentia.

Willenberg, I. (2014), 'It's Not Like in Apartheid: South African Children's Knowledge about their Rights', *International Journal of Children's Rights* 22: 446–66.

Williams, J. (2013), *The United Nations Convention on the Rights of the Child in Wales*, Cardiff: University of Wales Press.

Williams, P. (1991), *The Alchemy of Race and Rights*, Cambridge, MA: Harvard University Press.

(1998), *Seeing a Color-Blind Future: The Paradox of Race*, 1997 BBC Reith Lectures, New York: Farrar, Straus & Giroux.

Willow, C. (2015), 'Taking Account of Children: How Far Have We Come in England?' in A. B. Smith (ed.), *Enhancing Children's Rights*, Basingstoke: Palgrave Macmillan, 183–96.

Wolf, L. (2001), *Global Uprising: Confronting the Tyrannies of the 21st Century: Stories from a New Generation of Activists*, Gabriola Island: New Society Publishing.

Woll, L. (2000), 'Reporting to the UN Committee on the Rights of the Child: a Catalyst for Domestic Debate and Policy Change?' *International Journal of Children's Rights* 8: 71–81.

Women and Equalities Committee (2010), *Transgender Equality*, 1st Report, House of Commons Select Committee, London.

Wood, S. (1968), *Constitutional Politics in the Progressive Era: Child Labour and the Law*, University of Chicago Press.

Woodhead, M. and Faulkner, D. (2000), 'Subjects, Objects or Participants? Dilemmas of Psychological Research with Children', in P. Christensen, and A. James (eds), *Research with Children, Perspectives and Practices*, London: Falmer Press.

Woodhouse, B. B. (1993), 'Hatching the Egg: A Child-centered Perspective on Parents' Rights', *Cardozo Law Review* 14: 1747.

(2003). 'Enhancing Children's Participation in Policy Formation', *Arizona Law Review*, 45: 751–64.

(2008), *Hidden in Plain Sight*, Princeton University Press.

Woolf, J. (2012), *The Human Right to Health*, New York: W. W. Norton & Company Ltd.

Woolley, H. (2009), 'Every Child Matters in Public Open Spaces', in A. Millie (ed.), *Securing Respect: Behavioural Expectations and Anti-social Behaviour in the UK*, Bristol: Policy Press.

World Health Organisation (WHO) (2008), *Closing the Gap in a Generation: Health Equity through Action on the Social Determinants of Health, Commission on Social Determinants of Health Final Report* Geneva: WHO.

(2013), *World Health Statistics* Geneva: WHO.

Worsfold, V. (1974), 'A Philosophical Justification for Children's Rights', *Harvard Educational Review* 44: 142–57.

Wright Mills, C. (1959), *The Sociological Imagination*, Oxford University Press.

Wringe, C. (1981), *Children's Rights: A Philosophical Study*, London: RKP.

Wrong, D. (1991), 'The Oversocialized Conception of Man in Modern Sociology', *American Sociological Review* 26: 181.

Wyness, M. (2013), 'Children's Participation and Intergenerational Dialogue', *Childhood* 20: 429–42.

Wyness, M. et al. (2004), 'Childhood, Politics and Ambiguity: Towards an Agenda for Children's Political Inclusion', *Sociology* 38: 81, 82.

Young, I. M. (1990), *Justice and the Politics of Difference*, Princeton University Press.

(2000), *Inclusion and Democracy*, Oxford University Press.

Young-Bruehl, E. (2012), *Childism*, New Haven, CT: Yale University Press.

Yousafzai, M. (2013), *I am Malala*, London: Weidenfeld and Nicolson.

Zafran, R. (2010), 'Children's Rights and Relational Rights: the Case of Relocation', *Journal of Gender, Social Policy & the Law* 18(2): 163–215.

Zelizer, V. (1985), *Pricing the Priceless Child: the Changing Social Value of Children*, New York: Basic Books.

Zermatten, J. (2006), 'The Best Interests of the Child', *International Journal of Children's Rights* 13: 274–87.

Zigler, E. (1980), 'Controlling Child Abuse: Do We Have the Knowledge and/or the Will?' in G. Gerbner, C. J. Ross and E. Zigler (eds), *Child Abuse: An Agenda for Action*, New York: Oxford University Press.

Zimring, F. (1982), *The Changing World of Legal Adolescence*, New York: Free Press.